Words ...

Here are the words and writings of great Americans in forty-seven of the major documents which have shaped American history. Never before have these basic documents been available in one inexpensive volume, ideal for both student and general reader.

In addition to selecting and editing the actual texts of these documents, speeches and writings, historian Richard D. Heffner has written a series of brilliant interpolatory passages which explain the significance of each document together with its place in the events and developments of American history.

From these documents, which range from the Declaration of Independence to Gerald R. Ford's Inaugural Address, the social, political and intellectual patterns of American history emerge in sharp focus.

Both as a source book of hard-to-find basic documents and as a stimulating guide to a fuller understanding of America's past and present, *A Documentary History of the United States* is an invaluable volume for every intelligent reader.

A gifted historian, Richard D. Heffner is the recipient of an A.B. and M.A. from Columbia University. He has taught at the University of California, Columbia, Sarah Lawrence College and the New School for Social Research, and is the editor of the Mentor edition of Alexis de Tocqueville's *Democracy in America*. After a long career as a news commentator, a network and public broadcasting executive, and a producer of prize-winning television programs, Mr. Heffner is now Chairman of the Classification and Rating Administration of the Motion Picture Association of America, Inc.

MENTOR Books of Related Interest

A documentary
HISTORY OF THE UNITED STATES

Expanded and Updated
Bicentennial Edition

by

Richard D. Heffner

A MENTOR BOOK
NEW AMERICAN LIBRARY
TIMES MIRROR
NEW YORK AND SCARBOROUGH, ONTARIO

TO MY MOTHER AND FATHER
with love, honor and gratitude

 MENTOR TRADEMARK REG. U.S. PAT. OFF. AND FOREIGN COUNTRIES
REGISTERED TRADEMARK—MARCA REGISTRADA
HECHO EN CHICAGO, U.S.A.

SIGNET, SIGNET CLASSICS, MENTOR, PLUME, MERIDIAN AND NAL
BOOKS are published *in the United States* by
The New American Library, Inc.,
1633 Broadway, New York, New York 10019,
in Canada by The New American Library of Canada Limited,
81 Mack Avenue, Scarborough, Ontario M1L 1M8.

THIRD EDITION, JANUARY, 1976

24 25 26 27 28 29 30 31 32

PRINTED IN THE UNITED STATES OF AMERICA

Contents

FOREWORD

In this brief history of the United States many of the major sources of American political, economic and intellectual life are presented essentially as they were written. For the sake of clarity, liberties have been taken with punctuation and spelling, and ellipses indicate that some passages have been omitted. But what in the broadest sense are many of the tangible and unquestioned raw materials of American history are objectively presented here for examination and evaluation, so that each reader becomes truly his own historian. On the other hand, the connective commentary which places the various documents in their historical context is necessarily subjective, for the past as "fact" is to be clearly distinguished from recorded history, which is largely "opinion." Thus the commentary, as the late Charles A. Beard characterized written history generally, is pre-eminently an "act of faith" which embodies not the past itself, but simply the author's own changeable understanding of the sequence, motivation, and conceptual meaning of certain events in the American past.

In innumerable ways *A Documentary History of the United States* is a joint venture, and I wish to express deepest appreciation to my many friends, students, colleagues, and teachers who aided so generously in its preparation. Special thanks to Edward McN. Burns and to Richard V. Chase, for their thoughtfulness, kindness, and thoroughness in reading and checking the original manuscript. Thanks also to Lawrence H. Chamberlain, Arthur W. Macmahon, Harry J. Carman, Allan Nevins, Eduard C. Lindeman, and Martin Levin for their criticisms and constant encouragement; to Marc Jaffe, my editor, for wisdom and patience beyond the call of duty; and always to Elaine, my wife, for everything.

RICHARD D. HEFFNER

New York City
August 5, 1952

Various new documents have been added to the original edition of *A Documentary History of the United States*. Textual changes have also been made in the connective commentary to improve this Bicentennial edition and to bring it up to date.

New York City
January 1, 1976

REFERENCES

The author acknowledges his indebtedness to the following works in the preparation of *A Documentary History of the United States:*

The Selected Works of Tom Paine; Modern Library, 1946.

The Federalist, ed. by Edward Mead Earle; Modern Library, 1941.

Documents of American History, Henry Steele Commager (5th ed.); Appleton-Century-Crofts, Inc., 1949.

The Complete Jefferson, Saul K. Padover; Duell, Sloan & Pearce, Inc., 1943.

The Works of Alexander Hamilton, ed. by Henry Cabot Lodge; G. P. Putnam's Sons.

The Basic Writings of George Washington, ed. by Saxe Commins; Modern Library, 1948.

The Life and Selected Writings of Thomas Jefferson, ed. by Adrienne Koch and William Peden; Modern Library, 1944.

The People Shall Judge, selected and edited by the staff; The University of Chicago Press, 1950.

The Making of American Democracy, Ray Allen Billington and others; Rinehart & Company, Inc., 1950.

We Hold These Truths, ed. by Stuart Gerry Brown (2nd ed.); Harper & Bros., 1948.

American Issues, ed. by Willard Thorp, M. E. Curti, C. H. Baker; J. B. Lippincott Co., 1941.

The Life and Writings of Abraham Lincoln, ed. by Philip Van Doren Stern; Modern Library, 1942.

The Gospel of Wealth, Andrew Carnegie; Doubleday & Company, Inc., 1933.

The Complete Poetry and Prose of Walt Whitman, with an Introduction by Malcolm Cowley; Garden City Books, 1954.

The Frontier in American History, Frederick Jackson Turner; Henry Holt & Co., 1920, 1948.

Speeches of William Jennings Bryan; Funk & Wagnalls, 1909.

The Interest of America in Sea Power, Alfred T. Mahan; Little, Brown & Co., 1897.

The New Freedom, Woodrow Wilson; Doubleday & Company, Inc., 1913.

The New Day, Herbert Hoover; Stanford University Press, 1928.

Chapter 1

A NEW NATION

What then is the American, this new man? . . . He is an American, who leaving behind him all his ancient prejudices and manners, receives new ones from the new mode of life he has embraced, the new government he obeys, and the new rank he holds. He becomes an American by being received in the broad lap of our great Alma Mater. Here individuals of all nations are melted into a new race of men, whose labours and posterity will one day cause great changes in the world. . . . The American is a new man, who acts upon new principles; he must therefore entertain new ideas, and form new opinions. From involuntary idleness, servile dependence, penury, and useless labour, he has passed to toils of a very different nature, rewarded by ample subsistence.— This is an American. . . . HECTOR ST. JOHN DE CRÈVE-CŒUR, 1782.

Freed from the tyrannical economic, political, and ecclesiastical restraints of the Old World, and blessed with a bountiful environment whose rich and abundant resources, varied climate, and vast domain imbued in him an unquestioned faith in his own future, the American was in truth a "new man." Yet the roots of American society were firmly implanted in the great traditions of Western civilization, and ultimately American nationality was as heavily indebted to its European heritage of ideas and mode of life as it was to the new environment. Indeed, in its inception and its development, American colonial history was clearly a reflection of European experiences. The discovery of America resulted from the breakup of the feudal system, the rise of the nation-state, the revival of commerce, and the search for trade routes to the fabulous riches of the East. Later, the long process of English colonization of the New World was motivated both by the quest for free religious expression stemming largely from the Protestant Reformation of the

9

sixteenth century, and by that desire for economic opportunity which had its origins in the middle-class business ethic peculiar to the modern Western world.

The final chapter of American colonial history was also written abroad, for the restrictive policies of British mercantilism provided an economic impetus to the American Revolution, just as the natural rights philosophy of the European Enlightenment set its ideological framework. Mercantilism, an economic arm of the rising nationalism of the seventeenth and eighteenth centuries, had as its major objectives national self-sufficiency and prosperity for the dominant merchant and banking class. A favorable balance of trade was particularly important to the mercantilist doctrine, for if more goods and services were sold abroad than were imported, gold and silver would come into the country and the nation's total economic strength would be augmented rather than depleted. Each nation desired a favorable balance of trade, however, and so the great mercantilist powers of Europe soon turned to overseas possessions as a source of economic strength. For these colonies existed solely to be exploited by the mother country —to produce essential raw materials cheaply, to provide an unlimited market for surplus manufactured goods, and to offer a minimum of economic competition.

British colonial policy amply demonstrated the mother country's intention of molding her American possessions into this mercantilist pattern. To free herself from dependence upon foreign nations for needed raw materials, the Navigation Acts of the seventeenth and eighteenth centuries listed various "enumerated commodities" (such as sugar, tobacco, indigo, and naval stores) which the colonials had to export to England alone. And in an effort to retain exclusive control of the rapidly growing American markets for British manufactured goods, all foreign commodities bound for the colonies were required to pass through England, where prohibitive export duties and freight and handling charges made transshipment intolerably expensive. Competition by the industrious colonists themselves was nearly eliminated through laws such as the Woolens Act (1699), the Hat Act (1732), and the Iron Act (1750), which prohibited or discouraged local efforts at manufacturing.

Though mercantilism benefited the colonists in certain respects—generous bounties, for instance, were paid for indigo and badly needed naval stores, and a monopoly of the English tobacco market was insured to the American producer—the economic well-being of the colonies was for the most part harshly subordinated to the needs of the mother country. Even the Southern settlements, whose staple crops—such as tobacco—well suited them for the colonial role, were hard pressed by the one-sided mercantilist system. And by the eve of the American Revolution Thomas Jefferson estimated that a persistently unfavorable colonial balance of trade had placed at least half of the tobacco planters of Maryland and Virginia hopelessly in debt to British creditors. At the same time the various Navigation and Trade Acts attempted to restrict severely the trading, shipping, manufacturing, and other economic activities of the settlements in the North, where climate and soil were not capable of supporting the large scale cultivation of staple crops for the home market. Yet the colonies prospered, at least in the New England and Middle Atlantic regions. Smuggling and other evasions of mercantilist measures were prevalent, and for long decades before the conclusion of the French and Indian War in 1763, the British were too thoroughly immersed in a bitter imperial rivalry with France to enforce their restrictive legislation.

With the defeat of France, however, the British were able to bring to an end the era of "salutary neglect" and to turn their full attention once again to strict enforcement of colonial policy. Besides, Parliament now strongly reasserted its right to legislate for colonials who had long known virtual independence and self-rule and who were well versed in the liberal philosophy of the eighteenth-century Enlightenment. Political discontent was thus added to economic dislocation, and economic grievances soon found expression in the loftiest principles of political liberty. Royal (and even Parliamentary) efforts to enforce mercantilist policies were damned as contrary not only to the rights of Englishmen, but to the "natural rights of man" as well, while the colonists' fundamental antipathy to taxation of any kind achieved immortality in the idealistic slogan "no taxation without representation." The British were unmoved by these protests and in rapid succession the Sugar Act (1764), the Currency Act (1764), the Stamp Act (1765), the Townshend Duties (1767), the Tea Act (1773), and the Intolerable Acts (1774) taxed and regulated the colonial economy and imposed the severest restrictions upon colonial self-government.

The colonists were quick to reply. A Stamp Act Congress met in October, 1765, to denounce the hated tax on newspapers, magazines, commercial papers, and other documents, and an organization of patriots known as the Sons of Liberty directly forced the resignation of nearly all of the imperial stamp agents. American merchants agreed not to import British merchandise until the tax was repealed, and many persons stoutly refused to buy any stamps at all. Even though colonial pressures finally effected the repeal of the Stamp Tax, the tide of unrest continued to rise. Americans more and more frequently joined together to oppose imperial measures; and after British soldiers had fired into a jeering Boston mob (the "Boston Massacre" of March, 1770) popular resentment increased tremendously. Non-importation agreements, "Committees of Correspondence" (which Samuel Adams of Massachusetts organized to inform patriots throughout the colonies of current affairs), the "Boston Tea Party" of December, 1773, and finally the First Continental Congress that met in Philadelphia in September, 1774—all of these actions marked a growing sentiment for independence and separation from the mother country. And though there were many who still opposed the final break with England, the Revolution began in earnest in April, 1775, at Lexington and at Concord bridge, where "embattled farmers stood and fired the shot heard round the world."

Tom Paine's enormously popular and influential pamphlet, "Common Sense," published anonymously in January, 1776, quickly helped solidify Americans' rebellious spirit. And in June, 1776, a resolution that "these United Colonies are, and of right ought to be, free and independent states" was offered before the Second Continental Congress by Richard Henry Lee of Virginia. Then on July 4 the Congress formally adopted (with modifications) Thomas Jefferson's draft of the Declaration of Independence. The Declaration expressed certain fundamental precepts: that all men are equally endowed with the self-evident natural rights of life, liberty, and the pursuit of happiness, that civil government is merely an instrument to guarantee these rights within the framework of social order, that when government becomes tyrannical the social compact is broken and it is the "right of the people to alter or to abolish it." These were precepts which clearly embodied the political tenets of the European Enlightenment. Thus for Americans whose intellectual heritage was largely European, and whose free environment as well was conducive to libertarian ideas, the Declaration (as Jefferson himself later wrote) expressed not "new ideas altogether," but rather the "common sense of the matter . . . the harmonizing sentiment of the day." Pre-eminently it was an eloquent "expression of the American mind," and to those who cherished the democratic faith of their fathers it was to remain for all times the fountainhead of American ideology.

"Common Sense," *Tom Paine, 1776*

. . . In the following pages I offer nothing more than simple facts, plain arguments, and common sense: and have no other preliminaries to settle with the reader, than that he will divest himself of prejudice and prepossession, and suffer his reason and his feelings to determine for themselves: that he will put on, or rather that he will not put off, the true character of a man, and generously enlarge his views beyond the present day.

Volumes have been written on the subject of the struggle between England and America. Men of all ranks have embarked in the controversy, from different motives, and with various designs; but all have been ineffectual, and the period of debate is closed. Arms as the last resource decide the contest; the appeal was the choice of the King, and the Continent has accepted the challenge. . . .

The Sun never shined on a cause of greater worth. 'Tis not the affair of a City, a County, a Province, or a Kingdom; but of a Continent—of at least one-eighth part of the habitable Globe. 'Tis not the concern of a day, a year, or an age; posterity are virtually involved in the contest, and will be more or less affected even to the end of time, by the proceedings now. Now is the seedtime of Continental union, faith and honour. The least fracture now will be like a name engraved with the point of a pin on the tender rind of a young oak; the wound would enlarge with the tree, and posterity read in it full grown characters. . . .

I have heard it asserted by some, that as America has flourished under her former connection with Great Britain, the same connection is necessary towards her future happiness, and will always have the same effect. Nothing can be more fallacious than this kind of argument. We may as well assert that because a child has thrived upon milk, that it is never to have meat, or that the first twenty years of our lives is to become a precedent for the next twenty. But even this is admitting more than is true; for I answer roundly that America would have flourished as much, and probably much more, had no European power taken any notice of her. The commerce by which she hath enriched herself are the necessaries of life, and will always have a market while eating is the custom of Europe.

But she has protected us, say some. That she hath engrossed us is true, and defended the Continent at our expense as well as her own, is admitted; and she would have defended

Turkey from the same motive, *viz.* for the sake of trade and dominion.

Alas! we have been long led away by ancient prejudices and made large sacrifices to superstition. We have boasted the protection of Great Britain, without considering, that her motive was *interest* not *attachment;* and that she did not protect us from *our enemies* on *our account;* but from *her enemies* on *her own account,* from those who had no quarrel with us on any *other account,* and who will always be our enemies on the *same account.* Let Britain waive her pretentions to the Continent, or the Continent throw off the dependence, and we should be at peace with France and Spain, were they at war with Britain. . . .

But Britain is the parent country, say some. Then the more shame upon her conduct. Even brutes do not devour their young, nor savages make war upon their families. . . . Europe, and not England, is the parent country of America. . . .

I challenge the warmest advocate for reconciliation to show a single advantage that this Continent can reap by being connected with Great Britain. I repeat the challenge; not a single advantage is derived. Our corn will fetch its price in any market in Europe, and our imported goods must be paid for, buy them where we will.

But the injuries and disadvantages which we sustain by that connection, are without number; and our duty to mankind at large, as well as to ourselves, instructs us to renounce the alliance: because, any submission to, or dependence on, Great Britain, tends directly to involve this Continent in European wars and quarrels, and set us at variance with nations who would otherwise seek our friendship, and against whom we have neither anger nor complaint. As Europe is our market for trade, we ought to form no partial connection with any part of it. It is the true interest of America to steer clear of European contentions, which she never can do, while, by her dependence on Britain, she is made the makeweight in the scale of British politics. . . .

'Tis repugnant to reason, to the universal order of things, to all examples from former ages, to suppose that this Continent can long remain subject to any external power. The most sanguine in Britain doth not think so. The utmost stretch of human wisdom cannot, at this time, compass a plan, short of separation, which can promise the Continent even a year's security. Reconciliation is *now* a fallacious dream. Nature hath deserted the connection, and art cannot supply her place. For, as Milton wisely expresses, "never can true reconcilement grow where wounds of deadly hate have pierced so deep." . . .

To talk of friendship with those in whom our reason forbids us to have faith, and our affections wounded thro' a thousand pores instruct us to detest, is madness and folly. Every day wears out the little remains of kindred between us and them; and can there be any reason to hope, that as the relationship expires, the affection will encrease, or that we shall agree better when we have ten times more and greater concerns to quarrel over than ever?

Ye that tell us of harmony and reconciliation, can ye restore to us the time that is past? Can ye give to prostitution its former innocence? neither can ye reconcile Britain and America. The last cord now is broken, the people of England are presenting addresses against us. There are injuries which nature cannot forgive; she would cease to be nature if she did. As well can the lover forgive the ravisher of his mistress, as the Continent forgive the murders of Britain. . . .

O! ye that love mankind! Ye that dare oppose not only the tyranny but the tyrant, stand forth! Every spot of the old world is overrun with oppression. Freedom hath been hunted round the Globe. Asia and Africa have long expelled her. Europe regards her like a stranger, and England hath given her warning to depart. O! receive the fugitive, and prepare in time an asylum for mankind. . . .

The Declaration of Independence, 1776

In Congress, July 4, 1776
The unanimous Declaration of the thirteen
United States of America

When in the course of human events, it becomes necessary for one people to dissolve the political bands which have connected them with another, and to assume among the powers of the earth, the separate and equal station to which the Laws of Nature and of Nature's God entitle them, a decent respect to the opinions of mankind requires that they should declare the causes which impel them to the separation.

We hold these truths to be self-evident, that all men are created equal, that they are endowed by their Creator with certain unalienable rights, that among these are life, liberty and the pursuit of happiness. That to secure these rights, governments are instituted among men, deriving their just powers from the consent of the governed. That whenever any form of government becomes destructive of these ends, it is the right of the people to alter or to abolish it, and to institute new government, laying its foundation on such principles and organizing its powers in such form, as to them shall seem most likely to effect their safety and happiness. Prudence, indeed, will dictate that governments long established should not be changed for light and transient causes; and accordingly all experience hath shown, that mankind are more disposed to suffer, while evils are sufferable, than to right themselves by abolishing the forms to which they are accustomed. But when a long train of abuses and usurpations, pursuing invariably the same object evinces a design to reduce them under absolute despotism, it is their right, it is their duty, to throw off such government, and to provide new guards for their future security. Such has been the patient sufferance of these Colonies; and such is now the necessity which constrains them to alter their former systems of government. The history of the present King of Great Britain is a history of repeated injuries and usurpations, all having in direct object the establishment of an absolute tyranny over these States. To prove this, let facts be submitted to a candid world.

He has refused his assent to laws, the most wholesome and necessary for the public good.

He has forbidden his Governors to pass laws of immediate and pressing importance, unless suspended in their operation till his assent should be obtained; and when so suspended, he has utterly neglected to attend to them.

He has refused to pass other laws for the accommodation of large districts of people, unless those people would relinquish the right of representation in the Legislature, a right inestimable to them and formidable to tyrants only.

He has called together legislative bodies at places unusual, uncomfortable, and distant from the depository of their public records, for the sole purpose of fatiguing them into compliance with his measures.

He has dissolved representative houses repeatedly, for opposing with manly firmness his invasions on the rights of the people.

He has refused for a long time, after such dissolutions, to cause others to be elected; whereby the legislative powers, incapable of annihilation, have returned to the people at large for their exercise; the State remaining in the meantime exposed to all the dangers of invasion from without and convulsions within.

He has endeavoured to prevent the population of these States; for that purpose obstructing the laws of naturalization of foreigners; refusing to pass others to encourage their migration hither, and raising the conditions of new appropriations of lands.

He has obstructed the administration of justice, by refusing his assent to laws for establishing judiciary powers.

He has made judges dependent on his will alone, for the tenure of their offices, and the amount and payment of their salaries.

He has erected a multitude of new offices, and sent hither swarms of officers to harass our people, and eat out their substance.

He has kept among us, in times of peace, standing armies without the consent of our legislatures.

He has affected to render the military independent of and superior to the civil power.

He has combined with others to subject us to a jurisdiction foreign to our constitution, and unacknowledged by our laws; giving his assent to their acts of pretended legislation:

For quartering large bodies of armed troops among us:

For protecting them, by a mock trial, from punishment for any murders which they should commit on the inhabitants of these States:

For cutting off our trade with all parts of the world:

For imposing taxes on us without our consent:

For depriving us, in many cases, of the benefits of trial by jury:

For transporting us beyond seas to be tried for pretended offences:

For abolishing the free system of English laws in a neighbouring Province, establishing therein an arbitrary government, and enlarging its boundaries so as to render it at once an example and fit instrument for introducing the same absolute rule into these Colonies:

For taking away our Charters, abolishing our most valuable laws, and altering fundamentally the forms of our governments:

For suspending our own Legislatures, and declaring themselves invested with power to legislate for us in all cases whatsoever.

He has abdicated government here, by declaring us out of his protection and waging war against us.

He has plundered our seas, ravaged our coasts, burnt our towns, and destroyed the lives of our people.

He is at this time transporting large armies of foreign mercenaries to complete the works of death, desolation and tyranny, already begun with circumstances of cruelty and perfidy scarcely paralleled in the most barbarous ages, and totally unworthy the head of a civilized nation.

He has constrained our fellow citizens taken captive on the high seas to bear arms against their country, to become the executioners of their friends and brethren, or to fall themselves by their hands.

He has excited domestic insurrections amongst us, and has endeavoured to bring on the inhabitants of our frontiers, the merciless Indian savages, whose known rule of warfare, is an undistinguished destruction of all ages, sexes, and conditions.

In every stage of these oppressions we have petitioned for redress in the most humble terms: our repeated petitions have been answered only by repeated injury. A prince whose character is thus marked by every act which may define a tyrant is unfit to be the ruler of a free people.

Nor have we been wanting in attention to our British brethren. We have warned them from time to time of attempts by their legislature to extend an unwarrantable jurisdiction over us. We have reminded them of the circumstances of our emigration and settlement here. We have appealed to their native justice and magnanimity, and we have conjured them by the ties of our common kindred to disavow these usurpations, which would inevitably interrupt our connections and correspondence. They too have been deaf to the voice of justice and of consanguinity. We must, therefore, acquiesce in the necessity, which denounces our separation, and hold them, as we hold the rest of mankind, enemies in war, in peace friends.

We, therefore, the Representatives of the United States of America, in General Congress assembled, appealing to the Supreme Judge of the world for the rectitude of our intentions, do, in the name, and by authority of the good people of these Colonies, solemnly publish and declare, That these United Colonies are, and of right ought to be Free and Independent States; that they are absolved from all allegiance to the British Crown, and that all political connection between them and the State of Great Britain, is and ought to be totally dissolved; and that as Free and Independent States, they have full power to levy war, conclude peace, contract alliances, establish commerce, and to do all other acts and things which Independent States may of right do. And for the support of this declaration, with a firm reliance on the protection of Divine Providence, we mutually pledge to each other our lives, our fortunes, and our sacred honor.

JOHN HANCOCK.

New Hampshire
JOSIAH BARTLETT,
WM. WHIPPLE,
MATTHEW THORNTON.

Massachusetts Bay
SAML. ADAMS,
JOHN ADAMS,
ROBT. TREAT PAINE,
ELBRIDGE GERRY.

Rhode Island
STEP. HOPKINS,
WILLIAM ELLERY.

Maryland
SAMUEL CHASE,
WM. PACA,
THOS. STONE,
CHARLES CARROLL of Carrollton.

Virginia
GEORGE WYTHE,
RICHARD HENRY LEE,
TH. JEFFERSON,
BENJA. HARRISON,
THS. NELSON, JR.,
FRANCIS LIGHTFOOT LEE,
CARTER BRAXTON.

Connecticut
 ROGER SHERMAN,
 SAM'EL HUNTINGTON,
 WM. WILLIAMS,
 OLIVER WOLCOTT.

Georgia
 BUTTON GWINNETT,
 LYMAN HALL,
 GEO. WALTON.

Pennsylvania
 ROBT. MORRIS,
 BENJAMIN RUSH,
 BENJA. FRANKLIN,
 JOHN MORTON,
 GEO. CLYMER,
 JAS. SMITH,
 GEO. TAYLOR,
 JAMES WILSON,
 GEO. ROSS.

Delaware
 CAESAR RODNEY,
 GEO. READ,
 THO. M'KEAN.

New York
 WM. FLOYD,
 PHIL. LIVINGSTON,
 FRANS. LEWIS,
 LEWIS MORRIS.

North Carolina
 WM. HOOPER,
 JOSEPH HEWES,
 JOHN PENN.

South Carolina
 EDWARD RUTLEDGE,
 THOS. HEYWARD, JUNR.,
 THOMAS LYNCH, JUNR.,
 ARTHUR MIDDLETON.

New Jersey
 RICHD. STOCKTON,
 JNO. WITHERSPOON,
 FRAS. HOPKINSON,
 JOHN HART,
 ABRA. CLARK.

Chapter 2

THE LAW OF THE LAND

In 1783 the Treaty of Paris ended the Revolution and firmly secured American independence, but the enormously difficult problem of political reorganization remained to plague the erstwhile colonials. Though they had successfully swept away England's oppressive imperial rule, in its place they had yet to construct their own political system and to design a new equilibrium of liberty and order. The task of devising a constitution, formidable under the most favorable circumstances, proved particularly trying for the new nation. For beyond the single desire for independence there was little substantial agreement as to long-range political objectives amongst even the most fervid patriots.

Instead, a decided cleavage along class lines was evident throughout the Revolutionary crisis. A conservative group composed of wealthy Southern planters and Northern merchants, bankers, lawyers, and speculators sought independence to be free of British mercantilist restrictions and of an intolerable burden of debt to the mother country. But for the most part they wanted no fundamental social or economic change within the colonies themselves, and the status quo was to be maintained after independence was assured, with political power remaining in the possession of the well born, the educated, and the rich. On the other hand, the yeoman farmers, mechanics, artisans, and small businessmen who made up the radical patriots sought a *two-fold* revolution. Political ties to England were to be broken merely as a first step towards a revolution at home; and a new democratic government, based upon popular rule and responsive to the will of the people, was to destroy the social and economic privileges enjoyed by the colonial aristocracy.

Largely because Samuel Adams, Patrick Henry, and others of their leaders had played a prominent role in precipitating the final break with England, the radicals won important victories during and immediately after the war. Although conservatism was by no means completely routed, the radical viewpoint prevailed in many instances and there occurred a limited social revolution. Constitutions in the new states generally provided for more democracy than the colonial charters. Property qualifications for voting were lowered somewhat to permit a broader (though by no means universal) suffrage. Large estates were confiscated from loyalists, and though speculators secured much of these lands, a large quantity was made available to small farmers. The old feudal practices of entail—which kept huge land holdings intact by forbidding the division of an estate through inheritance—and primogeniture—which further fostered a landed aristocracy by making the first-born male heir to all land inheritances—were forbidden. In many states religious freedom received a considerable impetus from the separation of church and state. And generally the equalitarian principles of the Declaration of Independence were firmly impressed upon Americans who now sought to effect reforms in every aspect of national life.

The most significant radical victory, however, was the establishment of the Articles of Confederation. When independence was declared and the revolution begun, it was obvious that some form of permanent central authority must eventually supplant the Continental Congress. But the radicals well remembered British restraints upon democratic local self-government, and they were convinced that definitive political power must ultimately be concentrated in state legislatures susceptible to popular pressures rather than in a distant and less responsible strong central government. Thus the Articles of Confederation amply met the radicals' demands, for the common activities of the thirteen states were co-ordinated within a rather feeble "league of friendship" without significantly sacrificing local political control. Reflecting colonial experiences with tyrannical Royal governors, no provision was made for an independent executive department. Nor was a permanent federal judiciary created. Rather the sole organ of government was a one-house Congress in which each state retained its "sovereignty, freedom, and independence" and possessed but one vote. The agreement of nine states was necessary to pass legislation of importance, and a unanimous vote was required to amend the Articles. Besides, the powers granted to the government were severely limited. Congress might make war or peace, raise an army and navy by *requesting* quotas of men from the states, look after Indian affairs, borrow money, and administer a post office. But the government could not enforce its will or act directly upon the states or the people, and it totally lacked the essential powers to tax and to regulate commerce between the states.

Despite these severe limitations upon its power, the government under the Articles of Confederation did make lasting contributions to the national well-being, particularly in the creation of a permanent, democratic American colonial policy. In order to harmonize the various states' conflicting claims to Western lands, all of these territories were finally ceded to the central government (Maryland refused to ratify the Articles until 1781, when this decision was made). Then in the Ordinances of 1784 and 1785, and particularly in the famous Northwest Ordinance of 1787, provision was made for the organization of new lands into districts which were eventually to be admitted to the Union "on an equal footing with the original states in all respects whatsoever."

In all likelihood the majority of Americans were well satisfied with a government that had developed a liberal and far-sighted land policy and had faithfully administered its responsibilities without at all encroaching upon the liberties of its citizens. But the less numerous, though more articulate and powerful conservative elements in American society were grievously outraged at what they considered the "failures" of the Articles of Confederation. Though it was inevitable that long years of war and the destruction of the old colonial system would produce depression and severe economic dislocation, conservatives blamed the confusions of the "Critical Period" after the Revolution entirely upon inherent weaknesses in the radical-inspired Articles. The answers to many

of the nation's problems, they insisted, would be provided by
the establishment of a powerful national government free to
regulate interstate commerce, to tax, and to enforce its will
directly upon the people. Such a government would necessarily strengthen the nation, for it would assure economic
stability by bringing broad assistance to the conservative
propertied groups. For the manufacturer, a high national
tariff would protect his own goods from foreign competition
and serve as a retaliation against other nations for their restrictions. For the shipper and trader, there would be naval
protection for the nation's commerce, and favorable trade
treaties with foreign lands that despised the weak Confederation. For domestic businessmen, there would be an end to the
trade wars between the states, and the establishment of courts
would enforce the obligation of contracts. For land speculators, there would be military protection against Indians
whose ravages made Western settlement difficult and impaired
land values. And for the creditor class generally, a uniform,
controlled currency would put an end to the state legislatures' inflationary cheap money policies that devalued the
dollar and made debts meaningless.

Fortunately for the conservative cause, the radical movement had been largely dissipated after its initial victory in
the formulation of the weak Articles of Confederation. Now
it was the conservatives' turn to organize political victory, and
when in 1786 the Confederation government proved incapable of dealing with an agrarian insurrection in Western
Massachusetts (Shays' Rebellion), they took bold steps towards counterrevolution. Leading conservatives had very
early called for the revision of the Articles, and preliminary
meetings had been held at Mount Vernon in 1785 and at
Annapolis in 1786 to discuss ways and means of furthering
state cooperation on trade and other matters. Then at the
Annapolis Convention a resolution penned by Alexander
Hamilton called for a new meeting "to render the constitution of the federal government adequate to the exigencies of
the Union." And in February, 1787, the Congress invited all
of the states to send delegates to a convention at Philadelphia in the spring of that year for the "sole and express purpose of revising the Articles of Confederation."

That the Constitutional Convention was predominantly conservatives goes without saying, for determined men of property within the various state legislatures had chosen representatives of their own social and economic persuasion. None
of the old fiery radicals were present and of the fifty-five
delegates who participated in the deliberations of the Conven-

tion most were substantial men of affairs personally interested in creating a strong central government. That the delegates wrote large areas of their conservative views into the Constitution was equally true, for the document which became the "supreme law of the land" fully met most of the propertied classes' objections to the weak and supposedly inadequate Articles of Confederation. Vast powers (including those to regulate interstate commerce and to tax) were conferred upon the national government, while the powers of the individual states were severely curtailed. And the entire national political structure was itself carefully guarded against an "excess of democracy" by an intricate set of checks and balances, the separation of powers, a difficult amending process, the indirect election of the President and of the Senate, the equal representation of large and small states in the Senate, and by the presidential veto.

A bitter struggle remained, however, for the Constitution had yet to be approved by the necessary nine of the thirteen states. Now the radicals were thoroughly aroused as they studied the handiwork of the Convention whose instructions had been simply to revise the old Articles of Confederation. To a majority of Americans, the poorer classes generally, the consolidating character of the proposed federal Constitution smacked of despotism and class rule. But, with certain outstanding exceptions such as Patrick Henry and Richard Henry Lee of Virginia, the anti-Federalists were mostly inarticulate, and their strength in the state ratifying conventions was minimized by lack of systematic organization no less than by undemocratic restrictions upon voting. The Federalists, of course, were superbly organized, and they numbered amongst their most effective arguments for the Constitution a series of brilliant essays by Alexander Hamilton, James Madison, and John Jay. The *Federalist Papers* were read widely throughout the nation, and none more effectively defended the new government than Madison's Federalist Number Ten —a masterful statement of the founders' realistic appraisal of politics.

The skill and organization of the Federalists prevailed and the Constitution was ratified, but only after the first ten amendments, the "Bill of Rights," had been submitted to satisfy the demands of the majority of the people. Because of the radicals' fear of tyranny under the conservative constitution, bitter conflict between Federalists and anti-Federalists carried over into the early years of the Republic. Soon, however, popular victories at the polls proved these fears unfounded and demonstrated that the Founding Fathers had in fact possessed the vision and wisdom to create "a more perfect union" which did in time become truly a government "of the people, by the people, for the people."

The Constitution of the United States, *1787*

We the People of the United States, in order to form a more perfect union, establish justice, insure domestic tranquility, provide for the common defence, promote the general welfare, and secure the blessings of liberty to ourselves and our posterity, do ordain and establish this Constitution for the United States of America.

ARTICLE I

Sec. 1. All legislative powers herein granted shall be vested in a Congress of the United States, which shall consist of a Senate and House of Representatives.

Sec. 2. The House of Representatives shall be composed of members chosen every second year by the people of the several States, and the electors in each State shall have the qualifications requisite for electors of the most numerous branch of the State legislature.

No person shall be a Representative who shall not have attained to the age of twenty-five years, and been seven years a citizen of the United States, and who shall not, when elected, be an inhabitant of that State in which he shall be chosen.

Representatives and direct taxes shall be apportioned among the several States which may be included within this Union, according to their respective numbers, which shall be determined by adding to the whole number of free persons, including those bound to service for a term of years, and excluding Indians not taxed, three-fifths of all other persons. The actual enumeration shall be made within three years after the first meeting of the Congress of the United States, and within every subsequent term of ten years, in such manner as they shall by law direct. The number of Representatives shall not exceed one for every thirty thousand, but each State shall have at least one Representative; and until such enumeration shall be made, the State of New Hampshire shall be entitled to choose three, Massachusetts eight, Rhode Island and Providence Plantations one, Connecticut five, New York six, New Jersey four, Pennsylvania eight, Delaware one, Maryland six, Virginia ten, North Carolina five, South Carolina five, and Georgia three.

When vacancies happen in the representation from any State, the executive authority thereof shall issue writs of election to fill such vacancies.

The House of Representatives shall choose their Speaker and other officers; and shall have the sole power of impeachment.

Sec. 3. The Senate of the United States shall be composed of two Senators from each State, chosen by the legislature thereof, for six years; and each Senator shall have one vote.

Immediately after they shall be assembled in consequence of the first election, they shall be divided as equally as may be into three classes. The seats of the Senators of the first class shall be vacated at the expiration of the second year, of the second class at the expiration of the fourth year, and of the third class at the expiration of the sixth year, so that one-third may be chosen every second year; and if vacancies happen by resignation, or otherwise, during the recess of the legislature of any State, the executive thereof may make temporary appointments until the next meeting of the legislature, which shall then fill such vacancies.

No person shall be a Senator who shall not have attained to the age of thirty years, and been nine years a citizen of the United States, and who shall not, when elected, be an inhabitant of that State for which he shall be chosen.

The Vice-President of the United States shall be President of the Senate, but shall have no vote, unless they be equally divided.

The Senate shall choose their other officers, and also a President pro tempore, in the absence of the Vice-President, or when he shall exercise the office of President of the United States.

The Senate shall have the sole power to try all impeachments. When sitting for that purpose, they shall be on oath or affirmation. When the President of the United States is tried, the Chief Justice shall preside: and no person shall be convicted without the concurrence of two-thirds of the members present.

Judgment in cases of impeachment shall not extend further than to removal from office, and disqualification to hold and enjoy any office of honor, trust or profit under the United States: but the party convicted shall nevertheless be liable and subject to indictment, trial, judgment, and punishment, according to law.

Sec. 4. The times, places and manner of holding elections for Senators and Representatives, shall be prescribed in each State by the legislature thereof; but the Congress may at any time by law make or alter such regulations, except as to the places of choosing Senators.

The Congress shall assemble at least once in every year, and such meeting shall be on the first Monday in December, unless they shall by law appoint a different day.

Sec. 5. Each house shall be the judge of the elections, returns and qualifications of its own members, and a majority of each shall constitute a quorum to do business; but a smaller number may adjourn from day to day, and may be authorized to compel the attendance of absent members, in such manner, and under such penalties as each House may provide.

Each house may determine the rules of its proceedings, punish its members for disorderly behaviour, and, with the concurrence of two-thirds, expel a member.

Each house shall keep a journal of its proceedings, and from time to time publish the same, excepting such parts as may in their judgment require secrecy; and the yeas and nays of the members of either house on any question shall, at the desire of one-fifth of those present, be entered on the journal.

Neither house, during the session of Congress, shall, without the consent of the other, adjourn for more than three days, nor to any other place than that in which the two Houses shall be sitting.

Sec. 6. The Senators and Representatives shall receive a compensation for their services, to be ascertained by law, and paid out of the Treasury of the United States. They shall in all cases, except treason, felony and breach of the peace, be privileged from arrest during their attendance at the session of their respective Houses, and in going to and returning from the same; and for any speech or debate in either House, they shall not be questioned in any other place.

No Senator or Representative shall, during the time for which he was elected, be appointed to any civil office under the authority of the United States which shall have been created, or the emoluments whereof shall have been increased during such time; and no person holding any office under the United States, shall be a member of either House during his continuance in office.

Sec. 7. All bills for raising revenue shall originate in the House of Representatives; but the Senate may propose or concur with amendments as on other bills.

Every bill which shall have passed the House of Representatives and the Senate, shall, before it become a law, be presented to the President of the United States; if he approve he shall sign it, but if not he shall return it, with his objections to that house in which it shall have originated, who shall enter the objections at large on their journal, and proceed to reconsider it. If after such reconsideration two-thirds of that house shall agree to pass the bill, it shall be sent, together with the objections, to the other house, by which it shall likewise be reconsidered, and if approved by two-thirds of that house, it shall become a law. But in all such cases the votes of both houses shall be determined by yeas and nays, and the names of the persons voting for and against the bill shall be entered on the journal of each house respectively. If any bill shall not be returned by the President within ten days (Sundays excepted) after it shall have been presented to him, the same shall be a law, in like manner as if he had signed it, unless the Congress by their adjournment prevent its return, in which case it shall not be a law.

Every order, resolution, or vote to which the concurrence of the Senate and House of Representatives may be necessary (except on a question of adjournment) shall be presented to the President of the United States; and before the same shall take effect, shall be approved by him, or being disapproved by him, shall be repassed by two-thirds of the Senate and House of Representatives, according to the rules and limitations prescribed in the case of a bill.

Sec. 8. The Congress shall have power to lay and collect taxes, duties, imposts, and excises, to pay the debts and provide for the common defence and general welfare of the United States; but all duties, imposts, and excises shall be uniform throughout the United States;

To borrow money on the credit of the United States;

To regulate commerce with foreign nations, and among the several States, and with the Indian tribes;

To establish a uniform rule of naturalization, and uniform laws on the subject of bankruptcies throughout the United States;

To coin money, regulate the value thereof, and of foreign coin, and fix the standard of weights and measures;

To provide for the punishment of counterfeiting the securities and current coin of the United States;

To establish post-offices and post-roads;

To promote the progress of science and useful arts, by securing for limited times to authors and inventors the exclusive right to their respective writings and discoveries;

To constitute tribunals inferior to the Supreme Court;

To define and punish piracies and felonies committed on the high seas, and offences against the law of nations;

To declare war, grant letters of marque and reprisal, and make rules concerning captures on land and water;

To raise and support armies, but no appropriation of money to that use shall be for a longer term than two years;

To provide and maintain a navy;

To make rules for the government and regulation of the land and naval forces;

To provide for calling forth the militia to execute the laws of the Union, suppress insurrections and repel invasions;

To provide for organizing, arming, and disciplining the militia, and for governing such part of them as may be employed in the service of the United States, reserving to the States respectively the appointment of the officers, and the authority of training the militia according to the discipline prescribed by Congress;

To exercise exclusive legislation in all cases whatsoever, over such district (not exceeding ten miles square) as may, by cession of particular States, and the acceptance of Congress, become the seat of the Government of the United States, and to exercise like authority over all places purchased by the consent of the Legislature of the State in which the same shall be, for the erection of forts, magazines, arsenals, dockyards, and other needful buildings; and

To make all laws which shall be necessary and proper for carrying into execution the foregoing powers, and all other powers vested by this Constitution in the Government of the United States, or in any department or officer thereof.

Sec. 9. The migration or importation of such persons as any of the States now existing shall think proper to admit, shall not be prohibited by the Congress prior to the year one thousand eight hundred and eight, but a tax or duty may be imposed on such importation, not exceeding ten dollars for each person.

The privilege of the writ of habeas corpus shall not be suspended, unless when in cases of rebellion or invasion the public safety may require it.

No bill of attainder or ex post facto law shall be passed.

No capitation, or other direct, tax shall be laid, unless in proportion to the census or enumeration herein before directed to be taken.

No tax or duty shall be laid on articles exported from any State.

No preference shall be given by any regulation of commerce or revenue to the ports of one State over those of another: nor shall vessels bound to, or from, one State, be obliged to enter, clear, or pay duties in another.

No money shall be drawn from the Treasury but in consequence of appropriations made by law; and a regular statement and account of the receipts and expenditures of all public money shall be published from time to time.

No title of nobility shall be granted by the United States: and no person holding any office of profit or trust under them, shall, without the consent of the Congress, accept of any present, emolument, office, or title, of any kind whatever, from any king, prince or foreign State.

Sec. 10. No State shall enter into any treaty, alliance, or confederation; grant letters of marque and reprisal; coin money; emit bills of credit; make any thing but gold and silver coin a tender in payment of debts; pass any bill of attainder, ex post facto law, or law impairing the obligation of contracts, or grant any title of nobility.

No State shall, without the consent of the Congress, lay any imposts or duties on imports or exports, except what may be absolutely necessary for executing its inspection laws: and the net produce of all duties and imposts, laid by any State on imports or exports, shall be for the use of the Treasury of the United States; and all such laws shall be subject to the revision and control of the Congress.

No State shall, without the consent of Congress, lay any duty of tonnage, keep troops, or ships of war in time of peace, enter into any agreement or compact with another State, or with a foreign power, or engage in war, unless actually invaded, or in such imminent danger as will not admit of delay.

ARTICLE II

Sec. 1. The executive power shall be vested in a President of the United States of America. He shall hold his office during the term of four years, and, together with the Vice-President, chosen for the same term, be elected, as follows:

Each State shall appoint, in such manner as the legislature thereof may direct, a number of electors, equal to the whole number of Senators and Representatives to which the State may be entitled in the Congress: but no Senator or Representative, or person holding an office of trust or profit under the United States, shall be appointed an elector.

The electors shall meet in their respective States, and vote by ballot for two persons, of whom one at least shall not be an inhabitant of the same State with themselves. And they shall make a list of all the persons voted for, and of the number of votes for each; which list they shall sign and certify, and transmit sealed to the seat of the Government of the United States, directed to the President of the Senate. The President of the Senate shall, in the presence of the Senate and House of Representatives, open all the certificates, and the votes shall then be counted. The person having the greatest number of votes shall be the President, if such number be a majority of the whole number of electors appointed; and if there be more than one who have such majority, and have an equal number of votes, then the House of Representatives shall immediately choose by ballot one of them for President; and if no person have a majority, then from the five highest on the list the said house shall in like manner choose the President. But in choosing the President, the votes shall be taken by States, the representation from each State having one vote; a quorum for this purpose shall consist of a member or members from two-thirds of the States, and a majority of all the States shall be necessary to a choice. In every case, after the choice of the President, the person having the greatest number of votes of the electors shall be the Vice-President. But if there should remain two or more who have equal votes, the Senate shall choose from them by ballot the Vice-President.

The Congress may determine the time of choosing the electors, and the day on which they shall give their votes; which day shall be the same throughout the United States.

No person except a natural-born citizen, or a citizen of the United States, at the time of the adoption of this Constitution, shall be eligible to the office of President; neither shall any person be eligible to that office who shall not have attained to the age of thirty-five years, and been fourteen years a resident within the United States.

In case of the removal of the President from office, or of his death, resignation, or inability to discharge the powers and duties of the said office, the same shall devolve on the Vice-President, and the Congress may by law provide for the case of removal, death, resignation, or inability, both of the President and Vice-President, declaring what officer shall then act as President, and such officer shall act accordingly, until the disability be removed, or a President shall be elected.

The President shall, at stated times, receive for his services, a compensation, which shall neither be increased nor diminished during the period for which he shall have been elected, and he shall not receive within that period any other emolument from the United States, or any of them.

Before he enter on the execution of his office, he shall take the following oath or affirmation: 'I do solemnly swear (or affirm) that I will faithfully execute the office of President of the United States, and will to the best of my ability, preserve, protect, and defend the Constitution of the United States:'

Sec. 2. The President shall be Commander-in-Chief of the Army and Navy of the United States, and of the militia of the several States, when called into the actual service of the United States; he may require the opinion, in writing, of the principal officer in each of the executive departments, upon any subject relating to the duties of their respective offices, and he shall have power to grant reprieves and pardons for offences against the United States, except in cases of impeachment.

He shall have power, by and with the advice and consent of the Senate, to make treaties, provided two-thirds of the Senators present concur; and he shall nominate, and by and with the advice and consent of the Senate, shall appoint ambassadors, other public ministers and consuls, judges of the Supreme Court, and all other officers of the United States, whose appointments are not herein otherwise provided for, and which shall be established by law: but the Congress may by law vest the appointment of such inferior officers, as they think proper, in the President alone, in the courts of law, or in the heads of departments.

The President shall have power to fill up all vacancies that may happen during the recess of the Senate, by granting commissions which shall expire at the end of their next session.

Sec. 3. He shall from time to time give to the Congress information of the state of the Union, and recommend to their consideration such measures as he shall judge necessary and expedient; he may, on extraordinary occasions, convene both houses, or either of them, and in case of disagreement between them, with respect to the time of adjournment, he may adjourn them to such time as he shall think proper; he shall receive ambassadors and other public ministers; he shall take care that the laws be faithfully executed, and shall commission all the officers of the United States.

Sec. 4. The President, Vice-President and all civil officers of the United States, shall be removed from office on impeachment for, and conviction of, treason, bribery, or other high crimes and misdemeanors.

ARTICLE III

Sec. 1. The judicial power of the United States, shall be vested in one Supreme Court, and in such inferior courts as the Congress may from time to time ordain and establish. The judges, both of the supreme and inferior courts, shall hold their offices during good behaviour, and shall, at stated times, receive for their services, a compensation, which shall not be diminished during their continuance in office.

Sec. 2. The judicial power shall extend to all cases, in law and equity, arising under this Constitution, the laws of the United States, and treaties made, or which shall be made, under their authority; to all cases affecting ambassadors, other public ministers and consuls; to all cases of admiralty and maritime jurisdiction; to controversies to which the United

States shall be a party; to controversies between two or more States; between a State and citizens of another State; between citizens of different States, between citizens of the same State claiming lands under grants of different States, and between a State, or the citizen thereof, and foreign States, citizens or subjects.

In all cases affecting ambassadors, other public ministers and consuls, and those in which a State shall be party, the Supreme Court shall have original jurisdiction. In all the other cases before mentioned, the Supreme Court shall have appellate jurisdiction, both as to law and fact, with such exceptions, and under such regulations as the Congress shall make.

The trial of all crimes, except in cases of impeachment, shall be by jury; and such trial shall be held in the State where the said crimes shall have been committed; but when not committed within any State, the trial shall be at such place or places as the Congress may by law have directed.

Sec. 3. Treason against the United States, shall consist only in levying war against them, or in adhering to their enemies, giving them aid and comfort. No person shall be convicted of treason unless on the testimony of two witnesses to the same overt act, or on confession in open court.

The Congress shall have power to declare the punishment of treason, but no attainder of treason shall work corruption of blood, or forfeiture except during the life of the person attainted.

ARTICLE IV

Sec. 1. Full faith and credit shall be given in each State to the public acts, records, and judicial proceedings of every other State. And the Congress may by general laws prescribe the manner in which such acts, records, and proceedings shall be provided, and the effect thereof.

Sec. 2. The citizens of each State shall be entitled to all privileges and immunities of citizens in the several States.

A person charged in any State with treason, felony, or other crime, who shall flee from justice, and be found in another State, shall on demand of the executive authority of the State from which he fled, be delivered up, to be removed to the State having jurisdiction of the crime.

No person held to service or labor in one State, under the laws thereof, escaping into another, shall, in consequence of any law or regulation therein, be discharged from such service or labor, but shall be delivered up on claim of the party to whom such service or labor may be due.

Sec. 3. New States may be admitted by the Congress into this Union; but no new States shall be formed or erected within the jurisdiction of any other State; nor any State be formed by the junction of two or more states; or parts of States, without the consent of the legislatures of the States concerned as well as of the Congress.

The Congress shall have power to dispose of and make all needful rules and regulations respecting the territory or other property belonging to the United States; and nothing in this Constitution shall be so construed as to prejudice any claims of the United States, or of any particular State.

Sec. 4. The United States shall guarantee to every State in this Union a republican form of government, and shall protect each of them against invasion; and on application of the legislature, or of the executive (when the legislature cannot be convened) against domestic violence.

ARTICLE V

The Congress, whenever two-thirds of both houses shall deem it necessary, shall propose amendments to this Constitution, or, on the application of the legislature of two-thirds of the several States, shall call a convention for proposing amendments, which, in either case, shall be valid to all intents and purposes, as part of this Constitution, when ratified by the legislatures of three-fourths of the several States, or by conventions in three-fourths thereof, as the one or the other mode of ratification may be proposed by the Congress; provided that no amendment which may be made prior to the year one thousand eight hundred and eight shall in any manner affect the first and fourth clauses in the ninth section of the first article; and that no State, without its consent, shall be deprived of its equal suffrage in the Senate.

ARTICLE VI

All debts contracted and engagements entered into, before the adoption of this Constitution, shall be as valid against the United States under this Constitution, as under the Confederation.

This Constitution, and the laws of the United States which shall be made in pursuance thereof; and all treaties made, or which shall be made, under the authority of the United States, shall be the supreme law of the land; and the judges in every State shall be bound thereby, anything in the Constitution or laws of any State to the contrary notwithstanding.

The Senators and Representatives before mentioned, and the members of the several State legislatures, and all executive and judicial officers, both of the United States and of the several States, shall be bound by oath or affirmation, to support this Constitution; but no religious test shall ever be required as a qualification to any office or public trust under the United States.

ARTICLE VII

The ratification of the conventions of nine States, shall be sufficient for the establishment of this Constitution between the States so ratifying the same.

Done in convention by the unanimous consent of the States present, the seventeenth day of September in the year of our Lord one thousand seven hundred and eighty-seven and of the independence of the United States of America the twelfth. In witness whereof, we have hereunto subscribed our names,

Gº WASHINGTON—Presidᵗ and deputy from Virginia

New Hampshire
   JOHN LANGDON
   NICHOLAS GILMAN
Massachusetts
   NATHANIEL GORHAM
   RUFUS KING
Connecticut
   Wᴹ Samᴸ JOHNSON
   ROGER SHERMAN
New York
   ALEXANDER HAMILTON
New Jersey
   WIL: LIVINGSTON
   DAVID BREARLEY
   Wᴹ PATERSON
   JONA: DAYTON
Pennsylvania
   B. FRANKLIN
   THOMAS MIFFLIN
   ROBᵀ MORRIS
   GEO. CLYMER
   THOˢ FITZSIMONS
   JARED INGERSOLL
   JAMES WILSON
   GOUV MORRIS

Delaware
   GEO: READ
   GUNNING BEDFORD jun
   JOHN DICKINSON
   RICHARD BASSETT
   JACO: BROOM
Maryland
   JAMES MᶜHENRY
   DAN of Sᵀ THOˢ JENIFER
   DANᴸ CARROLL
Virginia
   JOHN BLAIR
   JAMES MADISON JR.
North Carolina
   Wᴹ BLOUNT
   RICHᴰ DOBBS SPAIGHT
   HU WILLIAMSON
South Carolina
   J. RUTLEDGE
   CHARLES COTESWORTH
      PINCKNEY
   CHARLES PINCKNEY
   PIERCE BUTLER
Georgia
   WILLIAM FEW
   ABR BALDWIN

AMENDMENTS TO THE CONSTITUTION

ARTICLES I-X (the Bill of Rights) 1791

ARTICLE I

Congress shall make no law respecting an establishment of religion, or prohibiting the free exercise thereof; or abridging the freedom of speech, or of the press; or the right of the people peaceably to assemble, and to petition the government for a redress of grievances.

ARTICLE II

A well regulated militia, being necessary to the security of a free State, the right of the people to keep and bear arms, shall not be infringed.

ARTICLE III

No soldier shall, in time of peace be quartered in any house, without the consent of the owner, nor in time of war, but in a manner to be prescribed by law.

ARTICLE IV

The right of the people to be secure in their persons, houses, papers, and effects, against unreasonable searches and seizures, shall not be violated, and no warrants shall issue, but upon probable cause, supported by oath or affirmation, and particularly describing the place to be searched, and the persons or things to be seized.

ARTICLE V

No person shall be held to answer for a capital, or otherwise infamous crime, unless on a presentment or indictment of a grand jury, except in cases arising in the land or naval forces, or in the militia, when in actual service in time of war or public danger; nor shall any person be subject for the same offence to be twice put in jeopardy of life or limb; nor shall be compelled in any criminal case to be a witness against himself, nor be deprived of life, liberty, or property, without due process of law; nor shall private property be taken for public use, without just compensation.

ARTICLE VI

In all criminal prosecutions, the accused shall enjoy the right to a speedy and public trial, by an impartial jury of the State and district wherein the crime shall have been committed, which district shall have been previously ascertained by law, and to be informed of the nature and cause of the accusation; to be confronted with the witnesses against him; to have compulsory process for obtaining witnesses in his favor, and to have the assistance of counsel for his defence.

ARTICLE VII

In suits at common law, where the value in controversy shall exceed twenty dollars, the right of trial by jury shall be preserved, and no fact tried by a jury, shall be otherwise reexamined in any court of the United States, than according to the rules of the common law.

ARTICLE VIII

Excessive bail shall not be required, nor excessive fines imposed, nor cruel and unusual punishments inflicted.

ARTICLE IX

The enumeration in the Constitution, of certain rights, shall not be construed to deny or disparage others retained by the people.

ARTICLE X

The powers not delegated to the United States by the Constitution, nor prohibited by it to the States, are reserved to the States respectively, or to the people.

ARTICLE XI (1798)

The judicial power of the United States shall not be construed to extend to any suit in law or equity, commenced or prosecuted against one of the United States by citizens of another State, or by citizens or subjects of any foreign State.

ARTICLE XII (1804)

The electors shall meet in their respective states, and vote by ballot for President and Vice-President, one of whom, at least, shall not be an inhabitant of the same state with themselves; they shall name in their ballots the person voted for as President, and in distinct ballots the person voted for as Vice-President, and they shall make distinct lists of all persons voted for as President, and of all persons voted for as Vice-President, and of the number of votes for each, which lists they shall sign and certify, and transmit sealed to the seat of the Government of the United States, directed to the President of the Senate; The President of the Senate shall, in the presence of the Senate and House of Representatives, open all the certificates and the votes shall then be counted; The person having the greatest number of votes for President, shall be the President, if such number be a majority of the whole number of electors appointed; and if no person have such majority, then from the persons having the highest numbers not exceeding three on the list of those voted for as President, the House of Representatives shall choose immediately, by ballot, the President. But in choosing the President, the votes shall be taken by states, the representation from each state having one vote; a quorum for this purpose shall consist of a member or members from two-thirds of the states, and a majority of all the states shall be necessary to a choice. And if the House of Representatives shall not choose a President whenever the right of choice shall devolve upon them, before the fourth day of March next following, then the Vice-President shall act as President, as in the case of death or other constitutional disability of the President. The person having the greatest number of votes as Vice-President, shall be the Vice-President, if such number be a majority of the whole number of electors appointed, and if no person have a majority, then from the two highest numbers on the list, the Senate shall choose the Vice-President; a quorum for the purpose shall consist of two-thirds of the whole number of Senators, and a majority of the whole number shall be necessary to a choice. But no person constitutionally ineligible to the office of President shall be eligible to that of Vice-President of the United States.

Article XIII (1865)

Sec. 1. Neither slavery nor involuntary servitude, except as a punishment for crime whereof the party shall have been duly convicted, shall exist within the United States, or any place subject to their jurisdiction.

Sec. 2. Congress shall have power to enforce this article by appropriate legislation.

Article XIV (1868)

Sec. 1. All persons born or naturalized in the United States, and subject to the jurisdiction thereof, are citizens of the United States and of the State wherein they reside. No State shall make or enforce any law which shall abridge the privileges or immunities of citizens of the United States; nor shall any State deprive any person of life, liberty, or property, without due process of law; nor deny to any person within its jurisdiction the equal protection of the laws.

Sec. 2. Representatives shall be appointed among the several States according to their respective numbers, counting the whole number of persons in each State, excluding Indians not taxed. But when the right to vote at any election for the choice of electors for President and Vice-President of the United States, Representatives in Congress, the executive and judicial officer of any State, to support the Constitution of the United States, is denied to any of the male inhabitants of such State, being twenty-one years of age, and citizens of the United States, or in any way abridged, except for participation in rebellion, or other crime, the basis of representation therein shall be reduced in the proportion which the number of such male citizens shall bear to the whole number of male citizens twenty-one years of age in such State.

Sec. 3. No person shall be a Senator or Representative in Congress, or elector of President and Vice-President, or hold any office, civil or military, under the United States, or under any State, who, having previously taken an oath, as a member of Congress, or as an officer of the United States, or as a member of any State legislature, or as an executive or judicial officer of any State, to support the Constitution of the United States, shall have engaged in insurrection or rebellion against the same, or given aid or comfort to the enemies thereof. But Congress may by a vote of two-thirds of each house, remove such disability.

Sec. 4. The validity of the public debt of the United States, authorized by law, including debts incurred for payment of pensions and bounties for services in suppressing insurrection or rebellion, shall not be questioned. But neither the United States nor any State shall assume or pay any debt or obligation incurred in aid of insurrection or rebellion against the United States, or any claim for the loss or emancipation of any slave; but all such debts, obligations and claims shall be held illegal and void.

Sec. 5. The Congress shall have power to enforce, by appropriate legislation, the provisions of this article.

ARTICLE XV (1870)

Sec. 1. The right of citizens of the United States to vote shall not be denied or abridged by the United States or by any State on account of race, color, or previous condition of servitude.

Sec. 2. The Congress shall have power to enforce this article by appropriate legislation.

ARTICLE XVI (1913)

The Congress shall have power to lay and collect taxes on incomes, from whatever source derived, without apportionment among the several States and without regard to any census or enumeration.

ARTICLE XVII (1913)

The Senate of the United States shall be composed of two Senators from each State, elected by the people thereof, for six years, and each Senator shall have one vote. The electors in each State shall have the qualifications requisite for electors of the most numerous branch of the State legislature.

When vacancies happen in the representation of any State in the Senate, the executive authority of such State shall issue writs of election to fill such vacancies: *Provided,* That the legislature of any State may empower the executive thereof to make temporary appointments until the people fill the vacancies by election as the legislature may direct.

This amendment shall not be so construed as to affect the election or term of any Senator chosen before it becomes valid as part of the Constitution.

ARTICLE XVIII (1919)

After one year from the ratification of this article, the manufacture, sale, or transportation of intoxicating liquors within, the importation thereof into, or the exportation thereof from the United States and all territory subject to the jurisdiction thereof for beverage purposes is hereby prohibited.

The Congress and the several States shall have concurrent power to enforce this article by appropriate legislation.

This article shall be inoperative unless it shall have been ratified as an amendment to the Constitution by the legislatures of the several States, as provided in the Constitution, within seven years from the date of the submission hereof to the States by Congress.

ARTICLE XIX (1920)

The right of citizens of the United States to vote shall not be denied or abridged by the United States or by any States on account of sex.

The Congress shall have power to appropriate legislation to enforce the provisions of this article.

ARTICLE XX (1933)

Sec. 1. The terms of the President and Vice-President shall end at noon on the twentieth day of January, and the terms of Senators and Representatives at noon on the third day of January, of the years in which such terms would have ended if this article had not been ratified; and the terms of their successors shall then begin.

Sec. 2. The Congress shall assemble at least once in every year, and such meeting shall begin at noon on the third day of January, unless they shall by law appoint a different day.

Sec. 3. If, at the time fixed for the beginning of the term of the President, the President-elect shall have died, the Vice-President-elect shall become President. If a President shall not have been chosen before the time fixed for the beginning of his term, or if the President-elect shall have failed to qualify, then the Vice-President-elect shall act as President until a President shall have qualified; and the Congress may by law provide for the case wherein neither a President-elect nor a Vice-President-elect shall have qualified, declaring who shall then act as President, or the manner in which one who is to act shall be elected, and such person shall act accordingly until a president or vice-president shall have qualified.

Sec. 4. The Congress may by law provide for the case of the death of any of the persons from whom the House of Representatives may choose a President whenever the right of choice shall have devolved upon them, and for the case of the death of any of the persons from whom the Senate may choose a Vice-President whenever the right of choice shall have devolved upon them.

Sec. 5. Selections 1 and 2 shall take effect on the Fifteenth day of October following the ratification of this article.

Sec. 6. This article shall be inoperative unless it shall have been ratified as an amendment to the Constitution by the legislatures of three-fourths of the several States within seven years from the date of its submission.

ARTICLE XXI (1933)

Sec. 1. The eighteenth article of amendment to the Constitution of the United States is hereby repealed.

Sec. 2. The transportation or importation into any State, territory or possession of the United States for delivery or use therein of intoxicating liquors, in violation of the laws thereof, is hereby prohibited.

Sec. 3. This article shall be inoperative unless it shall have been ratified as an amendment to the Constitution by convention in the several States, as provided in the Constitution, within seven years from the date of the submission thereof to the States by the Congress.

ARTICLE XXII (1951)

Sec. 1. No person shall be elected to the office of the President more than twice, and no person who has held the office of President, or acted as President, for more than two years of a term to which some other person was elected President shall be elected to the office of the President more than once. But this Article shall not apply to any person holding the office of President when this Article was proposed by the Congress, and shall not prevent any person who may be holding the office of President or acting as President during the term within which this Article becomes operative, from holding the office of President, or acting as President, during the remainder of such term.

Sec. 2. This article shall be inoperative unless it shall have been ratified as an amendment to the Constitution by the legislatures of three-fourths of the several States within seven years from the date of its submission to the States by the Congress.

ARTICLE XXIII (1961)

Sec. 1. The District constituting the seat of Government of the United States shall appoint in such manner as the Congress may direct:

A number of electors of President and Vice-President equal to the whole number of Senators and Representatives in Congress to which the District would be entitled if it were a State, but in no event more than the least populous State; they shall be in addition to those appointed by the States, but they shall be considered, for the purposes of the election of President and Vice-President, to be electors appointed by a State; and they shall meet in the District and perform such duties as provided by the twelfth article of amendment.

Sec. 2. The Congress shall have power to enforce this article by appropriate legislation.

ARTICLE XXIV (1964)

Sec. 1. The right of citizens of the United States to vote in any primary or other election for President or Vice-President, for electors for President or Vice-President, or for Senator or Representative in Congress, shall not be denied or abridged by the United States or any State by reason of failure to pay any poll tax or other tax.

Sec. 2. The Congress shall have the power to enforce this article by appropriate legislation.

ARTICLE XXV (1967)

Sec. 1. In case of the removal of the President from office or of his death or resignation, the Vice-President shall become President.

Sec. 2. Whenever there is a vacancy in the office of the Vice-President, the President shall nominate a Vice-President who shall take office upon confirmation by a majority vote of both Houses of Congress.

Sec. 3. Whenever the President transmits to the President pro tempore of the Senate and the Speaker of the House of Representatives his written declaration that he is unable to discharge the powers and duties of his office, and until he transmits to them a written declaration to the contrary, such powers and duties shall be discharged by the Vice-President as Acting President.

Sec. 4. Whenever the Vice-President and a majority of either of the principal officers of the executive departments or of such other body as Congress may by law provide, transmit to the President pro tempore of the Senate and the Speaker of the House of Representatives their written declaration that the President is unable to discharge the powers and duties of his office, the Vice-President shall immediately assume the powers and duties of the office as Acting President.

Thereafter, when the President transmits to the President pro tempore of the Senate and the Speaker of the House of Representatives his written declaration that no inability exists, he shall resume the powers and duties of his office unless the Vice-President and a majority of either the principal officers of the executive department or of such other body as Congress may by law provide, transmit within four days to the President pro tempore of the Senate and the Speaker of the House of Representatives their written declaration that the President is unable to discharge the powers and duties of his office. Thereupon Congress shall decide the issue, assembling within forty-eight hours for that purpose if not in session. If the Congress, within twenty-one days after receipt of the latter written declaration, or, if Congress is not in session, within twenty-one days after Congress is required to assemble, determines by two-thirds vote of both Houses that the President is unable to discharge the powers and duties of his office, the Vice-President shall continue to discharge the same as Acting President; otherwise, the President shall resume the powers and duties of his office.

ARTICLE XXVI (1971)

Sec. 1. The right of citizens of the United States, who are eighteen years of age or older, to vote shall not be denied or abridged by the United States or by any State on account of age.

Sec. 2. The Congress shall have power to enforce this article by appropriate legislation.

The Federalist Number Ten, *James Madison, 1787*

TO THE PEOPLE OF THE STATE OF NEW YORK: Among the numerous advantages promised by a well constructed Union, none deserves to be more accurately developed than its tendency to break and control the violence of faction. The friend of popular governments never finds himself so much alarmed for their character and fate, as when he contemplates their propensity to this dangerous vice. He will not fail, therefore, to set a due value on any plan which, without violating the principles to which he is attached, provides a proper cure for it. The instability, injustice, and confusion introduced into the public councils, have, in truth, been the mortal diseases under which popular governments have everywhere perished; as they continue to be the favorite and fruitful topics from which the adversaries to liberty derive their most specious declamations. The valuable improvements made by the American constitutions on the popular models, both ancient and modern, cannot certainly be too much admired; but it would be an unwarrantable partiality, to contend that they have as effectually obviated the danger on this side, as was wished and expected. Complaints are everywhere heard from our most considerate and virtuous citizens, equally the friends of public and private faiths, and of public and personal liberty, that our governments are too unstable, that the public good is disregarded in the conflicts of rival parties, and that measures are too often decided, not according to the rules of justice and the rights of the minor party, but by the superior force of an interested and overbearing majority. However anxiously we may wish that these complaints had no foundation, the evidence of known facts will not permit us to deny that they are in some degree true. It will be found, indeed, on a candid review of our situation, that some of the distresses under which we labor have been erroneously charged on the operation of our governments; but it will be found, at the same time, that other causes will not alone account for many of our heaviest misfortunes; and particularly, for that prevailing and increasing distrust of public engagements, and alarm for private rights, which are echoed from one end of the continent to the other. These must be chiefly, if not wholly, effects of the unsteadiness and injustice with which a factious spirit has tainted our public administrations.

By a faction, I understand a number of citizens, whether amounting to a majority or minority of the whole, who are united and actuated by some common impulse of passion, or of interest, adverse to the rights of other citizens, or to the permanent and aggregate interests of the community.

There are two methods of curing the mischiefs of faction: the one, by removing its causes; the other, by controlling its effects.

There are again two methods of removing the causes of faction: the one, by destroying the liberty which is essential to its existence; the other, by giving to every citizen the same opinions, the same passions, and the same interests.

It could never be more truly said than of the first remedy, that it was worse than the disease. Liberty is to faction what air is to fire, an ailment without which it instantly expires. But it could not be less folly to abolish liberty, which is essential to political life, because it nourishes faction, than it would be to wish the annihilation of air, which is essential to animal life, because it imparts to fire its destructive agency.

The second expedient is as impracticable as the first would be unwise. As long as the reason of man continues fallible, and he is at liberty to exercise it, different opinions will be formed. As long as the connection subsists between his reason and his self-love, his opinions and his passion will have a reciprocal influence on each other, and the former will be objects to which the latter will attach themselves. The diversity in the faculties of men, from which the rights of property originate, is not less an insuperable obstacle to a uniformity of interests. The protection of these faculties is the first object of government. From the protection of different and unequal faculties of acquiring property, the possession of different degrees and kinds of property immediately results; and from the influence of these on the sentiments and views of the respective proprietors, ensues a division of the society into different interests and parties.

The latent causes of faction are thus sown in the nature of man; and we see them everywhere brought into different degrees of activity, according to the different circumstances of civil society. A zeal for different opinions concerning religion, concerning government, and many other points, as well of speculation as of practise; an attachment to different leaders ambitiously contending for pre-eminence and power; or to persons of other descriptions whose fortunes have been interesting to the human passions, have, in turn, divided mankind into parties, inflamed them with mutual animosity, and rendered them much more disposed to vex and oppress each other than to co-operate for their common good. So strong is this propensity of mankind to fall into mutual animosities, that where no substantial occasion presents itself, the most frivolous and fanciful distinctions have been sufficient to kindle their unfriendly passions and excite their most violent conflicts. But the most common and durable source of factions has been the various and unequal distribution of property. Those who hold and those who are without property have ever formed distinct interests in society. Those who are creditors, and those who are debtors, fall under a like discrimination. A landed interest, a manufacturing interest, a mercantile interest, a moneyed interest, with many lesser interests, grow up of necessity in civilized nations, and divide them into different classes, actuated by different sentiments and views. The regulation of these various and interfering interests forms the principal task of modern legislation, and involves the spirit of party and faction in the necessary and ordinary operations of the government.

No man is allowed to be a judge in his own cause, because his interest would certainly bias his judgment, and, not improbably, corrupt his integrity. With equal, nay with greater reason, a body of men are unfit to be both judges and parties at the same time; yet what are many of the most important acts of legislation, but so many judicial determinations, not indeed concerning the rights of single persons, but concerning the rights of large bodies of citizens? And what are the different classes of legislators but advocates and parties to the causes which they determine? Is a law proposed concerning private debts? It is a question to which the creditors are parties on one side and the debtors on the other. Justice ought to hold the balance between them. Yet the parties are, and must be, themselves the judges; and the most numerous party, or, in other words, the most powerful faction, must be expected to prevail. Shall domestic manufactures be encouraged, and in what degree, by restrictions on foreign manufactures? These are questions which would be differently decided by the landed and the manufacturing classes, and probably by neither with a sole regard to justice and the public good. The apportionment of taxes on the various descriptions of property is an act which seems to require the most exact impartiality; yet there is, perhaps, no legislative act in which greater opportunity and temptation are given to a predominant party to trample on the rules of justice. Every shilling with which they overburden the interior number, is a shilling saved to their own pockets.

It is in vain to say that enlightened statesmen will be able to adjust these clashing interests, and render them all subservient to the public good. Enlightened statesmen will not always be at the helm. Nor, in many cases, can such an adjustment be made at all without taking into view indirect and remote considerations, which will rarely prevail over the immediate interest which one party may find in disregarding the rights of another or the good of the whole.

The inference to which we are brought is, that the *causes* of faction cannot be removed, and that relief is only to be sought in the means of controlling its *effects*.

If a faction consists of less than a majority, relief is supplied by the republican principle, which enables the majority to defeat its sinister view by regular vote. It may clog the administration, it may convulse the society, but it will be unable to execute and mask its violence under the forms of the Constitution. When a majority is included in a faction, the form of popular government, on the other hand, enables it to sacrifice to its ruling passion or interest both the public good and the rights of other citizens. To secure the public good and private rights against the danger of such a faction, and at the same time to preserve the spirit and the form of popular government, is then the great object to which our inquiries are directed. Let me add that it is the great desideratum by which this form of government can be rescued from the opprobrium under which it has so long labored, and be recommended to the esteem and adoption of mankind.

By what means is this object attainable? Evidently by one of two only. Either the existence of the same passion or interest in a majority at the same time must be prevented, or the majority, having such coexistent passion or interest, must be rendered, by their number and local situation, unable to concert and carry into effect schemes of oppression. If the impulse and the opportunity be suffered to coincide, we well know that neither moral nor religious motives can be relied on as an adequate control. They are not found to be such on the injustice and violence of individuals, and lose their efficacy in proportion to the number combined together, that is, in proportion as their efficacy becomes needful.

From this view of the subject it may be concluded that a pure democracy, by which I mean a society consisting of a small number of citizens, who assemble and administer the government in person, can admit of no cure for the mischiefs of fraction. A common passion or interest will, in almost every case, be felt by a majority of the whole; a communication and concert result from the form of government itself; and there is nothing to check the inducements to sacrifice the weaker party or an obnoxious individual. Hence it is that such democracies have ever been spectacles of turbulence and contention; have ever been found incompatible with personal security or the rights of property; and have in general been as short in their lives as they have been violent in their deaths. Theoretic politicians, who have patronized this species of government, have erroneously supposed that by reducing mankind to a perfect equality in their political rights, they would, at the same time, be perfectly equalized and assimilated in their possessions, their opinions, and their passions.

A republic, by which I mean a government in which the scheme of representation takes place, opens a different prospect, and promises the cure for which we are seeking. Let me examine the points in which it varies from pure democracy, and we shall comprehend both the nature of the cure and the efficacy which it must derive from the Union.

The two great points of difference between a democracy and a republic are: first, the delegation of the government, in the latter, to a small number of citizens, elected by the rest; secondly, the greater number of citizens, and greater sphere of country, over which the latter may be extended.

The effect of the first difference is, on the one hand, to refine and enlarge the public views, by passing them through the medium of a chosen body of citizens, whose wisdom may best discern the true interest of their country, and whose patriotism and love of justice will be least likely to sacrifice it to temporary or partial consideration. Under such a regulation, it may well happen that the public voice, pronounced by the representatives of the people, will be more consonant to the public good than if pronounced by the people themselves, convened for the purpose. On the other hand, the effect may be inverted. Men of factious tempers, of local prejudices, or of sinister designs, may, by intrigue, by corruption, or by other means, first obtain the suffrages, and then betray the interests, of the people. The question resulting is, whether small or extensive republics are more favorable to the election of proper guardians of the public weal; and it is clearly decided in favor of the latter by two obvious considerations:

In the first place, it is to be remarked that, however small the republic may be, the representatives must be raised to a certain number, in order to guard against the cabals of a few; and that, however large it may be, they must be limited to a certain number, in order to guard against the confusion of a multitude. Hence, the number of representatives in the two cases not being in proportion to that of the two constituents, and being proportionally greater in the small republic, it follows that, if the proportion of fit characters be not less in the large than in the small republic, the former will present a greater option, and consequently a greater probability of a fit choice.

In the next place, as each representative will be chosen by a greater number of citizens in the large than in the small republic, it will be more difficult for unworthy candidates to practice with success the vicious arts by which elections are too often carried; and the suffrages of the people being more free, will be more likely to centre in men who possess the most attractive merit and the most diffusive and established characters.

It must be confessed that in this, as in most other cases, there is a mean, on both sides of which inconveniences will be found to lie. By enlarging too much the number of electors, you render the representative too little acquainted with all their local circumstances and lesser interests; as by reducing it too much, you render him unduly attached to these, and too little fit to comprehend and pursue great and national objects. The federal Constitution forms a happy combination in this respect; the great and aggregate interests being referred to the national, the local and particular to the State legislatures.

The other point of difference is, the greater number of citizens and extent of territory which may be brought within the compass of republican than of democratic government; and it is this circumstance principally which renders factious combinations less to be dreaded in the former than in the latter. The smaller the society, the fewer probably will be the distinct parties and interests composing it; the fewer the distinct parties and interests, the more frequently will a majority be found of the same party; and the smaller the number of individuals composing a majority, and the smaller the compass within which they are placed, the more easily will they concert and execute their plans of oppression. Extend the sphere, and take in a greater variety of parties and interests; you make it less probable that a majority of the whole will have a common motive to invade the rights of other citizens; or if such a common motive exists, it will be more difficult for all who feel it to discover their own strength, and to act in unison with each other. Besides other impediments, it may be remarked that, where there is a consciousness of unjust or dishonorable purposes, communication is always checked by distrust in proportion to the number whose concurrence is necessary.

Hence, it clearly appears, that the same advantage which a republic has over a democracy, in controlling the effects of faction, is enjoyed by a large over a small republic—is enjoyed by the Union over the States composing it. Does the advantage consist in the substitution of representatives whose enlightened views and virtuous sentiments render them superior to local prejudices and to schemes of injustice? It will not be denied that the representation of the Union will be most likely to possess these requisite endowments. Does it consist in the greater security afforded by a greater variety of parties, against the event of any one party being able to outnumber and oppress the rest? In an equal degree does the increased variety of parties comprised within the Union, increase this security. Does it, in fine, consist in the greater obstacles opposed to the concert and accomplishment of the secret wishes of an unjust and interested majority? Here, again, the extent of the Union gives it the most palpable advantage.

The influence of factious leaders may kindle a flame within their particular States, but will be unable to spread a general conflagration through the other States. A religious sect may degenerate into a political faction in a part of the Confederacy; but the variety of sects dispersed over the entire face of it must secure the national councils against any danger from that source. A rage for paper money, for an abolition of debts, for an equal division of property, or for any other improper or wicked project, will be less apt to pervade the whole body of the Union than a particular member of it; in the same proportion as such a malady is more likely to taint a particular county or district, than an entire State.

In the extent and proper structure of the Union, therefore, we behold a republican remedy for the diseases most incident to republican government. And according to the degree of pleasure and pride we feel in being republicans, ought to be our zeal in cherishing the spirit and supporting the character of Federalists.   PUBLIUS

Chapter 3

FEDERALISTS VS. REPUBLICANS

Even when the Constitution had been ratified and George Washington unanimously chosen to preside over the destinies of the new republic, enormous difficulties faced those who sought to establish a "more perfect union." The Constitution provided merely a structural framework for the new government; the details of organization, procedure, and protocol had yet to be decided upon. Congress had to provide for its own organization, laws had to be passed to establish executive departments and a federal judiciary, and provision had to be made for an adequate revenue. Besides, precedents had to be set to answer those many questions on which the Constitution was silent: What was to be the relationship of the President to his department heads? In answer, Washington's practice of frequent consultation created the closely knit cabinet of advisers we know today. Was the "advice and consent" of the Senate to be sought before or after the President entered into treaty negotiations? The Senate's abrupt treatment when Washington came in person to seek prior advice on an Indian treaty convinced him—and his successors—that treaties should be submitted for ratification only after executive negotiations had been completed. In this fashion many of the extra-constitutional practices peculiar to American government today were derived from the experiences of Washington and his colleagues in the early years of the republic.

Final ratification of the Constitution and the establishment of the new government under Washington's leadership by no means resolved the severe conflict that had raged between Federalists and Anti-Federalists in the state ratifying conventions. Although the antagonists joined in support of Washington's efforts to set up the machinery of government, their intense struggle for control continued under the new Constitution, and soon political parties emerged to institutionalize old and deeply rooted antagonisms between classes and sections. Indeed, it was ironic that Washington, who sought so strenuously to avoid the dissensions of party, appointed as his chief cabinet officers the two distinguished Americans who were to be most closely identified with the rise of political factions. He chose as his Secretary of State the versatile and learned Thomas Jefferson, author of the Declaration of Independence, and as his Secretary of the Treasury the brilliant and dynamic Alexander Hamilton, who had so vigorously led the proponents of the Constitution. About these giants were to rage the party battles of the infant republic.

Hamilton's primary objective, as Secretary of the Treasury, was to make of the new government a powerful instrument for order and stability. He saw that "communities divide themselves into the few and the many. The first are the rich and well-born; the other the mass of the people." The masses are "turbulent and changing," but the "rich and well-born" seek order. Thus it was Hamilton's plan to secure for the federal government the active support not of the many—debtor farmers, artisans, and mechanics—but of the powerful few—merchants, bankers, and speculators who made up the creditor classes and formed the Federalist party. To assure that support to the new government, the Secretary very early submitted to Congress a series of brilliant Reports on the Public Credit. In rapid succession Hamilton's Reports called for the funding of the national debt and the assumption of state debts, measures that served not only to establish the nation's credit, but also to guarantee to speculating conservatives a new "interest" in the federal government; the passage of excise taxes, particularly a whiskey tax, harmless to the commercial East but so obnoxious to the agrarian West where bulky grain was converted into whiskey for easy transportation across the mountains; and the creation of a Bank of the United States, in whose stock the "rich and well-born" might invest most profitably. These measures were all quickly passed at Hamilton's insistence, but by a more and more angrily divided Congress. With them Hamilton achieved his immediate objectives, for they successfully wove an intricate net of profit that secured to the national government the enthusiastic support of wealthy Federalists. But even as his Reports were being written into law, Hamilton was arousing an opposition whose concern for popular interests would call forth widespread support which would finally drive the Federalist leader and his party from power.

Thomas Jefferson was no friend of anarchy or license—by birth, training and temperament no fiery partisan of mobs. But neither did he share Hamilton's desperate fear of the people as a "great beast." To the thoughtful Virginian, government need not stand primarily as a symbol of order and stability; rather, the end of "legitimate government" was "freedom and the happiness of its citizens." A political philosophy so antithetical to Hamilton's quickly led the Secretary of State to assume the leadership of those groups organizing to defeat the Federalist program. As Federalists represented creditor mercantile and commercial interests, so the opposition, emerging as the Republican party, represented the debtor agrarian interests of a nation still predominantly agricultural. Under Jefferson and James Madison the new party bitterly opposed Hamilton's legislative proposals and eagerly awaited the time when the sacred name of Washington no longer would sanction and protect Federalist policy. In 1792 Washington again received a unanimous electoral vote as President, but party divisions were already so intense that his Federalist Vice-President, John Adams, received only 77 votes to 55 for the Republican George Clinton. Thus national political parties, neither provided for nor even foreseen by the framers of the Constitution, had early come to be the dominant fact of American political life.

When in February, 1791, Washington called upon Jefferson and Hamilton to submit their opinions on the constitutionality of legislation chartering a Bank of the United States, national political affiliations had already been well defined in terms of broad and basic interests. Though the letters they wrote in reply were couched in the language of the Constitution, the rival Secretaries wrote primarily as leaders of their respective parties. Fearful of extending the powers of an administration so deeply committed to the interests of Federalism, Jefferson spoke the mind of his party when he declared for a "strict" construction of the Constitution: his was a philosophy of limited government. Congress, he argued, had been delegated specifically enumerated powers; its further power "to make all laws necessary and proper" for carrying them into execution must not be loosely defined. "Necessary and proper," wrote Jefferson, mean "essential." A bank was not essential for carrying out the enumerated powers; therefore the Bank Bill was clearly unconstitutional.

For those whose interests were so well served by the ever more powerful Federalist-dominated central government, Hamilton as vigorously defended the Bank Bill. His was a "loose" or "broad" construction of the Constitution. Implied in the Constitution, wrote the conservative Secretary, was the power to pass even those measures that were "no more than needful, requisite, incidental, useful, or conducive to" carrying out the enumerated powers; the Bank Bill fell into this category and therefore was constitutional. Ultimately Washington accepted Hamilton's opinion and signed the bill. Since that time the doctrine of "implied powers" has been used to extend the functions of government to a point even Hamilton could not have foreseen.

But before long Federalists and Republicans were to reverse their political—and therefore their constitutional—positions. A decade after the famous letters on the Bank Bill a combination of agrarians and poorer urban groups had made Jefferson President, and the Federalists no longer controlled the central government. The victorious Republicans, now in office, spoke enthusiastically about a generously broad and nationalistic interpretation of the Constitution. And the defeated, disgruntled Federalists, now out of office, sought to return to the "true" principles of the Founding Fathers—principles of limited government so well defended, in 1791, by Thomas Jefferson!

On the Constitutionality of the Bank of the United States, *1791*

Jefferson to Washington:

I consider the foundation of the Constitution as laid on this ground: That "all powers not delegated to the United States, by the Constitution, nor prohibited by it to the States, are reserved to the States or to the people . . ." To take a single step beyond the boundaries thus specially drawn around the powers of Congress is to take possession of a boundless field of power, no longer susceptible of any definition.

The incorporation of a bank, and the powers assumed by this bill, have not, in my opinion, been delegated to the United States by the Constitution.

I. They are not among the powers specially enumerated: for these are: 1. A power to lay taxes for the purpose of paying the debts of the United States; but no debt is paid by this bill, nor any tax laid. Were it a bill to raise money, its origination in the Senate would condemn it by the Constitution.

2. "To borrow money." But this bill neither borrows money nor insures the borrowing it. The proprietors of the bank will be just as free as any other money-holders to lend or not to lend their money to the public. The operation proposed in the bill, first, to lend them two millions, and then to borrow them back again, cannot change the nature of the latter act, which will still be a payment, and not a loan, call it by what name you please.

3. To "regulate commerce with foreign nations, and among the states, and with the Indian tribes." To erect a bank, and to regulate commerce, are very different acts. He who erects a bank creates a subject of commerce in its bills; so does he

who makes a bushel of wheat or digs a dollar out of the mines; yet neither of these persons regulates commerce thereby. To make a thing which may be bought and sold is not to prescribe regulations for buying and selling. Besides, if this was an exercise of the power of regulating commerce, it would be void, as extending as much to the internal commerce of every State, as to its external. For the power given to Congress by the Constitution does not extend to the internal regulation of the commerce of a State (that is to say of the commerce between citizen and citizen), which remain exclusively with its own legislature; but to its external commerce only, that is to say, its commerce with another State, or with foreign nations, or with the Indian tribes. Accordingly the bill does not propose the measure as a regulation of trade, but as "productive of considerable advantages to trade." Still less are these powers covered by any other of the special enumerations.

II. Nor are they within either of the general phrases, which are the two following:

1. To lay taxes to provide for the general welfare of the United States, that is to say, "to lay taxes for the purpose of providing for the general welfare." For the laying of taxes is the power, and the general welfare the purpose for which the power is to be exercised. They are not to lay taxes *ad libitum* for any purpose they please but only to pay the debts or provide for the welfare of the Union. In like manner, they are not to do anything they please to provide for the general welfare but only to lay taxes for that purpose. To consider the latter phrase, not as describing the purpose of the first, but as giving a distinct and independent power to do any act they please, which might be for the good of the Union, would render all the preceding and subsequent enumerations of power completely useless.

It would reduce the whole instrument to a single phrase, that of instituting a Congress with power to do whatever would be for the good of the United States; and, as they would be the sole judges of the good or evil, it would be also a power to do whatever evil they please.

It is an established rule of construction where a phrase will bear either of two meanings to give it that which will allow some meaning to the other parts of the instrument and not that which would render all the others useless. Certainly no such universal power was meant to be given them. It was intended to lace them up straitly within the enumerated powers, and those without which, as means, these powers could not be carried into effect. It is known that the very power now proposed as a means was rejected as an end by the Convention which formed the Constitution. A proposition was made to them to authorize Congress to open canals, and an amendatory one to empower them to incorporate. But the whole was rejected, and one of the reasons for rejection urged in debate was that then they would have a power to erect a bank, which would render the great cities, where there were prejudices and jealousies on the subject, adverse to the reception of the Constitution.

2. The second general phrase is "to make all laws necessary and proper for carrying into execution the enumerated powers." But they can all be carried into execution without a bank. A bank therefore is not necessary and consequently not authorized by this phrase.

It has been urged that a bank will give great facility or convenience in the collection of taxes. Suppose this were true: yet the Constitution allows only the names which are "necessary," not those which are merely "convenient" for effecting the enumerated powers. If such a latitude of construction be allowed to this phrase as to give any nonenumerated power, it will go to every one, for there is not one which ingenuity may not torture into a convenience in some instance or other, to some one of so long a list of enumerated powers. It would swallow up all the delegated powers and reduce the whole to one power, as before observed. Therefore it was that the Constitution restrained them to the *necessary* means, that is to say, to those means without which the grant of power would be nugatory. . . .

Perhaps, indeed, bank bills may be a more convenient vehicle than treasury orders. But a little difference in the degree of convenience cannot constitute the necessity which the Constitution makes the ground for assuming any nonenumerated power. . . .

It may be said that a bank whose bills would have a currency all over the States would be more convenient that one whose currency is limited to a single State. So it would be still more convenient that there should be a bank whose bills should have a currency all over the world. But it does not follow from this superior conveniency that there exists anywhere a power to establish such a bank or that the world may not get on very well without it.

Can it be thought that the Constitution intended that for a shade or two of convenience, more or less, Congress should be authorized to break down the most ancient and fundamental laws of the several States; such as those against mortmain, the laws of alienage, the rules of descent, the acts of distribution, the laws of escheat and forfeiture, the laws of monopoly? Nothing but a necessity invincible by any other means can justify such a prostitution of laws, which constitute the pillars of our whole system of jurisprudence. Will Congress be too strait-laced to carry the Constitution into honest effect, unless they may pass over the foundation laws of the State government for the slightest convenience of theirs?

The negative of the President is the shield provided by the Constitution to protect against the invasions of the legislature: 1. The right of the executive. 2. Of the judiciary. 3. Of the States and States legislatures. The present is the case of a right remaining exclusively with the States, and consequently one of those intended by the Constitution to be placed under its protection. . . .

Hamilton to Washington: *

. . . Now it appears to the Secretary of the Treasury that this general principle is inherent in the very definition of government and essential to every step of the progress to be made by that of the United States, namely: That every power vested in a government is in its nature sovereign and includes, by force of the term, a right to employ all the means requisite and fairly applicable to the attainment of the ends of such power, and which are not precluded by restrictions and exceptions specified in the Constitution, or not immoral, or not contrary to the essential ends of political society. . . .

. . . The circumstance that the powers of sovereignty are in this country divided between the national and state governments does not afford the distinction required. It does not follow from this that each of the portion of powers delegated to the one or to the other is not sovereign with regard to its proper objects. It will only follow from it that each has sovereign power as to certain things and not as to other things. To deny that the Government of the United States has sovereign power, as to its declared purposes and trusts, because its power does not extend to all cases, would be equally to deny that the State governments have sovereign power in any case, because their power does not extend to every case. The tenth section of the first article of the Constitution exhibits a long list of very important things which they may not do. And thus the United States would furnish the singular spectacle of a political society without sovereignty, or of a people governed without government.

If it would be necessary to bring proof to a proposition so clear, as that which affirms that the powers of the Federal Government, as to its objects, were sovereign, there is a clause of its Constitution which would be decisive. It is that which declares that the Constitution, and the laws of the United States made in pursuance of it, and all treaties made, or which shall be made, under their authority, shall be the supreme law of the land. The power which can create the

* From *The Works of Alexander Hamilton* (Vol. III), edited by Henry Cabot Lodge. Used by permission of G. P. Putnam's Sons.

supreme law of the land in any case is doubtless sovereign as to such case.

This general and indisputable principle puts at once an end to the abstract question whether the United States have power to erect a corporation; that is to say, to give a legal or artificial capacity to one or more persons, distinct from the natural. For it is unquestionably incident to sovereign power to erect corporations, and consequently to that of the United States, in relation to the objects intrusted to the management of the Government. The difference is this: where the authority of the Government is general, it can create corporations in all cases; where it is confined to certain branches of legislation, it can create corporations only in those cases. . . .

. . . It is not denied that there are implied as well as express powers and that the former are as effectually delegated as the latter. And for the sake of accuracy it shall be mentioned that there is another class of powers which may be properly denominated resulting powers. It will not be doubted that, if the United States should make a conquest of any of the territories of its neighbors, they would possess sovereign jurisdiction over the conquered territory. This would be rather a result, from the whole mass of the powers of the Government, and from the nature of political society, than a consequence of either of the powers specially enumerated. . . .

. . . It is conceded that implied powers are to be considered as delegated equally with express ones. Then it follows that, as a power of erecting a corporation may as well be implied as any other thing, it may as well be employed as an instrument or means of carrying into execution any of the specified powers, as any other instrument or means whatever. The only question must be, in this, as in every other case, whether the means to be employed or, in this instance, the corporation to be erected, has a natural relation to any of the acknowledged objects or lawful ends of the Government. Thus a corporation may not be erected by Congress for superintending the police of the city of Philadelphia, because they are not authorized to regulate the police of that city. But one may be erected in relation to the collection of taxes, or to the trade with foreign countries, or to the trade between the States, or with the Indian tribes; because it is the province of the Federal Government to regulate those objects, and because it is incident to a general sovereign or legislative power to regulate a thing, to employ all the means which relate to its regulation to the best and greatest advantage. . . .

Through this mode of reasoning respecting the right of employing all the means requisite to the execution of the specified powers of the Government, it is objected that none but necessary and proper means are to be employed; and the Secretary of State maintains that no means are to be considered as necessary but those without which the grant of the power would be nugatory. Nay, so far does he go in his restrictive interpretation of the word, as even to make the case of the necessity which shall warrant the constitutional exercise of the power to depend on casual and temporary circumstances; an idea which alone refutes the construction. The expediency of exercising a particular power, at a particular time, must, indeed, depend on circumstances; but the constitutional right of exercising it must be uniform and invariable, the same today as tomorrow.

All the arguments, therefore, against the constitutionality of the bill derived from the accidental existence of certain state banks—institutions which happen to exist today and, for aught that concerns the Government of the United States, may disappear tomorrow—must not only be rejected as fallacious but must be viewed as demonstrative that there is a radical source of error in the reasoning.

It is essential to the being of the national government that so erroneous a conception of the meaning of the word necessary should be exploded.

It is certain that neither the grammatical nor popular sense of the term requires that construction. According to both, necessary often means no more than needful, requisite, incidental, useful, or conducive to. It is a common mode of expression to say that it is necessary for a government or a person to do this or that thing, when nothing more is intended or understood than that the interests of the government or person require, or will be promoted by, the doing of this or that thing. The imagination can be at no loss for exemplifications of the use of the word in this sense. And it is the true one in which it is to be understood as used in the Constitution. The whole turn of the clause containing it indicates that it was the intent of the Convention, by that clause, to give a liberal latitude to the exercise of the specified powers. The expressions have peculiar comprehensiveness. They are, "to make all laws necessary and proper for carrying into execution the foregoing powers, and all other powers vested by the Constitution in the government of the United States, or in any department or officer thereof."

To understand the word as the Secretary of State does would be to depart from its obvious and popular sense and to give it a restrictive operation, an idea never before entertained. It would be to give it the same force as if the word absolutely or indispensably had been prefixed to it. . . .

The degree in which a measure is necessary can never be a test of the legal right to adopt it; that must be a matter of opinion and can only be a test of expediency. The relation between the measure and the end; between the nature of the means employed toward the execution of a power and the object of that power, must be the criterion of constitutionality, not the more or less of necessity or utility. . . .

This restrictive interpretation of the word necessary is also contrary to this sound maxim of construction; namely, that the powers contained in a constitution of government, especially those which concern the general administration of the affairs of a country, its finances, trade, defense, etc., ought to be construed liberally in advancement of the public good. This rule does not depend on the particular form of a government, or on the particular demarcation of the boundaries of its powers, but on the nature and objects of government itself. The means by which national exigencies are to be provided for, national inconveniences obviated, national prosperity promoted, are of such infinite variety, extent, and complexity, that there must of necessity be great latitude of discretion in the selection and application of those means. Hence, consequently, the necessity and propriety of exercising the authorities intrusted to a government on principles of liberal construction. . . .

But the doctrine which is contended for is not chargeable with the consequences imputed to it. It does not affirm that the national government is sovereign in all respects but that it is sovereign to a certain extent; that is, to the extent of the objects of its specified powers.

It leaves, therefore, a criterion of what is constitutional and of what is not so. This criterion is the end, to which the measure relates as a means. If the end be clearly comprehended within any of the specified powers, and if the measures have an obvious relation to that end, and is not forbidden by a particular provision of the Constitution, it may safely be deemed to come within the compass of the national authority. There is also this further criterion, which may materially assist the decision: Does the proposed measure abridge a pre-existing right of any State or of any individual? If it does not, there is a strong presumption in favor of its constitutionality, and slighter relations to any declared object of the Constitution may be permitted to turn the scale. . . .

It is presumed to have been satisfactorily shown in the course of the preceding observations:

1. That the power of the Government, as to the objects intrusted to its management, is, in its nature, sovereign.

2. That the right of erecting corporations is one inherent in, and inseparable from, the idea of sovereign power.

3. That the position that the Government of the United States can exercise no power but such as is delegated to it by its Constitution does not militate against this principle.

4. That the word necessary, in the general clause, can have no restrictive operation derogating from the force of this

principle; indeed, that the degree in which a measure is or is not necessary cannot be a test of constitutional right but of expediency only.

5. That the power to erect corporations is not to be considered as an independent or substantive power but as an incidental and auxiliary one and was therefore more properly left to implication that expressly granted.

6. That the principle in question does not extend the power of the Government beyond the prescribed limits, because it only affirms a power to incorporate for purposes within the sphere of the specified powers.

And, lastly, that the right to exercise such a power in certain cases is unequivocally granted in the most positive and comprehensive terms. . . .

A hope is entertained that it has, by this time, been made to appear, to the satisfaction of the President, that a bank has a natural relation to the power of collecting taxes—to that of regulating trade—to that of providing for the common defense—and that, as the bill under consideration contemplates the Government in the light of a joint proprietor of the stock of the bank, it brings the case within the provision of the clause of the Constitution which immediately respects the property of the United States.

Under a conviction that such a relation subsists, the Secretary of the Treasury, with all deference, conceives, that it will result as a necessary consequence from the position, that all the specified powers of Government are sovereign, as to the proper objects; that the incorporation of a bank is a constitutional measure; and that the objections taken to the bill, in this respect, are ill founded. . . .

Chapter 4

NEUTRALITY AND NATIONAL GROWTH

The maintenance of American neutrality in the perilous early years of the Republic was a profound tribute to the wisdom and foresight of Washington and his colleagues. However great the difficulties peculiar to the establishment of the new government and the determination of national domestic policy, they were equaled, if not surpassed, by the difficulty of preserving peace. It was Washington's objective that the new nation should grow and thrive in peace until the strength of union was a reality and a just and powerful United States could assume its rightful position among the nations of the world. But peace was precarious, for war raged almost incessantly among the great powers of England, France and Spain. And Washington's dual task of preserving peace and affirming the integrity of the new government was made even more burdensome by bitter disagreements on foreign policy among party factions at home. Most of the great leaders concurred with Washington's strong feeling that peace was indispensable to the young nation's well-being. Beyond that, however, the area of their agreement was small indeed, and the political parties very early came to be identified with the foreign antagonists, the Republican as pro-French, the Federalist as pro-English. The overwhelming intensity of the partisan conflict over foreign policy was alarming. Yet for nearly a quarter of a century of national progress under the new government, peace—if not absolute neutrality—was maintained, and time was secured to prove the experiment of American democracy successful. This, ultimately, was the supreme achievement of early American statesmanship.

When war broke out between England and France in 1793, the United States was forced to balance precariously between disastrous entanglements with the one or the other. Even before the war began, relations with the old mother country were marred by bad feelings. Antagonisms had been whipped up by England's refusal to abandon the Northwest forts and trading posts she had ceded at the end of the Revolutionary War. Americans were convinced that the English, intending to retain the posts permanently, were savagely encouraging the Indians to massacre oncoming settlers. Then after war between England and France started, explosive fuel was added to a long-range fire when the English seized American vessels and cargoes—even those having only the slightest connection with the French trade—and began the unhappy practice of impressing American sailors into the Royal Navy. Popular hatred of England, matched only by a widespread enthusiasm for Revolutionary France, grew very quickly to proportions that seemed to augur war. Even the beloved Washington suffered outrageous abuse at the hands of inflamed Anglophobes when in 1795 he supported the treaty which Federalist Chief Justice John Jay had negotiated with the English. Washington himself deplored the tenor of the Jay Treaty; for though it provided for final abandonment of the Northwest posts, it seemed to concede more to the English than it gained from them. But Washington correctly

estimated its real value to the nation: it provided a necessary breathing spell of peace. At his insistence, then, but
by an extremely close vote, a reluctant Senate ratified the
treaty and, at least for the immediate future, war with England was avoided.

Meanwhile relations with France were fast deteriorating.
In 1793 the French Minister, blundering "Citizen" Genêt,
though cheered wildly by a predominantly pro-French popu-
lace, had failed to win formal assistance from the American
government for its warring sister republic. Arrogantly, Genêt
then appealed for popular support over the President's head.
Washington, however, with the concurrence of his entire
cabinet, remained firm in the declaration of his recent Proclamation of Neutrality that the conduct of the United States
should be "impartial towards the belligerents," and Genêt's
mission remained a failure. Despairing of active assistance
from the United States, France soon came to treat American
neutral rights with the same studied disdain so long practiced
by the English. Later, in John Adams' administration, French
depredations threatened to turn the tide of popular feelings
so completely as even to bring war with the former ally. In
1798, when three unnamed French officials (designated as
X, Y, and Z) demanded bribes to receive a trio of American
envoys, popular fury at the French knew no bounds and
throughout the nation the angry cry echoed, "Millions for
defense, but not one cent for tribute." Only John Adams'
firm stand against this popular outcry saved the nation from
plunging headlong into a full-fledged war with France. Again
the new government was reprieved from a war that might
have destroyed it.

Washington, and after him Adams, had struggled courageously to preserve peace, but not without suffering the vilest
abuse from those whose personal or party interests opposed
the statesmen's insistence upon impartial relations with all
nations. Thus, when in 1796 Washington composed his
valedictory, the memorable Farewell Address, he had long
experienced the "baneful effects of the spirit of party" upon
the nation's foreign as well as domestic affairs. Unwilling
himself "to be longer buffeted in the public prints by a set of
infamous scribblers," Washington here sought to establish
principles of national behavior that were based upon unity
rather than party factionalism. Drafted and revised in part
by Madison, Jay, and particularly Hamilton, but always speaking the mind of the President, the Farewell Address embodied
Washington's sage counsel to his fellow countrymen to "observe good faith and justice towards all nations" and to shun

"permanent, inveterate antipathies against particular nations and passionate attachments for others." Of course, even as Washington bade farewell to the nation he had served so long and so well, pleading for the principles of unity, independence and good faith, opponents rejoiced that "the name of Washington ceases from this day to give currency to political iniquity and to legalize corruption." But if Washington's plea for an end to partisanship fell on deaf ears within both parties, nonetheless the Farewell Address stands as a profound tribute to his wisdom, sincerity, and statesmanship.

Washington's Farewell Address, *1796*

FRIENDS AND FELLOW-CITIZENS: The period for a new election of a citizen, to administer the executive government of the United States, being not far distant, and the time actually arrived, when your thoughts must be employed in designating the person, who is to be clothed with that important trust, it appears to me proper, especially as it may conduce to a more distinct expression of the public voice, that I should now apprise you of the resolution I have formed, to decline being considered among the number of those out of whom a choice is to be made. . . .

I rejoice that the state of your concerns, external as well as internal, no longer renders the pursuit of inclination incompatible with the sentiment of duty or propriety; and am persuaded, whatever partiality may be retained for my services, that, in the present circumstances of our country, you will not disapprove my determination to retire.

The impressions, with which I first undertook the arduous trust, were explained on the proper occasion. In the discharge of this trust, I will only say, that I have, with good intentions, contributed toward the organization and administration of the Government, the best exertions of which a very fallible judgment was capable. Not unconscious, in the outset, of the inferiority of my qualifications, experience in my own eyes, perhaps still more in the eyes of others, has strengthened the motives to diffidence of myself; and every day the increasing weight of years admonishes me more and more, that the shade of retirement is as necessary to me as it will be welcome. Satisfied that if any circumstances have given peculiar value to my services, they were temporary, I have the consolation to believe, that while choice and prudence invite me to quit the political scene, patriotism does not forbid it.

. . . Solicitude for your welfare, which cannot end but with my life, and the apprehension of danger, natural to that solicitude, urge me on an occasion like the present, to offer to your solemn contemplation, and to recommend to your frequent review, some sentiments; which are the result of much reflection, of no inconsiderable observation, and which appear to me all important to the permanency of your felicity as a people. These will be offered to you with the more freedom, as you can only see in them the disinterested warnings of a parting friend, who can possibly have no personal motive as his counsel. . . .

Interwoven as is the love of liberty with every ligament of your hearts, no recommendation of mine is necessary to fortify or confirm the attachment.

The unity of government which constitutes you one people is also now dear to you. It is justly so; for it is a main pillar in the edifice of your real independence, the support of your tranquility at home; your peace abroad; of your safety; of your prosperity; of that very liberty which you so highly prize. But as it is easy to foresee, that from different causes and from different quarters, much pains will be taken, many artifices employed, to weaken in your minds the conviction of this truth; as this is the point in your political fortress against which the batteries of internal and external enemies will be most constantly and actively (though often covertly and insidiously) directed, it is of infinite moment, that you should properly estimate the immense value of your national Union to your collective and individual happiness; that you should cherish a cordial, habitual and immoveable attachment to it; accustoming yourselves to think and speak of it as of the palladium of your political safety and prosperity; watching for its preservation with jealous anxiety; discountenancing whatever may suggest even a suspicion that it can in any event be abandoned, and indignantly frowning upon the first dawning of every attempt to alienate any portion of our country from the rest, or to enfeeble the sacred ties which now link together the various parts.

For this you have every inducement of sympathy and interest. Citizens by birth or choice, of a common country, that country has a right to concentrate your affections. The name of *American*, which belongs to you, in your national capacity, must always exalt the just pride of patriotism, more than any appellation derived from local discriminations. With slight shades of difference, you have the same religion, manners, habits and political principles. You have in a common cause fought and triumphed together. The independence and liberty you possess are the work of joint councils, and joint efforts; of common dangers, sufferings and successes.

But these considerations, however powerfully they address themselves to your sensibility are greatly outweighed by those which apply more immediately to your interest. Here every portion of our country finds the most commanding motives for carefully guarding and preserving the union of the whole.

The North, in an unrestrained intercourse with the South, protected by the equal laws of a common Government, finds in the productions of the latter, great additional resources of maritime and commercial enterprise and precious materials of manufacturing industry. The South in the same intercourse, benefitting by the agency of the North, sees its agriculture grow and its commerce expand. Turning partly into its own channels the seamen of the North, it finds its particular navigation envigorated; and while it contributes, in different ways, to nourish and increase the general mass of the national navigation, it looks forward to the protection of a maritime strength, to which itself is unequally adapted. The East, in a like intercourse with the West, already finds, and in the progressive improvement of interior communications, by land and water, will more and more find a valuable vent for the commodities which it brings from abroad, or manufactures at home. The West derives from the East supplies requisite to its growth and comfort, and what is perhaps of still greater consequence, it must of necessity owe the secure enjoyment of indispensable outlets for its own productions to the weight, influence, and the future maritime strength of the Atlantic side of the Union, directed by an indissoluble community of interest as one nation. Any other tenure by which the West can hold this essential advantage, whether derived from its own separate strength, or from an apostate and unnatural connection with any foreign power, must be intrinsically precarious.

While then every part of our country thus feels an immediate and particular interest in union, all the parts combined cannot fail to find in the united mass of means and efforts greater strength, greater resource, proportionably greater security from external danger, a less frequent interruption of their peace by foreign nations; and, what is of inestimable value, they must derive from union an exemption from those broils and wars between themselves, which so frequently afflict neighboring countries, not tied together by the same government; which their own rivalships alone would be sufficient to produce, but which opposite foreign alliances, attachments and intrigues would stimulate and imbitter. . . .

In contemplating the causes which may disturb our union, it occurs as a matter of serious concern, that any ground should have been furnished for characterizing parties by geographical discriminations: Northern and Southern; Atlantic and Western; whence designing men may endeavour to excite a belief that there is a real difference of local interests and views. One of the expedients of party to acquire influence, within particular districts, is to misrepresent the opinions and aims of other districts. You cannot shield yourselves too much against the jealousies and heart burnings which spring from these misrepresentations. . . .

To the efficacy and permanency of your union, a Government for the whole is indispensable. No alliances however strict between the parts can be an adequate substitute. They must inevitably experience the infractions and interruptions which all alliances in all times have experienced. Sensible of this momentous truth, you have improved upon your first essay, by the adoption of a Constitution of Government, better calculated than your former for an intimate union, and for the efficacious management of your common concerns. This Government, the offspring of your own choice uninfluenced and unawed, adopted upon full investigation and mature deliberation, completely free in its principles, in the distribution of its powers, uniting security with energy, and containing within itself a provision for its own amendment, has a just claim to your confidence and your support. Respect for its authority, compliance with its laws, acquiescence in its measures, are duties enjoined by the fundamental maxims of true liberty. . . .

Towards the preservation of your Government and the permanency of your present happy state, it is requisite, not only that you steadily discountenance irregular oppositions to its acknowledged authority, but also that you resist with care the spirit of innovation upon its principles however specious the pretexts. One method of assault may be to effect, in the forms of the Constitution, alterations which will impair the energy of the system, and thus to undermine what cannot be directly overthrown. In all the changes to which you may be invited, remember that time and habit are at least as necessary to fix the true character of governments, as of other human institutions; that experience is the surest standard, by which to test the real tendency of the existing Constitution of a country; that facility in changes upon the credit of mere hypothesis and opinion exposes to perpetual change, from the endless variety of hypothesis and opinion; and remember, especially, that for the efficient management of your common interests, in a country so extensive as ours, a government of as much vigor as is consistent with the perfect security of liberty is indispensable. Liberty itself will find in such a government, with powers properly distributed and adjusted, its surest guardian. . . .

I have already intimated to you the danger of parties in the State, with particular reference to the founding of them on geographical discriminations. Let me now take a more comprehensive view, and warn you in the most solemn manner against the baneful effects of the spirit of party, generally.

This spirit, unfortunately, is inseparable from our nature, having its root in the strongest passions of the human mind. It exists under different shapes in all governments, more or less stifled, controlled, or repressed; but, in those of the popular form it is seen in its greatest rankness and is truly their worst enemy. . . .

It serves always to distract the public councils and enfeeble the public administration. It agitates the community with ill-founded jealousies and false alarms, kindles the animosity of one part against another, foments occasionally riot and insurrection. It opens the door to foreign influence and corruption, which find a facilitated access to the government itself through the channels of party passions. Thus the policy and the will of one country, are subjected to the policy and will of another.

There is an opinion that parties in free countries are useful checks upon the administration of the Government and serve to keep alive the spirit of liberty. This within certain limits is probably true, and in governments of a monarchical cast, patriotism may look with indulgence, if not with favor, upon the spirit of party. But in those of the popular character, in governments purely elective, it is a spirit not to be encouraged. From their natural tendency, it is certain there will always be enough of that spirit for every salutary purpose. And there being constant danger of excess, the effort ought to be, by force of public opinion, to mitigate and assuage it. A fire not to be quenched; it demands a uniform vigilance to prevent its bursting into a flame, lest instead of warming it should consume. . . .

It is substantially true, that virtue or morality is a necessary spring of popular government. The rule indeed extends with more or less force to every species of free government. Who that is a sincere friend to it, can look with indifference upon attempts to shake the foundation of the fabric.

Promote then as an object of primary importance, institutions for the general diffusion of knowledge. In proportion as the structure of a government gives force to public opinion, it is essential that public opinion should be enlightened.

As a very important source of strength and security, cherish public credit. One method of preserving it is to use it as sparingly as possible; avoiding occasions of expense by cultivating peace, but remembering also that timely disbursements to prepare for danger frequently prevent much greater disbursements to repel it; avoiding likewise the accumulation of debt, not only by shunning occasions of expense, but by vigorous exertions in time of peace to discharge the debts which unavoidable wars may have occasioned, not ungenerously throwing upon posterity the burden which we ourselves ought to bear. . . .

Observe good faith and justice towards all nations; cultivate peace and harmony with all. Religion and morality enjoin this conduct; and can it be that good policy does not equally enjoin it? It will be worthy of a free, enlightened, and, at no distant period, a great nation, to give to mankind the magnanimous and too novel example of a people always guided by an exalted justice and benevolence. Who can doubt that in the course of time and things the fruits of such a plan would richly repay any temporary advantages which might be lost by a steady adherence to it? Can it be, that Providence has not connected the permanent felicity of a nation with its virtue? The experiment, at least, is recommended by every sentiment which ennobles human nature. Alas! is it rendered impossible by its vices?

In the execution of such a plan nothing is more essential than that permanent, inveterate antipathies against particular nations and passionate attachments for others should be excluded; and that in place of them just and amicable feelings towards all should be cultivated. The nation, which indulges towards another an habitual hatred, or an habitual fondness, is in some degree a slave. It is a slave to its animosity or to its affection, either of which is sufficient to lead it astray from its duty and its interest. Antipathy in one nation against another, disposes each more readily to offer insult and injury, to lay hold of slight causes of umbrage, and to be haughty and intractable, when accidental or trifling occasions of dispute occur. Hence frequent collisions, obstinate envenomed and bloody contests. . . .

So likewise, a passionate attachment of one nation for another produces a variety of evils. Sympathy for the favorite nation, facilitating the illusion of an imaginary common interest, in cases where no real common interest exists, and infusing into one the enmities of the other, betrays the former into a participation in the quarrels and wars of the latter, without adequate inducement or justification. It leads also to concessions to the favorite nation of privileges denied to others, which is apt doubly to injure the nation making the concessions; by unnecessarily parting with what ought to have been retained; and by exciting jealousy, ill-will, and a disposition to retaliate, in the parties from whom equal privileges are withheld. And it gives to ambitious, corrupted, or deluded citizens (who devote themselves to the favorite nation) facility to betray, or sacrifice the interests of their own country, without odium, sometimes even with popularity; gilding with the appearances of a virtuous sense of obligation, a commendable deference for public opinion, or a laudable zeal for public good, the base or foolish compliances of ambition, corruption or infatuation. . . .

Against the insidious wiles of foreign influence, (I conjure you to believe me fellow-citizens) the jealousy of a free people ought to be constantly awake; since history and experience prove that foreign influence is one of the most baneful foes of republican government. But that jealousy to be useful must be impartial; else it becomes the instrument of the very influence to be avoided, instead of a defence against it. Excessive partiality for one foreign nation and excessive dislike of another, cause those whom they actuate to see danger only on one side, and serve to veil and even second the arts of influence on the other. Real patriots, who may resist the intrigues of the favorite, are liable to become suspected and odious; while its tools and dupes usurp the applause and confidence of the people, to surrender their interests.

The great rule of conduct for us, in regard to foreign nations is in extending our commercial relations to have with them as little political connection as possible. So far as we have already formed engagements let them be fulfilled, with perfect good faith. Here let us stop.

Europe has a set of primary interests, which to us have none, or a very remote relation. Hence she must be engaged in frequent controversies, the causes of which are essentially foreign to our concerns. Hence therefore it must be unwise in us to implicate ourselves, by artificial ties, in the ordinary vicissitudes of her politics, or the ordinary combinations and collisions of her friendships, or enmities.

Our detached and distant situation invites and enables us to pursue a different course. If we remain one people, under an efficient government, the period is not far off, when we may defy material injury from external annoyance; when we may take such an attitude as will cause the neutrality we may at any time resolve upon to be scrupulously respected; when belligerent nations, under the impossibility of making acquisitions upon us, will not lightly hazard the giving us provocation; when we may choose peace or war, as our interest guided by our justice shall counsel.

Why forego the advantages of so peculiar a situation? Why quit our own to stand upon foreign ground? Why, by interweaving our destiny with that of any part of Europe, entangle our peace and prosperity in the toils of European ambition, rivalship, interest, humour, or caprice?

It is our true policy to steer clear of permanent alliances, with any portion of the foreign world. So far, I mean, as we are now at liberty to do it, for let me not be understood as capable of patronizing infidelity to existing engagements. I hold the maxim no less applicable to public than to private affairs, that honesty is always the best policy. I repeat it therefore, let those engagements be observed in their genuine sense. But in my opinion, it is unnecessary and would be unwise to extend them.

Taking care always to keep ourselves, by suitable establishments, on a respectably defensive posture, we may safely trust to temporary alliances for extraordinary emergencies.

Harmony, liberal intercourse with all nations, are recommended by policy, humanity and interest. But even our commercial policy should hold an equal and impartial hand; neither seeking nor granting exclusive favors or preferences; consulting the natural course of things; diffusing and diversifying by gentle means the streams of commerce, but forcing nothing; establishing with powers so disposed; in order to give to trade a stable course, to define the rights of our merchants, and to enable the Government to support them; conventional rules of intercourse, the best that present circumstances and mutual opinion will permit, but temporary, and liable to be from time to time abandoned or varied, as experience and circumstances shall dictate; constantly keeping in view, that it is folly in one nation to look for disinterested favors from another; that it must pay with a portion of its independence for whatever it may accept under that character; that by such acceptance, it may place itself in the condition of having given equivalents for nominal favors and yet of being reproached with ingratitude for not giving more. There can be no greater error than to expect, or calculate upon real favors from nation to nation. It is an illusion which experience must cure, which a just pride ought to discard. . . .

Though in reviewing the incidents of my administration, I am unconscious of intentional error, I am nevertheless too sensible of my defects not to think it probable that I may have committed many errors. Whatever they may be I fervently beseech the Almighty to avert or mitigate the evils to which they may tend. I shall also carry with me the hope that my country will never cease to view them with indulgence; and that after forty-five years of my life dedicated to its service, with an upright zeal, the faults of incompetent abilities will be consigned to oblivion, as myself must soon be to the mansions of rest. . . .

Chapter 5

THE JEFFERSONIAN REVOLUTION

In 1796 George Washington's refusal to seek a third term loosed a floodtide of partisanship that had been at least partially restrained during his administrations, and a bitterly contested Presidential campaign resulted in a narrow victory for the Federalist John Adams over the Republican Thomas Jefferson. Despite the narrowness of their victory, the Federalists made no effort in the next four years to relate their party's policy more closely to the will of the majority of Americans. Continuing to champion the wealthy commercial and mercantile creditor class, they ignored the needs and demands of the more numerous and less prosperous agrarians and urban workers and remained distinctly out of temper with the country at large. Yet they were determined to maintain political power and to that end employed oppression as an alternative to popular appeal. To undermine an increasingly powerful Republican party, the Federalist-dominated Congress in 1798 passed the infamous Alien and Sedition Acts. Aimed at foreigners who contributed much in numbers and leadership to the Republicans, the Alien Acts extended from five to fourteen years the naturalization period prior to citizenship (and the suffrage) and gave to the Federalist President extensive powers over aliens in peace as well as in war. The Sedition Act was intended to silence all opposition to the Federalists by providing fines and prison terms for "malicious" attacks on Congress or the President. These desperate acts threatened violent harm to the personal liberties essential to democracy, but in passing them the Federalists had signed their own death warrant, for each convicted Republican stood as a martyr to the cause of free speech, and the laws themselves were ample testimony to the undemocratic intentions of the party in power. In reply came the dramatic Kentucky and Virginia Resolutions, penned by Jefferson and James Madison. Arguing the right of the states to interpose their authority against an oppressive central government, they called upon their sister states to join in declaring unconstitutional the viciously discriminatory

70

Federalist Acts. Later the constitutional question of states' rights would time and again be invoked by both parties to rationalize conflict with the immediate policies of the central government. More important immediately, however, was the effectiveness of the Resolutions in their original intent: to provide the Republicans a winning platform for the election of 1800. In that year Jefferson had merely to point to the Federalists' record in office to win the Presidency in a decisive Republican victory.

Late in life, Jefferson described the election of 1800 thus: "as real a revolution in the principles of our government as that of 1776 was in its form." But in his Inaugural Address of March, 1801, the new President wisely sought to allay the bitter partisanship of recent years. To admirers gathered to witness the first Presidential Inauguration in the new capital city of Washington, Jefferson insisted that "We have called by different names brethren of the same principles. We are all Republicans—we are all Federalists." There was no hint of revolution, no threat of repudiation, in the conciliatory Inaugural; rather, Jefferson's address was a strong affirmation of faith in the young republic, although it had been dominated by Federalists since its inception. And to the dismay of many who had helped forge the victory of 1800, the new President's moderation was in act as well as word. National offices were not swept clean of Federalists appointed by Washington and Adams, for the notion that "to the victors belong the spoils" was peculiar to the later Jacksonian Democracy, not to Jeffersonianism. Fundamentally, the machinery of government bequeathed by the Federalists was kept intact. The fiscal system that Hamilton had contrived was not substantially altered—although the Treasury was no longer used to gain support for the government from the "rich and well-born"—and the public credit was as secure under Albert Gallatin, Jefferson's Secretary of the Treasury, as it had been under Hamilton. Besides, under a President who came to construe his powers so broadly as to allow him to purchase the vast expanse of the Louisiana Territory, the Hamiltonian-Federalist orientation towards a strong central government, though modified in many ways, was certainly not abandoned. Indeed, to many good Republicans it seemed that Jefferson had taken all too seriously his inaugural assertion that "We are all Republicans—we are all Federalists."

But if the structure and much of the content of government were not radically changed with Republican victory, and if, indeed, Hamilton's vision of a highly industrialized and centralized state was ultimately to prove more prophetic than Jefferson's early notions of limited govern-

ment and an agrarian economy, still in the most fundamental terms Jefferson's election marked a real revolution.
For it was a revolution in ideas—as Jefferson later wrote,
"in the principles of government"—that saw the national
government dedicated by the Jeffersonians to the principles of
democracy and liberty, as Federalists had made of it a
shrine to order and stability. No longer was the prime concern of government for the interests of the few, the wealthy
business class, but rather for the freedom and happiness of
all the people. Not that business interests were proscribed nor
even so subordinated to agrarianism as to be severely damaged, for the nation's industrial growth continued under
Jefferson and his Republican successors as it had before
them. With the ascendancy of the Republicans, however,
that growth was to continue without a strong control over
government. Finally, Jefferson's great achievement and the
real meaning of the "Revolution of 1800," was that he preserved the Federalists' tremendous steps toward national
economic and political power while he infused into government the ideals of democracy and liberty. That the nation
grew strong and became the great industrial power Hamilton
had envisaged remains the most meaningful tribute to Jeffersonian Democracy; for it did so, not under the auspices of
the oppressive plutocratic or aristocratic government Hamilton thought necessary, but rather within the context of a
free, democratic government whose principles were Jeffersonian. And a nation that had repudiated the tyranny of a
Federalist Sedition Act would long remember Jefferson's
famous plea for freedom of thought and expression: "Even if
there be any among us who would wish to dissolve this
Union or to change its republican form, let them stand
undisturbed as monuments of the safety with which error of
opinion may be tolerated when reason is left free to combat
it."

Jefferson's First Inaugural Address, 1801

FRIENDS AND FELLOW CITIZENS:—Called upon to undertake
the duties of the first executive office of our country, I avail
myself of the presence of that portion of my fellow citizens
which is here assembled, to express my grateful thanks for
the favor with which they have been pleased to look toward
me, to declare a sincere consciousness that the task is above
my talents, and that I approach it with those anxious and

awful presentiments which the greatness of the charge and the weakness of my powers so justly inspire. A rising nation, spread over a wide and fruitful land, traversing all the seas with the rich productions of their industry, engaged in commerce with nations who feel power and forget right, advancing rapidly to destinies beyond the reach of mortal eye—when I contemplate these transcendent objects, and see the honor, the happiness, and the hopes of this beloved country committed to the issue and the auspices of this day, I shrink from the contemplation, and humble myself before the magnitude of the undertaking. Utterly indeed, should I despair, did not the presence of many whom I here see remind me, that in the other high authorities provided by our constitution, I shall find resources of wisdom, of virtue, and of zeal, on which to rely under all difficulties. To you, then, gentlemen, who are charged with the sovereign functions of legislation, and to those associated with you, I look with encouragement for that guidance and support which may enable us to steer with safety the vessel in which we are all embarked amid the conflicting elements of a troubled world.

During the contest of opinion through which we have passed, the animation of discussion and of exertions has sometimes worn an aspect which might impose on strangers unused to think freely and to speak and to write what they think; but this being now decided by the voice of the nation, announced according to the rules of the constitution, all will, of course, arrange themselves under the will of the law, and unite in common efforts for the common good. All, too, will bear in mind this sacred principle, that though the will of the majority is in all cases to prevail, that will, to be rightful, must be reasonable; that the minority possess their equal rights, which equal laws must protect, and to violate which would be oppression. Let us, then, fellow citizens, unite with one heart and one mind. Let us restore to social intercourse that harmony and affection without which liberty and even life itself are but dreary things. And let us reflect that having banished from our land that religious intolerance under which mankind so long bled and suffered, we have yet gained little if we countenance a political intolerance as despotic, as wicked, and capable of as bitter and bloody persecutions. During the throes and convulsions of the ancient world, during the agonizing spasms of infuriated man, seeking through blood and slaughter his long-lost liberty, it was not wonderful that the agitations of the billows should reach even this distant and peaceful shore; that this should be more felt and feared by some and less by others; that this should divide opinions as to measures of safety. But every difference of opinion is not a difference

of principle. We have called by different names brethren of
the same principle. We are all Republicans—we are all
Federalists. If there be any among us who would wish to
dissolve this Union or to change its republican form, let
them stand undisturbed as monuments of the safety with
which error of opinion may be tolerated where reason is
left free to combat it. I know, indeed, that some honest
men fear that a republican government cannot be strong;
that this government is not strong enough. But would the
honest patriot, in the full tide of successful experiment,
abandon a government which has so far kept us free and
firm, on the theoretic and visionary fear that this government, the world's best hope, may by possibility want energy
to preserve itself? I trust not. I believe this, on the contrary, the strongest government on earth. I believe it is the
only one where every man, at the call of the laws, would
fly to the standard of the law, and would meet invasions
of the public order as his own personal concern. Sometimes
it is said that man cannot be trusted with the government
of himself. Can he, then, be trusted with the government of
others? Or have we found angels in the forms of kings to
govern him? Let history answer this question.

Let us, then, with courage and confidence pursue our own
federal and republican principles, our attachment to our
union and representative government. Kindly separated by
nature and a wide ocean from the exterminating havoc of
one quarter of the globe; too high-minded to endure the
degradations of the others; possessing a chosen country,
with room enough for entertaining a due sense of our equal
right to the use of our own faculties, to the acquisitions of
our industry, to honor and confidence from our fellow citizens, resulting not from birth but from our actions and
their sense of them; enlightened by a benign religion, professed, indeed, and practiced in various forms, yet all of
them including honesty, truth, temperance, gratitude, and
the love of man; acknowledging and adoring an overruling
Providence, which by all its dispensations proves that it de-
lights in the happiness of man here and his greater happiness hereafter; with all these blessings, what more is necessary to make us a happy and prosperous people? Still one
thing more, fellow citizens—a wise and frugal government,
which shall restrain men from injuring one another, which
shall leave them otherwise free to regulate their own pursuits of industry and improvement, and shall not take from
the mouth of labor the bread it has earned. This is the
sum of good government, and this is necessary to close the
circle of our felicities.

About to enter, fellow citizens, on the exercise of duties
which comprehend everything dear and valuable to you, it is

proper that you should understand what I deem the essential principles of our government, and consequently those which ought to shape its administration. I will compress them within the narrowest compass they will bear, stating the general principle, but not all its limitations. Equal and exact justice to all men, of whatever state or persuasion, religious or political; peace, commerce, and honest friendship, with all nations—entangling alliances with none; the support of the state governments in all their rights, as the most competent administrations for our domestic concerns and the surest bulwarks against anti-republican tendencies; the preservation of the general government in its whole constitutional vigor, as the sheet anchor of our peace at home and safety abroad; a jealous care of the right of election by the people—a mild and safe corrective of abuses which are lopped by the sword of the revolution where peaceable remedies are unprovided; absolute acquiescence in the decisions of the majority—the vital principle of republics, from which there is no appeal but to force, the vital principle and immediate parent of despotism; a well-disciplined militia—our best reliance in peace and for the first moments of war, till regulars may relieve them; the supremacy of the civil over the military authority; economy in the public expense, that labor may be lightly burdened; the honest payment of our debts and sacred preservation of the public faith; encouragement of agriculture, and of commerce as its handmaid; the diffusion of information and the arraignment of all abuses at the bar of public reason; freedom of religion; freedom of the press; freedom of person under the protection of the habeas corpus; and trial by juries impartially selected—these principles form the bright constellation which has gone before us, and guided our steps through an age of revolution and reformation. The wisdom of our sages and the blood of our heroes have been devoted to their attainment. They should be the creed of our political faith—the text of civil instruction—the touchstone by which to try the services of those we trust; and should we wander from them in moments of error or alarm, let us hasten to retrace our steps and to regain the road which alone leads to peace, liberty, and safety.

I repair, then, fellow citizens, to the post you have assigned me. With experience enough in subordinate offices to have seen the difficulties of this, the greatest of all, I have learned to expect that it will rarely fall to the lot of imperfect man to retire from this station with the reputation and the favor which bring him into it. Without pretensions to that high confidence reposed in our first and great revolutionary character, whose preeminent services had entitled him to the first place in his country's love, and destined for him the fairest page in the volume of faithful history, I ask so much confidence only as may give firmness and effect to the legal administration of your affairs. I shall often go wrong through defect of judgment. When right, I shall often be thought wrong by those whose positions will not command a view of the whole ground. I ask your indulgence for my own errors, which will never be intentional; and your support against the errors of others, who may condemn what they would not if seen in all its parts. The approbation implied by your suffrage is a consolation to me for the past; and my future solicitude will be to retain the good opinion of those who have bestowed it in advance, to conciliate that of others by doing them all the good in my power, and to be instrumental to the happiness and freedom of all.

Relying, then, on the patronage of your good will, I advance with obedience to the work, ready to retire from it whenever you become sensible how much better choice it is in your power to make. And may that Infinite Power which rules the destinies of the universe, lead our councils to what is best, and give them a favorable issue for your peace and prosperity.

Chapter 6

THE POWER OF THE COURT

For the Federalists, defeat in the election of 1800 was as decisive as it was bitter. Though they continued to intrigue against Jefferson's party, they would never again win national political power, and in 1815, after the ill-fated Hartford Convention, their party sank permanently into oblivion. At Hartford, desperate Federalists had abandoned their earlier nationalistic, loose interpretation of the Constitution, had protested the War of 1812 as "Madison's War," and in opposition to the war had espoused the very doctrines of states' rights and limited government they so vigorously opposed when in office. In 1815, however, most Americans were celebrating Jackson's bold victory in the Battle of New Orleans as the triumphant conclusion to the war with England, and their confidence in the now strongly nationalistic leadership of the Republican party was unbounded. Again, and for the last time, the Federalists had proved out of step with the majority of Americans. In the Presidential election of 1816 the nation overwhelmingly chose James Monroe, Madison's Secretary of State and the last of the distinguished Republican triumvirate of friends and neighbors which sarcastic Federalists had dubbed "the Virginia dynasty": Jefferson, Madison and Monroe. Thus for more than two decades—until in the 1820's it would split into National Republicans under John Quincy Adams and Henry Clay and Democrats under Andrew Jackson—the Republican party dominated the nation's political life. So complete and long lasting was the political victory Jefferson had won in 1800!

To Jefferson's chagrin and intense anger, however, in at least one branch of government, the federal judiciary, defeated Federalists were able to limit the Republican triumph at the polls. For in the last weeks before Jefferson's inauguration in 1801, "lame duck" Federalists had reorganized, expanded, and "packed" the courts with conservative judges whose decisions might be counted upon to "check" somewhat the will of the new President and Congress. Foremost among John Adams' "midnight appointments" was that of Secretary of State John Marshall as Chief Justice of the Supreme Court. For thirty-four years this implacable Federalist was to dominate the highest court of the land, establishing judicial precedents that did much to determine the destinies of the young nation. Marshall immediately ranked high among Jefferson's Federalist antagonists, and between the two, fellow Virginians and kinsmen, raged the first of the many battles between Supreme Court and President that characterized American political and constitutional history.

The most significant of John Marshall's early achievements on the bench was his establishment of the doctrine of judicial review in the case of Marbury v. Madison. William Marbury, a Federalist, had been among Adams' last-minute appointments to the lower federal courts, but in the hectic final days of Adams' administration, Secretary of State John Marshall had neglected to give Marbury his commission. Later, the new Republican Secretary, James Madison, refused to do so. Marbury appealed to the Supreme Court—now presided over by Marshall—for a writ of mandamus ordering Madison to surrender the commission. The writ was to be issued under powers conferred upon the Court by the Judiciary Act of 1789. In 1803 Marshall delivered his famous decision, insisting first that in right and in law Marbury was entitled to his commission. Nevertheless the Chief Justice went on to deny Marbury's petition, asserting that the Court could not issue such writs of mandamus. The justices had reviewed the section of the Judiciary Act granting that power to the Court and had found it unconstitutional and void. Previously the Court had declared state laws unconstitutional and many of the Founding Fathers had taken for granted its power to pass upon the constitutionality of national laws. But nowhere did the Constitution *specifically* grant that power to the highest court. Though the Court would not again nullify an act of Congress until 1857 in the Dred Scott case, Marshall's opinion in Marbury v. Madison thus set the most important of judicial precedents, that of judicial review of congressional legislation. Besides, the decision made brilliant strategy in the battle with the Republicans, for in declaring unconstitutional a law enacted by the Federalist Congress of 1789 and in rejecting the plea of a Federalist place-seeker, Marshall had cleverly removed from his decision the stigma of partisanship. Yet Jefferson fully appreciated the political significance of Marbury v. Madison and determined to attack the Court and particularly the Chief Justice, lest judicial review be employed to deny the will of the nation as expressed by its elected Republican legislators and Chief Executive. Jefferson's party even made efforts to remove the unfriendly justices. Justice Samuel Chase of the Supreme Court, an intemperately partisan Federalist, was actually impeached by the House of Representatives and only his acquittal by the Senate foiled the Republicans' plans to remove other obnoxious jurists and finally Marshall himself. But these schemes failed. Despite Jefferson's opposition, the Supreme Court under John Marshall had won its first important battle for judicial supremacy and had clearly emerged as a powerful factor in the American system of checks and balances.

For more than three decades after his famous decision in Marbury v. Madison, Marshall continued to lay the foundation of American constitutional law. Two of the most notable of his many opinions were delivered in 1819 in McCulloch v. Maryland and Dartmouth College v. Woodward. In question in the first case were the constitutionality of the Bank of the United States (Jefferson and Hamilton had debated the point in their famous letters to Washington in 1791) and the right of a state to tax the Bank. Maintaining his early nationalism—as other Federalists had not—Marshall fully accepted Hamilton's "loose" or "broad" construction of the Constitution to support federal powers that were "implied" rather than specifically enumerated in the Constitution. Sanctioning Hamilton's earlier opinion, Marshall wrote: "Let the end be legitimate, let it be within the scope of the constitution, and all means which are appropriate, which are plainly adapted to that end, which are not prohibited, but consist with the letter and spirit of the constitution, are constitutional. . . ." The Bank, then, though not provided for in the Constitution, was constitutional. Nor could Maryland tax the Bank, for "the power to tax involves the power to destroy" and a state could not be permitted to destroy the legitimate creature of what in Marshall's opinion was its superior, the national government.

At the same time, in Dartmouth College v. Woodward, the Chief Justice further limited state powers when he declared unconstitutional New Hampshire's efforts to revise Dartmouth's old colonial charter and place the college under state control. Charters were contracts, Marshall stated, and therefore inviolable by the states under the constitutional stricture against "impairing the obligation of contracts." Here too, precedent set by the early Chief Justice proved profoundly important to the nation's later development. For Marshall's decision in the Dartmouth College case did much to promote and protect the business interests of the nation. Under it, particularly in the period of tremendous industrial expansion after the Civil War, state legislatures were frequently prevented from controlling corporations to which they had granted charters, even those whose business practices were most abusive.

Not only had Marshall struck powerful blows for the supremacy of the nation over the states, but in the best Hamiltonian-Federalist tradition, he had extended the protection of the Constitution to the propertied classes and had made of the Supreme Court a bulwark of economic conservatism.

Marbury v. Madison: Chief Justice John Marshall for the Supreme Court, *1803*

In the order in which the court has viewed this subject, the following questions have been considered and decided:

1. Has the applicant a right to the commission he demands?

2. If he has a right, and that right has been violated, do the laws of his country afford him a remedy?

3. If they do afford him a remedy, is it a mandamus issuing from this court? . . .

The first object of enquiry is,

Has the applicant a right to the commission he demands? . . .

It is therefore decidedly the opinion of the court, that

when a commission has been signed by the President, the appointment is made; and that the commission is complete, when the seal of the United States has been affixed to it by the secretary of state. . . .

Mr. Marbury, then, since his commission was signed by the President, and sealed by the secretary of state, was appointed; and as the law creating the office, gave the officer a right to hold for five years, independent of the executive, the appointment was not revocable; but vested in the officer legal rights, which are protected by the laws of his country.

To withhold his commission, therefore, is an act deemed by the court not warranted by law, but violative of a vested legal right.

This brings us to the second enquiry: which is,

If he has a right, and that right has been violated, do the laws of his country afford him a remedy? . . .

The government of the United States has been emphatically termed a government of laws, and not of men. It will certainly cease to deserve this high appellation, if the laws furnish no remedy for the violation of a vested legal right.

By the constitution of the United States, the President is invested with certain important political powers, in the exercise of which he is to use his own discretion, and is accountable only to his country in his political character, and to his own conscience. To aid him in the performance of these duties, he is authorized to appoint certain officers, who act by his authority and in conformity with his orders.

In such cases, their acts are his acts; and whatever opinion may be entertained of the manner in which executive discretion may be used, still there exists, and can exist, no power to control that discretion. . . .

The conclusion from this reasoning is, that where the heads of departments are the political or confidential agents of the executive, merely to execute the will of the President, or rather to act in cases in which the executive possesses a constitutional or legal discretion, nothing can be more perfectly clear than that their acts are only politically examinable. But where a specific duty is assigned by law, and individual rights depend upon the performance of that duty, it seems equally clear that the individual who considers himself injured, has a right to resort to the laws of his country for a remedy. . . .

It is, then, the opinion of the Court,

1. That by signing the commission of Mr. Marbury, the President of the United States appointed him a justice of peace, for the county of Washington, in the district of Columbia; and that the seal of the United States, affixed thereto

by the secretary of state, is conclusive testimony of the
verity of the signature, and of the completion of the appointment; and that the appointment conferred on him a
legal right to the office for the space of five years.

2. That, having this legal title to the office, he has a
consequent right to the commission; a refusal to deliver
which, is a plain violation of that right, for which the laws
of his country afford him a remedy. . . .

This, then, is a plain case for a mandamus, either to
deliver the commission, or a copy of it from the record;
and it only remains to be inquired whether it can issue
from this court.

The act to establish the judicial courts of the United
States authorizes the Supreme Court "to issue writs of
mandamus, in cases warranted by the principles and usages
of law, to any courts appointed, or persons holding office,
under the authority of the United States."

The secretary of state, being a person holding an office
under the authority of the United States, is precisely within
the letter of the description; and if this court is not authorized to issue a writ of mandamus to such an officer, it
must be because the law is unconstitutional and therefore
absolutely incapable of conferring the authority and assigning the duties which its words purport to confer and assign.

The Constitution vests the whole judicial power of the
United States in one supreme court and such inferior courts
as Congress shall, from time to time, ordain and establish.
This power is expressly extended to all cases arising under
the laws of the United States and, consequently, in some
form, may be exercised over the present case because the
right claimed is given by a law of the United States.

In the distribution of this power it is declared that "the
Supreme Court shall have original jurisdiction in all cases
affecting ambassadors, other public ministers and consuls,
and those in which a state shall be a party. In all other
cases, the Supreme Court shall have appellate jurisdiction."

It has been insisted, at the bar, that as the original grant
of jurisdiction, to the supreme and inferior courts, is general,
and the clause, assigning original jurisdiction to the Supreme
Court, contains no negative or restrictive words, the power
remains to the legislature, to assign original jurisdiction to
that court, in other cases than those specified in the article
which has been recited, provided those cases belong to the
judicial power of the United States.

If it had been intended to leave it in the discretion of
the legislature to apportion the judicial power between the
supreme and inferior courts according to the will of that
body, it would certainly have been useless to have pro-
ceeded further than to have defined the judicial power and

the tribunals in which it should be vested. The subsequent part of the section is mere surplusage—is entirely without meaning—if such is to be the construction. If Congress remains at liberty to give this court appellate jurisdiction, where the Constitution has declared their jurisdiction shall be original, and original jurisdiction where the Constitution has declared it shall be appellate, the distribution of jurisdiction, made in the Constitution, is form without substance.

Affirmative words are often, in their operation, negative of other objects than those affirmed; and in this case, a negative or exclusive sense must be given to them, or they have no operation at all.

It cannot be presumed that any clause in the Constitution is intended to be without effect; and, therefore, such a construction is inadmissible, unless the words require it. . . .

The authority, therefore, given to the Supreme Court by the act establishing the judicial courts of the United States, to issue writs of mandamus to public officers, appears not to be warranted by the Constitution; and it becomes necessary to inquire whether a jurisdiction, so conferred, can be exercised.

The question whether an act, repugnant to the Constitution, can become the law of the land is a question deeply interesting to the United States but, happily, not of an intricacy proportioned to its interest. It seems only necessary to recognize certain principles, supposed to have been long and well established, to decide it.

That the people have an original right to establish, for their future government, such principles as, in their opinions, shall most conduce to their own happiness is the basis on which the whole American fabric has been erected. The exercise of this original right is a very great exertion; nor can it, nor ought it, to be frequently repeated. The principles, therefore, so established are deemed fundamental. And as the authority, from which they proceed, is supreme, and can seldom act, they are designed to be permanent.

This original and supreme will organizes the government and assigns to different departments their respective powers. It may either stop here or establish certain limits not to be transcended by those departments.

The government of the United States is of the latter description. The powers of the legislature are defined and limited; and that those limits may not be mistaken or forgotten, the Constitution is written. To what purpose are powers limited, and to what purpose is that limitation committed to writing, if these limits may, at any time, be passed by those intended to be restrained? The distinction between a government with limited and unlimited powers is abolished if those limits do not confine the persons on which they are imposed, and if acts prohibited and acts allowed are of equal obligation. It is a proposition too plain to be contested that the Constitution controls any legislative act repugnant to it or that the legislature may alter the Constitution by an ordinary act.

Between these alternatives there is no middle ground. The Constitution is either a superior paramount law, unchangeable by ordinary means, or it is on a level with ordinary legislative acts and, like other acts, is alterable when the legislature shall please to alter it.

If the former part of the alternative be true, then a legislative act contrary to the Constitution is not law; if the latter part be true, then written constitutions are absurd attempts, on the part of the people, to limit a power in its own nature illimitable.

Certainly, all those who have framed written constitutions contemplate them as forming the fundamental and paramount law of the nation, and, consequently, the theory of every such government must be, that an act of the legislature repugnant to the Constitution is void.

This theory is essentially attached to a written constitution and is, consequently, to be considered, by this court, as one of the fundamental principles of our society. It is not, therefore, to be lost sight of in the further consideration of this subject.

If an act of the legislature repugnant to the Constitution is void, does it, notwithstanding its invalidity, bind the courts and oblige them to give it effect? Or, in other words, though it be not law, does it constitute a rule as operative as if it was a law? This would be to overthrow, in fact, what was established in theory and would seem, at first view, an absurdity too gross to be insisted on. It shall, however, receive a more attentive consideration.

It is, emphatically, the province and duty of the judicial department to say what the law is. Those who apply the rule to particular cases must of necessity expound and interpret that rule. If two laws conflict with each other, the courts must decide on the operation of each.

So if a law be in opposition to the Constitution, if both the law and the Constitution apply to a particular case, so that the court must either decide that case conformably to the law, disregarding the Constitution, or conformably to the Constitution, disregarding the law, the court must determine which of these conflicting rules governs the case. This is of the very essence of judicial duty. If, then, the courts are to regard the Constitution, and the Constitution is superior to any ordinary act of the legislature, the Constitution, and not such ordinary act, must govern the case to which they both apply.

Those, then, who controvert the principle that the Constitution is to be considered, in court, as a paramount law are reduced to the necessity of maintaining that courts must close their eyes on the Constitution and see only the law.

This doctrine would subvert the very foundation of all written constitutions. It would declare that an act which, according to the principles and theory of our government, is entirely void, is yet, in practice, completely obligatory. It would declare that if the legislature shall do what is expressly forbidden, such act, notwithstanding the express prohibition, is in reality effectual. It would be giving to the legislature a practical and real omnipotence, with the same breath which professes to restrict their powers within narrow limits. It is prescribing limits and declaring that those limits may be passed at pleasure.

That it thus reduces to nothing what we have deemed the greatest improvement on political institutions, a written constitution would of itself be sufficient, in America, where written constitutions have been viewed with so much reverence, for rejecting the construction. But the peculiar expressions of the Constitution of the United States furnish additional arguments in favor of its rejection.

The judicial power of the United States is extended to all cases arising under the Constitution. Could it be the intention of those who gave this power to say that, in using it, the Constitution should not be looked into? That a case arising under the Constitution should be decided without examining the instrument under which it arises?

This is too extravagant to be maintained.

In some cases, then, the Constitution must be looked into by the judges. And if they can open it at all, what part of it are they forbidden to read or to obey?

There are many other parts of the Constitution which serve to illustrate this subject. It is declared that "no tax or duty shall be laid on articles exported from any state." Suppose a duty on the export of cotton, or tobacco, or of flour; and a suit instituted to recover it. Ought judgment to be rendered in such a case? Ought the judges to close their eyes on the Constitution and only see the law?

The Constitution declares that "no bill of attainder or ex post facto law shall be passed." If, however, such a bill should be passed and a person should be prosecuted under it, must the court condemn to death those victims whom the Constitution endeavors to preserve?

"No person," says the Constitution, "shall be convicted of treason, unless on the testimony of two witnesses to the same overt act, or on confession in open court." Here the language of the Constitution is addressed especially to the courts. It prescribes, directly for them, a rule of evidence not to be departed from. If the legislature should change that rule and declare one witness, or a confession out of court, sufficient for conviction, must the constitutional principle yield to the legislative act?

From these, and many other selections which might be made, it is apparent that the framers of the Constitution contemplated that instrument as a rule for the government of *courts* as well as of the legislature.

Why otherwise does it direct the judges to take an oath to support it? This oath certainly applies, in an especial manner, to their conduct in their official character. How immoral to impose it on them, if they were to be used as the instruments, and the knowing instruments, for violating what they swear to support!

The oath of office, too, imposed by the legislature is completely demonstrative of the legislative opinion on this subject. It is in these words: "I do solemnly swear that I will administer justice, without respect to persons, and do equal right to the poor and to the rich; and that I will faithfully and impartially discharge all the duties incumbent on me as, according to the best of my abilities and understanding, agreeably to the Constitution, and laws of the United States."

Why does a judge swear to discharge his duties agreeably to the Constitution of the United States if that Constitution forms no rule for his government? If it is closed upon him, and cannot be inspected by him? If such be the real state of things, this is worse than solemn mockery. To prescribe, or to take this oath, becomes equally a crime.

It is also not entirely unworthy of observation that, in declaring what shall be the supreme law of the land, the Constitution itself is first mentioned; and not the laws of the United States generally, but those only which shall be made in pursuance of the Constitution have that rank.

Thus, the particular phraseology of the Constitution of the United States confirms and strengthens the principle, supposed to be essential to all written constitutions, that a law repugnant to the Constitution is void and that courts, as well as other departments, are bound by that instrument.

The rule must be discharged.

Chapter 7

A BOLD FOREIGN POLICY

A dominant theme of American foreign policy in the early nineteenth century was a self-assertive and expansive nationalism. Earlier, under Washington and Adams, American statesmen had struggled to maintain neutrality for the infant republic. For the times their policy had been wise. In little more than a decade of peace the young nation had organized politically under the new constitution, had consolidated its human and material resources, and had prospered considerably. But by the 1800's a strong sense of American nationality had arisen and confident nationalists were more concerned with expansion than with consolidation. The westward movement contributed much to this new nationalism, and with the rapid development of frontier regions (Kentucky became a state in 1792, Tennessee in 1796, Ohio in 1803) there came an ever increasing demand for further expansion: into Canada, into the Floridas, across the Mississippi River and into the lands beyond.

The greatest triumph of western expansionism, and one of the most important achievements of Jefferson's presidency, was the Louisiana Purchase of 1803. From the time of the first American settlements in the Ohio valley, Westerners who shipped farm produce down the Mississippi had depended upon Spain's permission to "deposit" their goods in New Orleans for trans-shipment to market. But Napoleon, whose purpose was to make France a power once again in the New World, in 1800 extorted Louisiana from a weak and compliant Spain. And in 1802 the Americans' "right of deposit" in New Orleans was suspended. Under pressure from furious Westerners who thought war not too strong a remedy for this attack upon their interests, Jefferson authorized James Monroe and Robert R. Livingston to purchase from Napoleon the city of New Orleans (and possibly West Florida) for no more than $10,000,000. Actually, Jefferson's envoys paid Napoleon $15,000,000, but for New Orleans and the whole territory of Louisiana! So vast an expanse was this—all or part of 13 states would eventually be carved from it—that even Jefferson could not foresee its settlement "for a thousand years."

As the West grew in area and in population, so the section's political strength was enhanced and it came to play a determinant role in formulating American foreign policy. The War of 1812, traditionally associated with maritime New England as a struggle for the freedom of the seas, was in reality the West's war. Western "War Hawks" had demanded war, while New Englanders, fearing that their shipping interests would be more severely damaged by armed conflict with England than by her violation of their rights as neutrals, had actively opposed the war and at the Hartford Convention had threatened secession unless it were ended and the political power of the West curtailed. Nor were the bellicose Westerners disinterested, for they wanted much from the war with England: Canada to the north and Florida to the south. As John Randolph wrote, "Agrarian cupidity, not maritime right urges the war . . . we have heard but one word—like the whippoorwill, but one eternal monotonous tone—Canada! Canada! Canada!" But British military successes, capped by the seizure of Washington, the nation's capital, frustrated these ambitions. And when in 1815 the Treaty of Ghent ended the indecisive war the West secured no spoils, not Canada nor Florida. Nevertheless, most Americans quickly erased from memory all save such splendid victories as Andrew Jackson's at the Battle of New Orleans, and at the close of the war they were more than ever convinced of America's invincible might. Not less convinced of their nation's destiny and right to round out its borders, in 1818 they wildly cheered the hero of New Orleans when in subduing the Seminole Indians he swept through Spanish Florida, deposed the Spanish Governor, and executed two British citizens. Finally, in 1821, Spain accepted the inevitable and formally surrendered Florida to the determined American expansionists.

Thus, faith in the nation's strength, and pride in its vast Western empire, had nourished a bold sense of national destiny. And the upsurge of flamboyant nationalism that characterized the years following the Treaty of Ghent, the "Era of Good Feelings," could not fail to be reflected in relations with the powerful nations of Europe. Soon the monarchs of the Old World were to learn that in determining the fate of any part of the Western hemisphere the United States considered its will decisive. Although the Napoleonic invasion of Spain and the temporary collapse of the Spanish colonial system had given Latin Americans a taste of independence, with Napoleon's defeat, Spain's "legitimate" monarchy was restored and her old colonial empire reconstructed.

Led by San Martín, Bolívar and O'Higgins, the Latin Americans quickly rebelled against the mother country and, emulating their northern neighbor, established independent republics. With the ardent support of the great powers of Europe, whose "Holy Alliance" was dedicated to the suppression of revolution wherever it might occur, Spain sought to destroy these revolutionary governments. It was obvious to President Monroe and his Secretary of State, John Quincy Adams, that such an effort boded evil for the United States, whose interests were ever broadening. Were the European nations to succeed, they might well continue the colonization of the Americas; indeed they might soon establish new empires at the very borders of the United States. Determined to take a firm stand against European intervention in the Western hemisphere, the United States formally recognized the new republics.

Adams had no intention of stopping there, for the European powers must specifically be warned against intervention in the New World. Ever concerned with the "balance of power" in Europe, and with her important commercial ties to the new Latin-American Republics, England was equally opposed to intervention by Spain and her allies. Canning, the English foreign secretary, suggested that the two nations issue a joint warning to the other powers. Monroe was amenable to this suggestion, as were his venerable advisers, former Presidents Jefferson and Madison, but Adams would not have the United States seem a mere "cock-boat in the wake of a British man-of-war" and the Secretary successfully insisted upon unilateral action. In December, 1823, in two widely separated passages in a message to Congress, the President enunciated the principles that have become famous as the Monroe Doctrine. The "American continents," Monroe insisted, were ". . . not to be considered subjects for future colonization by any European powers. . . ." Besides, the monarchies of Europe were far different from the republics of the Americas and "any attempt on their part to extend their system to any portion of this hemisphere" would be considered "as dangerous to our peace and safety." The United States was without the power to support these bold principles, however, and for many years Latin-American independence was protected more by the British Navy than by the presidential pronouncement. Yet, as Adams intended, the Monroe Doctrine has long stood as one of the most fundamental principles of American foreign policy.

The Monroe Doctrine, *1823*

. . . At the proposal of the Russian Imperial Government, made through the minister of the Emperor residing here, a full power and instructions have been transmitted to the minister of the United States at St. Petersburg to arrange by amicable negotiation the respective rights and interests of the two nations on the northwest coast of this continent. A similar proposal had been made by His Imperial Majesty to the Government of Great Britain, which has likewise been acceded to. The Government of the United States has been desirous by this friendly proceeding of manifesting the great value which they have invariably attached to the friendship of the Emperor and their solicitude to cultivate the best understanding with his Government. In the discussions to which this interest has given rise and in the arrangements by which they may terminate the occasion has been judged proper for asserting, as a principle in which the rights and interests of the United States are involved, that the American continents, by the free and independent condition which they have assumed and maintain, are henceforth not to be considered as subjects for future colonization by any European powers. . . .

It was stated at the commencement of the last session that a great effort was then making in Spain and Portugal to improve the condition of the people of those countries, and that it appeared to be conducted with extraordinary moderation. It need scarcely be remarked that the result has been so far very different from what was then anticipated. Of events in that quarter of the globe, with which we have so much intercourse and from which we derive our origin, we have always been anxious and interested spectators. The citizens of the United States cherish sentiments the most friendly in favor of the liberty and happiness of their fellow-men on that side of the Atlantic. In the wars of the European powers in matters relating to themselves we have never taken any part, nor does it comport with our policy so to do. It is only when our rights are invaded or seriously menaced that we resent injuries or make preparation for our defense. With the movements in this hemisphere we are of necessity more immediately connected, and by causes which must be obvious to all enlightened and impartial observers. The political system of the allied powers is essentially different in this respect from that of America. This difference proceeds from that which exists in their respective Governments; and to the defense of our own, which has been achieved by the loss of so much blood and treasure, and matured by the wisdom of their most enlightened citizens, and under which we have enjoyed unexampled felicity, this whole nation is devoted. We owe it, therefore, to candor and to the amicable relations existing between the United States and those powers to declare that we should consider any attempt on their part to extend their system to any portion of this hemisphere as dangerous to our peace and safety. With the existing colonies or dependencies of any European power we have not interfered and shall not interfere. But with the Governments who have declared their independence and maintained it, and whose independence we have, on great consideration and on just principles, acknowledged, we could not view any interposition for the purpose of oppressing them, or controlling in any other manner their destiny, by any European power in any other light than as the manifestation of an unfriendly disposition toward the United States. In the war between those new Governments and Spain we declared our neutrality at the time of their recognition, and to this we have adhered, and shall continue to adhere, provided no change shall occur which, in the judgment of the competent authorities of this Government, shall make a corresponding change on the part of the United States indispensable to their security.

The late events in Spain and Portugal show that Europe is still unsettled. Of this important fact no stronger proof can be adduced than that the allied powers should have thought it proper, on any principle satisfactory to themselves, to have interposed by force in the internal concerns of Spain. To what extent such interposition may be carried, on the same principle, is a question in which all independent powers whose governments differ from theirs are interested, even those most remote, and surely none more so than the United States. Our policy in regard to Europe, which was adopted at an early stage of the wars which have so long agitated that quarter of the globe, nevertheless remains the same, which is, not to interfere in the internal concerns of any of its powers; to consider the government *de facto* as the legitimate government for us; to cultivate friendly relations with it, and to preserve those relations by a frank, firm, and manly policy, meeting in all instances the just claims of every power, submitting to injuries from none. But in regard to these continents circumstances are eminently and conspicuously different. It is impossible that the allied powers should extend their political system to any portion of either continent without endangering our peace and happiness; nor can anyone believe that our southern brethren, if left to themselves, would adopt it of their own accord. It is equally impossible, therefore, that we should behold such interposition in any form with indifference. If we look to the comparative strength and resources of Spain and those new Governments, and their distance from each other, it must be obvious that she can never subdue them. It is still the true policy of the United States to leave the parties to themselves, in the hope that other powers will pursue the same course.

Chapter 8

JACKSONIAN DEMOCRACY

Andrew Jackson's election in 1828—like Thomas Jefferson's in 1800 and Franklin D. Roosevelt's more than a century later—marked a significant change in American social and political thought, for Jackson thoroughly symbolized the widespread democratic impulse of the 1820's and 1830's. A half-century earlier Jefferson had declared as the philosophical basis of the Declaration of Independence the proposition that "all men are created equal"; and in the bloodless "Revolution of 1800" a crumbling Federalism had been laid low by the determined disciples of Jeffersonian Democracy. Yet the Jeffersonians were themselves essentially aristocratic in outlook and suspicious of popular rule. They believed in government *of* and *for* the people, but not necessarily *by* the people, and it was not until the Age of Jackson that equalitarianism became a pervasive theme of American life.

Now, however, political institutions underwent a profound transformation, and political control was rapidly transferred from an aristocracy of education, position, and wealth to the common man, the average American. Early in the republic's history each of the original states had imposed severe restrictions upon the suffrage, but the newly admitted Western states had enfranchised almost all of their adult white males and constitutional revisions soon brought the older states into line. Property qualifications for office were similarly abolished at the example of the West; terms of office were limited, as were the numbers of appointive or non-elective positions; and by the time of Jackson's first election each state, with the exception of Delaware and South Carolina, had provided that Presidential electors be chosen popularly rather than by the state legislatures. Important, too, was the widespread insistence that Presidential candidates be chosen by open party conventions instead of by tightly inbred legislative caucuses.

Jacksonian Democracy also brought a new equalitarian conception of public office: that all men were essentially of equal talents, that each American of normal intelligence was capable of holding any position in government, and that democracy required a rotation in office to prevent the development of an untouchable and undemocratic political bureaucracy. And though it was frequently abused by venal politicians for private gain, this notion that "to the victors belong the spoils" was a forthright expression of the simple democratic instinct for replacing office holders whose party had been repudiated with those who were more clearly "the people's choice." Leveling doctrines pervaded every area of social life as well, and there were some, like the French observer Alexis de Tocqueville in his classic "Democracy in America," who wondered whether Americans' liberties would long survive the nation's penchant for equality. For at times the tyranny of the majority proved even more oppressive than minority rule, and "King Numbers" seemed as despotic a sovereign as any in history.

Meanwhile Americans' democratic sympathies found ample expression in the myriad social and economic reform movements of the Jacksonian period. Determined to cleanse and purify the national life, they enthusiastically devoted their energies to such varied causes as free public education, women's rights, abolitionism, temperance, and the care of criminals and of the insane. With the steady growth of industry in the Northeast the labor movement also received an important impetus, for the squalor and impoverishment of the new urban working class were in striking contrast to contemporary ideals of equality and material well-being for all Americans.

Undoubtedly many of the new labor unions and workingmen's parties fervently supported the political ascendancy of Andrew Jackson. Yet the warrior-statesman's rough-and-tumble ways and his disdain for rank and ceremony identified him even more closely with the West, where a continuous frontier experience bred a firm faith in the capacity of the common man; and his hatred of privilege and monopoly made him equally the champion of the struggling entrepreneur. Thus in 1828 and again in 1832 Jackson, though a wealthy planter, was able to rally to his support the democratic forces of the nation—the workers, farmers and small businessmen—and to make the new Democratic party a symbol of the leveling spirit of the age.

Ultimately it was his spectacular war upon the second Bank of the United States that most clearly illustrated Jackson's libertarian instincts and his intolerance of monopoly. The charter of the first Bank of the United States (which Jefferson had emphatically opposed and Hamilton as firmly supported in their famous letters to Washington in 1791) had expired in 1811 and had not been immediately renewed. But in 1816, after the harsh fiscal experiences of the War of 1812, and in the midst of the nationalistic fervor that gripped the nation at the War's conclusion, Congress had enthusiastically chartered a second Bank, granting it important monopolies in the national banking business. By the 1820's, however, the "Era of Good Feelings" had been supplanted by a period of intense sectional and class conflict, and though conservative business leaders were well served by the Bank and by its aristocratic president, Nicholas Biddle, popular enthusiasm gave way to suspicion and distrust. Soon representatives of the underprivileged classes spoke of the Bank as a "financial octopus" and protested its vast power over the economic life of the nation.

Jackson fully shared this popular prejudice against the Bank, and like Jefferson before him he argued against its constitutionality. His real objections, however, were personal and political, for Biddle had used the Bank's resources to support anti-Jackson Congressmen and to defy the popular President. At the insistence of Henry Clay, Jackson's bitter rival in the West, Biddle actually precipitated the conflict himself. Jackson had early made known his hostility to the Bank, but there was no sure indication of his plans in regard to its recharter. Nevertheless in the early summer of 1832 Biddle forced a recharter bill through Congress. Since the old charter would not expire for four years, it was obvious that the Bank Bill had been timed to present Clay with a convenient campaign issue in the coming Presidential election, for the conservative National Republicans (soon to emerge as the new Whig party) erroneously believed that a Presidential veto would be extremely unpopular.

Instead, Jackson's forceful veto message gained him widespread support from all who feared the "concentration of power in the hands of a few men irresponsible to the people." Though his enemies denounced the Bank veto as "demagogic" and dictatorial and dubbed Jackson "King Andrew I," great numbers of "the humble members of society" saw in his veto message a clear expression of the era's growing democratic ideology. Once again they elected the hero of New Orleans to the highest office in the land.

Veto of the Bank Renewal Bill,
Andrew Jackson, 1832

The bill "to modify and continue" the act entitled "An act to incorporate the subscribers to the Bank of the United States" was presented to me on the 4th July instant. Having considered it with that solemn regard to the principles of the Constitution which the day was calculated to inspire, and come to the conclusion that it ought not to become a law, I herewith return it to the Senate, in which it originated, with my objections.

A bank of the United States is in many respects convenient for the Government and useful to the people. Entertaining this opinion, and deeply impressed with the belief that some of the powers and privileges possessed by the existing bank are unauthorized by the Constitution, subversive of the rights of the States, and dangerous to the liberties of the people, I felt it my duty at an early period of my Administration to call the attention of Congress to the practicability of organizing an institution combining all its advantages and obviating these objections. I sincerely regret that in the act before me I can perceive none of those modifications of the bank charter which are necessary, in my opinion, to make it compatible with justice, with sound policy, or with the Constitution of our country.

The present corporate body, denominated the president, directors, and company of the Bank of the United States, will have existed at the time this act is intended to take effect twenty years. It enjoys an exclusive privilege of banking under the authority of the General Government, a monopoly of its favor and support, and, as a necessary consequence, almost a monopoly of the foreign and domestic exchange. The powers, privileges, and favors bestowed upon it in the original charter, by increasing the value of the stock far above its par value, operated as a gratuity of many millions to the stockholders.

An apology may be found for the failure to guard against this result in the consideration that the effect of the original act of incorporation could not be certainly foreseen at the time of its passage. The act before me proposes another gratuity to the holders of the same stock, and in many cases to the same men, of at least seven millions more. This donation finds no apology in any uncertainty as to the effect of the act. On all hands it is conceded that its passage will increase at least 20 or 30 per cent more the market price of the stock, subject to the payment of the annuity of $200,000 per year secured by the act, thus adding in a moment one-fourth to its par value. It is not our own citizens only who are to receive the bounty of our Government. More than eight millions of the stock of this bank are held by foreigners. By this act the American Republic proposes virtually to make them a present of some millions of dollars. For these gratuities to foreigners, and to some of our own opulent citizens the act secures no equivalent whatever. They are the certain gains of the present stockholders under the operation of this act, after making full allowance for the payment of the bonus.

Every monopoly and all exclusive privileges are granted at the expense of the public, which ought to receive a fair equivalent. The many millions which this act proposes to bestow on the stockholders of the existing bank must come directly or indirectly out of the earnings of the American people. It is due to them, therefore, if their Government sell monopolies and exclusive privileges, that they should at least exact for them as much as they are worth in open market. The value of the monopoly in this case may be correctly ascertained. The twenty-eight millions of stock would probably be at an advance of 50 per cent, and command in market at least $42,000,000, subject to the payment of the present bonus. The present value of the monopoly, therefore, is $17,000,000, and this the act proposes to sell for three millions, payable in fifteen annual installments of $200,000 each.

It is not conceivable how the present stockholders can have any claim to the special favor of the Government. The present corporation has enjoyed its monopoly during the period stipulated in the original contract. If we must have such a corporation, why should not the Government sell out the whole stock and thus secure to the people the full market value of the privileges granted? Why should not Congress create and sell twenty-eight millions of stock, incorporating the purchases with all the powers and privileges secured in this act and putting the premium upon the sales into the Treasury?

But this act does not permit competition in the purchase of this monopoly. It seems to be predicated on the erroneous idea that the present stockholders have a prescriptive right not only to the favor but to the bounty of Government. It appears that more than a fourth part of the stock is held by foreigners and the residue is held by a few hundred of our own citizens, chiefly of the richest class. For their benefit does this act exclude the whole American people from competition in the purchase of this monopoly and dispose of it for many millions less than it is worth. This seems the less excusable because some of our citizens not now stockholders petitioned that the door of competition might be opened, and offered to take a charter on terms much more favorable to the Government and country.

But this proposition, although made by men whose aggregate wealth is believed to be equal to all the private stock in the existing bank, has been set aside, and the bounty of our Government is proposed to be again bestowed on the few who have been fortunate enough to secure the stock and at this moment wield the power of the existing institution. I can not perceive the justice or policy of this course. If our Government must sell monopolies, it would seem to be its duty to take nothing less than their full value, and if gratuities must be made once in fifteen or twenty years let them not be bestowed on the subjects of a foreign government nor upon a designated and favored class of men in our own country. It is but justice and good policy as far as the nature of the case will admit, to confine our favors to our own fellow-citizens, and let each in his turn enjoy an opportunity to profit by our bounty. In the bearings of the act before me upon these points I find ample reasons why it should not become a law.

It has been urged as an argument in favor of rechartering the present bank that the calling in its loans will produce great embarrassment and distress. The time allowed to close its concerns is ample, and if it has well managed its pressure will be light, and heavy only in case its management has been bad. If, therefore, it shall produce distress, the fault will be its own, and it would furnish a reason against renewing a power which has been so obviously abused. But will there ever be a time when this reason will be less powerful? To acknowledge its force is to admit that the bank ought to be perpetual, and as a consequence the present stockholders and those inheriting their rights as successors be established a privileged order, clothed both with great political power and enjoying immense pecuniary advantages from their connection with the Government.

The modifications of the existing charter proposed by this act are not such, in my view, as make it consistent with the rights of the States or the liberties of the people. The qualification of the right of the bank to hold real estate, the limitation of its power to establish branches, and the power reserved to Congress to forbid the circulation of small notes are restrictions comparatively of little value or importance. All the objectionable principles of the existing corporation, and most of its odious features, are retained without alleviation. . . .

In another of its bearings this provision is fraught with danger. Of the twenty-five directors of this bank five are chosen by the Government and twenty by the citizen stockholders. From all voice in these elections the foreign stockholders are excluded by the charter. In proportion, therefore, as the stock is transferred to foreign holders the extent of suffrage in the choice of directors is curtailed. Already is almost a third of the stock in foreign hands and not represented in elections. It is constantly passing out of the country, and this act will accelerate its departure. The entire control of the insitution would necessarily fall into the hands of a few citizen stockholders, and the ease with which the object would be accomplished would be a temptation to designing men to secure that control in their own hands by monopolizing the remaining stock. There is danger that a president and directors would then be able to elect themselves from year to year, and without responsibility or control manage the whole concerns of the bank during the existence of its charter. It is easy to conceive that great evils to our country and its institutions might flow from such a concentration of power in the hands of a few men irresponsible to the people.

Is there no danger to our liberty and independence in a bank that in its nature has so little to bind it to our country? The president of the bank has told us that most of the State banks exist by its forbearance. Should its influence become concentered, as it may under the operation of such an act as this, in the hands of a self-elected directory whose interests are identified with those of the foreign stockholders, will there not be cause to tremble for the purity of our elections in peace and for the independence of our country in war? Their power would be great whenever they might choose to exert it; but if this monopoly were regularly renewed every fifteen or twenty years on terms proposed by themselves, they might seldom in peace put forth their strength to influence elections or control the affairs of the nation. But if any private citizen or public functionary should interpose to curtail its powers or prevent a renewal of its privileges, it can not be doubted that he would be made to feel its influence.

Should the stock of the bank principally pass into the hands of the subjects of a foreign country, and we should unfortunately become involved in a war with that country, what would be our condition? Of the course which would be pursued by a bank almost wholly owned by the subjects of a foreign power, and managed by those whose interests, if not affections, would run in the same direction there can be no doubt. All its operations within would be in aid of the hostile fleets and armies without. Controlling our currency, receiving our public moneys, and holding thousands of our citizens in dependence, it would be more formidable and dangerous than the naval and military power of the enemy.

If we must have a bank with private stockholders, every consideration of sound policy and every impulse of American feeling admonishes that it should be *purely American*. Its stockholders should be composed exclusively of our own citizens, who at least ought to be friendly to our Government and willing to support it in times of difficulty and danger. So abundant is domestic capital that competition in subscribing for the stock of local banks has recently led almost to riots. To a bank exclusively of American stockholders, possessing the powers and privileges granted by this act, subscriptions for $200,000,000 could readily be obtained. Instead of sending abroad the stock of the bank in which the Government must deposit its funds and on which it must rely to sustain its credit in times of emergency, it would rather seem to be expedient to prohibit its sale to aliens under penalty of absolute forfeiture.

It is maintained by the advocates of the bank that its constitutionality in all its features ought to be considered as settled by precedent and by the decision of the Supreme Court. To this conclusion I can not assent. Mere precedent is a dangerous source of authority, and should not be regarded as deciding questions of constitutional power except where the acquiescence of the people and the States can be considered as well settled. So far from this being the case on this subject, an argument against the bank might be based on precedent. One Congress, in 1791, decided in favor of a bank; another, in 1811, decided against it. One Congress, in 1815, decided against a bank; another, in 1816, decided in its favor. Prior to the present Congress, therefore, the precedents drawn from that source were equal. If we resort to the States, the expressions of legislative, judicial, and executive opinions against the bank have been probably to those in its favor as 4 to 1. There is nothing in precedent, therefore, which, if its authority were admitted, ought to weigh in favor of the act before me.

If the opinion of the Supreme Court covered the whole ground of this act, it ought not to control the coordinate authorities of this Government. The Congress, the Executive, and the Court must each for itself be guided by its own opinion of the Constitution. Each public officer who takes an oath to support the Constitution swears that he will support it as he understands it, and not as it is understood by others. It is as much the duty of the House of Representatives, of the Senate, and of the President to decide upon the constitutionality of any bill or resolution which may be presented to them for passage or approval as it is of the supreme judges when it may be brought before them for judicial decision. The opinion of the judges has no more authority over Congress than one opinion of Congress has over the judges, and on that point the President is independent of both. The authority of the Supreme Court must not, therefore, be permitted to control the Congress or the Executive when acting in their legislative capacities, but to have only such influence as the force of their reasoning may deserve. . . .

The bank is professedly established as an agent of the executive branch of the Government, and its constitutionality is maintained on that ground. Neither upon the propriety of present action nor upon the provisions of this act was the Executive consulted. It has had no opportunity to say that it neither needs nor wants an agent clothed with such powers and favored by such exemptions. There is nothing in its legitimate functions which makes it necessary or proper. Whatever interest or influence, whether public or private, has given birth to this act, it can not be found either in the wishes or necessities of the executive department, by which present action is deemed premature, and the powers conferred upon its agent not only unnecessary, but dangerous to the Government and country.

It is to be regretted that the rich and powerful too often bend the acts of government to their selfish purposes. Distinctions in society will always exist under every just government. Equality of talents, of education, or of wealth can not be produced by human institutions. In the full enjoyment of the gifts of Heaven and the fruits of superior industry, economy, and virtue, every man is equally entitled to protection by law; but when the laws undertake to add to these natural and just advantages artificial distinctions, to grant titles, gratuities, and exclusive privileges, to make the rich richer and the potent more powerful, the humble members of society—the farmers, mechanics, and laborers—who have neither the time nor the means of securing like favors to themselves, have a right to complain of the injustice of their Government. There are no necessary evils in government. Its evils exist only in its abuses. If it would confine itself to equal protection, and, as Heaven does its rains, shower its favors alike on the high and the low, the rich and the poor, it would be an unqualified blessing. In the act before me there seems to be a wide and unnecessary departure from these just principles.

Nor is our Government to be maintained or our Union preserved by invasions of the rights and powers of the several States. In thus attempting to make our General Government strong we make it weak. Its true strength consists in leaving individuals and States as much as possible to themselves—in making itself felt, not in its power, but in its beneficence; not in its control, but in its protection; not in binding the States more closely to the center, but leaving each more unobstructed in its proper orbit.

Experience should teach us wisdom. Most of the difficulties our Government now encounters and most of the dangers which impend over our Union have sprung from an abandonment of the legitimate objects of Government by our national legislation, and the adoption of such principles as are embodied in this act. Many of our rich men have not been content with equal protection and equal benefits, but have besought us to make them richer by act of Congress. By attempting to gratify their desires we have in the results of our legislation arrayed section against section, interest against interest, and man against man, in a fearful commotion which threatens to shake the foundations of our Union. It is time to pause in our career to review our principles, and if possible revive that devoted patriotism and spirit of compromise which distinguished the sages of the Revolution and the fathers of our Union. If we can not at once, in justice to interests vested under improvident legislation, make our Government what it ought to be, we can at least take a stand against all new grants of monopolies and exclusive privileges, against any prostitution of our Government to the advancement of the few at the expense of the many, and in favor of compromise and gradual reform in our code of laws and system of political economy.

Chapter 9

LIBERTY OR UNION

Nationalism had been the keynote of the years immediately following the War of 1812—the period known as the "Era of Good Feelings"—for Americans seemed to be imbued with a profound sense of national identity that they had lacked before. Nowhere was this nationalism more completely expressed than in Congressional legislation sponsored by Republicans who had forsaken their earlier belief in states' rights and a severely limited national government. The permanent armed forces of the United States were strengthened; internal improvements, such as the construction of roads and canals, were authorized; a second Bank of the United States, which promised a stable and uniform national currency, was created; and, most significant for the future, high war-time tariffs were maintained and even increased to protect American industries that had sprung up during the war. Throughout the country there was widespread support for this impressive legislative program, and James Monroe's reelection to the Presidency in 1820 was a significant symbol of the period's vaunted political unity. For in that year Monroe received every electoral vote but one; lest another share with Washington the honor of a unanimous vote for President, one Republican elector had cast an opposing ballot.

Not far beneath this surface unity, however, there lay deeply rooted sectional antagonisms that within two generations were to erupt into civil war. And in 1820 an angry dispute over Missouri's admission to the Union gave Americans a foretaste of the conflict ahead. The country was torn by dissension when the South violently protested Northern efforts to prohibit the further introduction of slavery into Missouri as a condition for statehood. Though there were an equal number of slave and free states, with equal representation in the United States Senate, the South had consistently been outstripped by the North in population growth. By 1820 it could claim only 89 members in the House of Representatives to the North's 123. For this reason the South considered it essential to its interests that slave and free states be numerically equal, guaranteeing a sectional balance at least in the Senate, and it bitterly resented the Northern proposals that would eventually make Missouri a free state. Besides, with the tremendous expansion of cotton cultivation that followed Eli Whitney's invention of the cotton gin in 1793, slavery had once again become an integral part of the Southern economy and the North's attempt to limit it was taken as a direct attack upon the South's well-being. But the scene had not yet been set for a prolonged open struggle between the sections, and the issue was soon settled by the Missouri Compromise. Missouri was admitted to the Union as a slave state without restrictions, and at the same time, to maintain the sectional balance, Maine was admitted as a free state. The historic Compromise further provided that with the exception of Missouri, slavery was to be prohibited permanently in all of the Louisiana Purchase territory above the 36° 30″ line and permitted below it. The nation rejoiced that the immediate problem had been resolved peacefully, but those whose insight into the dynamics of the sectional conflict was more profound saw that the Missouri question was only a prelude to a later, more fundamental—and possibly tragic—struggle.

Nevertheless both slavery itself and the burning question of a balance of political power between the sections were secondary and merely symptomatic of the more basic cleavage between the South's agrarian economy and the industrial economy of the North. After the War of 1812, Southern Congressmen like John C. Calhoun of South Carolina hoped to promote industrial development in their own section and supported nationalistic legislation such as high tariffs. Industrial failures and a tremendous increase in cotton production quickly disabused Southerners of this idea, however, and they returned to a defense of traditional agrarian ways. Indeed Calhoun and other Southern leaders soon came to champion states' rights and to oppose the nationalistic, industrial measures they so recently had advanced. Their conversion had its parallel in the North, where Calhoun's early arguments for a high tariff had been brilliantly countered by Daniel Webster, who at that time represented New England's mercantile and shipping interests in their opposition to industrialization. But by the 1820's the older mercantile interests were giving way to industrialism in the North, and the opportunistic Webster had shifted his allegiance to become the pro-industrial nationalist we remember today. Fundamentally Calhoun and Webster were at all times "sectionalists," each deeply committed to the immediate interests of his own section. Their respective metamorphoses—Calhoun's from nationalist to agrarian states' righter, and Webster's from mercantile states' righter to nationalist—provide us with the clearest possible picture of the realignment of their sections' economic interests. And later political struggles between the great leaders and their followers, whether over slavery or over the nature of the Union, were never more than ancillary to the basic sectional conflict between plantation agrarianism and industrialism.

One of the most memorable of these political struggles was the Webster-Hayne Debate of January, 1830. The immediate issue was an attempt by Senator Foot of Connecticut to limit Western land sales. Seizing upon the Foot Resolution as a vehicle for alienating the West from the North and winning support for Southern policies, Senator Hayne of South Carolina had launched a violent attack upon New England, questioning its patriotism and charging that section (particularly Massachusetts) with a selfish antipathy to the South and West alike. As presiding officer of the Senate, Vice-President Calhoun actually took no part in the debate. But it was evident to all that Hayne was Calhoun's spokesman as the younger Carolinian went on to espouse the superiority of the states over the national government and to insist that for the West no less than for the South nullification of national legislation by the "sovereign" states was a final answer to Northern tyranny. Then Webster rose in defense of his state, his section, and his new nationalism and delivered one of the most eloquent of American orations. The states had not created the Union, the Senator from Massachusetts proclaimed; rather it was the creature of all of the people, whose political organ (the national government) was superior to all others. Thus nullification could find no sanction in history and must be forsworn in favor of a firm devotion to the binding force of national authority. To those who cried "Liberty first and Union afterwards" the "Godlike Daniel" replied in a magnificent peroration with "that other sentiment, dear to every true American heart—Liberty *and* Union, now and forever, one and inseparable."

Three months later, at a dinner celebrating Jefferson's birthday, the West replied, through the greatest of its spokesmen, to the South's bid for political support. Andrew Jackson— his eyes fixed on Calhoun—rose dramatically to offer the Presidential toast: "Our Federal Union—it must be preserved!" The implications of Jackson's reply were unmistakable; the West, keenly national in its feelings and interests, had rejected the Southern lure of states' rights and sectionalism. Two years later North and West joined in support of Jackson's firm stand against the efforts of South Carolina to nullify the tariff of 1832. In his fiery appeal for patriotism and Union, Webster clearly had touched upon what Lincoln would later call the "mystic chords of memory"; he had spoken the heart no less than the mind of the nation.

Daniel Webster's Second Reply to Hayne, *1830*

. . . So, Sir, I understood the gentleman and am happy to find that I did not misunderstand him. What he contends for is that it is constitutional to interrupt the administration of the Constitution itself, in the hands of those who are chosen and sworn to administer it, by the direct interference, in form of law, of the states, in virtue of their sovereign capacity. The inherent right in the people to reform their government I do not deny; and they have another right, and that is to resist unconstitutional laws without overturning the government. It is no doctrine of mine that unconstitutional laws bind the people. The great question is: Whose prerogative is it to decide on the constitutionality or unconstitutionality of the laws? On that, the main debate hinges. The proposition that, in case of a supposed violation of the Constitution by Congress, the states have a constitutional right to interfere and annul the law of Congress is the proposition of the gentleman. I do not admit it. If the gentleman had intended no more than to assert the right of revolution for justifiable cause, he would have said only what all agree to. But I cannot conceive that there can be a middle course, between submission to the laws, when regularly pronounced constitutional, on the one hand, and open resistance, which is revolution or rebellion, on the other. I say the right of a state to annul a law of Congress cannot be maintained but on the ground of the inalienable right of man to resist oppression; that is to say, upon the ground of revolution. I admit that there is an ultimate violent remedy, above the Constitution and in defiance of the Constitution, which may be resorted to when a revolution is to be justified. But I do not admit that, under the Constitution and in conformity with it, there is any mode in which a state government, as a member of the Union, can interfere and stop the progress of the general government, by force of her own laws, under any circumstances whatever.

This leads us to inquire into the origin of this government and the source of its power. Whose agent is it? Is it the creature of the state legislatures or the creature of the people? If the government of the United States be the agent of the state governments, then they may control it, provided they can agree in the manner of controlling it; if it be the agent of the people, then the people alone can control it, restrain it, modify, or reform it. . . . It is, Sir, the people's Constitution, the people's government, made for the people, made by the people, and answerable to the people. The people of the United States have declared that this Constitution shall be the supreme law. We must either admit the proposition or dispute their authority. The states are, unquestionably, sovereign so far as their sovereignty is not affected by this supreme law. But the state legislatures, as political bodies, however sovereign, are yet not sovereign over the people. So far as the people have given power to the general government, so far the grant is unquestionably good, and the government holds of the people and not of the state governments. We are all agents of the same supreme power, the people. The general government and the state governments derive their authority from the same source. Neither can, in relation to the other, be called primary, though one is definite and restricted, and the other general and residuary. The national government possesses those powers which it can be shown the people have conferred on it, and no more. All the rest belongs to the state governments or to the people themselves. So far as the people have restrained state sovereignty, by the expression of their will, in the Constitution of the United States, so far, it must be admitted, state sovereignty is effectually controlled. I do not contend that it is, or ought to be, controlled further. The sentiment to which I have referred propounds that state sovereignty is only to be controlled by its own "feeling of justice"; that is to say, it is not to be controlled at all, for one who is to follow his own feelings is under no legal control. Now, however, men may think this ought to be, the fact is that the people of the United States have chosen to impose control on state sovereignties. There are those, doubtless, who wish they had been left without restraint; but the Constitution has ordered the matter differently. To make war, for instance, is an exercise of sovereignty; but the Constitution declares that no state shall make war. To coin money is another exercise of sovereign power; but no state is at liberty to coin money. Again, the Constitution says that no sovereign state shall be so sovereign as to make a treaty. These prohibitions, it must be confessed, are a control on the state sovereignty of South Carolina, as well as of the other states, which does not arise "from her own feelings of honorable justice." The opinion referred to, therefore, is in defiance of the plainest provisions of the Constitution.

. . . The Carolina doctrine, which the honorable member has now stood up on this floor to maintain . . . resolved that

> the tariff of 1828, and every other tariff designed to promote one branch of industry at the expense of others, is contrary to the meaning and intention of the federal compact; and such a dangerous, palpable, and deliberate usurpation of power, by a determined majority, wielding the general government beyond the limits of its delegated powers, as calls upon the states which compose the suffering minority, in their sovereign capacity, to exercise the powers which, as sovereigns, necessarily devolve upon them, when their compact is violated.

. . . This resolution holds the tariff of 1828, and every other tariff designed to promote one branch of industry at the expense of another, to be such a dangerous, palpable, and deliberate usurpation of power, as calls upon the states, in their sovereign capacity, to interfere by their own authority. . . . Let us suppose the state of South Carolina to express this same opinion by the voice of her legislature. That would be very imposing; but what then? Is the voice of one state conclusive? It so happens that, at the very moment when South Carolina resolves that the tariff laws are unconstitutional, Pennsylvania and Kentucky resolve exactly the reverse. *They* hold those laws to be both highly proper and strictly constitutional. . . .

In Carolina the tariff is a palpable, deliberate usurpation; Carolina, therefore, may nullify it and refuse to pay the duties. In Pennsylvania it is both clearly constitutional and highly expedient; and there the duties are to be paid.

And yet we live under a government of uniform laws and under a Constitution too which contains an express provision, as it happens, that all duties shall be equal in all the states. Does not this approach absurdity?

If there be no power to settle such questions, independent of either of the states, is not the whole Union a rope of sand? Are we not thrown back again, precisely, upon the old Confederation?

It is too plain to be argued. Four-and-twenty interpreters of constitutional law, each with a power to decide for itself, and none with authority to bind anybody else, and this constitutional law the only bond of their union! What is such a state of things but a mere connection during pleasure or, to use the phraseology of the times, "during feeling"? And that feeling too, not the feeling of the people, who established the Constitution, but the feeling of the state governments. . . .

The people, then, Sir, erected this government. They gave it a Constitution, and in that Constitution they have enumerated the powers which they bestow on it. They have made it a limited government. They have defined its authority. They have restrained it to the exercise of such powers as are granted; and all others, they declare, are reserved to the states or the people. But, Sir, they have not stopped here. If they had, they would have accomplished but half their work. No definition can be so clear, as to avoid possibility of doubt; no limitation so precise, as to exclude all uncertainty. Who, then, shall construe this grant of the people? Who shall interpret their will, where it may be supposed they have left it doubtful? With whom do they repose this ultimate right of deciding on the powers of the government? Sir, they have settled all this in the fullest manner. They have left it with the government itself, in its appropriate branches. Sir, the very chief end, the main design, for which the whole Constitution was framed and adopted, was to establish a government that should not be obliged to act through state agency, or depend on state opinion and state discretion. The people had had quite enough of that kind of government under the Confederation. Under that system, the legal action, the application of law to individuals, belonged exclusively to the states. Congress could only recommend; their acts were not of binding force, till the states had adopted and sanctioned them. Are we in that condition still? Are we yet at the mercy of state discretion and state construction? Sir, if we are, then vain will be our attempt to maintain the Constitution under which we sit.

But, Sir, the people have wisely provided, in the Constitution itself, a proper, suitable mode and tribunal for settling questions of constitutional law. There are in the Constitution grants of powers to Congress and restrictions on these powers. There are, also, prohibitions on the states. Some authority must, therefore, necessarily exist having the ultimate jurisdiction to fix and ascertain the interpretation of these grants, restrictions, and prohibitions. The Constitution has itself pointed out, ordained, and established that authority. How has it accomplished this great and essential end? By declaring, Sir, that "the Constitution, and the laws of the United States made in pursuance thereof, shall be the supreme law of the land, anything in the constitution or laws of any state to the contrary notwithstanding."

This, Sir, was the first great step. By this the supremacy of the Constitution and laws of the United States is declared. The people so will it. No state law is to be valid which comes in conflict with the Constitution, or any law of the United States passed in pursuance of it. But who shall decide this question of interference? To whom lies the last appeal? This, Sir, the Constitution itself decides also, by declaring, that *the judicial power shall extend to all cases arising under the Constitution and laws of the United States.* These two provisions cover the whole ground. They are, in truth, the keystone of the arch! With these it is a government; without them it is a confederation. In pursuance of these clear and express provisions, Congress established, at its very first session, in the judicial act, a mode for carrying them into full effect, and for bringing all questions of constitutional power to the final decision of the Supreme Court. It then, Sir, became a government. It then had the means of self-protection; and but for this, it would, in all probability, have been now among things which are past. Having constituted the government, and declared its powers, the people have further said that since somebody must decide on the extent of these powers, the government itself shall decide; subject, always, like other popular governments, to its responsibility to the people. And now, Sir, I repeat, how is it that a state legislature acquires any power to interfere? Who, or what, gives them the right to say to the people "We, who are your agents and servants for one purpose, will undertake to decide, that your other agents and servants, appointed by you for another purpose, have transcended the authority you gave them!" The reply would be, I think, not impertinent: "Who made you a judge over another's servants? To their own masters they stand or fall."

Sir, I deny this power of state legislatures altogether. It cannot stand the test of examination. Gentlemen may say that, in an extreme case, a state government might protect the people from intolerable oppression. Sir, in such a case, the people might protect themselves, without the aid of the state governments. Such a case warrants revolution. It must

make, when it comes, a law for itself. A nullifying act of a
state legislature cannot alter the case, nor make resistance
any more lawful. In maintaining these sentiments, Sir, I am
but asserting the rights of the people. I state what they have
declared and insist on their right to declare it. They have
chosen to repose this power in the general government and
I think it my duty to support it, like other constitutional
powers.

. . . If, sir, the people in these respects had done otherwise than they have done, their Constitution could neither
have been preserved, nor would it have been worth preserving. And if its plain provisions shall now be disregarded,
and these new doctrines interpolated in it, it will become as
feeble and helpless a being as its enemies, whether early or
more recent, could possibly desire. It will exist in every
State, but as a poor dependent on State permission. It must
borrow leave to be, and will be no longer than State pleasure or State discretion sees fit to grant the indulgence and
to prolong its poor existence.

But, sir, although there are fears, there are hopes also.
The people have preserved this, their own chosen Constitution, for forty years, and have seen their happiness, prosperity, and renown grow with its growth and strengthen
with its strength. They are now, generally, strongly attached
to it. Overthrown by direct assault it cannot be; evaded,
undermined, *nullified,* it will not be, if we and those who
shall succeed us here as agents and representatives of the
people shall conscientiously and vigilantly discharge the two
great branches of our public trust—faithfully to preserve
and wisely to administer it.

Mr. President, I have thus stated the reasons of my dis-
sent to the doctrines which have been advanced and maintained. I am conscious of having detained you and the Senate much too long. I was drawn into the debate with no
previous deliberation, such as is suited to the discussion of
so grave and important a subject. But it is a subject of
which my heart is full, and I have not been willing to suppress the utterance of its spontaneous sentiments. I cannot, even now, persuade myself to relinquish it without
expressing once more my deep conviction that, since it respects nothing less than the Union of the State, it is of most
vital and essential importance to the public happiness. I
profess, sir, in my career hitherto, to have kept steadily
in view the prosperity and honor of the whole country and
the preservation of our Federal Union. It is to that Union
we owe our safety at home and our consideration and
dignity abroad. It is to that Union that we are chiefly indebted for whatever makes us most proud of our country.
That Union we reached only by the discipline of our virtues

in the severe school of adversity. It had its origin in the necessities of disordered finance, prostrate commerce, and ruined credit. Under its benign influences these great interests immediately awoke as from the dead, and sprang forth with newness of life. Every year of its duration has teemed with fresh proofs of its utility and its blessings; and although our territory has stretched out wider and wider, and our population spread farther and farther, they have not outrun its protection or its benefits. It has been to us all a copious fountain of national, social, and personal happiness.

I have not allowed myself, sir, to look beyond the Union, to see what might lie hidden in the dark recess behind. I have not coolly weighed the chances of preserving liberty when the bonds that unite us together shall be broken asunder. I have not accustomed myself to hang over the precipice of disunion, to see whether, with my short sight, I can fathom the depth of the abyss below; nor could I regard him as a safe counselor in the affairs of this government whose thoughts should be mainly bent on considering, not how the Union may be best preserved, but how tolerable might be the condition of the people when it shall be broken up and destroyed. While the Union lasts, we have high, exciting, gratifying prospects spread out before us for us and our children. Beyond that I seek not to penetrate the veil. God grant that in my day, at least, that curtain may not rise! God grant that on my vision never may be opened what lies behind! When my eyes shall be turned to behold for the last time the sun in heaven, may I not see him shining on the broken and dishonored fragments of a once glorious Union; on States dissevered, discordant, belligerent; on a land rent with civil feuds, or drenched, it may be, in fraternal blood! Let their last feeble and lingering glance rather behold the gorgeous ensign of the republic, now known and honored throughout the earth, still full high advanced, its arms and trophies streaming in their original lustre, not a stripe erased or polluted nor a single star obscured, bearing for its motto no such miserable interrogatory as "What is all this worth?" nor those other words of delusion and folly, "Liberty first and Union afterwards"; but everywhere, spread all over in characters of living light, blazing on all its ample folds, as they float over the sea and over the land, and in every wind under the whole heavens, that other sentiment, dear to every true American heart—Liberty *and* Union, now and forever, one and inseparable!

Chapter 10

THE ABOLITIONIST CRUSADE

From the Missouri Compromise to the Civil War, the American political scene was almost continuously dominated by some aspect of the slavery question. But the sectional conflict was basically economic rather than political in nature, and in the final analysis even the ideological controversy over slavery was secondary to the struggle for national predominance between defensive adherents of Southern agrarianism and aggressive champions of Northern industrialism. For both sides, however, feelings could be raised more easily to the highest pitch and fiery partisans could be recruited with greatest dispatch if the issues were protested as moral rather than bluntly political or crassly economic. Besides, whatever its origins, for many Americans the slavery question had very early assumed the proportions of an intensely ideological contest—as the untiring and sometimes fanatical activities of both Southern apologists for slavery and Northern Abolitionists bear witness. During the four decades prior to the Civil War the sectional conflict most frequently took the form of a moral issue. And when finally the sections chose war to resolve their "irrepressible conflict," both were to make of it a great and holy crusade, for good against evil, for right against wrong.

Negro slavery had first been introduced into the American colonies in 1619 when a Dutch ship brought its cargo of human chattels to Virginia. Throughout the seventeenth and most of the eighteenth centuries, as the plantation system came to be an integral part of the Southern economy, slavery as the source of plantation labor seemed more and more closely identified with the South's economic well-being. Towards the end of the eighteenth century, however, depression struck at the plantation region, and Southern leaders lost confidence in their system of land and labor. After the American Revolution many Southerners, imbued with the ideals of liberty and equality expressed in the Declaration of Independence and disgruntled at what seemed the inadequacy of slave labor, urged at least the gradual abolition of slavery.

One great Southern spokesman for liberty, Patrick Henry, openly proclaimed his guilt as a slaveholder: "Would anyone believe that I am Master of Slaves of my own purchase! I am drawn along by the general inconvenience of living without them; I will not, I cannot justify it." More and more frequently Southerners provided in their wills for the emancipation of their slaves, and in the years immediately after the Revolution the number of free Negroes increased considerably. An observer might have noted that slavery no longer played a vital role in the Southern economy; the barbaric institution seemed doomed.

Then in 1793 the Yankee Eli Whitney breathed new life into the plantation-slave system with his invention of the cotton gin. Previous laborious and expensive hand methods of separating the seed from the cotton had limited cotton production to the more easily separated long staple crop that could be grown only in the rich lowlands of the seacoast. But Whitney's remarkable machine for separating seed from cotton made possible the large scale cultivation of the short staple crop that could be grown throughout almost the entire South. In 1790 Americans produced 4,000 bales of cotton; two decades later annual production was upwards of 175,000 bales; and by 1860 the figure had reached nearly 4,000,000 bales. This remarkable productive spurt marked a revitalization of the plantation system which in turn created a new demand for slave labor, and soon gradual emancipation was supplanted by a frantic search for an ever larger slave labor force. To a limited extent the planters' demands for more slaves were met—often by the disreputable practice of slave breeding and by the illegal slave trade—and the slave population increased from about one and a half million in 1820 to approximately four million in 1860. But with the tremendous westward expansion of "King Cotton" the demand for slaves constantly outstripped the supply, and a prime field hand who cost five to seven hundred dollars in 1820 brought over eighteen hundred dollars in 1860. In 1790 slavery had appeared moribund, but by the 1820's to many wealthy Southerners human bondage seemed the foundation of their prosperity.

As their human chattels once again came to play a vital role in the plantation economy, the Southerners felt pressed to translate the slaves' new function into moral terms. Earlier apologies for slavery as a "necessary evil" were manifestly unsuitable for this period of expansion; now Negro slavery was proclaimed altogether righteous, moral and even beneficial to the slave himself. Slavery was no longer merely defended; rather it was defiantly pronounced a "positive good," and soon Southerners formulated an elaborate pro-slavery argument that found sanction for slavery in selections from Scripture, in historical references to slavery among ancient peoples, and in "scientific" theories of the slaves' "biological inferiority."

There were numbers of Americans, however, who remained unconvinced by the slaveholders' rationalizations and who abhorred the South's "peculiar institution" as vicious, brutalizing and immoral. Many of them joined the numerous Northern societies dedicated to the abolition of slavery, and the sincere, though sometimes unreasoning, intensity of purpose of the Abolitionists offered proof of the moral, if not the numerical, strength of the anti-slavery cause.

Closely identified with the Abolition movement was the aggressive and fearless William Lloyd Garrison, a New England journalist who had lent his pen and energies to the cause of many other contemporary reform movements, such as temperance, pacifism and women's rights. On January 1, 1831, even before he organized the powerful New England Anti-Slavery Society, Garrison gave voice to America's conscience when he dedicated his new journal, *The Liberator*, to abolitionism. Recanting his earlier acceptance of the "popular but pernicious doctrine of *gradual* abolition," Garrison demanded the immediate emancipation and enfranchisement of the slaves. "On this subject I do not wish to think, speak, or write, with moderation," he wrote. "I am in earnest—I will not equivocate—I will not excuse—I will not retreat a single inch—AND I WILL BE HEARD."

Throughout the length and breadth of the land Garrison and his followers were heard, but they met the angry opposition of most Northerners as well as Southerners. Before the Civil War the Abolitionists were seldom truly representative of Northern thought, for they had too closely identified themselves with radicalism generally. Above the Mason-Dixon line they were ridiculed as fanatics, ostracized from polite society and sometimes violently assaulted for their activities. In 1835 a frenzied mob attacked Garrison, tied a rope around his neck, and dragged him through the streets of Boston; two years later an Illinois mob killed the Abolitionist editor, Elijah P. Lovejoy. As the "irrepressible conflict" approached the proportions of war, however, the Abolitionists were making more and more converts to their cause. Most important, through constant vilification of the slaveholders they were creating in Northern minds an image of Southern life that did much to aggravate sectional antagonisms. Then, when compromise was finally abandoned and the war came, Northern leaders more easily made of it a holy crusade against a "slaveocracy" that had already been stereotyped as cruel, godless and immoral. Though they had by no means created it, the Abolitionists had done much to intensify the sectional conflict.

The First Issue of *The Liberator, 1831*

In the month of August, I issued proposals for publishing *The Liberator* in Washington city; but the enterprise, though hailed in different sections of the country, was palsied by public indifference. Since that time, the removal of the *Genius of Universal Emancipation* to the Seat of Government has rendered less imperious the establishment of a similar periodical in that quarter.

During my recent tour for the purpose of exciting the minds of the people by a series of discourses on the subject of slavery, every place that I visited gave fresh evidence of the fact, that a greater revolution in public sentiment was to be effected in the free states—*and particularly in New England*—than at the south. I found contempt more bitter, opposition more active, detraction more relentless, prejudice more stubborn, and apathy more frozen, than among slave owners themselves. Of course, there were individual exceptions to the contrary. This state of things afflicted, but did not dishearten me. I determined, at every hazard, to lift up the standard of emancipation in the eyes of the nation, *within sight of Bunker Hill and in the birth place of liberty.* That standard is now unfurled; and long may it float, unhurt by the spoliations of time or the missiles of a desperate foe—yea, till every chain be broken, and every bondman set free! Let Southern oppressors tremble—let their secret abettors tremble—let their Northern apologists tremble—let all the enemies of the persecuted blacks tremble.

I deem the publication of my original Prospectus unnecessary, as it has obtained a wide circulation. The principles therein inculcated will be steadily pursued in this paper, excepting that I shall not array myself as the political partisan of any man. In defending the great cause of human rights, I wish to derive the assistance of all religions and of all parties.

Assenting to the "self evident truth" maintained in the American Declaration of Independence, "that all men are created equal, and endowed by their Creator with certain unalienable rights—among which are life, liberty and the pursuit of happiness," I shall strenuously contend for the immediate enfranchisement of our slave population. In Park Street Church, on the Fourth of July, 1829, in an address on slavery, I unreflectingly assented to the popular but pernicious doctrine of *gradual* abolition. I seize this opportunity to make a full and unequivocal recantation, and thus publicly to ask pardon of my God, of my country, and of my brethren the poor slaves, for having uttered a sentiment so full of timidity, injustice and absurdity. A similar recantation, from my pen, was published in the *Genius of Universal Emancipation* at Baltimore, in September, 1829. My conscience is now satisfied.

I am aware, that many object to the severity of my language; but is there not cause for severity? I *will be* as harsh as truth, and as uncompromising as justice. On this subject, I do not wish to think, or speak, or write, with moderation. No! no! Tell a man whose house is on fire, to give a moderate alarm; tell him to moderately rescue his wife from the hands of the ravisher; tell the mother to gradually extricate her babe from the fire into which it has fallen;— but urge me not to use moderation in a cause like the present. I am in earnest—I will not equivocate—I will not excuse—I will not retreat a single inch—AND I WILL BE HEARD. The apathy of the people is enough to make every statue leap from its pedestal, and to hasten the resurrection of the dead.

It is pretended, that I am retarding the cause of emancipation by the coarseness of my invective and the precipitancy of my measures. *The charge is not true.* On this question my influence,—humble as it is,—is felt at this moment to a considerable extent, and shall be felt in coming years—not perniciously, but beneficially—not as a curse, but as a blessing; and posterity will bear testimony that I was right. I desire to thank God, that he enables me to disregard "the fear of man which bringeth a snare," and to speak his truth in its simplicity and power.

And here I close with this fresh dedication:

"Oppression! I have seen thee, face to face,
And met thy cruel eye and cloudy brow;
But thy soul-withering glance I fear not now—
For dread to prouder feelings doth give place
Of deep abhorrence! Scorning the disgrace
Of slavish knees that at thy footstool bow,
I also kneel—but with far other bow
Do hail thee and thy herd of hirelings base:—
I swear, while life-blood warms my throbbing veins,
Still to oppose and thwart, with heart and hand,
Thy brutalizing sway—till Afric's chains

Are burst, and Freedom rules the rescued land,—
Trampling Oppression and his iron rod:
Such is the vow I take—SO HELP ME GOD!"

Chapter 11

THE SECTIONAL CONFLICT

As an articulate minority the South had no greater spokesman than John C. Calhoun. Indeed of all Southerners it was
the coldly logical South Carolinian who had most systematical-
ly analyzed the dynamics of the South's position in the Union.
Calhoun had clearly perceived that the rapidly industrializing,
creditor North was relegating the agrarian, debtor South to a
minor role in the nation's economy. He saw realistically that
political subjugation would follow, and that as the South
became more and more of an economic and political minority
within the nation, its whole social structure would be
jeopardized by the aggressive and numerically superior North.
Besides, even within the South the ruling, slave-owning planter
class which Calhoun represented was threatened by the
specter of majority rule, since the owners of many slaves and
large plantations were few in number. Out of a total Southern
white population of 8,000,000 in 1860 there were only 384,-
000 who actually owned any slaves, while more than three-
fourths of the white population had no direct interest in the
plantation-slave system at all. Of the slave-owning group,
300,000 owned fewer than 10 slaves each, while only 2500
owned more than 100 slaves and could be considered members of the dominant planter aristocracy. Here, too, the
South's rulers were a small minority and feared majority rule.
But the majority of Southern whites, impressed by a carefully
contrived pro-slavery argument and loath to surrender the
"superiority" that color alone provided, seemed more concerned with keeping the legal bonds of slavery between themselves and the Negroes than in disrupting a slave economy
that served the purposes of the wealthy planters alone. Therefore, though acutely conscious of the class as well as sectional status of the planting aristocracy, Calhoun first addressed himself to the more immediate sectional conflict and
formulated a philosophy of minority rights that was designed,

through constitutional checks, to prevent a Northern controlled majority from imposing its will upon the South. At the same time his affirmation of the South's rights within the nation helped to maintain unbroken the power of the minority planting class within the South itself.

Ultimately Calhoun's theorizing led to the repudiation of majority rule and to the doctrines of nullification and secession. In 1832 South Carolina actually proclaimed the tariff of that year null and void within her borders and warned that any attempt to enforce the national law would be met with armed resistance. At length the crisis was met by compromise: the ordinance of nullification was withdrawn and the tariff was lowered. More important, however, was the fact that Carolina planters had found a way of denying the nation's will, and nearly three decades later they would lead ten other Southern states in embracing secession as the logical conclusion to Calhoun's arguments for minority rights. It was ironic that Calhoun should contrive this philosophic framework of a sectionalism that eventually would be the rationale for dismemberment of the Union, for he had begun his career as the staunchest of nationalists. Yet his metamorphosis from nationalist to sectionalist was in keeping with his recognition of basic economic changes within the nation. The nationalism he had espoused in the early decades of the nineteenth century had then been consistent with the economic interests of the South, but Calhoun saw that the new high-tariff nationalism of the 1830's and 1840's was geared solely to the interests of the industrial North. It was to this later nationalism that he objected so strongly and in answer to which he changed from ardent nationalist to redoubtable sectionalist.

In 1850, at the very end of Calhoun's life, North and South joined in battle once more on what seemed to the philosopher of sectionalism the most crucial question of all: should slavery be permitted to expand freely, with the full protection of the national government, into the new lands acquired in 1848 at the end of the Mexican War? Again Calhoun looked to political realities. If the Southern "slave power" were to be denied free and protected access to the nation's new territories, the North would people these regions, would organize them politically, and eventually would bring them into the Union under its own aegis. Then, with its new allies, the North would so completely overwhelm the Southern minority in Congress that slavery and eventually all of the South's interests and institutions would be destroyed by the tyrannical majority. If this were not ultimately to be her lot, Calhoun insisted, the South must accept nothing less than an unconditional guarantee of slavery in all of the Territories.

And when the "Great Compromiser," Henry Clay, offered his famous Compromise of 1850—providing for the organization of lands ceded by Mexico without such a guarantee, though conceding to the South its long desired stringent Fugitive Slave Law—Calhoun prepared to raise an angry if enfeebled voice against it.

Unaware that for ten years the sectional conflict would increase in intensity and bitterness until finally the last bonds of union would be severed by cannon fire, the giants of America's past and of her future were gathered in the Congress that on March 4, 1850, heard Calhoun's last and most famous speech on the slavery question. Clay, Webster, and Benton—they were from the past. Seward, Chase, Douglas, and Jefferson Davis—they were of the future. It was to these leaders that Calhoun made his final plea for what he considered the rights of his beloved South. As if prophetic of the fate of his section's cause, Calhoun's words, immediately directed against the Compromise of 1850, were his dying words. As the courageous but aged statesman was helped into the Senate Chamber, the galleries were jammed with those who came to hear the great spokesman of the Old South for the last time. But Calhoun, who would live but four weeks more, was too weak to deliver his address and begged leave for Senator Mason of Virginia to read it for him.

It was obvious on all sides, Calhoun maintained, that the Union was breaking up; the great political parties were sectional rather than national, and even the churches were being divided into Northern and Southern branches. It was actually the North that had disrupted the Union by destroying the earlier equilibrium between sections and interests. The North had grown many times more rapidly than the South in resources and population and had in consequence seized political and economic control of the nation. The North had imposed tariffs upon an unwilling but helpless South, had monopolized offices in the national government, had prohibited Southerners from equal access to the nation's territories, and had viciously and unremittingly attacked the South's domestic institutions. As matters stood the South could not with honor and safety remain within the Union. If the Union were to be preserved in its original intent, the North must enforce the fugitive slave laws, must end its anti-slavery agitation, must grant the South equal rights in the territories, and must accept constitutional changes designed to restore equality between the sections. Primarily these constitutional changes were based upon the concept of "concurrent majorities"—a majority of each section must concur in enacting national legislation. And, as he revealed elsewhere, Calhoun would provide for a dual Presidency: one President to represent the South and the other to represent the North, each with an independent veto power. Thus the South, though numerically a distinct minority, would have a voice in the national government equal to that of the rapidly expanding North. Thus minority rights would become minority rule, or at least minority control.

The alternative to such concessions by the North, Calhoun warned, would be disunion. But the Compromise of 1850, which was warmly supported by Daniel Webster in his famous "Seventh of March" speech, was accepted by the nation despite the violent opposition of extremists in both sections. Ten years later the nation well remembered Calhoun's somber prophecy as his native South Carolina led her sister states in secession from the Union.

John C. Calhoun on the Slavery Question, *1850*

I have, Senators, believed from the first that the agitation of the subject of slavery would, if not prevented by some timely and effective measure, end in disunion. Entertaining this opinion, I have, on all proper occasions, endeavored to call the attention of both the two great parties which divide the country to adopt some measure to prevent so great a disaster, but without success. The agitation has been permitted to proceed, with almost no attempt to resist it, until it has reached a point when it can no longer be disguised or denied that the Union is in danger. You have thus had forced upon you the greatest and the gravest question that can ever come under your consideration: How can the Union be preserved?

To give a satisfactory answer to this mighty question, it is indispensable to have an accurate and thorough knowledge of the nature and the character of the cause by which the Union is endangered. Without such knowledge it is impossible to pronounce, with any certainty, by what measure it can be saved; just as it would be impossible for a physician to pronounce, in the case of some dangerous disease, with any certainty, by what remedy the patient could be saved, without similar knowledge of the nature and character of the cause which produced it. The first question, then, presented for consideration, in the investigation I propose to make, in order to obtain such knowledge, is, What is it that has endangered the Union?

To this question there can be but one answer: that the

immediate cause is the almost universal discontent which pervades all the States composing the Southern section of the Union. This widely extended discontent is not of recent origin. It commenced with the agitation of the slavery question, and has been increasing ever since. The next question, going one step further back, is—What has caused this widely diffused and almost universal discontent?

It is a great mistake to suppose, as is by some, that it originated with demagogues, who excited the discontent with the intention of aiding their personal advancement, or with the disappointed ambition of certain politicians, who resorted to it as the means of retrieving their fortunes. On the contrary, all the great political influences of the section were arrayed against excitement, and exerted to the utmost to keep the people quiet. The great mass of the people of the South were divided, as in the other section, into Whigs and Democrats. The leaders and the presses of both parties in the South were very solicitous to prevent excitement and to preserve quiet; because it was seen that the effects of the former would necessarily tend to weaken, if not destroy, the political ties which united them with their respective parties in the other section. Those who know the strength of party ties will readily appreciate the immense force which this cause exerted against agitation, and in favor of preserving quiet. But, great as it was, it was not sufficient to prevent the widespread discontent which now pervades the section. No; some cause, far deeper and more powerful than the one supposed, must exist, to account for discontent so wide and deep. The question then recurs, What is the cause of this discontent? It will be found in the belief of the people of the Southern States, as prevalent as the discontent itself, that they cannot remain, as things now are, consistently with honor and safety, in the Union. The next question to be considered is, What has caused this belief?

One of the causes is, undoubtedly, to be traced to the long-continued agitation of the slave question on the part of the North, and the many aggressions which they have made on the rights of the South during the time. . . .

There is another lying back of it, with which this is intimately connected, that may be regarded as the great and primary cause. This is to be found in the fact that the equilibrium between the two sections, in the Government as it stood when the constitution was ratified and the Government put in action, has been destroyed. At that time there was nearly a perfect equilibrium between the two, which afforded ample means to each to protect itself against the aggression of the other; but, as it now stands, one section has the exclusive power of controlling the Government, which leaves the other without any adequate means of protecting itself against its encroachment and oppression. To place this subject distinctly before you, I have, Senators, prepared a brief statistical statement, showing the relative weight of the two sections in the Government under the first census of 1790 and the last census of 1840.

According to the former, the population of the United States, including Vermont, Kentucky, and Tennessee, which then were in their incipient condition of becoming States, but were not actually admitted, amounted to 3,929,827. Of this number the Northern States had 1,997,899, and the Southern 1,952,072, making a difference of only 45,827 in favor of the former States. The number of States, including Vermont, Kentucky, and Tennessee, were sixteen; of which eight, including Vermont, belonged to the Northern section, and eight, including Kentucky and Tennessee, to the Southern—making an equal division of the States between the two sections under the first census. There was a small preponderance in the House of Representatives, and in the Electoral College, in favor of the Northern, owing to the fact that, according to the provisions of the constitution, in estimating federal numbers five slaves count but three; but it was too small to affect sensibly the perfect equilibrium which, with that exception, existed at the time. Such was the equality of the two sections when the States composing them agreed to enter into a Federal Union. Since then the equilibrium between them has been greatly disturbed.

According to the last census the aggregate population of the United States amounted to 17,063,357, of which the Northern section contained 9,728,920, and the Southern 7,334,437, making a difference, in round numbers, of 2,-400,000. The number of States has increased from sixteen to twenty-six, making an addition of ten States. In the meantime the position of Delaware had become doubtful as to which section she properly belonged. Considering her as neutral, the Northern States will have thirteen and the Southern States twelve, making a difference in the Senate of two Senators in favor of the former. According to the apportionment under the census of 1840, there were two hundred and twenty-three members of the House of Representatives, of which the Northern States had one hundred and thirty-five, and the Southern States (considering Delaware as neutral) eighty-seven, making a difference in favor of the former in the House of Representatives of forty-eight. The difference in the Senate of two members, added to this, gives to the North in the electoral college, a majority of fifty. Since the census of 1840, four States have been added to the Union—Iowa, Wisconsin, Florida, and Texas. They leave the difference in the Senate as it stood when the census was taken; but add two to the side of the North in the House, making the present majority in the House in its favor fifty, and in the electoral college fifty-two.

The result of the whole is to give the Northern section a predominance in every department of the Government, and thereby concentrate in the two elements which constitute the Federal Government—majority of States, and a majority of their population, estimated in federal numbers. Whatever section concentrates the two in itself possesses the control of the entire Government.

But we are just at the close of the sixth decade, and the commencement of the seventh. The census is to be taken this year, which must add greatly to the decided preponderance of the North in the House of Representatives and in the electoral college. The prospect is, also, that a great increase will be added to its present preponderance in the Senate, during the period of the decade, by the addition of new States. Two territories, Oregon and Minnesota, are already in progress, and strenuous efforts are making to bring in three additional States from the territory recently conquered from Mexico; which, if successful, will add three other States in a short time to the Northern section, making five States; and increasing the present number of its States from fifteen to twenty, and of its Senators from thirty to forty. On the contrary, there is not a single territory in progress in the Southern section, and no certainty that any additional State will be added to it during the decade. The prospect then is that the two sections in the Senate, should the efforts now made to exclude the South from the newly acquired territories succeed, will stand, before the end of the decade, twenty Northern States to fourteen Southern (considering Delaware as neutral), and forty Northern Senators to twenty-eight Southern. This great increase of Senators, added to the great increase of members of the House of Representatives and the electoral college on the part of the North, which must take place under the next decade, will effectually and irretrievably destroy the equilibrium which existed when the Government commenced.

Had this destruction been the operation of time, without the interference of government, the South would have had no reason to complain; but such was not the fact. It was caused by the legislation of this Government, which was appointed, as the common agent of all, and charged with the protection of the interests and security of all. The legislation by which it has been effected, may be classed under three heads. The first, is that series of acts by which the South has been excluded from the common territory belonging to all the States as members of the Federal Union—which have had the effect of extending vastly the portion allotted to the Northern section, and restricting within nar-

row limits the portion left the South. The next consists in
adopting a system of revenue and disbursements, by which
an undue proportion of the burden of taxation has been
imposed upon the South, and an undue proportion of its
proceeds appropriated to the North; and the last is a system
of political measures, by which the original character of the
Government has been radically changed. I propose to bestow
upon each of these, in the order they stand, a few remarks,
with the view of showing that it is owing to the action of
this Government, that the equilibrium between the two sections has been destroyed, and the whole powers of the system centered in a sectional majority. . . .

The result of the whole of these causes combined is,
that the North has acquired a decided ascendency over every
department of this Government, and through it a control
over all the powers of the system. A single section governed
by the will of the numerical majority, has now, in fact,
the control of the Government and the entire powers of
the system. . . .

As, then, the North has the absolute control over the
Government, it is manifest, that on all questions between it
and the South, where there is a diversity of interests, the
interest of the latter will be sacrificed to the former, however oppressive the effects may be; as the South possesses
no means by which it can resist, through the action of the
Government. But if there was no question of vital importance
to the South, in reference to which there was a diversity
of views between the two sections, this state of things might
be endured, without the hazard of destruction to the South.
But such is not the fact. There is a question of vital importance to the Southern section, in reference to which the
views and feelings of the two sections are as opposite and
hostile as they can possibly be.

I refer to the relation between the two races in the Southern section, which constitutes a vital portion of her social
organization. Every portion of the North entertains views
and feelings more or less hostile to it. Those most opposed
and hostile, regard it as a sin, and consider themselves
under the most sacred obligation to use every effort to destroy it. Indeed, to the extent that they conceive that they
have power, they regard themselves as implicated in the sin,
and responsible for not suppressing it by the use of all and
every means. Those less opposed and hostile, regard it as a
crime—an offence against humanity, as they call it; and although not so fanatical, feel themselves bound to use all
efforts to effect the same object; while those who are least
opposed and hostile, regard it as a blot and a stain on the
character of what they call the Nation, and feel themselves
accordingly bound to give it no countenance or support. On

the contrary, the Southern section regards the relation as one which cannot be destroyed without subjecting the two races to the greatest calamity; and the section to poverty, desolation, and wretchedness; and accordingly they feel bound, by every consideration of interest and safety, to defend it.

This hostile feeling on the part of the North towards the social organization of the South long lay dormant, but it only required some cause to act on those who felt most intensely that they were responsible for its continuance, to call it into action. The increasing power of this Government, and of the control of the Northern section over all its departments, furnished the cause. It was this which made an impression on the minds of many, that there was little or no restraint to prevent the Government from doing whatever it might choose to do. This was sufficient of itself to put the most fanatical portion of the North in action, for the purpose of destroying the existing relation between the two races in the South.

The first organized movement towards it commenced in 1835. Then, for the first time, societies were organized, presses established, lecturers sent forth to excite the people of the North, and incendiary publications scattered over the whole South through the mail. The South was thoroughly aroused. Meetings were held everywhere, and resolutions adopted, calling upon the North to apply a remedy to arrest the threatened evil, and pledging themselves to adopt measures for their own protection, if it was not arrested. . . .

As for myself, I believed at that early period . . . that agitation would follow, and that it would in the end, if not arrested, destroy the Union. I then so expressed myself in debate . . . but in vain. Had my voice been heeded . . . the agitation which followed would have been prevented, and the fanatical zeal . . . which has brought us to our present perilous condition, would have become extinguished, from the want of fuel to feed the flame. That was the time for the North to have shown her devotion to the Union; but, unfortunately, both of the great parties of that section were so intent on obtaining or retaining party ascendency, that all other considerations were overlooked or forgotten.

What has since followed are but natural consequences. With the success of their first movement, this small fanatical party began to acquire strength; and with that, to become an object of courtship to both the great parties. The necessary consequence was, a further increase of power, and a gradual tainting of the opinions of both of the other parties with their doctrines, until the infection has extended over both; and the great mass of the population of the North, who, whatever may be their opinion of the original abolition party, which still preserves its distinctive organization, hardly ever fail, when it comes to acting, to co-operate in carrying out their measures. . . .

Such is a brief history of the agitation, as far as it has yet advanced. Now I ask, Senators, what is there to prevent its further progress, until it fulfills the ultimate end proposed, unless some decisive measure should be adopted to prevent it? Has any one of the causes, which has added to its increase from its original small and contemptible beginning until it has attained its present magnitude, diminished in force? Is the original cause of the movement—that slavery is a sin, and ought to be suppressed—weaker now than at the commencement? Or is the abolition party less numerous or influential, or have they less influence with, or control over the two great parties of the North in elections? Or has the South greater means of influencing or controlling the movements of this Government now, than it had when the agitation commenced? To all these questions but one answer can be given: No, no, no. The very reverse is true. Instead of being weaker, all the elements in favor of agitation are stronger now than they were in 1835, when it first commenced, while all the elements of influence on the part of the South are weaker. Unless something decisive is done, I again ask what is to stop this agitation, before the great and final object at which it aims—the abolition of slavery in the States—is consummated? Is it, then, not certain, that if something is not done to arrest it, the South will be forced to choose between abolition and secession? Indeed, as events are now moving, it will not require the South to secede, in order to dissolve the Union. Agitation will of itself effect it, of which its past history furnishes abundant proof—as I shall next proceed to show.

It is a great mistake to suppose that disunion can be effected by a single blow. The cords which bound these States together in one common Union, are far too numerous and powerful for that. Disunion must be the work of time. It is only through a long process, and successively, that the cords can be snapped, until the whole fabric falls asunder. Already the agitation of the slavery question has snapped some of the most important, and has greatly weakened all the others, as I shall proceed to show.

The cords that bind the States together are not only many, but various in character. Some are spiritual or ecclesiastical; some political; others social. Some appertain to the benefit conferred by the Union, and others to the feeling of duty and obligation.

The strongest of those of a spiritual and ecclesiastical nature, consisted in the unity of the great religious denominations, all of which originally embraced the whole Union. All these denominations, with the exception, perhaps, of the

Catholics, were organized very much upon the principle of our political institutions. Beginning with smaller meetings, corresponding with the political divisions of the country, their organization terminated in one great central assemblage, corresponding very much with the character of Congress. At these meetings the principal clergymen and lay members of the respective denominations, from all parts of the Union, met to transact business relating to their common concerns. It was not confined to what appertained to the doctrines and discipline of the respective denominations, but extended to plans for disseminating the Bible, establishing missions, distributing tracts, and of establishing presses for the publications of tracts, newspapers, and periodicals, with a view of diffusing religious information, and for the support of their respective doctrines and creeds. All this combined contributed greatly to strengthen the bonds of the Union. The ties which held each denomination together formed a strong cord to hold the whole Union together; but, powerful as they were, they have not been able to resist the explosive effect of slavery agitation. . . .

The strongest cord, of a political character, consists of the many and powerful ties that have held together the two great parties which have, with some modifications, existed from the beginning of the Government. They both extended to every portion of the Union, and strongly contributed to hold all its parts together. But this powerful cord has fared no better than the spiritual. It resisted, for a long time, the explosive tendency of the agitation, but has finally snapped under its force—if not entirely, in a great measure. Nor is there one of the remaining cords which has not been greatly weakened. To this extent the Union has already been destroyed by agitation, in the only way it can be, sundering and weakening the cords which bind it together.

If the agitation goes on, the same force, acting with increased intensity, as has been shown, will finally snap every cord, when nothing will be left to hold the States together except force. But surely, that can, with no propriety of language, be called a Union, when the only means by which the weaker is held connected with the stronger portion is force. It may, indeed, keep them connected; but the connection will partake much more of the character of subjugation, on the part of the weaker to the stronger, than the union of free, independent, and sovereign States, in one confederation as they stood in the early stages of the Government, and which only is worthy of the sacred name of Union.

Having now, Senators, explained what it is that endangers the Union, and traced it to its cause, and explained its nature and character, the question again recurs, How can the Union be saved? To this I answer: There is but one way by which it can be, and that is, by adopting such measures as will satisfy the States belonging to the Southern section, that they can remain in the Union consistently with their honor and their safety. There is, again, only one way by which this can be effected, and that is by removing the causes by which this belief has been produced. Do this, and discontent will cease, harmony and kind feelings between the sections be restored, and every apprehension of danger to the Union removed. The question then, is, How can this be done? But, before I undertake to answer this question, I propose to show by what the Union cannot be saved.

It cannot, then, be saved by eulogies on the Union, however splendid or numerous. The cry of "Union, Union, the glorious Union!" can no more prevent disunion than the cry of "Health, health, glorious health!" on the part of the physician, can save a patient lying dangerously ill. So long as the Union, instead of being regarded as a protector, is regarded in the opposite character, by not much less than a majority of the States, it will be in vain to attempt to conciliate them by pronouncing eulogies on it.

Besides, this cry of Union comes commonly from those whom we cannot believe to be sincere. It usually comes from our assailants. But we cannot believe them to be sincere; for, if they loved the Union, they would necessarily be devoted to the constitution. It made the Union, and to destroy the constitution would be to destroy the Union. But the only reliable and certain evidence of devotion to the constitution is, to abstain, on the one hand, from violating it, and to repel, on the other, all attempts to violate it. It is only by faithfully performing these high duties that the constitution can be preserved, and with it the Union.

But how stands the profession of devotion to the Union by our assailants, when brought to this test? Have they abstained from violating the constitution? Let the many Acts passed by the Northern States to set aside and annul the clause of the Constitution providing for the delivery up of fugitive slaves answer. I cite this, not that it is the only instance (for there are many others), but because the violation in this particular is too notorious and palpable to be denied. Again, have they stood forth faithfully to repel violations of the constitution? Let their course in reference to the agitation of the slavery question, which was commenced and has been carried on for fifteen years, avowedly for the purpose of abolishing slavery in the States—an object all acknowledged to be unconstitutional—answer. Let them show a single instance, during this long period, in which they have denounced the agitators or their attempts to effect what is admitted to be unconstitutional, or a single measure which they have brought forward for that purpose. How can we, with all these facts before us, believe that they are sincere in their profession of devotion to the Union, or avoid believing their profession is but intended to increase the vigor of their assaults and to weaken the force of our resistance?

Nor can we regard the profession of devotion to the Union, on the part of those who are not our assailants, as sincere, when they pronounce eulogies upon the Union, evidently with the intent of charging us with disunion, without uttering one word of denunciation against our assailants. If friends of the Union, their course should be to unite with us in repelling these assaults, and denouncing the authors as enemies of the Union. Why they avoid this, and pursue the course they do, it is for them to explain.

Nor can the Union be saved by invoking the name of the illustrious Southerner whose mortal remains repose on the western bank of the Potomac. He was one of us—a slaveholder and a planter. We have studied his history, and find nothing in it to justify submission to wrong. On the contrary, his great fame rests on the solid foundation, that, while he was careful to avoid doing wrong to others, he was prompt and decided in repelling wrong. I trust that, in this respect, we profited by his example.

Nor can we find any thing in his history to deter us from seceding from the Union, should it fail to fulfill the objects for which it was instituted, by being permanently and hopelessly converted into the means of oppressing instead of protecting us. On the contrary, we find much in his example to encourage us, should we be forced to the extremity of deciding between submission and disunion. . . .

Having now shown what cannot save the Union, I return to the question with which I commenced. How can the Union be saved? There is but one way by which it can with any certainty; and that is, by a full and final settlement, on the principle of justice, of all the questions at issue between the two sections. The South asks for justice, simple justice, and less she ought not to take. She has no compromise to offer, but the Constitution; and no concession or surrender to make. She has already surrendered so much that she has little left to surrender. Such a settlement would go to the root of the evil, and remove all cause of discontent, by satisfying the South, that she could remain honorably and safely in the Union, and thereby restore the harmony and fraternal feeling between the sections, which existed anterior to the Missouri agitation. Nothing else can, with any certainty, finally and for ever settle the questions at issue, terminate agitation, and save the Union.

But can this be done? Yes, easily; not by the weaker party, for it can of itself do nothing, not even protect itself, but by the stronger. The North has only to will it to accomplish it, to do justice by conceding to the South an equal right in the acquired territory, and to do her duty by causing the stipulations relative to fugitive slaves to be faithfully fulfilled, to cease the agitation of the slave question, and to provide for the insertion of a provision in the Constitution, by an amendment, which will restore to the South, in substance, the power she possessed of protecting herself, before the equilibrium between the sections was destroyed by the action of this Government. There will be no difficulty in devising such a provision, one that will protect the South, and which, at the same time, will improve and strengthen the Government, instead of impairing and weakening it.

But will the North agree to this? It is for her to answer the question. But, I will say, she cannot refuse, if she has half the love of the Union which she professes to have, or without justly exposing herself to the charge that her love of power and aggrandizement is far greater than her love of the Union. At all events, the responsibility of saving the Union rests on the North, and not on the South. The South cannot save it by any act of hers, and the North may save it without any sacrifice whatever, unless to do justice, and to perform her duties under the Constitution, should be regarded by her as a sacrifice.

It is time, Senators, that there should be an open and manly avowal on all sides, as to what is intended to be done. If the question is not now settled, it is uncertain whether it ever can hereafter be; and we, the representatives of the States of this Union, regarded as governments, should come to a distinct understanding as to our respective views, in order to ascertain whether the great questions at issue can be settled or not. If you, who represent the stronger portion, cannot agree to settle them on the broad principle of justice and duty, say so; and let the States we both represent agree to separate and part in peace. If you are unwilling we should part in peace, tell us so; and we shall know what to do, when you reduce the question to submission or resistance. If you remain silent, you will compel us to infer by your acts what you intend. In that case, California will become the test question. If you admit her, under all the difficulties that oppose her admission, you compel us to infer that you intend to exclude us from the whole of the acquired territories, with the intention of destroying, irretrievably, the equilibrium between the two sections. We would be blind not to perceive in that case, that your real objects are power and aggrandizement, and infatuated not to act accordingly.

I have now, Senators, done my duty in expressing my opinions fully, freely, and candidly, on this solemn occasion. In doing so, I have been governed by the motives which have governed me in all the stages of the agitation of the slavery question since its commencement. I have exerted myself, during the whole period, to arrest it, with the intention of saving the Union, if it could be done; and if it could not, save the section where it has pleased Providence to cast my lot, and which I sincerely believe has justice and the Constitution on its side. Having faithfully done my duty to the best of my ability, both to the Union and my section, throughout this agitation, I shall have the consolation, let what will come, that I am free from all responsibility.

Chapter 12

THE FATEFUL DECADE

The dramatic gold rush of the Forty-Niners, the phenomenal growth of a vast railroad network joining distant regions of the country, the conquest of the oceans by Yankee clipper ships, the rapid transformation of the upper Mississippi Valley into the nation's most important agricultural region, and a tremendous boom in industry and commerce—all of these made the 1850's years of prosperity and plenty. Yet they were also fitful, angry, and divisive years, in which tempers grew shorter and more heated, in which the personal ties of kinship and friendship were often broken by the deep emotionalism that marked the persistent debate over the morality of slavery. And when in 1858 Abraham Lincoln warned that "A house divided against itself cannot stand," there were already many Americans who feared that the bitterness of the ideological conflict was evidence that the house was in truth divided.

Throughout this fateful decade before secession and war the most intensely emotional area of conflict between the sections concerned the fugitive slaves. Though the number of Negroes who escaped the brutal regimen of slavery was small,

Southerners were particularly infuriated at the assistance rendered their chattels by the Northern "Underground Railroad," a carefully guarded route of farm houses from which Abolitionists sped the fortunate fugitives northward to freedom. Frequently, however, the slaveholder had his revenge when long-suffering fugitives were seized by federal officers and returned to bondage under the stringent Fugitive Slave Act of 1850. But thoughtful Southerners may have tempered their immediate satisfaction with fearful concern for the future when in 1854 they beheld the spectacle of usually staid Boston roused to fury by the apprehension of a fugitive slave, one Anthony Burns. Burns was surrendered to his master, but in the face of an angry mob that was restrained from freeing him only by the presence of four platoons of marines, United States artillery, cavalry units and the police, one thousand men strong. That it cost up to $100,000 to return this one fugitive was far less significant than that Northern attitudes towards slavery were visibly changing—two decades before, another Boston mob had savagely attacked the arch-Abolitionist, William Lloyd Garrison. The new Northern temper boded ill for the slaveholders.

The North's enthusiastic reception of Harriet Beecher Stowe's *Uncle Tom's Cabin* was further testimony to the increasingly bad feelings between the sections. This classic indictment of slavery made innumerable friends for the anti-slavery cause as Little Eva, Topsy, Uncle Tom and Simon Legree called forth compassion for the oppressed slaves and hatred for the oppressors. Three hundred thousand copies of the novel were sold in the first year after publication, and some years later, when the sections were already joined in mortal combat, it is reported that President Lincoln remarked to Mrs. Stowe: "So you're the little woman who wrote the book that made this great war!" But constantly mounting emotions found their outlet in bloodshed long before the war came. Even within the halls of Congress sectional tempers had led to violence and Congressmen who were outspoken on the slavery question frequently carried a brace of pistols or a bowie knife in self-defense.

Essentially human slavery was no more pleasing to Southerners than to Northerners; rather the South had rationalized its "peculiar institution" as just and altogether righteous only when slave labor had come to seem essential to the plantation system and thus to the section's prosperity. Slavery was the focus of attention, but the basic conflict was between Northern industrialism and Southern plantation agrarianism, and it was to find its most immediate expression in the fiercely debated political question of the expansion of slavery into the Territories. If slavery were permitted to expand into the new Territories, these areas would be settled and organized politically by Southerners; if the expansion of slavery were prohibited, the new Territories would be politically controlled by Northerners. And when statehood was achieved the Territories would provide the one section or the other with important new Congressional power to enact or reject the economic program of high tariffs, subsidies and internal improvements that the industrial North demanded and the agrarian South bitterly opposed. By the 1850's, confronted by an already numerically—and thus politically—superior North, desperate Southerners were insisting that they would remain within the Union only as long as slavery was unconditionally *guaranteed* in the Territories. They damned the Compromise of 1850, which provided for "squatter sovereignty," the right of the settlers themselves to determine whether slavery should be permitted or prohibited. But in 1854, the Southerners applauded the Kansas-Nebraska Act that again provided for "popular sovereignty," this time because the Act at least opened to the possibility of slavery territory from which it had previously been prohibited by the Missouri Compromise of 1820. And soon the nation was appalled at the spectacle of "Bleeding Kansas," as Northerners and Southerners opened battle to determine which section should organize the Territory, whether Kansas would ultimately bring additional political power to the free or to the slave states.

Actually, it was in the Supreme Court, not in Congress, that the pro-slavery forces won their most decisive victory. In March, 1857, speaking for a court that was predominantly Southern, Chief Justice Roger B. Taney delivered his famous decision in Dred Scott v. Sanford. Scott, a Missouri Negro, was suing his master, arguing that he had automatically attained his freedom when taken to Illinois, a free state, and then to Minnesota Territory, where slavery had specifically been forbidden by the Missouri Compromise. The case had long been before the Court, and the nation had anxiously awaited its decision; now the momentous importance of Taney's words was obvious to all. Taney first declared that Scott, as a Negro, was not a citizen and therefore could not sue in the Federal courts. The Chief Justice might have stopped there and simply dismissed Scott's petition for freedom, but he went on to delight the Southern expansionists by insisting —and this was the crucial part of the opinion—that Scott could not possibly have been freed by his stay in Minnesota Territory, because Minnesota was not free territory! In fact, Congress had no power to create a free Territory! Thus the Missouri Compromise had been unconstitutional, for, contrary to the Fifth Amendment, it had deprived Southerners of their slave property without due process of law. Under the new decision slavery could not be forbidden in the Territories.

Southerners were overjoyed at the decision. The question of the expansion of slavery seemed to have been settled for all time: now it might spread freely through all of the Territories with the sanction of a Court that had read Southern extremism into the Constitution. But that the Court had by no means effectually disposed of the issue was evident in the North's vehement opposition to Taney's decision. There were increasingly large numbers of Northerners who now would agree with one prominent Republican that "There is a higher law than the Constitution." And soon many of them would fight to uphold that "higher law."

Dred Scott v. Sanford:

Chief Justice Roger B. Taney

for the Supreme Court, 1857

. . . There are two leading questions presented by the record:

1. Had the Circuit Court of the United States jurisdiction to hear and determine the case between these parties? And,

2. If it had jurisdiction, is the judgment it has given erroneous or not?

The plaintiff in error was, with his wife and children, held as slaves by the defendant, in the State of Missouri, and he brought this action in the Circuit Court of the United States for that district, to assert the title of himself and his family to freedom.

The declaration is . . . that he and the defendant are citizens of different States; that is, that he is a citizen of Missouri, and the defendant a citizen of New York.

The defendant pleaded in abatement to the jurisdiction of the court, that the plaintiff was not a citizen of the State of Missouri, as alleged in his declaration, being a Negro of African descent whose ancestors were of pure African blood, and who were brought into this country and sold as slaves. . . .

Before we speak of the pleas in bar, it will be proper to dispose of the questions which have arisen on the plea in abatement.

That plea denies the right of the plaintiff to sue in a court of the United States, for the reasons therein stated.

If the question raised by it is legally before us, and the court should be of opinion that the facts stated in it disqualify the plaintiff from becoming a citizen, in the sense in which that word is used in the Constitution of the United States, then the judgment of the Circuit Court is erroneous, and must be reversed. . . .

The question to be decided is, whether the plaintiff is not entitled to sue as a citizen in a court of the United States. . . .

The question is simply this: Can a Negro, whose ancestors were imported into this country, and sold as slaves, become a member of the political community formed and brought into existence by the Constitution of the United States, and as such become entitled to all the rights, and privileges, and immunities, guaranteed by that instrument to the citizen? One of which rights is the privilege of suing in a court of the United States in the cases specified in the Constitution.

It will be observed, that the plea applies to that class of persons only whose ancestors were Negroes of the African race, and imported into this country, and sold and held as slaves. The only matter in issue before the court, therefore, is whether the descendants of such slaves, when they shall be emancipated, or who are born of parents who had become free before their birth, are citizens of a State, in the sense in which the word citizen is used in the Constitution of the United States. . . .

The words "people of the United States" and "citizens" are synonymous terms, and mean the same thing. They both describe the political body who, according to our republican institutions, form the sovereignty, and who hold the power and conduct the government through their representatives. They are what we familiarly call the "sovereign people," and every citizen is one of this people, and a constituent member of this sovereignty. The question before us is, whether the class of persons described in the plea in abatement compose a portion of this people, and are constituent members of this sovereignty? We think they are not, and that they are not included, and were not intended to be included, under the word "citizens" in the Constitution, and can, therefore, claim none of the rights and privileges which that instrument provides for and secures to citizens of the United States. On the contrary, they were at that time considered as a subordinate and inferior class of beings, who had been subjugated by the dominant race, and whether emancipated or not, yet remained subject to their authority, and had no rights or privileges but such as those who held the power and the government might choose to grant them. . . .

In discussing this question, we must not confound the rights of citizenship which a State may confer within its own limits, and the rights of citizenship as a member of the Union. It does not by any means follow, because he has all the rights and privileges of a citizen of a State, that he must be a citizen of the United States. He may have all of the rights and privileges of the citizen of a State, and yet not be entitled to the rights and privileges of a citizen in any other State. For, previous to the adoption of the Constitution of the United States, every State had the undoubted right to confer on whomsoever it pleased the character of a citizen, and to endow him with all its rights. But this character, of course, was confined to the boundaries of the State, and gave him no rights or privileges in other States beyond those secured to him by the laws of nations and the comity of States. Nor have the several States surrendered the power of conferring these rights and privileges by adopting the Constitution of the United States. Each State may still confer them upon an alien, or any one it thinks proper, or upon any class or description of persons; yet he would not be a citizen in the sense in which that word is used in the Constitution of the United States, nor entitled to sue as such in one of its courts, nor to the privileges and immunities of a citizen in the other States. The rights which he would acquire would be restricted to the State which gave them. . . .

It is very clear, therefore, that no State can, by any Act or law of its own, passed since the adoption of the Constitution, introduce a new member into the political community created by the Constitution of the United States. It cannot make him a member of this community by making him a member of its own. And for the same reason it cannot introduce any person, or description of persons, who were not intended to be embraced in this new political family, which the Constitution brought into existence, but were intended to be excluded from it.

The question then arises, whether the provisions of the Constitution, in relation to the personal rights and privileges to which the citizen of a State should be entitled, embraced the Negro African race, at that time in this country, or who might afterwards be imported, who had then or should afterwards be made free in any State; and to put it in the power of a single State to make him a citizen of the United States, and endue him with the full rights of citizenship in every other State without their consent. Does the Constitution of the United States act upon him whenever he shall be made free under the laws of a State, and raised there to the rank of a citizen, and immediately clothe him with all the privileges of a citizen in every other State, and in its own courts?

The court think the affirmative of these propositions cannot be maintained. And if it cannot, the plaintiff in error could not be a citizen of the State of Missouri, within the meaning of the Constitution of the United States, and, consequently, was not entitled to sue in its courts.

It is true, every person, and every class and description of persons, who were at the time of the adoption of the Constitution recognized as citizens in the several States, became also citizens of this new political body; but none other; it was formed by them, and for them and their posterity, but for no one else. And the personal rights and privileges guaranteed to citizens of this new sovereignty were intended to embrace those only who were then members of the several state communities, or who should afterwards, by birthright or otherwise, become members, according to the provisions of the Constitution and the principles on which it was founded. . . .

It becomes necessary, therefore, to determine who were citizens of the several States when the Constitution was adopted. And in order to do this, we must recur to the governments and institutions of the thirteen Colonies, when they separated from Great Britain and formed new sovereignties. . . . We must inquire who, at that time, were recognized as the people or citizens of a State. . . .

In the opinion of the court, the legislation and histories of the times, and the language used in the Declaration of Independence, show, that neither the class of persons who had been imported as slaves, nor their descendants, whether they had become free or not, were then acknowledged as a part of the people, nor intended to be included in the general words used in that memorable instrument.

It is difficult at this day to realize the state of public opinion in relation to that unfortunate race, which prevailed in the civilized and enlightened portions of the world at the time of the Declaration of Independence, and when the Constitution of the United States was framed and adopted. . . .

They had for more than a century before been regarded as beings of an inferior order and altogether unfit to associate with the white race, either in social or political relations; and so far inferior that they had no rights which the white man was bound to respect; and that the Negro might justly and lawfully be reduced to slavery for his benefit. He was bought and sold and treated as an ordinary article of merchandise and traffic whenever a profit could be made by it. This opinion was at that time fixed and universal in the civilized portion of the white race. It was regarded as an axiom in morals as well as in politics, which no one thought of disputing, or supposed to be open to dispute; and men in every grade and position in society daily and habitually acted upon it in their private pursuits, as well as in matters of public concern, without doubting for a moment the correctness of this opinion.

. . . A Negro of the African race was regarded . . . as an article of property and held and bought and sold as such in every one of the thirteen Colonies which united in the Declaration of Independence and afterward formed the Constitution of the United States. The slaves were more or less numerous in the different Colonies, as slave labor was found more or less profitable. But no one seems to have doubted the correctness of the prevailing opinion of the time.

The legislation of the different Colonies furnished positive and indisputable proof of this fact. . . .

The language of the Declaration of Independence is equally conclusive:

It begins by declaring that "When, in the course of human events, it becomes necessary for one people to dissolve the political bands which have connected them with another, and to assume, among the powers of the earth the separate and equal station to which the laws of nature and nature's God entitle them, a decent respect for the opinions of mankind requires that they should declare the causes which impel them to the separation."

It then proceeds to say: "We hold these truths to be self-evident: that all men are created equal; that they are endowed by their Creator with certain inalienable rights; that among these are life, liberty, and the pursuit of happiness; that to secure these rights, governments are instituted, deriving their just powers from the consent of the governed."

The general words above quoted would seem to embrace the whole human family, and if they were used in a similar instrument at this day would be so understood. But it is too clear for dispute that the enslaved African race were not intended to be included and formed no part of the people who framed and adopted this declaration; for if the language, as understood in that day, would embrace them, the conduct of the distinguished men who framed the Declaration of Independence would have been utterly and flagrantly inconsistent with the principles they asserted; and instead of the sympathy of mankind, to which they so confidently appealed, they would have deserved and received universal rebuke and reprobation.

Yet the men who framed this declaration were great men —high in literary acquirements—high in their sense of honor, and incapable of asserting principles inconsistent with those on which they were acting. They perfectly understood the meaning of the language they used and how it would be understood by others; and they knew that it would not in any part of the civilized world be supposed to embrace the Negro race, which, by common consent, had been excluded from civilized governments and the family of nations and doomed to slavery. They spoke and acted according to the then established doctrine and principles and in the ordinary language of the day, and no one misunderstood them. The unhappy black race were separated from the white by indelible marks, and laws long before established, and were never thought of or spoken of except as property and when the claims of the owner or the profit of the trader were supposed to need protection.

This state of public opinion had undergone no change when the Constitution was adopted, as is equally evident from its provisions and language.

The brief preamble sets forth by whom it was formed, for what purposes, and for whose benefit and protection. It declares that it is formed by the *people* of the United States; that is to say, by those who were members of the different political communities in the several states; and its great object is declared to be to secure the blessing of liberty to themselves and their posterity. It speaks in general terms of the *people* of the United States, and of *citizens* of the several states, when it is providing for the exercise of the powers granted or the privileges secured to the citizen. It does not define what description of persons are intended to be included under these terms, or who shall be regarded as a citizen and one of the people. It uses them as terms so well understood that no further description or definition was necessary. . . .

But there are two clauses in the Constitution which point directly and specifically to the Negro race as a separate class of persons, and show clearly that they were not regarded as a portion of the people or citizens of the Government then formed.

One of these clauses reserves to each of the thirteen States the right to import slaves until the year 1808, if it thinks it proper. And the importation which it thus sanctions was unquestionably of persons of the race of which we are speaking, as the traffic in slaves in the United States had always been confined to them. And by the other provision the States pledge themselves to each other to maintain the right of property of the master, by delivering up to him any slave who may have escaped from his service, and be found within their respective territories. . . . And these two provisions show, conclusively, that neither the description of persons therein referred to, nor their descendants, were embraced in any of the other provisions of the Constitution; for certainly these two clauses were not intended to confer on them or their posterity the blessings of liberty, or any of the personal rights so carefully provided for the citizen. . . .

Indeed, when we look to the condition of this race in the several States at the time, it is impossible to believe that these rights and privileges were intended to be extended to them. . . .

The legislation of the States therefore shows, in a manner not to be mistaken, the inferior and subject condition of that race at the time the Constitution was adopted, and long afterwards, throughout the thirteen States by which that instrument was framed; and it is hardly consistent with the respect due to these States, to suppose that they regarded at that time, as fellow-citizens and members of the sovereignty, a class of beings whom they had thus stigmatized. . . . More especially, it cannot be believed that the large slave-holding States regarded them as included in the word "citizens," or would have consented to a constitution which might compel them to receive them in that character from another State. For if they were so received, and entitled to the privileges and immunities of citizens, it would exempt them from the operation of the special laws and from the police regulations which they considered to be necessary for their own safety. . . . And all of this would be done in the face of the subject race of the same color, both free and slaves, inevitably producing discontent and insubordination among them, and endangering the peace and safety of the State. . . .

. . . Upon a full and careful consideration of the subject, the court is of opinion that, upon the facts stated in the plea in abatement, Dred Scott was not a citizen of Missouri within the meaning of the Constitution of the United States, and not entitled as such to sue in its courts; and, consequently, that the Circuit Court had no jurisdiction of the case, and that the judgment on the plea in abatement is erroneous. . . .

We proceed, therefore, to inquire whether the facts relied on by the plaintiff entitled him to his freedom. . . .

In considering this part of the controversy, two questions arise: 1. Was he, together with his family, free in Missouri by reason of the stay in the territory of the United States hereinbefore mentioned? 2. If they were not, is Scott himself free by reason of his removal to Rock Island, in the State of Illinois, as stated in the above admissions?

We proceed to examine the first question.

The Act of Congress, upon which the plaintiff relies, declares that slavery and involuntary servitude, except as a punishment for crime, shall be forever prohibited in all that part of the territory ceded by France, under the name of Louisiana, which lies north of thirty-six degrees thirty minutes north latitude, and not included within the limits of Missouri. And the difficulty which meets us at the threshold of this part of the inquiry is, whether Congress was authorized to pass this law under any of the powers granted to it by the Constitution; for if the authority is not given by that instrument, it is the duty of this court to declare it void and inoperative, and incapable of conferring freedom upon any one who is held as a slave under the laws of any one of the States.

The counsel for the plaintiff has laid much stress upon that article in the Constitution which confers on Congress the power "to dispose of and make all needful rules and regulations respecting the territory or other property belonging to the United States;" but, in the judgment of the court, that provision has no bearing on the present controversy, and the power there given, whatever it may be, is confined, and was intended to be confined, to the territory which at that time belonged to, or was claimed by, the United States, and was within their boundaries as settled by the treaty with Great Britain, and can have no influence upon a territory afterwards acquired from a foreign Government. It was a special provision for a known and particular territory, and to meet a present emergency, and nothing more. . . .

If this clause is construed to extend to territory acquired by the present Government from a foreign nation, outside of the limits of any charter from the British Government to a colony, it would be difficult to say, why it was deemed necessary to give the Government the power to sell any vacant lands belonging to the sovereignty which might be found within it; and if this was necessary, why the grant of this power should precede the power to legislate over it and establish a Government there; and still more difficult to say, why it was deemed necessary so specially and particularly to grant the power to make needful rules and regulations in relation to any personal or movable property it might acquire there. For the words, *other property* necessarily, by every known rule of interpretation, must mean property of a different description from territory or land. And the difficulty would perhaps be insurmountable in endeavoring to account for the last member of the sentence, which provides that "nothing in this Constitution shall be so construed as to prejudice any claims of the United States or any particular State," or to say how any particular State could have claims in or to a territory ceded by a foreign Government, or to account for associating this provision with the preceding provisions of the clause, with which it would appear to have no connection. . . .

But the power of Congress over the person or property of a citizen can never be a mere discretionary power under our Constitution and form of Government. The powers of the Government and the rights and privileges of the citizen are regulated and plainly defined by the Constitution itself. And when the Territory becomes a part of the United States, the Federal Government enters into possession in the character impressed upon it by those who created it. It enters upon it with its powers over the citizen strictly defined, and limited by the Constitution, from which it derives its own existence, and by virtue of which alone it continues to exist and act as a government and sovereignty. It has no power of any kind beyond it; and it cannot, when it enters a Territory of the United States, put off its character, and assume discretionary or despotic powers which the Constitution has denied to it. It cannot create for itself a new character separated from the citizens of the United States, and the duties it owes them under the provisions of the Constitution. The Territory being a part of the United States, the Government and the citizen both enter it under the authority of the Constitution, with their respective rights defined and marked out; and the Federal Government can exercise no power over his person or property, beyond what that instrument confers, nor lawfully deny any right which it has reserved. . . .

The rights of private property have been guarded with equal care. Thus the rights of property are united with the rights of person, and placed on the same ground by the fifth amendment to the Constitution. . . . An Act of Congress which deprives a person of the United States of his liberty or property merely because he came himself or brought his property into a particular Territory of the United States, and who had committed no offense against the laws, could hardly be dignified with the name of due process of law. . . .

And this prohibition is not confined to the States, but the words are general, and extend to the whole territory over which the Constitution gives it power to legislate, including those portions of it remaining under territorial government, as well as that covered by States. It is a total absence of power everywhere within the dominion of the United States, and places the citizens of a territory, so far as these rights are concerned, on the same footing with citizens of the States, and guards them as firmly and plainly against any inroads which the general government might attempt, under the plea of implied or incidental powers. And if Congress itself cannot do this—if it is beyond the powers conferred on the Federal Government—it will be admitted, we presume, that it could not authorize a territorial government to exercise them. It could confer no power on any local government, established by its authority, to violate the provisions of the Constitution.

It seems, however, to be supposed, that there is a difference between property in a slave and other property, and that different rules may be applied to it in expounding the Constitution of the United States.

But . . . if the Constitution recognizes the right of property of the master in a slave, and makes no distinction between that description of property and other property owned by a citizen, no tribunal, acting under the authority of the United States, whether it be legislative, executive, or judicial, has a right to draw such a distinction, or deny to it the benefit of the provisions and guarantees which have been provided for the protection of private property against the encroachments of the Government.

Now . . . the right of property in a slave is distinctly and expressly affirmed in the Constitution. The right to traffic in it, like an ordinary article of merchandise and property, was guaranteed to the citizens of the United States, in every State that might desire it, for twenty years. And the Government in express terms is pledged to protect it in all future time, if the slave escapes from his owner. . . . And no word can be found in the Constitution which gives Congress a greater power over slave property, or which entitles property of that kind to less protection than property of any other description. The only power conferred is the power coupled with the duty of guarding and protecting the owner in his rights.

Upon these considerations, it is the opinion of the court that the Act of Congress which prohibited a citizen from holding and owning property of this kind in the territory of the United States north of the line therein mentioned, is not warranted by the Constitution, and is therefore void; and that neither Dred Scott himself, nor any of his family, were made free by being carried into this territory; even if they had been carried there by the owner, with the intention of becoming a permanent resident. . . .

Upon the whole, therefore, it is the judgment of this court, that it appears by the record before us that the plaintiff in error is not a citizen of Missouri, in the sense in which that word is used in the Constitution; and that the Circuit Court of the United States, for that reason, had no jurisdiction in the case, and could give no judgment in it.

Its judgment for the defendant must, consequently, be reversed, and a mandate issued directing the suit to be dismissed for want of jurisdiction.

Chapter 13

WAR!

Even as Abraham Lincoln took his solemn oath on March 4, 1861, to "preserve, protect and defend" the government of all the states, secession was a reality and the Union, to many, was a meaningless and anachronistic misnomer. The election of 1860, a final political battle within the Union between sections long joined in bitter conflict, had resulted in an impressive victory for a Republican party that had been founded only six years earlier and that was completely and wholeheartedly Northern in its orientation. Opposed by the Northern Democrat Stephen A. Douglas and two other candidates, Lincoln had received only 40 per cent of the popular vote and was therefore a minority President; but he had won a substantial majority in the Electoral College despite the fact that not a single Southern or Border state voted for him. To the South this victory of an avowed Northern party in a national election completed the political imbalance between the sections that her statesmen had long feared and deplored. Besides, in their steadfast opposition to the further expansion of slavery, Republicans could prevent the South from ever redressing that imbalance, for now slaveholders might not organize and bring into the Union new slave states to bolster their section's waning political power. Republicans disclaimed any intentions of interfering with slavery in the states; indeed, even after Lincoln's election and with his full approval they proposed an amendment to the Constitution that would guarantee slavery forever within the South. But they were determined above all else to set aside the Dred Scott decision that protected slavery in the nation's new territories. And many Southerners were certain that Lincoln's sectional victory prophesied as well the eventual writing into law of the whole Republican platform with its demand for economic measures (such as high tariffs, free land for Western settlers, and internal improvements) so opposed to what the South considered its necessary and legitimate plantation-economy interests. Thus in anger and disgust, with South Carolina once again in the vanguard, the disaffected Southern states began their long threatened secession from the Union. When Lincoln became the 16th President of the United States, seven states had already seceded, more were in the process, and Jefferson Davis and Alexander H. Stephens had been selected President and Vice-President under a provisional constitution of the Confederate States of America.

The interregnum between Lincoln's election and his inauguration was filled with excitement, bewilderment, and tension in the North as well as the South. Many Northerners had voted for Lincoln without fully realizing that his election might finally result in secession. Now the die had been cast and, as President Buchanan struggled desperately to maintain peace and the Union, all the North, indeed all the world, awaited Lincoln's Inaugural Address as a pronouncement of the new administration's policy in the secession crisis. During these fateful months Lincoln suffered much abuse at the hands of those who saw him only as a political unknown, an awkward and incompetent party wheel-horse to whom they referred variously as a "Simple Susan," an "Ape," or a "Baboon." All were quick with advice; from all sides, from high places and low, Lincoln received demands that he meet the crisis in this way or that. Some wanted to let the South secede in peace; others wanted immediate military coercion of the secessionists; still others hoped for peaceful reconciliation after concessions by Lincoln on the vital question of the expansion of slavery into the Territories. Lincoln listened patiently to all but remained the master of his own house, and in his Inaugural Address maintained the same moderate but determined position he had long espoused.

Ironically, the venerable Chief Justice of the Supreme Court, Roger B. Taney, whose Dred Scott decision Lincoln had so derided, administered the oath of office on this fine, brisk March day. And it is reported that Stephen A. Douglas, recently Lincoln's bitter opponent, reached forward, took, and held on his lap Lincoln's immense stove-pipe hat when the new President could find no place for it during the ceremonies. These acts were symbolic, for the address was conciliatory in tone. The President saw no need for secession; he and his party had "no purpose, directly or indirectly, to interfere with the institution of slavery in the States where it exists." Besides, disunion was impossible, Lincoln insisted, for the Union was perpetual; ordinances of secession were meaningless, and the Union remained unbroken. No person or state would be coerced by the national Government; there would be no invasion of the South; no use of force—but the laws would be enforced. Would the Southerners obey them? for there would be no war unless the South were to violate the laws of the nation. The "momentous issue of civil war" was not, Lincoln maintained, in his hands, but in those of his "dissatisfied fellow-countrymen." This was superb political strategy on Lincoln's part, for he had deliberately maneuvered the South into a position of responsibility for war or peace.

Thus, the war did not come because of ineptitude; Lincoln's generation did not blunder into war. Nor was the Civil War "inevitable," an "irrepressible conflict." Bitterness, antagonism, and conflict between societies whose economic, political and cultural patterns were so opposed—these were irrepressible, but war was not. Rather conciliation failed in this last crisis because both sections had determined what their basic interests were and, when they were at stake, refused to make those compromises necessary to prevent war. Six weeks after Lincoln's inauguration Southern batteries fired on Fort Sumter, and the war came.

Abraham Lincoln's First Inaugural Address, 1861

Fellow-Citizens of the United States: In compliance with a custom as old as the government itself, I appear before you to address you briefly, and to take in your presence the oath prescribed by the Constitution of the United States to be taken by the President "before he enters on the execution of his office."

I do not consider it necessary at present for me to discuss those matters of administration about which there is no special anxiety or excitement.

Apprehension seems to exist among the people of the Southern States that by the accession of a Republican administration their property and their peace and personal security are to be endangered. There has never been any reasonable cause for such apprehension. Indeed, the most ample evidence to the contrary has all the while existed and been open to their inspection. It is found in nearly all the published speeches of him who now addresses you. I do but quote from one of those speeches when I declare that "I have no purpose, directly or indirectly, to interfere with the institution of slavery in the States where it exists. I believe I have no lawful right to do so, and I have no inclination to do so." Those who nominated and elected me did so with full knowledge that I had made this and many similar declarations, and had never recanted them.

And, more than this, they placed in the platform for my

acceptance, and as a law to themselves and to me, the clear and emphatic resolution which I now read:

> RESOLVED, That the maintenance inviolate of the rights of the States, and especially the right of each State to order and control its own domestic institutions according to its own judgment exclusively, is essential to that balance of power on which the perfection and endurance of our political fabric depend, and we denounce the lawless invasion by armed force of the soil of any State or Territory, no matter under what pretext, as among the gravest of crimes.

I now reiterate these sentiments; and, in doing so, I only press upon the public attention the most conclusive evidence of which the case is susceptible, that the property, peace, and security of no section are to be in any wise endangered by the now incoming administration. I add, too, that all the protection which, consistently with the Constitution and the laws, can be given, will be cheerfully given to all the States when lawfully demanded, for whatever cause—as cheerfully to one section as to another.

There is much controversy about the delivering up of fugitives from service or labor. The clause I now read is as plainly written in the Constitution as any other of its provisions:

> No person held to service or labor in one State, under the laws thereof, escaping into another, shall in consequence of any law or regulation therein be discharged from such service or labor, but shall be delivered up on claim to the party to whom such service or labor may be due.

It is scarcely questioned that this provision was intended by those who made it for the reclaiming of what we call fugitive slaves; and the intention of the lawgiver is the law. All members of Congress swear their support to the whole Constitution—to this provision as much as to any other. To the proposition then, that slaves whose cases come within the terms of this clause "shall be delivered up," their oaths are unanimous. Now, if they would make the effort in good temper, could they not with nearly equal unanimity frame and pass a law by means of which to keep good that unanimous oath?

There is some difference of opinion whether this clause should be enforced by national or by State authority; but surely that difference is not a very material one. If the slave is to be surrendered, it can be of little consequence to him or to others by which authority it is done. And should any one in any case be content that his oath shall go unkept on a merely unsubstantial controversy as to how it shall be kept?

Again, in any law upon this subject, ought not all the safeguards of liberty known in civilized and humane jurisprudence to be introduced, so that a free man be not, in any case, surrendered as a slave? And might it not be well at the same time to provide by law for the enforcement of that clause in the Constitution which guarantees that "the citizens of each State shall be entitled to all privileges and immunities of citizens in the several States"?

I take the official oath today with no mental reservations, and with no purpose to construe the Constitution or laws by any hypercritical rules. And while I do not choose now to specify particular acts of Congress as proper to be enforced, I do suggest that it will be much safer for all, both in official and private stations, to conform to and abide by all those acts which stand unrepealed, than to violate any of them, trusting to find impunity in having them held to be unconstitutional.

It is seventy-two years since the first inauguration of a President under our National Constitution. During that period fifteen different and greatly distinguished citizens have, in succession, administered the executive branch of the government. They have conducted it through many perils, and generally with great success. Yet, with all this scope of precedent, I now enter upon the same task for the brief constitutional term of four years under great and peculiar difficulty. A disruption of the Federal Union, heretofore only menaced, is now formidably attempted.

I hold that, in contemplation of universal law and of the Constitution, the Union of these States is perpetual. Perpetuity is implied, if not expressed, in the fundamental law of all national governments. It is safe to assert that no government proper ever had a provision in its organic law for its own termination.

Continue to execute all the express provisions of our National Constitution, and the Union will endure forever—it being impossible to destroy it except by some action not provided for in the instrument itself.

Again, if the United States be not a government proper, but an association of States in the nature of contract merely, can it, as a contract, be peaceably unmade by less than all the parties who made it? One party to a contract may violate it —break it, so to speak; but does it not require all to lawfully rescind it?

Descending from these general principles, we find the proposition that, in legal contemplation, the Union is perpetually confirmed by the history of the Union itself. The Union is much older than the Constitution. It was formed, in fact, by the Articles of Association in 1774. It was matured and continued by the Declaration of Independence in 1776. It was further matured, and the faith of all the then thirteen States expressly plighted and engaged that it should be perpetual, by the Articles of Confederation in 1778. And, finally, in 1787 one of the declared objects for ordaining and establishing the Constitution was "to form a more perfect Union."

But if the destruction of the Union by one or by a party only of the States be lawfully possible, the Union is less perfect than before the Constitution, having lost the vital element of perpetuity.

It follows from these views that no State upon its own mere motion can lawfully get out of the Union; that resolves and ordinances to that effect are legally void; and that acts of violence, within any State or States, against the authority of the United States, are insurrectionary or revolutionary, according to circumstances.

I therefore consider that, in view of the Constitution and the laws, the Union is unbroken; and to the extent of my ability I shall take care, as the Constitution itself expressly enjoins upon me, that the laws of the Union be faithfully executed in all the States. Doing this I deem to be only a simple duty on my part; and I shall perform it so far as practicable, unless my rightful masters, the American people, shall withhold the requisite means, or in some authoritative manner direct the contrary. I trust this will not be regarded as a menace, but only as the declared purpose of the union that it will constitutionally defend and maintain itself.

In doing this there needs to be no bloodshed or violence; and there shall be none, unless it be forced upon the national authority. The power confided to me will be used to hold, occupy, and possess the property and places belonging to the Government, and to collect the duties and imposts; but beyond what may be necessary for these objects, there will be no invasion, no using of force against or among the people anywhere. Where hostility to the United States, in any interior locality, shall be so great and universal as to prevent competent resident citizens from holding the Federal offices, there will be no attempt to force obnoxious strangers among the people for that object. While the strict legal right may exist in the Government to enforce the exercise of these offices, the attempt to do so would be so irritating, and so nearly impracticable withal, that I deem it better to forego for the time the uses of such offices.

The mails, unless repelled, will continue to be furnished in all parts of the Union. So far as possible, the people everywhere shall have that sense of perfect security which is most favorable to calm thought and reflection. The course here indicated will be followed unless current events and experience shall show a modification or change to be proper, and in every case and exigency my best discretion will be exercised according to circumstances actually existing, and with a view and a hope of a peaceful solution of the national troubles and the restoration of fraternal sympathies and affections.

That there are persons in one section or another who seek to destroy the Union at all events, and are glad of any pretext to do it, I will neither affirm nor deny; but if there be such, I need address no word to them. To those, however, who really love the Union may I not speak?

Before entering upon so grave a matter as the destruction of our national fabric, with all its benefits, its memories, and its hopes, would it not be wise to ascertain precisely why we do it? Will you hazard so desperate a step while there is any possibility that any portion of the ills you fly from have no real existence? Will you, while the certain ills you fly to are greater than all the real ones you fly from—will you risk the commission of so fearful a mistake?

All profess to be content in the Union if all constitutional rights can be maintained. Is it true, then, that any right, plainly written in the Constitution, has been denied? I think not. Happily the human mind is so constituted that no party can reach to the audacity of doing this. Think, if you can, of a single instance in which a plainly written provision of the Constitution has ever been denied. If by the mere force of numbers a majority should deprive a minority of any clearly written constitutional right, it might, in a moral point of view, justify revolution—certainly would if such a right were a vital one. But such is not our case. All the vital rights of minorities and of individuals are so plainly assured to them by affirmations and negations, guarantees and prohibitions, in the Constitution, that controversies never arise concerning them. But no organic law can ever be framed with a provision specifically applicable to every question which may occur in practical administration. No foresight can anticipate, nor any document of reasonable length contain, express provisions for all possible questions. Shall fugitives from labor be surrendered by national or by State authority? The Constitution does not expressly say. *May* Congress prohibit slavery in the Territories? The Constitution does not expressly say. *Must* Congress protect slavery in the Territories? The Constitution does not expressly say.

From questions of this class spring all our constitutional controversies, and we divide upon them into majorities and minorities. If the minority will not acquiesce, the majority must, or the Government must cease. There is no other alternative; for continuing the Government is acquiescence on one side or the other.

If a minority in such case will secede rather than acquiesce, they make a precedent which in turn will divide and ruin them; for a minority of their own will secede from them whenever a majority refuses to be controlled by such minority. For instance, why may not any portion of a new confederacy a year or two hence arbitrarily secede again, precisely as portions of the present Union now claim to secede from it? All who cherish disunion sentiments are now being educated to the exact temper of doing this.

Is there such perfect identity of interests among the States to compose a new Union, as to produce harmony only, and prevent renewed secession?

Plainly, the central idea of secession is the essence of anarchy. A majority held in restraint by constitutional checks and limitations, and always changing easily with deliberate changes of popular opinions and sentiments, is the only true sovereign of a free people. Whoever rejects it does, of necessity, fly to anarchy or to despotism. Unanimity is impossible; the rule of a minority, as a permanent arrangement, is wholly inadmissible; so that, rejecting the majority principle, anarchy or despotism in some form is all that is left.

I do not forget the position, assumed by some, that constitutional questions are to be decided by the Supreme Court; nor do I deny that such decision must be binding, in any case, upon the parties to a suit, as to the object of that suit, while they are also entitled to very high respect and consideration in all parallel cases by all other departments of the government. And while it is obviously possible that such decision may be erroneous in any given case, still the evil effect following it, being limited to that particular case, with the chance that it may be overruled and never become a precedent for other cases, can better be borne than could the evils of a different practice.

At the same time, the candid citizen must confess that if the policy of the Government, upon vital questions affecting the whole people, is to be irrevocably fixed by decisions of the Supreme Court, the instant they are made, in ordinary litigation between parties in personal actions, the people will have ceased to be their own rulers, having to that extent practically resigned their government into the hands of that eminent tribunal. Nor is there in this view any assault upon the court or the judges. It is a duty from which they may not shrink to decide cases properly brought before them, and it is no fault of theirs if others seek to turn their decisions to political purposes.

One section of our country believes slavery is right, and ought to be extended, while the other believes it is wrong, and ought not to be extended. This is the only substantial dispute. The fugitive slave clause of the Constitution, and the law for the suppression of the foreign slave trade, are each as well enforced, perhaps, as any law can ever be in a community where the moral sense of the people imperfectly supports the law itself. The great body of the people abide by the dry legal obligation in both cases, and a few break over in each. This, I think, cannot be perfectly cured; and it would be worse in both cases after the separation of the sections than before. The foreign slave trade, now imperfectly suppressed, would be ultimately revived, without restriction, in one section, while fugitive slaves, now only partially surrendered, would not be surrendered at all by the other.

Physically speaking, we cannot separate. We cannot remove our respective sections from each other, nor build an impassable wall between them. A husband and wife may be divorced, and go out of the presence and beyond the reach of each other; but the different parts of our country cannot do this. They cannot but remain face to face, and intercourse, either amicable or hostile, must continue between them. Is it possible, then, to make that intercourse more advantageous or more satisfactory after separation than before? Can aliens make treaties easier than friends can make laws? Can treaties be more faithfully enforced between aliens than laws can among friends? Suppose you go to war, you cannot fight always; and when, after much loss on both sides, and no gain on either, you cease fighting, the identical old questions as to terms of intercourse are again upon you.

This country, with its institutions, belongs to the people who inhabit it. Whenever they shall grow weary of the existing Government, they can exercise their constitutional right of amending it, or their revolutionary right to dismember or overthrow it. I cannot be ignorant of the fact that many worthy and patriotic citizens are desirous of having the National Constitution amended. While I make no recommendation of amendments, I fully recognize the rightful authority of the people over the whole subject, to be exercised in either of the modes prescribed in the instrument itself; and I should, under existing circumstances, favor rather than oppose a fair opportunity being afforded the people to act upon it. I will venture to add that to me the convention mode seems preferable, in that it allows amendments to originate with the people themselves, instead of only permitting them to take or reject propositions originated by others not specially chosen for the purpose, and which might not be precisely such as they would wish to either accept or refuse. I understand a proposed amendment to the Constitution—which amendment, however, I have not seen—has passed Congress, to the effect that the Federal Government shall never interfere with the domestic institutions of the States, including that of persons held to service. To avoid misconstruction of what I have said, I depart from my purpose not to speak of particular amendments so far as to say that, holding such a provision to now be implied constitutional law, I have no objection to its being made express and irrevocable.

The chief magistrate derives all his authority from the people, and they have conferred none upon him to fix terms for the separation of the States. The people themselves can do this also if they choose; but the executive, as such, has nothing to do with it. His duty is to administer the present Government, as it came to his hands, and to transmit it, unimpaired by him, to his successor.

Why should there not be a patient confidence in the ultimate justice of the people? Is there any better or equal hope in the world? In our present differences is either party without faith of being in the right? If the Almighty Ruler of Nations, with his eternal truth and justice, be on your side of the North, or on yours of the South, that truth and that justice will surely prevail by the judgment of this great tribunal of the American people.

By the frame of the Government under which we live, this same people have wisely given their public servants but little power for mischief; and have, with equal wisdom, provided for the return of that little to their own hands at very short intervals. While the people retain their virtue and vigilance, no administration, by any extreme of wickedness or folly, can very seriously injure the Government in the short space of four years.

My countrymen, one and all, think calmly and well upon this whole subject. Nothing valuable can be lost by taking time. If there be an object to hurry any of you in hot haste to a step which you would never take deliberately, that object will be frustrated by taking time; but no good object can be frustrated by it. Such of you as are now dissatisfied, still have the old Constitution unimpaired, and, on the sensitive point, the laws of your own framing under it; while the new administration will have no immediate power, if it would, to change either. If it were admitted that you who are dissatisfied hold the right side in the dispute, there still is no single good reason for precipitate action. Intelligence, patriotism, Christianity, and a firm reliance on Him who has never yet forsaken this favored land, are still competent to adjust in the best way all our present difficulty.

In your hands, my dissatisfied fellow-countrymen, and not in mine, is the momentous issue of civil war. The Government will not assail you. You can have no conflict without being yourselves the aggressors. You have no oath registered in heaven to destroy the Government, while I shall have

the most solemn one to "preserve, protect, and defend it."
I am loathe to close. We are not enemies, but friends.
We must not be enemies. Though passion may have strained,
it must not break our bonds of affection. The mystic chords
of memory, stretching from every battlefield and patriot grave
to every living heart and hearthstone all over this broad
land, will yet swell the chorus of the Union when again
touched, as surely they will be, by the better angels of our
nature.

Chapter 14

THE PROPHET OF DEMOCRACY

Though Abraham Lincoln's election in 1860 was followed
by secession, the formation of a Southern Confederacy, and
ultimately by civil war, it did not resolve—even in the North
—the ever perplexing slavery question. The Abolitionist Crusade had made innumerable converts to the anti-slavery cause
since the 1830's. But many, if not most, Northerners continued to espouse the cause of Union even more fervently
than that of the Negro slave, and throughout the entire war
Northern politics reflected a bitter conflict between anti-
slavery and Unionist sentiments. If the war were to be won,
the administration must be assured the political support of
both groups; thus Lincoln's supreme wartime task was to
strike a balance between Radicals who would first free the
slaves, and Conservatives who would first preserve the Union.

Traditionally, of course, the Emancipation Proclamation
has identified Lincoln most closely with the anti-slavery
cause, and he remains enshrined in the hearts of free men
the world over as the "Great Emancipator." Lincoln *did*
thoroughly despise slavery; he thought it a vicious, brutalizing
anachronism. "As I would not be a slave," Lincoln wrote,
"so I would not be a master." Yet his opposition to slavery
was based less on humanitarian grounds than on his acute
realization that human bondage was corruptive of the very
principles that had made the nation great. To Lincoln, America was democracy, and if slavery were to expand, it would
destroy democracy. Again and again Lincoln warned his fellow countrymen that America's democratic tradition, based

on "our ancient faith" that all men are created equal, could not long survive the extension of slavery. If Americans were further to deny their forefathers' faith in liberty and equality they would eventually lose their own freedom:

> Destroy this spirit and you have planted the seeds of despotism at your own doors. Familiarize yourselves with the chains of bondage and you prepare your own limbs to wear them. Accustomed to trample on the rights of others, you . . . become the fit subjects of the first cunning tyrant who rises among you.

Thus it was to preserve democracy in America and ultimately to foster its principles throughout the world that Lincoln was uncompromisingly opposed to the further spread of slavery.

But Lincoln was no friend of the Abolitionists. He decried their radical demand for immediate emancipation and proposed instead gradual emancipation, compensation for the owners and, perhaps, colonization abroad for the freedmen. Besides, though he would not permit slavery to expand, Lincoln had denied neither the Southerners' constitutional right to hold chattels within the Southern states nor the Northerners' obligation to return fugitive slaves.

Even limited to the Southern states slavery was oppressively an evil, but Lincoln would accept it where it already existed to avoid the still greater evil of secession and disunion. For to Lincoln the American Union was a magnificent experiment in democracy, the "last, best hope of earth." Still, the Union was sacred only as it remained an expression of freedom and democracy, and when in 1860-1861 the price of union was the further expansion of slavery, Lincoln chose disunion and war.

But when the war came Lincoln resisted the Radicals' demand that he proclaim it a moral crusade against slavery. Thus he risked their enmity and angry opposition by revoking a military order that would free the slaves of rebellious citizens in Missouri and by severely rebuking the popular General John C. Frémont for this unauthorized action. In the summer of 1862 Lincoln clearly set forth his position on the slavery question. On August 19th, in his widely read and extremely influential *New York Tribune*, Horace Greeley published a "Prayer of Twenty Millions." Addressed to the President, Greeley's famous "Prayer" demanded that the Federal Government make emancipation its announced policy. To this radical proposal Lincoln replied in a widely reprinted letter:

If there be those who would not save the Union unless they could at the same time *save* slavery, I do not agree with them. If there be those who would not save the Union unless they could at the same time *destroy* slavery, I do not agree with them. My paramount object in this struggle *is* to save the Union, and is *not* either to save or destroy slavery. If I could save the Union without freeing *any* slave, I would do it; if I could save it by freeing *all* the slaves, I would do it; and if I could do it by freeing some and leaving others alone, I would also do that. What I do about slavery and the colored race, I do because I believe it helps to save this Union; and what I forbear, I forbear because I do *not* believe it would help to save the Union. I shall do *less* whenever I shall believe what I am doing hurts the cause, and I shall do *more* whenever I believe doing more will help the cause. I shall try to correct errors when shown to be errors; and I shall adopt new views so fast as they shall appear to be true views.

Actually, Lincoln almost immediately adopted "new views," but only because he had re-assayed the pressures of Northern politics and the need for foreign support. He now concluded that he could no longer dare Radical opposition without seriously endangering the Union cause. Well organized and determined, the Radicals were possessed of political power disproportionate to their actual numbers, and it had become evident to the war President that the Confederacy could be defeated only with their ungrudging support. Besides, at a time when European powers had yet to be impressed by Northern military prowess, Lincoln saw that a statement of lofty war aims would go far to gain their respect and moral support. Thus on September 22, after Confederate troops under Robert E. Lee had been defeated at Antietam (it had been Secretary of State Seward's wise suggestion that the bold proclamation be postponed until military victory should make it meaningful) Lincoln issued his preliminary Emancipation Proclamation. Southerners were called upon to end their rebellion by January 1, 1863. Were they to surrender within the remaining 100 days, their slaves, as well as those of the loyal slaveholders, would be protected; but on that date "all persons held as slaves within any State or designated part of a State the people whereof shall then be in rebellion . . . shall be then, thenceforward, and forever free." And on the first day of 1863, that the Union might more surely be preserved, Abraham Lincoln issued his final Emancipation Proclamation and the Civil War became a crusade for freedom.

Lincoln is remembered as the "Great Emancipator" and remains universally a symbol of Union. Yet the martyred President might more appropriately and consistently be honored first as America's prophet of democracy. For it was on the great battlefield at Gettysburg, on November 19, 1863, that this giant amongst men taught that he had struck the chains of bondage from the slaves and had preserved his beloved Union, only to the end that "government of the people, by the people, for the people, shall not perish from the earth."

The Emancipation Proclamation, *1863*

WHEREAS on the twenty-second day of September, in the year of our Lord one thousand eight hundred and sixty-two, a proclamation was issued by the President of the United States, containing, among other things, the following, to wit:

> That on the first day of January, in the year of our Lord one thousand eight hundred and sixty-three, all persons held as slaves within any State, or designated part of a State, the people whereof shall then be in rebellion against the United States, shall be then, thenceforward, and forever free; and the Executive Government of the United States, including the military and naval authority thereof, will recognize and maintain the freedom of such persons, and will do no act or acts to repress such persons, or any of them, in any efforts they may make for their actual freedom.

> That the Executive will, on the first day of January aforesaid, by proclamation, designate the States and parts of States, if any, in which the people thereof respectively shall then be in rebellion against the United States; and the fact that any State, or the people thereof, shall on that day be in good faith represented in the Congress of the United States by members chosen thereto at elections wherein a majority of the qualified voters of such State shall have participated, shall in the absence of strong countervailing testimony be deemed conclusive evidence that such State and the people thereof are not then in rebellion against the United States.

Now, therefore, I, Abraham Lincoln, President of the United States, by virtue of the power in me vested as Commander-in-Chief of the Army and Navy of the United States, in time of actual armed rebellion against the authority and government of the United States, and as a fit and necessary war measure for suppressing said rebellion, do, on this first day of January, in the year of our Lord one thousand eight hundred and sixty-three, and in accordance with my purpose so to do, publicly proclaimed for the full period of 100 days from the day first above mentioned, order and designate as the States and parts of States wherein the people thereof, respectively, are this day in rebellion against the United States, the following, to wit:

Arkansas, Texas, Louisiana (except the parishes of St. Bernard, Plaquemines, Jefferson, St. John, St. Charles, St. James, Ascension, Assumption, Terre Bonne, Lafourche, St. Mary, St. Martin, and Orleans, including the city of New Orleans), Mississippi, Alabama, Florida, Georgia, South Carolina, North Carolina, and Virginia (except the forty-eight counties designated as West Virginia, and also the counties of Berkeley, Accomac, Northampton, Elizabeth City, York, Princess Anne, and Norfolk, including the cities of Norfolk and Portsmouth), and which excepted parts are for the present left precisely as if this proclamation were not issued.

And by virtue of the power and for the purpose aforesaid, I do order and declare that all persons held as slaves within said designated States and parts of States are, and henceforward shall be, free; and that the Executive Government of the United States, including the military and naval authorities thereof, shall recognize and maintain the freedom of said persons.

And I hereby enjoin upon the people so declared to be free to abstain from all violence, unless in necessary self-defense; and I recommend to them that, in all cases where allowed, they labor faithfully for reasonable wages.

And I further declare and make known that such persons of suitable condition will be received into the armed service of the United States to garrison forts, positions, stations, and other places, and to man vessels of all sorts in said service.

And upon this act, sincerely believed to be an act of justice, warranted by the Constitution upon military necessity, I invoke the considerate judgment of mankind and the gracious favor of Almighty God.

In witness whereof, I have hereunto set my hand and caused the seal of the United States to be affixed.

Done at the city of Washington, the first day of January,

in the year of our Lord one thousand eight hundred and sixty-three, and of the independence of the United States of America the eighty-seventh.

By the President: ABRAHAM LINCOLN
  WILLIAM H. SEWARD, Secretary of State.

The Gettysburg Address, *1863*

Fourscore and seven years ago our fathers brought forth on this continent a new nation, conceived in liberty, and dedicated to the proposition that all men are created equal.

Now we are engaged in a great civil war, testing whether that nation, or any nation so conceived and so dedicated, can long endure. We are met on a great battlefield of that war. We have come to dedicate a portion of that field as a final resting-place for those who here gave their lives that that nation might live. It is altogether fitting and proper that we should do this.

But, in a larger sense, we cannot dedicate—we cannot consecrate—we cannot hallow—this ground. The brave men, living and dead, who struggled here, have consecrated it far above our poor power to add or detract. The world will little note nor long remember what we say here, but it can never forget what they did here. It is for us, the living, rather, to be dedicated here to the unfinished work which they who fought here have thus far so nobly advanced. It is rather for us to be here dedicated to the great task remaining before us—that from these honored dead we take increased devotion to that cause for which they gave the last full measure of devotion; that we here highly resolve that these dead shall not have died in vain; that this nation, under God, shall have a new birth of freedom; and that government of the people, by the people, for the people, shall not perish from the earth.

Chapter 15

THE CONFLICT OVER RECONSTRUCTION

On April 9, 1865, in the town of Appomattox Court House in Virginia, the gallant Robert E. Lee surrendered his armies—and the Southern cause—to General Ulysses S. Grant. The war was over; the Union had been preserved. And eight months later, in the Thirteenth Amendment to the Constitution, a reunited nation proclaimed that "Neither slavery nor involuntary servitude . . . shall exist within the United States, or any place subject to their jurisdiction." Finally and unequivocally, slavery was destroyed and four million freedmen became a living monument to the more than six hundred thousand young men who had laid down their lives in the great conflict. But in its ultimate meaning for the nation the final legacy of the four long and tragic years of civil war was even more far reaching than emancipation. For the war had wrought such profound changes in American life that Appomattox as much symbolized the transformation of an old and familiar America into a new nation as it marked the destruction of the Old South.

Of all the revolutionary changes that heralded the emergence of modern America, none was more fundamental nor more dramatic than the triumph of industrial capitalism. During the bitter years of sectional controversy that preceded secession and war, Southern agrarians had steadfastly opposed Northern industrialists. Yet, ironically enough, it was the South's very act of secession that guaranteed the final defeat of agrarianism and the rise to power of the new industrial class. For only in disunion and in the absence of the South's large Congressional delegation, could the Republican party, as the political agent of this dynamic new group, muster enough power to push its desired legislation through Congress. The war years saw the passage of innumerable bills—raising tariffs, granting subsidies, and establishing national fiscal agencies—whose effect, and probably whose design, was not only to rally the nation's economic power to meet the needs of war, but also thoroughly and irrevocably to intrench in power the aggressively self-seeking industrial group. And when the war ended the agrarian South had been defeated even more decisively in the Halls of Congress than on the battlefields. By the time of Appomattox the United States, her destinies now firmly in the hands of Northern businessmen and those who would do their political bidding, was rapidly abandoning her traditional agrarian ways and becoming a predominantly industrial nation.

It was, in large part, to protect the fruits of this economic revolution, not to defend the freedman's new rights nor even to wreak vengeance upon the defeated Southerners, that Radical Republicans imposed military and political control on the South in the tragic era of Reconstruction that followed the war. The earlier, humanitarian Radicals, the fiery

Abolitionists to whom the Republican party served only as a means for attaining emancipation, had been supplanted in party councils by new Radicals whose concern was material rather than humanitarian. To these new Radicals emancipation and Negro suffrage were themselves merely means; the end was consolidation of the enormous gains made in wartime by the triumphant industrial class. But consolidation could be achieved only through continued Republican control of Congress, and this control would be completely upset were the South to send back to the national legislature the same anti-industrialist representatives who had so persistently opposed Republican measures before the war. Throughout Reconstruction, therefore, the objective of the Radical Republicans was to translate emancipation into a political weapon and to impose Negro suffrage upon a violently protesting South, not in consideration of the freedman's undeniable rights, but out of concern for Republican strength. Negro votes were Republican votes, and as long as they were needed no measure, not even rigorous military reorganization of the South, was too harsh to guarantee the Negroes' political and civil rights under the Fourteenth and Fifteenth Amendments to the Constitution. But later, when Negro suffrage no longer served Republican ends, zeal for the Negroes' rights disappeared.

Radical Reconstruction was not, of course, totally unopposed. Unsympathetic to the Radicals' motives, Abraham Lincoln had rejected as a pernicious abstraction their purposefully vindictive theory that seceded Southern states had "committed suicide" and as "conquered territories" were under the jurisdiction and the mercy of the Republican Congress. Lincoln had very early presented his own moderate plan of presidential reconstruction, but the Radicals bitterly resented it as unwarranted presidential interference. Similarly, they scorned the fervent plea of his Second Inaugural Address, delivered shortly before Appomattox, that the nation strive toward reunion "With malice toward none, with charity for all." Six weeks later, on April 14, 1865, when the great war leader was struck down by an assassin's bullet, Radical Republicans exclaimed that it was "God's will." And even as the nation mourned the tragic death of "Father Abraham," Radical Republicans rejoiced, singing the praises of the new President, Andrew Johnson of Tennessee, for his violent denunciations of wealthy and aristocratic Southern secessionists. But in their expectation that Johnson would approve Radical Reconstruction, the Republicans had clearly misjudged him. He was, in truth, bitterly opposed to the great slaveowning planters, but only as he was representative of poor white farmers who had no interest in slavery. Johnson was still a Southerner and, more importantly, an agrarian who equally disliked the Northern industrial plutocracy and the Southern plantation aristocracy. Like Lincoln before him, but without his predecessor's shrewdness and political adeptness, Johnson soon openly opposed the Radicals' program. Immediately the vindictive Republican leaders turned upon him in fury. In 1868 Radicals in the House of Representatives impeached the President for "high crimes and misdemeanors," and in the Senate they failed by only one vote to secure the necessary two-thirds for conviction of these charges. Johnson was acquitted, but his enemies had shown their strength. Radicalism was undeniably King, and the harshest of Reconstruction governments had been imposed by military force upon the Southern states.

Largely dominated by uneducated and inexperienced Negroes, sympathetic local whites known as "scalawags," and opportunistic Northern "carpetbaggers," these Radical state governments were frequently extravagant and corrupt. Nevertheless, the Ku Klux Klan and other instruments designed by the Southern whites to terrorize Negroes who supported the "carpetbag" governments expressed far more than a simple mass reaction to political corruption. Misconduct in high office, after all, was by no means peculiar to the South during Reconstruction, for public morals were deplorably low throughout the nation. Actually, in adopting their violently oppressive tactics Southern whites were indicating their basic hostility to *any* free and equal participation in the political process by the Negroes whom they had so recently, and so unwillingly, emancipated. Besides, in the debate over corruption, the great liberal and humanitarian accomplishments of the Reconstruction governments were often lost sight of: they had granted social and economic, as well as political rights to the freedmen; they had established much-needed schools and welfare agencies for Negroes and whites alike; and they had made important efforts at reforming the archaic and undemocratic practices of Southern state governments.

Protected by Federal troops, these governments could remain in power only at the pleasure of Northern Republicans. And by the mid-1870's the Republicans were sufficiently disturbed at growing Western and laborite opposition to their conservative economic policies to seek less precarious Southern cooperation. The disputed presidential election of 1876, in which both the Republican Hayes and the Democratic Tilden claimed victory, provided the setting for a compromise between the conservative elements among both Southern Democrats and Northern Republicans. Immediately, Southerners would help make Hayes President and grateful Republicans would withdraw the remaining Federal troops from the South. Of far greater significance, the supposed antagonists recognized a common interest in the maintenance of the new economic order and its profitable expansion into the South. Conservative Southerners were to share in the fruits of industrial capitalism, and the South was to become a great prop to the new order it had once opposed. Thus, as the supreme economic result of the Civil War was the triumph of industrial capitalism, its great political achievement was the emergence of a tacit but nonetheless effective coalition of conservatives North and South. And it was to secure this alliance that the North abandoned the Negro and brought Radical Reconstruction to an end.

Had Lincoln lived, the course of Reconstruction might possibly have been far different. For the magnificent statesman's only concern had been "to bind up the nation's wounds . . . to do all which may achieve and cherish a just and lasting peace." Besides, Lincoln was the master politician where Johnson was inept. Yet, such virulent economic and political forces dominated this "tragic era," that individual men counted for little. Had the wartime leader continued to oppose Radical Reconstruction he probably would not have been spared the vindictiveness with which the Radicals in Congress attacked the powers and prerogatives of the Chief Executive. And there were those who gave thanks that Lincoln had fallen early in victory rather than later in defeat.

Abraham Lincoln's Second Inaugural Address, *1865*

Fellow-Countrymen: At this second appearing to take the oath of the Presidential office, there is less occasion for an extended address than there was at the first. Then a statement, somewhat in detail, of a course to be pursued, seemed fitting and proper. Now, at the expiration of four years, during which public declarations have been constantly called forth on every point and phase of the great contest which still absorbs the attention and engrosses the energies of the nation, little that is new could be presented. The progress of our arms, upon which all else chiefly depends, is as well known to the public as to myself; and it is, I trust, reasonably satisfactory and encouraging to all. With high hope for the future, no prediction in regard to it is ventured.

On the occasion corresponding to this four years ago, all thoughts were anxiously directed to an impending civil war. All dreaded it—all sought to avert it. While the inaugural address was being delivered from this place, devoted altogether to saving the Union without war, insurgent agents were in the city seeking to destroy it without war—seeking to dissolve the Union, and divide effects, by negotiation. Both parties deprecated war; but one of them would make war rather than let the nation survive; and the other would accept war rather than let it perish. And the war came.

One-eighth of the whole population were colored slaves, not distributed generally over the Union, but localized in the Southern part of it. These slaves constituted a peculiar and powerful interest. All knew that this interest was, somehow, the cause of the war. To strengthen, perpetuate, and extend this interest was the object for which the insurgents would rend the Union, even by war; while the government claimed no right to do more than to restrict the territorial enlargement of it.

Neither party expected for the war the magnitude or the duration which it has already attained. Neither anticipated that the cause of the conflict might cease with, or even before, the conflict itself should cease. Each looked for an easier triumph, and a result less fundamental and astounding. Both read the same Bible, and pray to the same God; and each invokes His aid against the other. It may seem strange that any men should dare to ask a just God's assistance in wringing their bread from the sweat of other men's faces; but let us judge not, that we be not judged. The prayers of both could not be answered. That of neither has been answered fully. The Almighty has His own purposes. "Woe unto the world because of offenses! for it must needs be that offenses come; but woe to that man by whom the offense cometh." If we shall suppose that American slavery is one of those offenses which, in the providence of God, must needs come, but which, having continued through His appointed time, He now wills to remove, and that He gives to both North and South this terrible war, as the woe due to those by whom the offense came, shall we discern therein any departure from those divine attributes which the believers in a living God always ascribe to Him? Fondly do we hope, fervently do we pray, that this mighty scourge of war may speedily pass away. Yet, if God wills that it continue until all the wealth piled by the bondsman's two hundred and fifty years of unrequited toil shall be sunk, and until every drop of blood drawn with the lash shall be paid by another drawn with the sword, as was said three thousand years ago, so still it must be said, "The judgments of the Lord are true and righteous altogether."

With malice toward none, with charity for all, with firmness in the right, as God gives us to see the right, let us strive on to finish the work we are in, to bind up the nation's wounds, to care for him who shall have borne the battle, and for his widow, and his orphan—to do all which may achieve and cherish a just and lasting peace among ourselves and with all nations.

Chapter 16

THE GILDED AGE

Industrial expansion—ruthless, audacious, and unrelenting—was undeniably a major theme of American life in the decades from Appomattox to the end of the nineteenth century. Characterized by industry's rapid exploitation of the nation's vast human and material resources, and by the feverish accumulation of huge personal and corporate fortunes, this was America's great Age of Enterprise. But it was also America's Gilded Age, an age of aggressiveness, of unbridled acquisitiveness, of coarseness and vulgarity, when concern for the traditional principles of public and private morality had been supplanted by the worship of Mammon. By 1900 American businessmen had guided the nation to such heights of material success that she entered the new century a stridently powerful industrial giant. But to some thoughtful Americans it seemed that the high human values of an earlier America had been tragically sacrificed in the process.

By the end of the Civil War the scene had been well set for the phenomenal growth of business and for the ideological as well as physical conquest of America by her mighty captains of industry. Investment capital was readily available, for numbers of entrepreneurs had made large profits in the war years. Incredibly rich natural resources in timber, fertile lands, metals, coal, iron, and oil were at the disposal of business. A practically unlimited supply of cheap labor, increased yearly by an ever growing stream of immigrants from distant shores, waited to serve the industrial colossus. An enormous continent guaranteed a profitable and seemingly insatiable domestic market, and a rapidly developing railroad network provided an extensive transportation system to bring together these abundant resources. But the triumph of business enterprise cannot be accounted for in these terms alone. Three other factors played a particularly decisive role: the personalities and genius of American business leaders, the constant assistance rendered business by a friendly national government, and the nation's acceptance of an ethic that transformed its social order into a business civilization.

In the harsh competitiveness of an industrial age, business leaders rose rapidly to positions of prestige and power: Andrew Carnegie in steel, John D. Rockefeller in oil, Philip D. Armour in meat-packing, J. Pierpont Morgan in finance, and James J. Hill, Leland Stanford, and Edward H. Harriman in railroads. These were the leaders of a new American aristocracy, the giants who controlled the nation's industries, its wealth, and, some maintained, its very destinies. Family, education and gentility were not, however, the usual adornments of America's new overlords. Most often they were of humble origin, without education or training. Yet almost to a man they possessed aggressive personal traits and an unlimited capacity for business affairs that went far to secure them treasure in a brutally piratical age. They were hardheaded, hard-working, enterprising, domineering and imaginative men. Their extravagant visions of personal gain were seldom beclouded with concern for the welfare of their laborers or the many weaker competitors whom they frequently destroyed by fair means or foul. They combined shrewdness in the manipulation of men and materials with a genius for organization to create fabulous industrial empires that astounded the world. And the business elite's thorough mastery of the art of monopolization was clearly evidenced in Rockefeller's consolidation of the nation's oil industry into the Standard Oil trust and Carnegie's domination of almost the entire steel industry.

To these lords of industry and their admirers, the boldness and the enormity of their accomplishments, the development of the continent's natural riches, the construction of an immense national productive plant, and the creation of unheard-of wealth, raised them to heroic stature. But to the critics of the Gilded Age they were simply Robber Barons whose arts were those of the rapacious, though often romantic, highwayman. The magnitude of their achievements could not be gainsaid, yet the cost seemed truly appalling. And their critics argued cogently that to admire the Robber Barons was not only to condone trickery, cruelty, and frequently robbery, but also to applaud men whose very fortunes proved them most adept at these practices.

Those who criticized and would restrain the venal spirit of the age were to find no effective recourse in the political arena, however, for there the cunning of the entrepreneur found its counterpart in the chicanery of the politician. Like her *nouveaux riches*, America's politicos were fiercely dedicated to private profit and unconcerned with the public good. Throughout the period unscrupulous national and state legislators were openly bought and sold by the highest bidders, and during Ulysses S. Grant's administrations (1869-1877) a large segment of the Executive branch of the national government was viciously corrupt. The disgraceful Credit Mobilier railroad scandal—involving among others two Vice-Presidents of the United States, Schuyler Colfax and Henry Wilson, as well as a future President, James A. Garfield—proved to be truly symptomatic of the times. American political life, with many of its practitioners engaged in an orgy of thievery that permeated every level of government activity, was at its lowest ebb.

Though businessmen spent large sums to purchase vulnerable politicians, their investments in political power paid lush dividends in governmental assistance to industry's unrestrained expansion. Railroad interests alone received from friendly Federal and state governments land grants and subsidies that attained staggering proportions. These land grants equaled in size the state of Texas, and their value, together with direct money grants made to the railroads, totalled almost three-quarters of a billion dollars! Meanwhile the industrial community at large profited enormously from steep tariff walls erected against foreign competitors. And government assistance was by no means limited only to such positive forms. For government again served industry well in maintaining a consistently negative, hands-off attitude toward steadily mushrooming trusts and monopolies that trampled indifferently over all who stood in the path to profit. And when, under the pressures of an aroused and angry citizenry, some state legislatures did actually pass regulatory acts, these acts were swept aside as unconstitutional by a conservative Supreme Court that later emerged as industry's most ardent champion. Supported by the highest court in the land, the alliance between business and government seemed truly impregnable.

These economic and political developments were greatly facilitated by equally significant changes in the whole course of American thought. Embracing the ideological and ethical assumptions that underlay the Gilded Age, Americans generally viewed with enthusiasm the triumphant emergence of a business civilization whose most appropriate symbol was the dollar sign. And the coarse standards of the business community were clearly reflected in almost every aspect of American behavior. Yet men like E. L. Godkin, the caustic editor of the *Nation,* Henry Adams, grandson and great-grandson of Presidents, the poet James Russell Lowell, and others of their circle who composed America's older, declining intellectual aristocracy, inveighed bitterly against what Godkin termed a "chromo civilization."

Even Walt Whitman, the poet who once had sung most exuberantly of America's democratic virtues, strength and cultural creativeness, now pondered whether his nation's rampant, materialistic post-war individualism hadn't bequeathed her a "hollowness of heart" that in the Gilded Age was manifest everywhere in deceit, faithlessness, cruelty, corruption. Whitman's "Democratic Vistas," published in 1871, lacked the broad optimism of *Leaves of Grass* and his other early affirmations of faith in democracy. Now Whitman felt that "vulgarians" dominated America and that the democratic individualism which a generation before seemed to have promised great national poetry, art, creativeness, had actually degenerated into petty and depraved self-seeking. Not that Whitman had lost all faith in democracy—which for him, as for Lincoln, was synonymous with America— but now he saw its promise and true grandeur in the future only, its materialistic failures in the "chromo civilization" around him.

Despite these criticisms, however, the very materialistic "values" that Whitman and the others deplored were widely accepted. And most Americans, though separated from the rising plutocracy by a vast gulf of riches, came fervently to share its material standards of success. Thus, when the multimillionaire steel magnate, Andrew Carnegie, propounded an elaborate rationalization of the new highly competitive economic order, he faithfully reflected the temper of contemporary America.

Though concerned in large part with the philanthropic duties of the man of wealth as the "mere agent and trustee for his poorer brethren," Carnegie's essay, "Wealth," was significantly couched in the language of Darwinian evolutionary ideas that had already made a deep impression upon American thought. In his *Origin of Species,* the English scientist Charles Darwin had explained the evolution from low to higher living forms in terms of Nature's inexorable struggle for existence and the consequent survival of the fittest. Immediately industry's apologists seized upon these ideas in self-justification, seeking to translate Darwin's observations of natural phenomena into laws of social behavior. As a major spokesman for the Social Darwinists, Carnegie wrote that though competitiveness "may be sometimes hard for the individual, it is best for the race, because it insures the survival of the fittest in every department." We must accept "great inequality of environment, the concentration of business . . . in the hands of a few, and the law of competition between these as being not only beneficial, but essential for the future progress of the race." Thus the cut-throat competition of the Age of Enterprise was equated with Nature's own struggle for existence and sanctioned as natural and right. The giants who survived the struggle, the economic masters of the nation, were judged the "fittest" of the race; and even the most brutal business practices were esteemed as tools of survival and human progress.

Yet the Social Darwinists were not wholly consistent. They demanded for themselves positive assistance from government in the form of tariffs, land grants and subsidies. At the same time they condemned regulatory or social legislation as unwarranted interference with the law of the jungle, fraught with the most dire consequences for the "future progress of the race." Despite these inconsistencies, however, until the advent of Progressivism at the end of the century, large numbers of Americans remained imbued with the ideas of the Social Darwinists.

Democratic Vistas, *Walt Whitman*, 1871

. . . America, filling the present with greatest deeds and problems, cheerfully accepting the past, including feudalism (as, indeed, the present is but the legitimate birth of the past, including fuedalism), counts, as I reckon, for her justification and success, (for who, as yet, dare claim success?) almost entirely on the future. Nor is that hope unwarranted. To-day, ahead, though dimly yet, we see, in vistas, a copious, sane, gigantic offspring. For our New World I consider far less important for what it has done, or what it is, than for results to come. Sole among nationalities, these States have assumed the task to put in forms of lasting power and practicality, on areas of amplitude rivaling the operations of the physical kosmos, the moral political speculations of ages, long, long deferr'd, the democratic republican principle, and the theory of development and perfection by voluntary standards and self-reliance. Who else, indeed, except the United States, in history, so far, have accepted in unwitting faith, and, as we now see, stand, act upon, and go security for, these things?

But preluding no longer, let me strike the key-note of the following strain. First premising that, though the passages of it have been written at widely different times, (it is, in fact, a collection of memoranda, perhaps for future designers, comprehenders,) and though it may be open to the charge of one part contradicting another—for there are opposite sides to the great question of democracy, as to every great question—I feel the parts harmoniously blended in my own realization and convictions, and present them to be read only in such oneness, each page and each claim and assertion modified and temper'd by the others. Bear in mind, too, that they are not the result of studying up in political economy, but of the ordinary sense, observing, wandering among men, these States, these stirring years of war and peace. I will not gloss over the appalling dangers of universal suffrage in the United States. In fact, it is to admit and face these dangers I am writing. To him or her within whose thought rages the battle, advancing, retreating, between democracy's convictions, aspirations, and the people's crudeness, vice, caprices, I mainly write this essay. I shall use the words America and democracy as convertible terms. Not an ordinary one is the issue. The United States are destined either to surmount the gorgeous history of feudalism, or else prove the most tremendous failure of time. Not the least doubtful am I on any prospects of their material success. . . .

Admitting all this, with the priceless value of our political institutions, general suffrage, (and fully acknowledging the latest, widest opening of the doors,) I say that, far deeper than these, what finally and only is to make of our western world a nationality superior to any hither known, and outtopping the past, must be vigorous, yet unsuspected Literatures, perfect personalities, and sociologies, original, transcendental, and expressing (what, in highest sense, are not yet express'd at all,) democracy and the modern. With these, and out of these, I promulge new races of Teachers, and of perfect Women, indispensable to endow the birth-stock of a New World. For feudalism, caste, the ecclesiastic traditions, though palpably retreating from political institutions, still hold essentially, by their spirit, even in this country, entire possession of more important fields, indeed the very subsoil, of education, and of social standards and literature.

I say that democracy can never prove itself beyond cavil, until it founds and luxuriantly grows its own forms of art, poems, schools, theology, displacing all that exists, or that has been produced anywhere in the past, under opposite influences. . . . Our fundamental want to-day in the United

States, with closest, amplest reference to present conditions, and to the future, is of a class, and the clear idea of a class, of native authors, literatuses, far different, far higher in grade than any yet known, sacerdotal, modern, fit to cope with our occasions, lands, permeating the whole mass of American mentality, taste, belief, breathing into it a new breath of life, giving it decision, affecting politics far more than the popular superficial suffrage, with results inside and underneath the elections of Presidents or Congresses—radiating, begetting appropriate teachers, schools, manners, and, as its grandest result, accomplishing, (what neither the schools nor the churches and their clergy have hitherto accomplish'd, and without which this nation will no more stand, permanently, soundly, than a house will stand without a substratum,) a religious and moral character beneath the political and productive and intellectual bases of the States. . . .

I say we had best look our times and lands searchingly in the face, like a physician diagnosing some deep disease. Never was there, perhaps, more hollowness at heart than at present, and here in the United States. Genuine belief seems to have left us. The underlying principles of the States are not honestly believ'd in, (for all this hectic glow, and these melodramatic screamings,) nor is humanity itself believ'd in. What penetrating eye does not everywhere see through the mask? The spectacle is appalling. We live in an atmosphere of hypocrisy throughout. The men believe not in the women, nor the women in the men. A scornful superciliousness rules in literature. The aim of all the *littérateurs* is to find something to make fun of. A lot of churches, sects, &c., the most dismal phantasms I know, usurp the name of religion. Conversation is a mass of badinage. From deceit in the spirit, the mother of all false deeds, the offspring is already incalculable. . . . The depravity of the business classes of our country is not less than has been supposed, but infinitely greater. The official services of America, national, state, and municipal, in all their branches and departments, except the judiciary, are saturated in corruption, bribery, falsehood, maladministration; and the judiciary is tainted. The great cities reek with respectable as much as non-respectable robbery and scoundrelism. In fashionable life, flippancy, tepid amours, weak infidelism, small aims, or no aims at all, only to kill time. In business, (this all-devouring modern word, business,) the one sole object is, by any means, pecuniary gain. The magician's serpent in the fable ate up all the other serpents; and moneymaking is our magician's serpent, remaining to-day sole master of the field. The best class we show, is but a mob of fashionably dress'd speculators and vulgarians. True, indeed, behind this fantastic farce, enacted on the visible stage of society, solid things and stupendous labors are to be discover'd, existing crudely and going on in the background, to advance and tell themselves in time. Yet the truths are none the less terrible. I say that our New World democracy, however great a success in uplifting the masses out of their sloughs, in materialistic development, products, and in a certain highly-deceptive superficial popular intellectuality, is, so far, an almost complete failure in its social aspects, and in really grand religious, moral, literary, and esthetic results. . . .

Then still the thought returns, (like the thread-passage in overtures,) giving the key and echo to these pages. When I pass to and fro, different latitudes, different seasons, beholding the crowds of the great cities, New York, Boston, Philadelphia, Cincinnati, Chicago, St. Louis, San Francisco, New Orleans, Baltimore—when I mix with these interminable swarms of alert, turbulent, good-natured, independent citizens, mechanics, clerks, young persons—at the idea of this mass of men, so fresh and free, so loving and so proud, a singular awe falls upon me. I feel, with dejection and amazement, that among our geniuses and talented writers or speakers, few or none have yet really spoken to this people, created a single image-making work for them, or absorb'd the central spirit and the idiosyncrasies which are theirs—and which, thus, in highest ranges, so far remain entirely uncelebrated, unexpress'd.

Dominion strong is the body's; dominion stronger is the mind's. What has fill'd, and fills to-day our intellect, our fancy, furnishing the standards therein, is yet foreign. The great poems, Shakspere included, are poisonous to the idea of the pride and dignity of the common people, the life-blood of democracy. The models of our literature, as we get it from other lands, ultra-marine, have had their birth in courts, and bask'd and grown in castle sunshine; all smells of princes' favors. Of workers of a certain sort, we have, indeed, plenty, contributing after their kind; many elegant, many learn'd, all complacent. But touch'd by the national test, or tried by the standards of democratic personality, they wither to ashes. I say I have not seen a single writer, artist, lecturer, or what not, that has confronted the voiceless but ever erect and active, pervading, underlying will and typic aspiration of the land, in a spirit kindred to itself. Do you call those genteel little creatures American poets? Do you term that perpetual, pistareen, paste-pot work, American art, American drama, taste, verse? I think I hear, echoed as from some mountaintop afar in the west, the scornful laugh of the Genius of these States. . . .

America has yet morally and artistically originated nothing. She seems singularly unaware that the models of persons, books, manners, &c., appropriate for former conditions and for European lands, are but exiles and exotics here. No current of her life, as shown on the surfaces of what is authoritatively called her society, accepts or runs into social or esthetic democracy; but all the currents set squarely against it. Never, in the Old World, was thoroughly upholster'd exterior appearance and show, mental and other, built entirely on the idea of caste, and on the sufficiency of mere outside acquisition—never were glibness, verbal intellect, more the test, the emulation—more loftily elevated as head and sample —than they are on the surface of our republican States this day. The writers of a time hint the mottoes of its gods. The word of the modern, say these voices, is the word Culture.

We find ourselves abruptly in close quarters with the enemy. This word Culture, or what it has come to represent, involves, by contrast, our whole theme, and has been, indeed, the spur, urging us to engagement. Certain questions arise. As now taught, accepted and carried out, are not the processes of culture rapidly creating a class of supercilious infidels, who believe in nothing? Shall a man lose himself in countless masses of adjustments, and be so shaped with reference to this, that, and the other, that the simply good and healthy and brave parts of him are reduced and clipped away, like the bordering of box in a garden? You can cultivate corn and roses and orchards—but who shall cultivate the mountain peaks, the ocean, and the tumbling gorgeousness of the clouds? Lastly—is the readily-given reply that culture only seeks to help, systematize, and put in attitude, the elements of fertility and power, a conclusive reply?

I do not so much object to the name, or word, but I should certainly insist, for the purposes of these States, on a radical change of category, in the distribution of precedence. I should demand a programme of culture, drawn out, not for a single class alone, or for the parlors or lecture-rooms, but with an eye to practical life, the west, the working-men, the facts of farms and jack-planes and engineers, and of the broad range of the women also of the middle and working strata, and with reference to the perfect equality of women, and of a grand and powerful motherhood. I should demand of this programme or theory a scope generous enough to include the widest human area. It must have for its spinal meaning the formation of a typical personality of character, eligible to the uses of the high average of men—and *not* restricted by conditions ineligible to the masses. The best culture will always be that of the manly and courageous instincts, and loving perceptions, and of self-respect—aiming to form, over this continent, an idiocrasy of universalism, which, true child of America, will bring joy to its mother, returning to her in her own spirit, recruiting myriads of offspring, able, natural, perceptive, tolerant, devout believers in her, America, and with some definite instinct why and for what she has arisen, most vast, most formidable of historic births, and is, now and here, with wonderful step, journeying through Time. . . .

Wealth, *Andrew Carnegie, 1889*

The problem of our age is the proper administration of wealth, so that the ties of brotherhood may still bind together the rich and poor in harmonious relationship. The conditions of human life have not only been changed, but revolutionized within the past few hundred years. In former days there was little difference between the dwelling, dress, food, and environment of the chief and those of his retainers. The Indians are today where civilized man then was. When visiting the Sioux I was led to the wigwam of the chief. It was just like the others in external appearance, and even within the difference was trifling between it and those of the poorest of his braves. The contrast between the palace of the millionaire and the cottage of the laborer with us today measures the change which has come with civilization.

This change, however, is not to be deplored, but welcomed as highly beneficial. It is well, nay, essential for the progress of the race, that the houses of some should be homes for all that is highest and best in literature and the arts, and for all the refinements of civilization, rather than that none should be so. Much better this great irregularity than universal squalor. Without wealth there can be no Maecenas. The "good old times" were not good old times. Neither master nor servant was as well situated then as today. A relapse to old conditions would be disastrous to both—not the least so to him who serves—and would sweep away civilization with it. But whether the change be for good or ill, it is upon us, beyond our power to alter, and therefore to be accepted and made the best of. It is a waste of time to criticise the inevitable.

It is easy to see how the change has come. One illustration will serve for almost every phase of the cause. In the manufacture of products we have the whole story. It applies to all combinations of human industry, as stimulated and enlarged by the inventions of this scientific age. Formerly articles were manufactured at the domestic hearth or in small shops which formed part of the household. The master and his apprentices worked side by side, the latter living with the master, and therefore subject to the same conditions. When these apprentices rose to be masters, there was little or no change in their mode of life, and they, in turn, educated in the same routine succeeding apprentices. There was, substantially, social equality, and even political equality, for those engaged in industrial pursuits had then little or no political voice in the State.

But the inevitable result of such a mode of manufacture was crude articles at high prices. Today the world obtains commodities of excellent quality at prices which even the generation preceding this would have deemed incredible. In the commercial world similar causes have produced similar results, and the race is benefited thereby. The poor enjoy what the rich could not before afford. What were the luxuries have become the necessities of life. The laborer has now more comforts than the farmer had a few generations ago. The farmer has more luxuries than the landlord had, and is more richly clad and better housed. The landlord has books and pictures rarer, and appointments more artistic, than the King could then obtain.

The price we pay for this salutary change is, no doubt, great. We assemble thousands of operatives in the factory, in the mine, and in the counting-house, of whom the employer can know little or nothing, and to whom the employer is little better than a myth. All intercourse between them is at an end. Rigid castes are formed, and, as usual, mutual ignorance breeds mutual distrust. Each caste is without sympathy for the other, and ready to credit anything disparaging in regard to it. Under the law of competition, the employer of thousands is forced into the strictest economies, among which the rates paid to labor figure prominently, and often there is friction between the employer and the employed, between capital and labor, between rich and poor. Human society loses homogeneity.

The price which society pays for the law of competition, like the price it pays for cheap comforts and luxuries, is also great; but the advantages of this law are also greater still, for it is to this law that we owe our wonderful material development, which brings improved conditions in its train. But, whether the law be benign or not, we must say of it, as we say of the change in the conditions of men to which we have referred: It is here; we cannot evade it; no substitutes for it have been found; and while the law may be sometimes hard for the individual, it is best for the race, because it insures the survival of the fittest in every department. We accept and welcome, therefore, as conditions to which we must accommodate ourselves, great inequality of environment, the concentration of business, industrial and commercial, in the hands of a few, and the law of competition between these, as being not only beneficial, but essential for the future progress of the race. Having accepted these, it follows that there must be great scope for the exercise of special ability in the merchant and in the manufacturer who has to conduct affairs upon a great scale. That this talent for organization and management is rare among men is proved by the fact that it invariably secures for its possessor enormous rewards, no matter where or under what laws or conditions. The experienced in affairs always rate the *man* whose services can be obtained as a partner as not only the first consideration, but such as to render the question of his capital scarcely worth considering, for such men soon create capital; while, without the special talent required, capital soon takes wings. Such men become interested in firms or corporations using millions; and estimating only simple interest to be made upon the capital invested, it is inevitable that their income must exceed their expenditures, and that they must accumulate wealth. Nor is there any middle ground which such men can occupy, because the great manufacturing or commercial concern which does not earn at least interest upon its capital soon becomes bankrupt. It must either go forward or fall behind: to stand still is impossible. It is a condition essential for its successful operation that it should be thus far profitable, and even that, in addition to interest on capital, it should make profit. It is a law, as certain as any of the others named, that men possessed of this peculiar talent for affairs, under the free play of economic forces, must, of necessity, soon be in receipt of more revenue than can be judiciously expended upon themselves; and this law is as beneficial for the race as the others.

Objections to the foundations upon which society is based are not in order, because the condition of the race is better with these than it has been with any others which have been tried. Of the effect of any new substitutes proposed we cannot be sure. The socialist or anarchist who seeks to overturn present conditions is to be regarded as attacking the foundation upon which civilization itself rests, for civilization took its start from the day that the capable, industrious workman said to his incompetent and lazy fellow, "If thou dost not sow, thou shalt not reap," and thus ended primitive communism by separating the drones from the bees. One who studies this subject will soon be brought face to face with the conclusion that upon the sacredness of property civilization itself depends—the right of the laborer to his hundred dollars in the savings bank, and equally the legal right of the millionaire to his millions. To those who propose to substitute communism for this intense individualism the answer, therefore, is: The race has tried that. All progress from that barbarous day to the present time has resulted from its displacement. Not evil, but good, has come to the race from the accumulation of wealth by those who have the ability and energy that produce it. But even if we admit for a moment that it might be better for the race to discard its present foundation, individualism—that it is a nobler ideal that man should labor, not for himself alone, but in and for a brotherhood of his fellows, and share with them all in common, realizing Swedenborg's idea of Heaven, where, as he says, the angels derive their happiness, not from laboring for self, but for each other—even admit all this, and a sufficient answer is: This is not evolution, but revolution. It necessitates the changing of human nature itself—a work of aeons, even if it were good to change it, which we cannot know. It is not practicable in our day or in our age. Even if desirable theoretically, it belongs to another and long-succeeding sociological stratum. Our duty is with what is practicable now; with the next step possible in our day and generation. It is criminal to waste our energies in endeavoring to uproot, when all we can profitably or possibly accomplish is to bend the universal tree of humanity a little in the direction most favorable to the production of good fruit under existing circumstances. We might as well urge the destruction of the highest existing type of man because he failed to reach our ideal as to favor the destruction of Individualism, Private Property, the Law of Accumulation of Wealth, and the Law of Competition; for these are the highest results of human experience, the soil in which society so far has produced the best fruit. Unequally or unjustly, perhaps, as these laws sometimes operate, and imperfect as they appear to the Idealist, they are, nevertheless, like the highest type of man, the best and most valuable of all that humanity has yet accomplished.

We start, then, with a condition of affairs under which the best interests of the race are promoted, but which inevitably gives wealth to the few. Thus far, accepting conditions as they exist, the situation can be surveyed and pronounced good. The question then arises—and, if the foregoing be correct, it is the only question with which we have to deal: What is the proper mode of administering wealth after the laws upon which civilization is founded have thrown it into the hands of the few? And it is of this great question that I believe I offer the true solution. . . .

There are but three modes in which surplus wealth can be disposed of. It can be left to the families of the decedents; or it can be bequeathed for public purposes; or finally, it can be administered during their lives by its possessors. Under the first and second modes most of the wealth of the world that has reached the few has hitherto been applied. Let us in turn consider each of these modes. The first is the most injudicious. In monarchical countries, the estates and the greatest portion of the wealth are left to the first son, that the vanity of the parent may be gratified by the thought that his name and title are to descend to succeeding generations unimpaired. The condition of this class in Europe today teaches the futility of such hopes or ambitions. The successors have become impoverished through their follies or from the fall in the value of land. Even in Great Britain the strict law of entail has been found inadequate to maintain the status of an hereditary class. Its soil is rapidly passing into the hands of the stranger. Under republican institutions the division of property among the children is much fairer, but the question which forces itself upon thoughtful men in all lands is: Why should men leave great fortunes to their children? If this is done from affection, is it not misguided affection? Observation teaches that, generally speaking, it is not well for the children that they should be so burdened. Neither is it well for the state. Beyond providing for the wife and daughters moderate sources of income, and very moderate allowances indeed, if any, for the sons, men may well hesitate, for it is no longer questionable that great sums bequeathed oftener work more for the injury than for the good of the recipients. . . .

As to the second mode, that of leaving wealth at death for public uses, it may be said that this is only a means for the disposal of wealth, provided a man is content to wait until he is dead before it becomes of much good in the world. Knowledge of the results of legacies bequeathed is not calculated to inspire the brightest hopes of much posthumous good being accomplished. The cases are not few in which the real object sought by the testator is not attained, nor are they few in which his real wishes are thwarted. In many cases the bequests are so used as to become only monuments of his folly. It is well to remember that it requires the exercise of not less ability than that which acquired the wealth to use it so as to be really beneficial to the community. Besides this, it may fairly be said that no man is to be extolled for doing what he cannot help doing, nor is he to be thanked by the community to which he only leaves wealth at death. Men who leave vast sums in this way may fairly be thought men who would not have left it at all, had they been able to take it with them. . . .

The growing disposition to tax more and more heavily large estates left at death is a cheering indication of the growth of a salutary change in public opinion. The State of Pennsylvania now takes—subject to some exceptions—one-tenth of the property left by its citizens. The budget presented in the British Parliament the other day proposes to increase the death duties; and, most significant of all, the new tax is to be a graduated one. Of all forms of taxation, this seems the wisest. Men who continue hoarding great sums all their lives, the proper use of which for public ends would work good to the community, should be made to feel that the community, in the form of the state, cannot thus be deprived of its proper share. By taxing estates heavily at death the state marks its condemnation of the selfish millionaire's unworthy life. . . . This policy would work powerfully to induce the rich man to attend to the administration of wealth during his life, which is the end that society should always have in view as being that by far most fruitful for the people. Nor need it be feared that this policy would sap the root of enterprise and render men less anxious to accumulate, for to the class whose ambition it is to leave great fortunes and be talked about after their death, it will attract even more attention, and, indeed, be a somewhat nobler ambition to have enormous sums paid over to the state from their fortunes.

There remains, then, only one mode of using great fortunes; but in this we have the true antidote for the temporary unequal distribution of wealth, the reconciliation of the rich and the poor—a reign of harmony—another ideal, differing, indeed, from that of the communist in requiring only the further evolution of existing conditions, not the total overthrow of our civilization. It is founded upon the present most intense individualism, and the race is prepared to put it in practice by degrees whenever it pleases. Under its sway we shall have an ideal state, in which the surplus wealth of the few will become, in the best sense, the property of the many, because administered for the common good, and this wealth, passing through the hands of the few, can be made a much more potent force for the elevation of our race than if it had been distributed in small sums to the people themselves. Even the poorest can be made to see this, and to agree that great sums gathered by some of their fellow-citizens and spent for public purposes, from which the masses reap the principal benefit, are more valuable to them than if scattered among themselves in trifling amounts through the course of many years. . . .

This, then, is held to be the duty of the man of wealth: First, to set an example of modest, unostentatious living, shunning display or extravagance; to provide moderately for the legitimate wants of those dependent upon him; and after doing so to consider all surplus revenues which come to him simply as trust funds, which he is called upon to administer, and strictly bound as a matter of duty to administer in the manner which, in his judgment, is best calculated to produce the most beneficial results for the community—the man of wealth thus becoming the mere agent and trustee for his poorer brethren, bringing to their service his superior wisdom, experience, and ability to administer, doing for them better than they would or could do for themselves. . . .

The best uses to which surplus wealth can be put have already been indicated. Those who would administer wisely must, indeed, be wise, for one of the serious obstacles to the improvement of our race is indiscriminate charity. It were better for mankind that the millions of the rich were thrown into the sea than so spent as to encourage the slothful, the drunken, the unworthy. Of every thousand dollars spent in so-called charity today, it is probable that $950 is unwisely spent; so spent, indeed, as to produce the very evils which it proposes to mitigate or cure. A well-known writer of philosophic books admitted the other day that he had given a quarter of a dollar to a man who approached him as he was coming to visit the house of his friend. He knew nothing of the habits of this beggar; knew not the use that would be made of this money, although he had every reason to suspect that it would be spent improperly. This man professed to be a disciple of Herbert Spencer; yet the quarter-dollar given that night will probably work more injury than all the money which its thoughtless donor will ever be able to give in true charity will do good. He only gratified his own feelings, saved himself from annoyance—and this was probably one of the most selfish and very worst actions of his life, for in all respects he is most worthy.

In bestowing charity, the main consideration should be to help those who will help themselves; to provide part of the means by which those who desire to improve may do so; to give those who desire to rise the aids by which they may rise; to assist, but rarely or never to do all. Neither the individual nor the race is improved by alms-giving. Those worthy of assistance, except in rare cases, seldom require assistance. The really valuable men of the race never do, except in cases of accident or sudden change. . . . The best means of benefiting the community is to place within its reach the ladders upon which the aspiring can rise—parks, and means of recreation, by which men are helped in body and mind; works of art, certain to give pleasure and improve the public taste, and public institutions of various kinds, which will improve the general condition of the people—in this manner returning their surplus wealth to the mass of their fellows in the forms best calculated to do them lasting good.

Thus is the problem of rich and poor to be solved. The laws of accumulation will be left free; the laws of distribution free. Individualism will continue, but the millionaire will be but a trustee of the poor; intrusted for a season with a great part of the increased wealth of the community, but administering it for the community far better than it could or would have done for itself. The best minds will thus have reached a stage in the development of the race in which it is clearly seen that there is no mode of disposing of surplus wealth creditable to thoughtful and earnest men into whose hands it flows save by using it year by year for the general good. This day already dawns. But a little while, and although, without incurring the pity of their fellows, men may die sharers in great business enterprises from which their capital cannot be or has not been withdrawn, and is left chiefly at death for public uses, yet the man who dies leaving behind him millions of available wealth, which was his to administer during life, will pass away "unwept, unhonored, and unsung," no matter to what uses he leaves the dross which he cannot take with him. Of such as these the public verdict will then be: "The man who dies thus rich dies disgraced."

Such, in my opinion, is the true Gospel concerning Wealth, obedience to which is destined some day to solve the problem of the Rich and the Poor, and to bring "Peace on earth, among men Good Will."

Chapter 17

FROM FRONTIER TO FACTORY

From the earliest English settlements at Jamestown in 1607 to the end of the nineteenth century the westward movement provided succeeding generations of Americans with a common frontier experience. First the further reaches of the low country along the Atlantic seaboard, then the Allegheny Mountains, the Mississippi River, the Missouri River, the Great Plains, and finally the Rocky Mountains: these were the great frontier lines between virgin wilderness and an ever-expanding American civilization. At all times there were new frontiers to explore, new lands to conquer. And the seeming boundlessness of the West called forth a buoyant American optimism that Jefferson expressed in his vision of ample room within the public domain for the free and unlimited settlement of "our descendants to the hundredth and thousandth generation."

This characteristic optimism proved unfounded. Less than a century after Jefferson purchased the extensive Louisiana Territory in 1803, America's free Western lands were largely exhausted and the frontier had become less reality than myth or memory. The reasons were clear, for at mid-century the discovery of gold in California had inaugurated some four decades of unparalleled westward expansion. Boisterous Forty-Niners were followed by tens and then hundreds of thousands of native pioneers who made the long trek westward in search of free or cheap land under the generous Homestead Act of 1862. And the great transcontinental railroads, seeking first a supply of cheap labor and then settled Western communities to serve, encouraged millions of oppressed Europeans to migrate to the New World, where land was plentiful and the streets were supposedly "paved with gold." As natives and immigrants alike poured into the West the burdens of settlement were immeasurably lightened by the effective, though brutal, elimination of hostile Indian tribes. Meanwhile a booming cattle industry and continuing discoveries of rich gold and silver deposits throughout the Far West lured others who sought fortune. Only the frenzied rise of industry surpassed the sweeping intensity of this last thrust westward. But finally, and inevitably, the West was devoured by its settlers, and early in the 1890's the Superintendent of the Census announced the passing of the frontier. Land was still available in many parts of the nation, but the Great West—familiar to Americans of all generations—had been exhausted.

Few Americans were aware of the Census Report or of its meaning. But Frederick Jackson Turner, a brilliant young scholar at the University of Wisconsin, saw the passing of the frontier as an event of great national importance. And in 1893 he read before the American Historical Association a perceptive and challenging paper on "The Significance of the Frontier in American History." Rejecting historians' traditional view of American civilization as a simple continuation of European beginnings, Turner stated his own frontier thesis briefly but effectively: "The existence of an area of free land, its continuous recession, and the advance of American settlement westward explain American development." To Turner, American ideals and institutions were not the legacy of the Old World. Rather they were the creatures of the psychological and material demands of a uniquely American frontier. It was to the West, then, not to the East or to Europe, that Americans were indebted for their sense of nationality, their instinct for democracy, and particularly their characteristic independence and individualism.

In the 1890's Turner's frontier thesis seemed immediately appropriate. The western frontier had been pushed to its farthest limits. Yet Turner saw traditional American values as largely western in origin. What would be their fate now that the West was gone? In answer there were already unmistakable signs of change in the whole tenor of American life. As the nation soberly turned its energies from the exploitation to the consolidation and conservation of its human and material resources, the boom psychology that had earlier marked the westward movement was gradually supplanted by a more responsible sense of group or social values. And a subtle shift in emphasis from an exuberant and excessive individualism to unfamiliar patterns of collective thought and action was particularly evident. To some these fundamental changes in the American climate of opinion seemed to bear out Turner's thesis. Yet it remains difficult to determine whether the relationship of these changes to the passing of the frontier was causal or coincidental. Indeed, to a considerable extent industrialization and urbanization, which had begun three decades before when westward expansion was at its highest peak, were responsible for this new orientation. For the rapid development of industrial capitalism and the mass movement from rural to urban areas had been accompanied by complex social and economic problems that defied solution within the ideological framework of an older, individualistic agrarianism.

Bitter conflict between capital and labor was the gravest of these problems. Industrialization had already brought great riches to a number of rising businessmen, and ultimately it would bring material well-being to the nation at large. But immediately the wealth of the entrepreneur had been matched only by the growing impoverishment and insecurity of the workingman. Business profits and dividends had increased prodigiously, but wages remained pitifully low; large industrial combinations had limited competition to make capital investments secure, but workers continuously faced unemployment incidental to technological improvement and to depression; industry had enjoyed the generous favors of government, but Federal and state troops frequently deprived workers of their one weapon against capital, the strike. In short, as the lot of the laborer grew increasingly harsh, progress and poverty seemed inextricably bound together. Still, during this early phase of industrialization the availability of free Western land had served somewhat as a psychological safety valve for the frustrations of factory life, though only an occasional discontented laborer had actually been able to pull up stakes and make his way westward. Now, however, the disappearance of the open frontier shattered even the illusion of choice, compounding labor's difficulties and kindling class conflict, and the 1890's proved to be a nervous and turbulent decade, deeply scarred by unrelenting economic warfare between capital and labor.

Earlier, of course, there had been important, though generally confused and inadequate efforts to organize the growing armies of labor on a national scale. Solidarity amongst workingmen had not been achieved, but these first union experiences and failures provided the later labor movement important lessons. In 1866, under the impetus of rising prices and lagging wages, the National Labor Union had consolidated various national trade unions into one great federation designed to promote social and political reform. Large numbers of workers were attracted at first; the delegates to the 1868 convention represented 600,000 members. But its loose organization and vague, general efforts at reform did not meet the immediate needs of overworked and under-paid laborers. And in 1872 the National Labor Union formally deserted its trade-union orientation when its leaders formed the National Labor Reform party and entered national politics. For the next decade and a half American labor was represented by the Noble Order of the Knights of Labor. Highly centralized, emphasizing industrial rather than trade unionism, and embracing all members of the working class in one big union, the new organization grew rapidly, and in 1886 membership totaled 700,000. For a number of years the Knights proved to be a powerful force in American life, particularly as an articulate pressure group. Ultimately, however, overcentralization, confusion between immediate economic objectives and utopian reforms, and conflicting interests between skilled and unskilled workers led to the Knights' downfall. But in the late 1880's the American Federation of Labor stood ready to carry on labor's battles. Learning bitter lessons from its forerunners, the new union maintained organizational authority and responsibility without overcentralization, confined its membership generally to skilled workers, eschewed politics except to reward its friends and punish its enemies, and concentrated on immediate objectives such as higher wages, shorter hours, and better working conditions. Steadily and consistently doing battle to win for the workingman a larger and fairer share of industrial America's vast wealth, under the energetic leadership of Samuel Gompers the Federation quickly emerged as labor's leading champion.

By the 1890's American labor had yet to win its major battles. Bringing to bear every weapon at its disposal—the lockout, the "yellow-dog" contract, the blacklist, strike-breaking troops or armed thugs, the injunction—industry still bitterly fought labor's right to bargain collectively and to strike. In the bloody Homestead strike against the Carnegie Steel Company in 1892, when management used Pinkerton detectives to break the grip of the union, and in the Pullman strike in 1894, when injunctions and Federal troops destroyed the valiant efforts of Eugene V. Debs' American Railway Union, labor lost its most violent encounters with organized capital. Yet industry's victories proved futile—or worse. For they not only spurred labor on to greater organizational efforts, but they also impressed fair-minded and frightened Americans with the need for collective social action to redress the growing imbalance between capital and labor, between rich and poor. Whether fundamentally the cause was to be found in the passing of the frontier and the Great West, or in the development of industry and the rise of the city, it was obvious that the free economic opportunities of an earlier America were fast disappearing. Now most middle-class Americans seemed determined to recapture economic democracy and secure social justice for all, though to do so they had to abandon older ideas of individual self-help and look to government for direction and even control. By the turn of the new century the nation was obviously preparing to commit itself as enthusiastically to new conceptions of social responsibility and general welfare as earlier it had espoused the principles of laissez-faire.

The Significance of the Frontier in American History,* *Frederick Jackson Turner, 1893*

In a recent bulletin of the Superintendent of the Census for 1890 appear these significant words: "Up to and including 1880 the country had a frontier of settlement, but at present the unsettled area has been so broken into by isolated bodies of settlement that there can hardly be said to be a frontier line. In the discussion of its extent, its westward movement, etc., it can not, therefore, any longer have a place in the census reports." This brief official statement marks the closing of a great historic movement. Up to our own day American history has been in a large degree the history of the colonization of the Great West. The existence of an area of free land, its continuous recession, and the advance of American settlement westward, explain American development.

Behind institutions, behind constitutional forms and modifications, lie the vital forces that call these organs into life and shape them to meet changing conditions. The peculiarity of American institutions is the fact that they have been compelled to adapt themselves to the changes of an expanding people—to the changes involved in crossing a con-

* From *The Frontier in American History* by Frederick Jackson Turner. Copyright, 1920, by Frederick J. Turner. Copyright, 1948, by Caroline Mae S. Turner. Used by permission of Henry Holt and Company.

tinent, in winning a wilderness, and in developing at each area of this progress out of the primitive economic and political conditions of the frontier into the complexity of city life. Said Calhoun in 1817, "We are great, and rapidly—I was about to say fearfully—growing!" So saying, he touched the distinguishing feature of American life. All peoples show development; the germ theory of politics has been sufficiently emphasized. In the case of most nations, however, the development has occurred in a limited area; and if the nation has expanded, it has met other growing peoples whom it has conquered. But in the case of the United States we have a different phenomenon. Limiting our attention to the Atlantic coast, we have the familiar phenomenon of the evolution of institutions in a limited area, such as the rise of representative government; the differentiation of simple colonial governments into complex organs; the progress from primitive industrial society, without division of labor, up to manufacturing civilization. But we have in addition to this a recurrence of the process of evolution in each western area reached in the process of expansion. Thus American development has exhibited not merely advance along a single line, but a return to primitive conditions on a continually advancing frontier line, and a new development for that area. American social development has been continually beginning over again on the frontier. This perennial rebirth, this fluidity of American life, this expansion westward with its new opportunities, its continuous touch with the simplicity of primitive society, furnish the forces dominating American character. The true point of view in the history of this nation is not the Atlantic coast, it is the Great West. Even the slavery struggle . . . occupies its important place in American history because of its relation to westward expansion.

In this advance, the frontier is the outer edge of the wave, the meeting point between savagery and civilization. Much has been written about the frontier from the point of view of border warfare and the chase, but as a field for the serious study of the economist and the historian it has been neglected.

The American frontier is sharply distinguished from the European frontier, a fortified boundary line running through dense populations. The most significant thing about the American frontier is, that it lies at the hither edge of free land. In the census reports it is treated as the margin of that settlement which has a density of two or more to the square mile. The term is an elastic one, and for our purposes does not need sharp definition. We shall consider the whole frontier belt, including the Indian country and the outer margin of the "settled area" of the census reports.

This paper will make no attempt to treat the subject exhaustively; its aim is simply to call attention to the frontier as a fertile field for investigation, and to suggest some of the problems which arise in connection with it.

In the settlement of America we have to observe how European life entered the continent, and how America modified and developed that life and reacted on Europe. Our early history is the study of European germs developing in an American environment. Too exclusive attention has been paid by institutional students to the Germanic origins, too little to the American factors. The frontier is the line of most rapid and effective Americanization. The wilderness masters the colonist . . . at the frontier the environment is at first too strong for the man. He must accept the conditions which it furnishes, or perish, and so he fits himself into the Indian clearings and follows the Indian trails. Little by little he transforms the wilderness, but the outcome is not the old Europe, not simply the development of Germanic germs. . . . The fact is, that here is a new product that is American. At first, the frontier was the Atlantic coast. It was the frontier of Europe in a very real sense. Moving westward, the frontier became more and more American. As successive terminal moraines result from successive glaciations, so each frontier leaves its traces behind it, and when it becomes a settled area the region still partakes of the frontier characteristics. Thus the advance of the frontier has meant a steady movement away from the influence of Europe, a steady growth of independence on American lines. And to study this advance, the men who grow up under these conditions, and the political, economic, and social results of it, is to study the really American part of our history. . . .

In these successive frontiers we find natural boundary lines which have served to mark and to affect the characteristics of the frontiers, namely: the "fall line"; the Allegheny Mountains; the Mississippi; the Missouri where its direction approximates north and south; the line of the arid lands, approximately the ninety-ninth meridian; and the Rocky Mountains. The fall line marked the frontier of the seventeenth century; the Alleghenies that of the eighteenth; the Mississippi that of the first quarter of the nineteenth; the Missouri that of the middle of this century (omitting the California movement); and the belt of the Rocky Mountains and the arid tract, the present frontier. Each was won by a series of Indian wars.

At the Atlantic frontier one can study the germs of processes repeated at each successive frontier. We have the complex European life sharply precipitated by the wilderness into the simplicity of primitive conditions. The first frontier had to meet its Indian question, its question of the disposition of the public domain, of the means of intercourse with older settlements, of the extension of political organization, of religious and educational activity. And the settlement of these and similar questions for one frontier served as a guide for the next. The American student needs not to go to the "prim little townships of Sleswick" for illustrations of the law of continuity and development. For example, he may study the origin of our land policies in the colonial land policy; he may see how the system grew by adapting the statutes to the customs of the successive frontiers. He may see how the mining experience in the lead regions of Wisconsin, Illinois, and Iowa was applied to the mining laws of the Sierras, and how our Indian policy has been a series of experimentations on successive frontiers. Each tier of new States has found in the older ones material for its constitutions. Each frontier has made similar contributions to American characters. . . .

But with all these similarities there are essential differences, due to the place element and the time element. . . .

It would be a work worth the historian's labors to mark these various frontiers and in detail compare one with another. Not only would there result a more adequate conception of American development and characteristics, but invaluable additions would be made to the history of society.

Loria, the Italian economist, has urged the study of colonial life as an aid in understanding the stages of European development, affirming that colonial settlement is for economic science what the mountain is for geology, bringing to light primitive stratifications. "America," he says, "has the key to the historical enigma which Europe has sought for centuries in vain, and the land which has no history reveals luminously the course of universal history." There is much truth in this. The United States lies like a huge page in the history of society. Line by line as we read this continental page from West to East we find the record of social evolution. It begins with the Indian and the hunter; it goes on to tell of the disintegration of savagery by the entrance of the trader, the pathfinder of civilization; we read the annals of the pastoral stage in ranch life; the exploitation of the soil by the raising of unrotated crops of corn and wheat in sparsely settled farming communities; the intensive culture of the denser farm settlement; and finally the manufacturing organization with city and factory system. This page is familiar to the student of census statistics, but how little of it has been used by our historians. Particularly in eastern States this page is a palimpsest. What is now a manufacturing State was in an earlier decade an area of intensive farming. Earlier yet it had been a wheat area, and still earlier the "range" had attracted the cattle-herder. Thus Wisconsin, now developing manufacture, is a State with varied agricultural interests. But earlier it was given over to almost exclusive grain-raising, like North Dakota at the present time.

. . . Having now roughly outlined the various kinds of frontiers, . . . we may next inquire what were the influences on the East and on the Old World. . . .

First, we note that the frontier promoted the formation of a composite nationality for the American people. The coast was preponderantly English, but the later tides of continental immigration flowed across to the free lands. This was the case from the early colonial days. The Scotch-Irish and the Palatine Germans, or "Pennsylvania Dutch," furnished the dominant element in the stock of the colonial frontier. With these peoples were also the freed indented servants, or redemptioners, who at the expiration of their time of service passed to the frontier. . . . Very generally these redemptioners were of non-English stock. In the crucible of the frontier the immigrants were Americanized, liberated, and fused into a mixed race, English in neither nationality nor characteristics. The process has gone on from the early days to our own. Burke and other writers in the middle of the eighteenth century believed that Pennsylvania was "threatened with the danger of being wholly foreign in language, manners and perhaps even inclinations." The German and Scotch-Irish elements in the frontier of the South were only less great. In the middle of the present century the German element in Wisconsin was already so considerable that leading publicists looked to the creation of a German state out of the commonwealth by concentrating their colonization. Such examples teach us to beware of misinterpreting the fact that there is a common English speech in America into a belief that the stock is also English.

In another way the advance of the frontier decreased our dependence on England. The coast, particularly of the South, lacked diversified industries, and was dependent on England for the bulk of its supplies. In the South there was even a dependence on the Northern colonies for articles of food. . . . Before long the frontier created a demand for merchants. As it retreated from the coast it became less and less possible for England to bring her supplies directly to the consumer's wharfs, and carry away staple crops, and staple crops began to give way to diversified agriculture for a time. The effect of this phase of the frontier upon the northern section is perceived when we realize how the advance of the frontier aroused seaboard cities like Boston, New York, and Baltimore to engage in rivalry for what

Washington called "the extensive and valuable trade of a rising empire."

The legislation which most developed the powers of the national government, and played the largest part in its activity, was conditioned on the frontier. Writers have discussed the subjects of tariff, land, and internal improvement, as subsidiary to the slavery question. . . . This is a wrong perspective. The pioneer needed the goods of the coast, and so the grand series of internal improvement and railroad legislation began, with potent nationalizing effects. Over internal improvements occurred great debates, in which grave constitutional questions were discussed. Sectional groupings appear in the votes, profoundly significant for the historian. Loose construction increased as the nation marched westward. But the West was not content with bringing the farm to the factory. Under the lead of Clay—"Harry of the West" —protective tariffs were passed, with the cry of bringing the factory to the farm. The disposition of the public lands was a third important subject of national legislation influenced by the frontier. . . .

It is safe to say that the legislation with regard to land, tariff, and internal improvements—the American system of the nationalizing Whig party—was conditioned on frontier ideas and needs. But it was not merely in legislative action that the frontier worked against the sectionalism of the coast. The economic and social characteristics of the frontier worked against sectionalism. The men of the frontier had closer resemblances to the Middle region than to either of the other sections. Pennsylvania had been the seed-plot of frontier emigration, and, although she passed on her settlers along the Great Valley into the west of Virginia and the Carolinas, yet the industrial society of these Southern frontiersmen was always more like that of the Middle region than like that of the tide water portion of the South, which later came to spread its industrial type throughout the South.

The Middle region, entered by New York harbor, was an open door to all Europe. The tide water part of the South represented typical Englishmen, modified by a warm climate and servile labor, and living in baronial fashion on great plantations; New England stood for a special English movement, Puritanism. The Middle region was less English than the other sections. It had a wide mixture of nationalities, a varied society, the mixed town and county system of local government, a varied economic life, many religious sects. In short, it was a region mediating between New England and the South, and the East and the West. It represented that composite nationality which the contemporary United States exhibits, that juxtaposition of non-English groups, occupying a valley or a little settlement, and presenting reflections of the map of Europe in their variety. It was democratic and non-sectional, if not national; "easy, tolerant, and contented"; rooted strongly in material prosperity. It was typical of the modern United States. It was least sectional, not only because it lay between North and South, but also because with no barriers to shut out its frontiers from its settled region, and with a system of connecting waterways, the Middle region mediated between East and West as well as between North and South. Thus it became the typically American region. Even the New Englander, who was shut out from the frontier by the Middle region, tarrying in New York or Pennsylvania on his westward march, lost the acuteness of his sectionalism on the way.

. . . This nationalizing tendency . . . transformed the democracy of Jefferson into the national republicanism of Monroe and the democracy of Andrew Jackson. The West of the War of 1812, the West of Clay, and Benton and Harrison, and Andrew Jackson, shut off by the Middle States and the mountains from the coast sections, had a solidarity of its own with national tendencies. On the tide of the Father of Waters, North and South met and mingled into a nation. Interstate migration went steadily on—a process of cross-fertilization of ideas and institutions. The fierce struggle of the sections over slavery on the western frontier does not diminish the truth of this statement; it proves the truth of it. Slavery was a sectional trait that would not down, but in the West it could not remain sectional. It was the greatest of frontiersmen who declared: "I believe this Government can not endure permanently half slave and half free. It will become all of one thing or all of the other." Nothing works for nationalism like intercourse within the nation. Mobility of population is death to localism, and the western frontier worked irresistibly in unsettling population. The effect reached back from the frontier and affected profoundly the Atlantic coast and even the Old World.

But the most important effect of the frontier has been in the promotion of democracy here and in Europe. As has been indicated, the frontier is productive of individualism. Complex society is precipitated by the wilderness into a kind of primitive organization based on the family. The tendency is anti-social. It produces antipathy to control, and particularly to any direct control. The tax-gatherer is viewed as a representative of oppression. . . . Frontier conditions prevalent in the colonies are important factors in the explanation of the American Revolution, where individual liberty was sometimes confused with absence of all effective government. The same conditions aid in explaining the difficulty of instituting a strong government in the period of the confederacy. The frontier individualism has from the beginning promoted democracy.

The frontier States that came into the Union in the first quarter of a century of its existence came in with democratic suffrage provisions, and had reactive effects of the highest importance upon the older States whose peoples were being attracted there. An extension of the franchise became essential. It was *western* New York that forced an extension of suffrage in the constitutional convention of that State in 1821; and it was *western* Virginia that compelled the tide water region to put a more liberal suffrage provision in the constitution framed in 1830, and to give to the frontier region a more nearly proportionate representation with the tide water aristocracy. The rise of democracy as an effective force in the nation came in with western preponderance under Jackson and William Henry Harrison, and it meant the triumph of the frontier—with all of its good and with all of its evil elements. . . .

So long as free land exists, the opportunity for a competency exists, and economic power secures political power. But the democracy born of free land, strong in selfishness and individualism, intolerant of administrative experience and education, and pressing individual liberty beyond its proper bounds, has its dangers as well as its benefits. Individualism in America has allowed a laxity in regard to governmental affairs which has rendered possible the spoils system and all the manifest evils that follow from the lack of a highly developed civic spirit. In this connection may be noted also the influence of frontier conditions in permitting lax business honor, inflated paper currency and wild-cat banking. The colonial and revolutionary frontier was the region whence emanated many of the worst forms of an evil currency. The West in the War of 1812 repeated the phenomenon on the frontier of that day, while the speculation and wild-cat banking of the period of the crisis of 1837 occurred on the new frontier belt of the next tier of States. Thus each one of the periods of lax financial integrity coincides with periods when a new set of frontier communities had arisen, and coincides in area with these successive frontiers, for the most part. The recent Populist agitation is a case in point. Many a State that now declines any connection with the tenets of the Populists, itself adhered to such ideas in an earlier stage of the development of the State. A primitive society can hardly be expected to show the intelligent appreciation of the complexity of business interests in a developed society. The continual recurrence of these areas of paper money agitation is another evidence that the frontier can be isolated and studied as a factor in American history of the highest importance. . . .

From the conditions of frontier life came intellectual traits of profound importance. The works of travelers along each frontier from colonial days onward describe certain common traits, and these traits have, while softening down, still persisted as survivals in the place of their origin, even when a higher social organization succeeded. The result is that to the frontier the American intellect owes its striking characteristics. That coarseness and strength combined with acuteness and inquisitiveness; that practical, inventive turn of mind, quick to find expedients; that masterful grasp of material things, lacking in the artistic but powerful to effect great ends; that restless, nervous energy; that dominant individualism, working for good and for evil, and withal that buoyancy and exuberance which comes with freedom—these are traits of the frontier, or traits called out elsewhere because of the existence of the frontier. Since the days when the fleet of Columbus sailed into the waters of the New World, America has been another name for opportunity, and the people of the United States have taken their tone from the incessant expansion which has not only been open but has even been forced upon them. He would be a rash prophet who would assert that the expansive character of American life has now entirely ceased. Movement has been its dominant fact, and, unless this training has no effect upon a people, the American energy will continually demand a wider field for its exercise. But never again will such gifts of free land offer themselves. For a moment, at the frontier, the bonds of custom are broken and unrestraint is triumphant. There is no *tabula rasa*. The stubborn American environment is there with its imperious summons to accept its conditions; the inherited ways of doing things are also there; and yet, in spite of environment, and in spite of custom, each frontier did indeed furnish a new field of opportunity, a gate of escape from the bondage of the past; and freshness, and confidence, and scorn of older society, impatience of its restraints and its ideas, and indifference to its lessons, have accompanied the frontier. What the Mediterranean Sea was to the Greeks, breaking the bond of custom, offering new experiences, calling out new institutions and activities, that, and more, the ever retreating frontier has been to the United States directly, and to the nations of Europe more remotely. And now, four centuries from the discovery of America, at the end of a hundred years of life under the Constitution, the frontier has gone, and with its going has closed the first period of American history.

Chapter 18

GRASS-ROOTS REBELLION

Although industrial capitalism and its laissez-faire business ethic largely dominated American life and thought throughout the last half of the nineteenth century, protest and nonconformity were not unknown. Indeed, America had hardly embarked upon her great Age of Enterprise when reformers and militant protesters emerged to challenge her formidable new overlords, the mighty captains of industry and their political henchmen. But protest was amorphous and ill-defined, and as the political and economic abuses that accompanied industrialization became more pronounced, Americans were confronted with a bewildering array of reform movements that in principle and practice differed radically among themselves. At one extreme, under the leadership of E. L. Godkin of the *Nation* and George William Curtis of *Harper's Weekly,* a small group of aristocratic eastern intellectuals devoted themselves almost entirely to immediate political reform, proposing simply an extensive civil service and high public morals to redress the rank corruption that permeated every level of American government. Though appalled at the abject materialism of America's new business civilization, these good-government leaders (contemptuous politicos dubbed them "goo-goos") seemed totally unaware of the close connection between political corruption and the abusive business practices of unfettered, competitive industrialism, and they inveterately shunned any suggestion of governmental interference in the economic life of the nation. At the opposite extreme were groups of radical reformers who as consistently refused to work within the existing framework of laissez-faire industrial capitalism. Thus Marxian Socialists, Single-Taxers who championed the confiscatory single tax on unearned land values that Henry George urged in his widely read *Progress and Poverty,* and Nationalists who were inspired by Edward Bellamy's popular novel of utopian totalitarianism, *Looking Backward,* all proposed basic economic reforms that would utilize the full coercive power of the State to root out the poverty, inequality, and insecurity that had been fostered by America's economic revolution.

But the most significant and widespread area of discontent and protest in the post-Civil War period was agrarian in origin and orientation, and the American farmer seemed determined to steer a middle course between "goo-goos" and radicals. Like the civil service reformer, the farmer avoided long-range considerations of social planning and control, and he had no direct purpose to abandon free enterprise capitalism. Like his radical contemporaries, however, he was fully prepared to attain immediate objectives through State action, and throughout the period his angry cries for governmental intervention to secure economic and political reform seriously threatened and frightened the industrial ruling class.

Nor were the farmer's demands for reform without cause. Constantly subjected to the vicissitudes of drought and storm —and market—in many ways the farm population was even more deprived than the propertyless workers who crowded into the city. For as the farmer continued his barren, isolated, and culturally impoverished life, rural areas lagged far behind in the enjoyment of a higher standard of living, and the benefits of the industrial revolution seemed largely confined to the rapidly growing cities. Agriculture suffered a particularly severe depression during the thirty years before 1897, and the farmer's economic situation had grown increasingly more desperate as his costs mounted and prices for farm products tumbled. Cotton that cost 6 or 7 cents per pound to produce sold for 4 or 5 cents, while wheat that had brought $1.45 per bushel at the end of the Civil War brought 49 cents thirty years later, and corn that sold for 75 cents in 1869 fell to 28 cents in 1889. Crushed between minimal farm prices and the intolerable burden of debts assumed in prosperous, expansive years, it was the oppressed and disgruntled farmer who spearheaded America's crusade for reform.

Fundamentally, declining farm prices and income were due to a vastly increased competition of farm products on the world market and to the overexpansion of agriculture that had taken place during the Civil War. In assaying his plight, however, the farmer almost invariably attributed hard times to an inadequate money supply and to the immediate, tangible abuses he suffered at the hands of his economic masters, the railroads and the banks. Against the railroads his grievances were real enough. The carriers not only charged the farmer exorbitant rates that frequently took the value of one bushel of wheat or corn to pay the freight on another, but through rebates and other secret agreements they viciously discriminated against him in favor of larger and wealthier shippers. The bankers, too, as money became scarcer, as interest rates on loans and mortgages soared, and as foreclosures multiplied, seemed the farmer's mortal enemies. As one Nebraska farm editor lamented, "We have three crops—corn, freight rates, and interest. The farmers farm the land, and the businessmen farm the farmers."

These, then, were the embattled farmer's "devils," and the Granger laws of the 1870's and 1880's represented his early attempts to wield the power of government against their evil practices. Commonly known as the Grange, the Patrons of Husbandry had been founded in 1867 primarily as a social organization. But by the 1870's, when its members numbered one and a half million, agrarian distress and discontent had been so intensified that inevitably the Granger movement assumed political proportions. Rousing themselves to enormous political activity, in many Western states the Grangers elected large delegations of farm representatives to state legislatures that now for the first time subjected the railroads to stringent public control. Typically the Granger laws established state railroad commissions to set fair rates and to abolish discrimination between small and large shippers, and for some years—in 1876 the Supreme Court upheld their validity in Munn v. Illinois—they encountered no insurmountable constitutional barriers. But in the famous Wabash case of 1886 the Supreme Court reversed its earlier position and initiated a series of judicial decisions that for all practical purposes ended effective state regulation. Holding that the railroads were interstate enterprises beyond state control, and that state regulatory acts violated the "due process" clause of the 14th Amendment ("No State shall . . . deprive any person of life, liberty, or property, without due process of law"), in case after case the judges declared against the constitutionality of Granger legislation. By the 1890's, then, through severe limitations on the states' "police" powers, the high court had effectually nullified two decades of agrarian efforts to secure economic democracy.

Rebuffed by a conservative judiciary in these first steps towards relief and reform, the embattled farmer turned next to the national government. In response to a great wave of indignation that followed the Wabash case, Congress passed the Interstate Commerce Act of 1887, outlawing such railroad abuses as rebates, preferential rates, and pooling agreements that eliminated effective competition among the carriers. At the same time an Interstate Commerce Commission was created to investigate and prosecute violations of the new law. Then in 1890, in part as a further concession to farmers who attributed their higher living costs to monopolies and trusts, the Sherman Anti-Trust Act declared illegal "every contract, combination . . . or conspiracy in restraint of trade." Superficially the farmers seemed to have accomplished a great deal, for Congress had at least filled the legislative void left by the Court's denial of state powers and had taken an important initial step towards Federal regulation of industry. Yet, because of continued judicial opposition and legislative as well as administrative indifference, both of these acts proved ineffectual. Not only did Congress fail to grant to the Interstate Commerce Commission the essential power to fix rates, but consistently adverse judicial interpretations of the law tended to restrict whatever statutory power the Commission did possess. Similarly, enforcement of the Sherman Act was hampered by a hostile judiciary—in 1895 the Supreme Court ruled that the Sugar Trust's control of 95% of the nation's sugar refining did *not* constitute a violation of the anti-trust law—and particularly by the lack of any real enthusiasm on the part of Democratic and Republican politicians alike for a vigorous campaign against the trusts.

Essentially the leaders of both major parties were unsympathetic to agrarian needs and demands, and the farmer quickly concluded that little was to be accomplished within the framework of a do-nothing two-party system. Quadrennially the parties performed their traditional political rituals: "ins" solemnly met to "point with pride" at their record in office, while "outs" noisily assembled to "view with alarm" the same four years. But basic issues were only occasionally debated and even the personalities around whom the heated campaigns raged were generally undistinguished and lacking in important political principle. Thus the stage seemed set for a party of revolt, and for some years before the decisive election of 1896 angry Western and Southern farmers rallied together under the banner of Populism to "raise less corn and more Hell." Earlier third party movements, such as the Greenback Party, had failed to make any appreciable impression on American political life, but these first local Populist groups achieved considerable success in the state and Congressional elections of 1890. And on July 4, 1892, their representatives met at Omaha, Nebraska, to organize a national People's party and to formulate the decisive Omaha platform that, appropriate to the date, was to serve as the farmer's Declaration of Independence.

Polling more than a million popular votes, and obtaining 22 votes in the electoral college for General James B. Weaver of Iowa, the Populist party made a spectacular showing in the Presidential election of 1892. In the off-year elections of 1894, when a widespread depression that followed the

Panic of 1893 had convinced even greater numbers of dissatisfied farmers and laborers to desert the conservative older parties, the Populists repeated these astounding triumphs. Obviously the Populist Revolt had attained serious proportions, and the nation anxiously awaited the Presidential election of 1896, when Democrats and Republicans must either succumb to agrarian and labor demands for reform or battle to preserve the *status quo*. The issue was clear-cut, for protest had already been largely focused on the money question. Since the Civil War, debtor farmers had persistently advocated an expanded money supply as an inflationary measure to raise farm prices and relieve farm distress. Now the farmer almost entirely subordinated his other demands to the cry for "free silver": currency expansion through the free and unlimited coinage of silver as well as gold.

Thoroughly dominated by conservative "hard-money" men, in 1896 the Republicans nominated Governor William McKinley of Ohio for the Presidency, and adopted a platform that defiantly took up the Populist challenge, declaring unequivocally for the Gold Standard and for the entire economic and political structure to which agrarian and labor dissenters took such violent exception. The Democrats, too, had their share of conservative "Gold Bugs," among whom they numbered the incumbent President, Grover Cleveland. But when the party met to choose a platform and a Presidential candidate, it was controlled instead by reform groups who repudiated Cleveland, adopted much of the Populist platform of 1892, and rallied around the magnificent William Jennings Bryan, whose stirring "Cross of Gold" speech helped win the party to the cause of silver and the Democratic nomination for the "Boy Orator." Later the Populists also nominated Bryan as their candidate and the choice before the American people was clear: McKinley, the "advance agent of prosperity," was the candidate of business and conservatism, while Bryan spoke for the farmer, the laborer, and the underprivileged classes generally in their efforts to put the Government of the United States once again at the service of all of the American people.

Supported by most of the nation's great industries under the generalship of the fabulous Mark ("Dollar Mark") Hanna, McKinley won in an exceedingly bitter campaign that was marred by vicious attacks upon Bryan and his followers as "fanatics," "communists," and "revolutionaries." Of course Populism was not "revolutionary" in Marxian terms, for the farmer had no intention of destroying fundamental American political and economic institutions. Indeed, within a few decades both major parties had adopted a substantial portion of the Populist demands and the threat of a formidable third party disappeared altogether. Yet in 1896 a successful Bryan would have made strenuous efforts to alter the tone and orientation of the national government from an industrial to an agrarian bias. Besides, the Populist insistence that government extend its authority to protect the interests of all the people had a strong influence on the development of contemporary conceptions of the proper role of the State. And, although farm agitation diminished after 1897 with the return of prosperity and the rise of farm prices, ultimately the real significance of the Populist Revolt can best be measured in terms of the important inroads the social, economic, and political reforms of the twentieth century have made upon the abuses against which the farmer battled so desperately in the last decades of the nineteenth century.

The Populist Party Platform, *1892*

Assembled upon the 116th anniversary of the Declaration of Independence, the People's Party of America, in their first national convention, invoking upon their action the blessing of Almighty God, put forth in the name and on behalf of the people of this country, the following preamble and declaration of principles:

PREAMBLE

The conditions which surround us best justify our co-operation; we meet in the midst of a nation brought to the verge of moral, political, and material ruin. Corruption dominates the ballot-box, the legislatures, the Congress, and touches even the ermine of the bench. The people are demoralized; most of the States have been compelled to isolate the voters at the polling places to prevent universal intimidation and bribery. The newspapers are largely subsidized or muzzled, public opinion silenced, business prostrated, homes covered with mortgages, labor impoverished, and the land concentrated in the hands of capitalists. The urban workmen are denied the right to organize for self-protection, imported pauperized labor beats down their wages, a hireling standing army, unrecognized by our laws, is established to shoot them down, and they are rapidly degenerating into European conditions. The fruits of the toil of millions are boldly stolen to build up colossal fortunes for a few, unprecedented in the history of mankind; and the possessors of those, in turn, despise the Republic and endanger liberty. From the same prolific womb of governmental injustice we breed the two great classes—tramps and millionaires.

The national power to create money is appropriated to enrich bondholders; a vast public debt payable in legal tender currency has been funded into gold-bearing bonds, thereby adding millions to the burdens of the people.

Silver, which has been accepted as coin since the dawn of history, has been demonetized to add to the purchasing power of gold by decreasing the value of all forms of property as well as human labor, and the supply of currency is purposely abridged to fatten usurers, bankrupt enterprise, and enslave industry. A vast conspiracy against mankind has been organized on two continents, and it is rapidly taking possession of the world. If not met and overthrown at once it forebodes terrible social convulsions, the destruction of civilization, or the establishment of an absolute despotism.

We have witnessed for more than a quarter of a century the struggles of the two great political parties for power and plunder, while grievous wrongs have been inflicted upon the suffering people. We charge that the controlling influences dominating both these parties have permitted the existing dreadful conditions to develop without serious effort to prevent or restrain them. Neither do they now promise us any substantial reform. They have agreed together to ignore, in the coming campaign, every issue but one. They propose to drown the outcries of a plundered people with the uproar of a sham battle over the tariff, so that capitalists, corporations, national banks, rings, trusts, watered stock, the demonetization of silver and the oppressions of the usurers may all be lost sight of. They propose to sacrifice our homes, lives, and children on the altar of mammon; to destroy the multitude in order to secure corruption funds from the millionaires.

Assembled on the anniversary of the birthday of the nation, and filled with the spirit of the grand general and chief who established our independence, we seek to restore the government of the Republic to the hands of "the plain people," with which class it originated. We assert our purposes to be identical with the purposes of the National Constitution; to form a more perfect union and establish justice, insure domestic tranquillity, provide for the common defence, promote the general welfare, and secure the blessings of liberty for ourselves and our posterity.

We declare that this Republic can only endure as a free government while built upon the love of the whole people for each other and for the nation; that it cannot be pinned together by bayonets; that the Civil War is over, and that every passion and resentment which grew out of it must die with it, and that we must be in fact, as we are in name, one united brotherhood of free men.

Our country finds itself confronted by conditions for which there is no precedent in the history of the world; our annual agricultural productions amount to billions of dollars in value, which must, within a few weeks or months, be exchanged for billions of dollars' worth of commodities consumed in their production; the existing currency supply is wholly inadequate to make this exchange; the results are falling prices, the formation of combines and rings, the impoverishment of the producing class. We pledge ourselves that if given power we will labor to correct these evils by wise and reasonable legislation, in accordance with the terms of our platform.

We believe that the power of government—in other words, of the people—should be expanded (as in the case of the postal service) as rapidly and as far as the good sense of an intelligent people and the teachings of experience shall justify, to the end that oppression, injustice, and poverty shall eventually cease in the land.

While our sympathies as a party of reform are naturally upon the side of every proposition which will tend to make men intelligent, virtuous, and temperate, we nevertheless regard these questions, important as they are, as secondary to the great issues now pressing for solution, and upon which not only our individual prosperity but the very existence of free institutions depend; and we ask all men to first help us to determine whether we are to have a republic to administer before we differ as to the conditions upon which it is to be administered, believing that the forces of reform this day organized will never cease to move forward until every wrong is remedied and equal rights and equal privileges securely established for all the men and women of this country.

PLATFORM

We declare, therefore:

First.—That the union of the labor forces of the United States this day consummated shall be permanent and perpetual; may its spirit enter into all hearts for the salvation of the Republic and the uplifting of mankind.

Second.—Wealth belongs to him who creates it, and every dollar taken from industry without an equivalent is robbery. "If any will not work, neither shall he eat." The interests of rural and civic labor are the same; their enemies are identical.

Third.—We believe that the time has come when the railroad corporations will either own the people or the people must own the railroads, and should the Government enter upon the work of owning and managing all railroads, we should favor an amendment to the Constitution by which all persons engaged in the Government service shall be placed under a civil service regulation of the most rigid character, so as to prevent the increase of the power of the national administration by the use of such additional Government employees.

Finance.—We demand a national currency, safe, sound, and flexible, issued by the general Government only, a full legal tender for all debts, public and private, and that without the use of banking corporations, a just, equitable, and efficient means of distribution direct to the people, at a tax not to exceed 2 per cent per annum, to be provided as set forth in the sub-treasury plan of the Farmers' Alliance, or a better system; also by payments in discharge of its obligations for public improvements.

1. We demand free and unlimited coinage of silver and gold at the present legal ratio of 16 to 1.

2. We demand that the amount of circulating medium be speedily increased to not less than $50 per capita.

3. We demand a graduated income tax.

4. We believe that the money of the country should be kept as much as possible in the hands of the people, and hence we demand that all State and national revenues shall be limited to the necessary expenses of the Government, economically and honestly administered.

5. We demand that postal savings banks be established by the Government for the safe deposit of the earnings of the people and to facilitate exchange.

Transportation.—Transportation being a means of exchange and a public necessity, the Government should own and operate the railroads in the interest of the people. The telegraph, telephone, like the post-office system, being a necessity for the transmission of news, should be owned and operated by the Government in the interest of the people.

Land.—The land, including all the natural resources of wealth, is the heritage of the people, and should not be monopolized for speculative purposes, and alien ownership of land should be prohibited. All land now held by railroads and other corporations in excess of their actual needs, and all lands now owned by aliens should be reclaimed by the Government and held for actual settlers only.

EXPRESSION OF SENTIMENTS

Your Committee on Platform and Resolutions beg leave unanimously to report the following:

WHEREAS, Other questions have been presented for our consideration, we hereby submit the following, not as a part of the Platform of the People's Party, but as resolutions expressive of the sentiment of this Convention:

1. *Resolved,* That we demand a free ballot and a fair count in all elections, and pledge ourselves to secure it to every legal voter without Federal intervention, through the adoption by the States of the unperverted Australian or secret ballot system.

2. *Resolved,* That the revenue derived from a graduated income tax should be applied to the reduction of the burden of taxation now levied upon the domestic industries of this country.

3. *Resolved,* That we pledge our support to fair and liberal pensions to ex-Union soldiers and sailors.

4. *Resolved,* That we condemn the fallacy of protecting American labor under the present system, which opens our ports to the pauper and criminal classes of the world and crowds out our wage-earners; and we denounce the present ineffective laws against contract labor, and demand the further restriction of undesirable emigration.

5. *Resolved,* That we cordially sympathize with the efforts of organized workingmen to shorten the hours of labor, and demand a rigid enforcement of the existing eight-hour law on Government work, and ask that a penalty clause be added to the said law.

6. *Resolved,* That we regard the maintenance of a large standing army of mercenaries, known as the Pinkerton system, as a menace to our liberties, and we demand its abolition; and we condemn the recent invasion of the Territory of Wyoming by the hired assassins of plutocracy, assisted by Federal officers.

7. *Resolved,* That we commend to the favorable consideration of the people and the reform press the legislative system known as the initiative and referendum.

8. *Resolved,* That we favor a constitutional provision limiting the office of President and Vice-President to one term, and providing for the election of Senators of the United States by a direct vote of the people.

9. *Resolved,* That we oppose any subsidy or national aid to any private corporation for any purpose.

10. *Resolved,* That this convention sympathizes with the Knights of Labor and their righteous contest with the tyrannical combine of clothing manufacturers of Rochester, and declare it to be the duty of all who hate tyranny and oppression to refuse to purchase the goods made by the said manufacturers, or to patronize any merchants who sell such goods.

The "Cross of Gold" Speech,*
William Jennings Bryan, 1896

I would be presumptuous, indeed, to present myself against the distinguished gentlemen to whom you have listened if this were a mere measuring of abilities; but this is not a contest between persons. The humblest citizen in all the land, when clad in the armor of a righteous cause, is stronger than all the hosts of error. I come to speak to you in defense of a cause as holy as the cause of liberty—the cause of humanity.

When this debate is concluded, a motion will be made to lay upon the table the resolution offered in commendation of the administration, and also the resolution offered in condemnation of the administration. We object to bringing this question down to the level of persons. The individual is but an atom; he is born, he acts, he dies; but principles are eternal; and this has been a contest over a principle.

Never before in the history of this country has there been witnessed such a contest as that through which we have just passed. Never before in the history of American politics has a great issue been fought out as this issue has been, by the voters of a great party. On the fourth of March 1895 a few Democrats, most of them members of Congress, issued an address to the Democrats of the nation, asserting that the money question was the paramount issue of the hour; declaring that a majority of the Democratic party had the right to control the action of the party on this paramount issue; and concluding with the request that the believers in the free coinage of silver in the Democratic party should organize, take charge of, and control the policy of the Democratic party. Three months later, at Memphis, an organization was perfected, and the silver Democrats went forth openly and courageously proclaiming their belief, and declaring that, if successful, they would crystallize into a platform the declaration which they had made. Then began the conflict. With a zeal approaching the zeal which inspired the crusaders who followed Peter the Hermit, our silver Democrats went forth from victory unto victory until they are now assembled, not to discuss, not to debate, but to enter up the judgment already rendered by the plain people of this country. In this contest brother has been arrayed against brother, father against son. The warmest ties of love, acquaintance and as-

* Reprinted from *Speeches of William Jennings Bryan.* Copyright 1909. Used by permission of Funk & Wagnalls Company.

sociation have been disregarded; old leaders have been cast aside when they have refused to give expression to the sentiments of those whom they would lead, and new leaders have sprung up to give direction to this cause of truth. Thus has the contest been waged, and we have assembled here under as binding and solemn instructions as were ever imposed upon representatives of the people.

We do not come as individuals. As individuals we might have been glad to compliment the gentleman from New York, but we know that the people for whom we speak would never be willing to put him in a position where he could thwart the will of the Democratic party. I say it was not a question of persons; it was a question of principle, and it is not with gladness, my friends, that we find ourselves brought into conflict with those who are now arrayed on the other side.

The gentleman who preceded me spoke of the State of Massachusetts; let me assure him that not one present in all this convention entertains the least hostility to the people of the State of Massachusetts, but we stand here representing people who are the equals, before the law, of the greatest citizens in the State of Massachusetts. When you come before us and tell us that we are about to disturb your business interests, we reply that you have disturbed our business interests by your course.

We say to you that you have made the definition of a business man too limited in its application. The man who is employed for wages is as much a business man as his employer, the attorney in a country town is as much a business man as the corporation counsel in a great metropolis; the merchant at the cross-roads store is as much a business man as the merchant of New York; the farmer who goes forth in the morning and toils all day—who begins in the spring and toils all summer—and who by the application of brain and muscle to the natural resources of the country creates wealth, is as much a business man as the man who goes upon the board of trade and bets upon the price of grain; the miners who go down a thousand feet into the earth, or climb two thousand feet upon the cliffs, and bring forth from their hiding places the precious metals to be poured into the channels of trade are as much business men as the few financial magnates who, in a back room, corner the money of the world. We come to speak for this broader class of business men.

Ah, my friends, we say not one word against those who live upon the Atlantic coast, but the hardy pioneers who have braved all the dangers of the wilderness, who have made the desert to blossom as the rose—the pioneers away out there (pointing to the West), who rear their children near to Nature's heart, where they can mingle their voices with the voices of the birds—out there where they have erected schoolhouses for the education of their young, churches where they praise their Creator, and cemeteries where rest the ashes of their dead—these people, we say, are as deserving of the consideration of our party as any people in this country. It is for these that we speak. We do not come as aggressors. Our war is not a war of conquest; we are fighting in the defense of our homes, our families, and posterity. We have petitioned, and our petitions have been scorned; we have entreated, and our entreaties have been disregarded; we have begged, and they have mocked when our calamity came. We beg no longer; we entreat no more; we petition no more. We defy them.

The gentleman from Wisconsin has said that he fears a Robespierre. My friends, in this land of the free you need not fear that a tyrant will spring up from among the people. What we need is an Andrew Jackson to stand, as Jackson stood, against the encroachments of organized wealth.

They tell us that this platform was made to catch votes. We reply to them that changing conditions make new issues; that the principles upon which Democracy rests are as everlasting as the hills, but that they must be applied to new conditions as they arise. Conditions have arisen, and we are here to meet these conditions. They tell us that the income tax ought not to be brought in here; that it is a new idea. They criticize us for our criticism of the Supreme Court of the United States. My friends, we have not criticized; we have simply called attention to what you already know. If you want criticisms, read the dissenting opinions of the court. There you will find criticisms. They say that we passed an unconstitutional law; we deny it. The income tax law was not unconstitutional when it was passed; it was not unconstitutional when it went before the Supreme Court for the first time; it did not become unconstitutional until one of the judges changed his mind, and we cannot be expected to know when a judge will change his mind. The income tax is just. It simply intends to put the burdens of government justly upon the backs of the people. I am in favor of an income tax. When I find a man who is not willing to bear his share of the burdens of the government which protects him, I find a man who is unworthy to enjoy the blessings of a government like ours.

They say that we are opposing national bank currency; it is true. If you will read what Thomas Benton said, you will find he said that, in searching history, he could find but one parallel to Andrew Jackson; that was Cicero, who destroyed the conspiracy of Cataline and saved Rome. Benton said that Cicero only did for Rome what Jackson did for us when he destroyed the bank conspiracy and saved America. We say in our platform that we believe that the right to coin and issue money is a function of government. We believe it. We believe that it is a part of sovereignty, and can no more with safety be delegated to private individuals than we could afford to delegate to private individuals the power to make penal statutes or levy taxes. Mr. Jefferson, who was once regarded as good Democratic authority, seems to have differed in opinion from the gentleman who has addressed us on the part of the minority. Those who are opposed to this proposition tell us that the issue of paper money is a function of the bank, and that the Government ought to go out of the banking business. I stand with Jefferson rather than with them, and tell them, as he did, that the issue of money is a function of government, and that the banks ought to go out of the governing business.

They complain about the plank which declares against life tenure in office. They have tried to strain it to mean that which it does not mean. What we oppose by that plank is the life tenure which is being built up in Washington, and which excludes from participation in official benefits the humbler members of society.

Let me call your attention to two or three important things. The gentleman from New York says that he will propose an amendment to the platform providing that the proposed change in our monetary system shall not affect contracts already made. Let me remind you that there is no intention of affecting those contracts which according to present laws are made payable in gold; but if he means to say that we cannot change our monetary system without protecting those who have loaned money before the change was made, I desire to ask him where, in law or in morals, he can find justification for not protecting the debtors when the act of 1873 was passed, if he now insists that we must protect the creditors.

He says he will also propose an amendment which will provide for the suspension of free coinage if we fail to maintain the parity within a year. We reply that when we advocate a policy which we believe will be successful, we are not compelled to raise a doubt as to our own sincerity by suggesting what we shall do if we fail. I ask him, if he would apply his logic to us, why he does not apply it to himself. He says he wants this country to try to secure an international agreement. Why does he not tell us what he is going to do if he fails to secure an international agreement? There is more reason for him to do that than there is for us to provide against the failure to maintain the parity. Our opponents have tried for twenty years to secure an international agreement, and those are waiting for it most patiently who do not want it at all.

And now, my friends, let me come to the paramount issue. If they ask us why it is that we say more on the money question than we say upon the tariff question, I reply that, if protection has slain its thousands, the gold standard has slain its tens of thousands. If they ask us why we do not embody in our platform all the things that we believe in, we reply that when we have restored the money of the Constitution all other necessary reforms will be possible; but that until this is done there is no other reform that can be accomplished.

Why is it that within three months such a change has come over the country? Three months ago, when it was confidently asserted that those who believe in the gold standard would frame our platform and nominate our candidates, even the advocates of the gold standard did not think that we could elect a President. And they had good reason for their doubt, because there is scarcely a State here today asking for the gold standard which is not in the absolute control of the Republican party. But note the change. Mr. McKinley was nominated at St. Louis upon a platform which declared for the maintenance of the gold standard until it can be changed into bimetalism by international agreement. Mr. McKinley was the most popular man among the Republicans, and three months ago everybody in the Republican party prophesied his election. How is it today? Why, the man who was once pleased to think that he looked like Napoleon, that man shudders today when he remembers that he was nominated on the anniversary of the battle of Waterloo. Not only that, but as he listens he can hear with ever-increasing distinctness the sound of the waves as they beat upon the lonely shores of St. Helena.

Why this change? Ah, my friends, is not the reason for the change evident to any one who will look at the matter? No private character, however pure, no personal popularity, however great, can protect from the avenging wrath of an indignant people a man who will declare that he is in favor of fastening the gold standard upon this country, or who is willing to surrender the right of self-government and place the legislative control of our affairs in the hands of foreign potentates and powers.

We go forth confident that we shall win. Why? Because upon the paramount issue of this campaign there is not a spot of ground upon which the enemy will dare to challenge battle. If they tell us that the gold standard is a good thing, we shall point to their platform and tell them that their platform pledges the party to get rid of the gold standard and substitute bimetalism. If the gold standard is a good thing, why try to get rid of it? I call your attention to the fact that some of the very people who are in this convention today and who tell us that we ought to declare in favor of international bimetalism—thereby declaring that the gold standard is wrong and that the principle of bimetalism is better—these very people four months ago were open and avowed advocates of the gold standard, and were then telling us that we could not legislate two metals together, even with the aid of all the world. If the gold standard is a good thing, we ought to declare in favor of its retention and not in favor of abandoning it; and if the gold standard is a bad thing why should we wait until other nations are willing to help us to let go? Here is the line of battle, and we care not upon which issue they force the fight; we are prepared to meet them on either issue or on both. If they tell us that the gold standard is the standard of civilization, we reply to them that this, the most enlightened of all the nations of the earth, has never declared for a gold standard and that both the great parties this year are declaring against it. If the gold standard is the standard of civilization, why, my friends, should we not have it? If they come to meet us on that issue we can present the history of our nation. More than that; we can tell them that they will search the pages of history in vain to find a single instance where the common people of any land have ever declared themselves in favor of the gold standard. They can find where the holders of fixed investments have declared for a gold standard, but not where the masses have.

Mr. Carlisle said in 1878 that this was a struggle between "the idle holders of idle capital" and "the struggling masses, who produce the wealth and pay the taxes of the country"; and, my friends, the question we are to decide is: Upon which side will the Democratic party fight; upon the side of "the idle holders of idle capital" or upon the side of "the struggling masses"? That is the question which the party must answer first, and then it must be answered by each individual hereafter. The sympathies of the Democratic party, as shown by the platform, are on the side of the struggling masses who have ever been the foundation of the Democratic party. There are two ideas of government. There are those who believe that, if you will only legislate to make the well-to-do prosperous, their prosperity will leak through on those below. The Democratic idea, however, has been that if you legislate to make the masses prosperous, their prosperity will find its way up through every class which rests upon them.

You come to us and tell us that the great cities are in favor of the gold standard; we reply that the great cities rest upon our broad and fertile prairies. Burn down your cities and leave our farms, and your cities will spring up again as if by magic; but destroy our farms and the grass will grow in the streets of every city in the country.

My friends, we declare that this nation is able to legislate for its own people on every question, without waiting for the aid or consent of any other nation on earth; and upon that issue we expect to carry every State in the Union. I shall not slander the inhabitants of the fair State of Massachusetts nor the inhabitants of the State of New York by saying that, when they are confronted with the proposition, they will declare that this nation is not able to attend to its own business. It is the issue of 1776 over again. Our ancestors, when but three millions in number, had the courage to declare their political independence of every other nation; shall we, their descendants, when we have grown to seventy millions, declare that we are less independent than our forefathers? No, my friends, that will never be the verdict of our people. Therefore, we care not upon what lines the battle is fought. If they say bimetalism is good, but that we cannot have it until other nations help us, we reply that, instead of having a gold standard because England has, we will restore bimetalism, and then let England have bimetalism because the United States has it. If they dare to come out in the open field and defend the gold standard as a good thing, we will fight them to the uttermost. Having behind us the producing masses of this nation and the world, supported by the commercial interests, the laboring interests, and the toilers everywhere, we will answer their demand for a gold standard by saying to them: You shall not press down upon the brow of labor this crown of thorns, you shall not crucify mankind upon a cross of gold.

Chapter 19

IMPERIAL AMERICA

America's late-nineteenth-century venture in imperialism marked a decisive turning point in the nation's history. A vigorous and rather flamboyant expansionism had long characterized American foreign policy, but with the major exception of Alaska (purchased in 1867) this earlier expansion had been into contiguous rather than outlying territories, and new lands had all eventually been admitted to the Union with rights and privileges equal to those of older states. Besides, these coveted regions were generally sparsely populated and presented neither the serious problem of assimilation of native cultures nor the need for a burdensome bureaucracy to administer the affairs of subject colonial peoples. To the expansionists of the 1890's, however, the vision of America's "Manifest Destiny" was not limited to continental shores alone. As the passing of the frontier and the rounding out of the nation's furthermost boundaries signaled the final conquest of the continent, many Americans eagerly turned their eyes outward to champion a "large policy" for the republic. On every hand they were urged to recognize the "Mission of America" to carry the benefits and blessings of an advanced civilization to their numerous less fortunate brethren in the backward areas of the world, particularly the Far East and the Caribbean. Such plans for overseas expansion had been put before the American public before, but not until this last decade of the nineteenth century were most Americans convinced that their nation's destiny was inextricably bound up in securing, civilizing, humanizing, "sanitizing," Christianizing, and maintaining overseas possessions. In short, in the nineties Americans were finally to assume what Rudyard Kipling had called "the white man's burden"—and incidentally to acquire a vast colonial empire.

America's new willingness, or need, to assert herself imperially was probably connected very closely with the rapid development of industrial capitalism. For thirty years since the end of the Civil War an expanding, dynamic capitalism had safely and profitably engaged the nation in domestic projects of imperial proportions. A widespread network of railroads had spanned the continent; the Trans-Mississippi West had been thoroughly explored and colonized; the nation's vast natural resources, the raw materials of a factory civilization, had been thoroughly exploited; and great industrial empires had been created to serve an ever-expanding domestic market. But by the 1890's American industry was producing a surplus over what the domestic market, with purchasing power at the prevailing low level, could absorb; manufacturers were seeking supplies of certain raw materials that were not produced domestically; and business leaders generally were complaining that internal investment in an already well developed nation no longer provided the fantastic opportunities for profit of earlier decades. Now the business community turned its attention and energies to investments abroad, and American capital poured first into Hawaii and Cuba, and then at the turn of the century into other distant, underdeveloped areas of the world. Inevitably the flag followed the dollar, and foreign trade and investments brought extensive overseas possessions and protectorates in their wake. Then a large navy was deemed necessary to protect new possessions or "spheres of influence," and more island bases were sought to service this far-flung navy; and so the imperial circle went, ever widening. Nor was the imperialist pattern unfamiliar. For England, France, Germany, and several lesser nations had long since joined in bitter rivalry for the raw materials, the markets, and the investment potentials of the "uncivilized" world. America was merely a belated participant in the scramble for empire.

These overseas ventures were not, however, motivated by economic drives alone, and the expansionism of the nineties is to be explained less in terms of economic interests forcing a pliant government's hand than of intellectual and particularly emotional forces that gripped the entire nation. Indeed, the most blatant example of American aggressiveness, the Spanish-American War of 1898, was emphatically popular in origin and was waged despite the vehement objections of the larger portion of the business community. At the end of the brief war, when the spoils were well in hand and popular enthusiasm had already carried America well along the path to empire, businessmen were quick to make the nation's new possessions economically advantageous, and in the twentieth century their concern for profit considerably influenced America's imperial plans. But business had for the most part opposed the coming of war at the very moment that "jingoes" and the "yellow press" were making much of the nation's psychological readiness for aggression to whip up explosive feelings against Spanish misrule in Cuba.

Thus the tempo of acquisition quickened for reasons more deeply rooted in popular feeling than in private greed, and every bellicose act of national self-assertion was widely cheered. But Americans' aggressiveness did not stem from genuine feelings of security and self-esteem. Instead their boastful sense of "mission," their racism, and their nativism stemmed largely from fear rather than faith. For this was no "age of confidence"; rather it was an age of internal chaos and turbulence, when depression, farm revolt, labor strife, the specter of monopolization, and continuous conflict between older agrarian values and the material symbols of a new industrial urbanism beset middle-class Americans with overwhelming confusion and anxiety. The nervous energies that popular leaders channeled into a wild enthusiasm for expansion were less the product of a real feeling for mastery and world domination than an expression of immaturity, insecurity and fear.

Foremost among the "jingoes" who advocated a "large policy" for the United States was Theodore Roosevelt, an aristocratic and Harvard-bred young historian, reformer and

politician whose early association with the Dakota badlands
had given him the frontiersman's generally belligerent outlook and a taste for the "strenuous life." These were characteristics that thoroughly endeared him to a public ripe for
aggressive self-reliance. Responding to popular acclaim, the
inflammatory Roosevelt vigorously preached the expansionist doctrines of the eminent naval historian and philosopher of imperialism, Captain Alfred T. Mahan, whose volumes
on the influence of sea power in history had made a profound
impression on educated Americans. Affirming America's destiny to "look outward" beyond national borders, Mahan argued that the nation's honor and prestige as well as her
defense and trade, depended upon the acquisition of numerous overseas naval bases, the control of the Caribbean and
trade routes to the Far East, and the creation of an insur-
passable naval force. There were some Americans, of course,
who took violent exception to Mahan's doctrines and to the
bombastic, flag-waving jingoism of Roosevelt and his followers. But the anti-imperialists were hopelessly out of temper with their times, and when in 1897 Assistant Secretary of
the Navy Roosevelt delivered his famous Naval War College speech on preparedness ("Washington's Forgotten Maxim"), he met with widespread approval throughout the country. In this classic expression of naval expansionism Roosevelt
asked for "a great navy . . . an armament fit for the nation's
needs, not primarily to fight, but to avert fighting." Roosevelt declared that "preparation for war is the surest guaranty
for peace," and he extolled the "soldierly virtues" as the
"most valuable of all qualities." One year later the "glorious
little war" with Spain secured an empire for America and
swept the indomitable Colonel of the "Rough Riders" into
the Governorship of New York. From there he rose rapidly
to the Vice-Presidency, and then, in 1901, to the Presidency
of the United States.

Fantastically energetic and ebullient—John Morley once
described the President as "an interesting combination of St.
Vitus and St. Paul"—Roosevelt played a particularly vital role
in sparking and directing America's expansionist drive. But
Roosevelt's greatest significance in this period was as a folk-
hero, as a living, fighting symbol of the nervous energies
that dominated America. Earlier statesmen of a very different turn of mind and character had at times surrendered
to the expansionist demands of an anxiety-ridden public.
In 1893 the anti-imperialist Grover Cleveland had successfully opposed the annexation of Hawaii when American
sugar planters, without regard for the native majority, staged
a revolution in an attempt to protect their own extensive

investments in the islands, and sought admission to the Union. Nevertheless two years later even the courageous Cleveland submitted to the jingoist fervor in an act of national self-assertion that momentarily endeared him to the most violent expansionists. For in the Olney Doctrine of 1895 Cleveland peremptorily ordered the British to arbitrate a disturbing boundary dispute with Venezuela, claiming that "Today the United States is practically sovereign on this continent, and its fiat is law upon the subjects to which it confines its interposition." Ultimately England succumbed to Cleveland's bellicose demands, and the President was wildly applauded for twisting the lion's tail so ferociously. The un-warlike McKinley, too, had surrendered to the tide of popular feeling when he took the nation to war with Spain and presided over the acquisition of Guam, Puerto Rico and the Philippines, the annexation of the Hawaiian Islands, and the establishment of a protectorate over Cuba. Thus Cleveland and McKinley had contributed largely to America's emergence as a great imperial power. But they had done so half-heartedly and under intense pressure from an aroused public, while Roosevelt so thoroughly embodied the national temper that his every thought and act, however childlike or warlike, unhesitatingly bespoke the swashbuckling spirit of adolescent America.

Anti-imperialists violently denounced the colonial bequest of the war with Spain, but most Americans retorted with cries of "Don't haul down the flag" and turned to Theodore Roosevelt to half-lead, half-follow them into the expansive years of the early-twentieth century. The keystone of Roosevelt's foreign policy was his injunction that the nation "speak softly and carry a big stick." But Americans seldom spoke softly in those feverish years. In 1899-1900 Secretary of State John Hay had demanded an "Open Door" policy in China, insisting that American traders be treated equally with the nationals of those countries that had forcibly extorted trade concessions from the defenseless Chinese. Then in 1903 Roosevelt actively interfered in the internal affairs of Colombia, aiding and abetting a revolution in that Latin-American republic that left Panama free to negotiate an isthmian canal route with the impatient "Colossus of the North." And in 1904-5 the "Roosevelt Corollary" to the Monroe Doctrine warned our Latin neighbors that "Chronic wrong-doing, or an impotence which results in a general loosening of the ties of civilized society . . . may force the United States, however reluctantly . . . to the exercise of an international police power." This bold enlargement of American prerogatives throughout the Western hemisphere was frequently invoked in the following two decades to justify armed interference in the domestic as well as foreign affairs of the republics to the South. But by the late 1920's and early 1930's America's youthful aggressiveness had been largely dissipated by the tremendous burdens of world power. Under the guidance of Herbert Hoover and Franklin D. Roosevelt the nation's attitude toward the sovereign powers of the Western hemisphere underwent profound change, and a genuine sense of mutual respect and responsibility among equals—the "Good Neighbor" policy—was substituted for the "Big Stick" and "Dollar Diplomacy." America had finally come of age.

The United States Looking Outward*
Alfred T. Mahan, 1890

Indications are not wanting of an approaching change in the thoughts and policy of Americans as to their relations with the world outside their own borders. For the past quarter of a century, the predominant idea, which has asserted itself successfully at the polls and shaped the course of the Government, has been to preserve the home market for the home industries. The employer and the workman alike have been taught to look at the various economical measures proposed from this point of view, to regard with hostility any step favoring the intrusion of the foreign producer upon their own domain, and rather to demand increasingly rigorous measures of exclusion than to acquiesce in any loosening of the chain that binds the consumer to them. The inevitable consequence has followed, as in all cases when the mind or the eye is exclusively fixed in one direction, that the danger of loss or the prospect of advantage in another quarter has been overlooked; and although the abounding resources of the country have maintained the exports at a high figure, this flattering result has been due more to the superabundant bounty of Nature than to the demand of other nations for our protected manufactures.

For nearly the lifetime of a generation, therefore, American industries have been thus protected, until the practice has assumed the force of a tradition, and is clothed in the mail of conservatism. In their mutual relations, these industries resemble the activities of a modern ironclad that has heavy armor, but inferior engines and guns; mighty for defense, weak for offense. Within, the home market is se-

* From *The Interest of America in Sea Power*, Alfred T. Mahan; Little Brown & Co., 1897.

cured; but outside, beyond the broad seas, there are the markets of the world, that can be entered and controlled only by a vigorous contest, to which the habit of trusting to protection by statute does not conduce.

At bottom, however, the temperament of the American people is essentially alien to such a sluggish attitude. Independently of all bias for or against protection, it is safe to predict that, when the opportunities for gain abroad are understood, the course of American enterprise will cleave a channel by which to reach them. . . .

The interesting and significant feature of this changing attitude is the turning of the eyes outward, instead of inward only, to seek the welfare of the country. To affirm the importance of distant markets, and the relation to them of our own immense powers of production, implies logically the recognition of the link that joins the products and the markets—that is, the carrying trade; the three together constituting that chain of maritime power to which Great Britain owes her wealth and greatness. Further, is it too much to say that, as two of these links, the shipping and the markets, are exterior to our own borders, the acknowledgment of them carries with it a view of the relations of the United States to the world radically distinct from the simple idea of self-sufficingness? We shall not follow far this line of thought before there will dawn the realization of America's unique position, facing the older worlds of the East and West, her shores washed by the oceans which touch the one or the other, but which are common to her alone.

Coincident with these signs of change in our own policy there is restlessness in the world at large which is deeply significant, if not ominous. It is beside our purpose to dwell upon the internal state of Europe, whence, if disturbances arise, the effect upon us may be but partial and indirect. But the great seaboard powers there do not stand on guard against their continental rivals only; they cherish also aspirations for commercial extension, for colonies, and for influence in distant regions, which may bring, and, even under our present contracted policy, already have brought them into collision with ourselves. The incident of the Samoa Islands, trivial apparently, was nevertheless eminently suggestive of European ambitions. America then roused from sleep as to interests closely concerning her future. At this moment internal troubles are imminent in the Sandwich Islands, where it should be our fixed determination to allow no foreign influence to equal our own. All over the world German commercial and colonial push is coming into collision with other nations: witness the affair of the Caroline Islands with Spain; the partition of New Guinea with England; the yet more recent negotiation between these two powers concerning their share in Africa viewed with deep distrust and jealousy by France; the Samoa affair; the conflict between German control and American interests in the islands of the western Pacific; and the alleged progress of German influence in Central and South America. . . .

There is no sound reason for believing that the world has passed into a period of assured peace outside the limits of Europe. Unsettled political conditions, such as exist in Haiti, Central America, and many of the Pacific Islands, especially the Hawaiian group, when combined with great military or commercial importance as is the case with most of these positions, involve, now as always, dangerous germs of quarrel, against which it is prudent at least to be prepared. Undoubtedly, the general temper of nations is more averse from war than it was of old. If no less selfish and grasping than our predecessors, we feel more dislike to the discomforts and sufferings attendant upon a breach of peace; but to retain that highly valued repose and the undisturbed enjoyment of the returns of commerce, it is necessary to argue upon somewhat equal terms of strength with an adversary. It is the preparedness of the enemy, and not acquiescence in the existing state of things, that now holds back the armies of Europe.

On the other hand, neither the sanctions of international law nor the justice of a cause can be depended upon for a fair settlement of differences, when they come into conflict with a strong political necessity on the one side opposed to comparative weakness on the other. In our still pending dispute over the seal-fishing of Bering Sea, whatever may be thought of the strength of our argument, in view of generally admitted principles of international law, it is beyond doubt that our contention is reasonable, just, and in the interest of the world at large. But in the attempt to enforce it we have come into collision not only with national susceptibilities as to the honor of the flag, which we ourselves very strongly share, but also with a state governed by a powerful necessity, and exceedingly strong where we are particularly weak and exposed. Not only has Great Britain a mighty navy and we a long defenseless seacoast, but it is a great commercial and political advantage to her that her larger colonies, and above all Canada, should feel that the power of the mother country is something which they need, and upon which they can count. . . . Whatever arrangement of this question is finally reached, the fruit of Lord Salisbury's attitude scarcely can fail to be a strengthening of the sentiments of attachment to, and reliance upon, the mother country, not only in Canada, but in the other great colonies. These feelings of attachment and mutual dependence supply the living spirit, without which the nascent schemes for imperial federation are but dead mechanical contrivances; nor are they without influence upon such generally unsentimental considerations as those of buying and selling, and the course of trade.

This dispute, seemingly paltry yet really serious, sudden in its appearance and dependent for its issue upon other considerations than its own merits, may serve to convince us of many latent and yet unforeseen dangers to the peace of the western hemisphere, attendant upon the opening of a canal through the Central American Isthmus. In a general way, it is evident enough that this canal, by modifying the direction of trade routes, will induce a great increase of commercial activity and carrying trade throughout the Caribbean Sea; and that this now comparatively deserted nook of the ocean will become, like the Red Sea, a great thoroughfare of shipping, and will attract, as never before in our day, the interest and ambition of maritime nations. Every position in that sea will have enhanced commercial and military value, and the canal itself will become a strategic centre of the most vital importance. Like the Canadian Pacific Railroad, it will be a link between the two oceans; but, unlike it, the use, unless most carefully guarded by treaties, will belong wholly to the belligerent which controls the sea by its naval power. In case of war, the United States will unquestionably command the Canadian Railroad, despite the deterrent force of operations by the hostile navy upon our seaboard; but no less unquestionably will she be impotent, as against any of the great maritime powers, to control the Central American canal. Militarily speaking, and having reference to European complications only, the piercing of the Isthmus is nothing but a disaster to the United States, in the present state of her military and naval preparation. It is especially dangerous to the Pacific coast; but the increased exposure of one part of our seaboard reacts unfavorably upon the whole military situation.

Despite a certain great original superiority conferred by our geographical nearness and immense resources—due, in other words, to our natural advantages, and not to our intelligent preparations—the United States is woefully unready, not only in fact but in purpose to assert in the Caribbean and Central America a weight of influence proportioned to the extent of her interests. We have not the navy, and, what is worse, we are not willing to have the navy, that will weigh seriously in any disputes with those nations whose interests will conflict there with our own. We have not, and we are not anxious to provide, the defense of the seaboard which will leave the navy free for its work at sea. We have not, but many other powers have, positions, either within or on the borders of the Caribbean which not only possess great natural advantages for the control of that sea, but have received and are receiving that artificial strength of fortification and armament which will make them practically inexpugnable. On the contrary, we have not on the Gulf of Mexico even the beginning of a navy yard which could serve as the base of our operations. Let me not be misunderstood. I am not regretting that we have not the means to meet on terms of equality the great navies of the Old World. I recognize, what few at least say, that despite its great surplus revenue, this country is poor in proportion to its length of seaboard and its exposed points. That which I deplore, and which is a sober, just, and reasonable cause of deep national concern is that the nation neither has nor cares to have its sea frontier so defended, and its navy of such power, as shall suffice, with the advantages of our position, to weigh seriously when inevitable discussions arise—such as we have recently had about Samoa and Bering Sea, and which may at any moment come up about the Caribbean Sea or the canal. Is the United States, for instance, prepared to allow Germany to acquire the Dutch stronghold of Curaçao, fronting the Atlantic outlet of both the proposed canals of Panama and Nicaragua? Is she prepared to acquiesce in any foreign power purchasing from Haiti a naval station on the Windward Passage, through which pass our steamer routes to the Isthmus? Would she acquiesce in a foreign protectorate over the Sandwich Islands, that great central station of the Pacific, equidistant from San Francisco, Samoa, and the Marquesas, and an important post on our lines of communication with both Australia and China? Or will it be maintained that any one of these questions, supposing it to arise, is so exclusively one-sided, the arguments of policy and right so exclusively with us, that the other party will at once yield his eager wish, and gracefully withdraw? Was it so at Samoa? Is it so as regards the Bering Sea? The motto seen on so many ancient cannon, *Ultima ratio regum,* is not without its message to republics.

It is perfectly reasonable and legitimate, in estimating our needs of military preparation, to take into account the remoteness of the chief naval and military nations from our shores, and the consequent difficulty of maintaining operations at such a distance. It is equally proper, in framing our policy, to consider the jealousies of the European family of states, and their consequent unwillingness to incur the enmity of a people so strong as ourselves; their dread of our revenge in the future, as well as their inability to detach more than a certain part of their forces to our shores without losing much of their own weight in the councils of Europe. In truth, a careful determination of the force that Great Britain or France could probably spare for operations against our coasts, if the latter were suitably defended, without weakening their European position or unduly exposing their colonies and commerce, is the starting-point from which to calculate the strength of our own navy. . . .

While, therefore, the advantages of our own position in the western hemisphere, and the disadvantages under which the operations of a European state would labor, are undeniable and just elements in the calculations of the statesman, it is folly to look upon them as sufficient alone for our security. Much more needs to be cast into the scale that it may incline in favor of our strength. They are mere defensive factors, and partial at that. Though distant, our shores can be reached; being defenseless, they can detain but a short time a force sent against them. With a probability of three months' peace in Europe, no maritime power would fear to support its demands by a number of ships with which it would be loath indeed to part for a year.

Yet, were our sea frontier as strong as it now is weak, passive self-defense, whether in trade or war, would be but a poor policy, so long as this world continues to be one of struggle and vicissitude. All around us now is strife; "the struggle of life," "the race of life," are phrases so familiar that we do not feel their significance till we stop to think about them. Everywhere nation is arrayed against nation; our own no less than others. What is our protective system but an organized warfare? In carrying it on, it is true, we have only to use certain procedures which all states now concede to be a legal exercise of the national power, even though injurious to themselves. It is lawful, they say, to do what we will with our own. Are our people, however, so unaggressive that they are likely not to want their own way in matters where their interests turn on points of disputed right, or so little sensitive as to submit quietly to encroachment by others in quarters where they long have considered their own influence should prevail?

Our self-imposed isolation in the matter of markets, and the decline of our shipping interest in the last thirty years, have coincided singularly with an actual remoteness of this continent from the life of the rest of the world. . . .

When the Isthmus is pierced, this isolation will pass away, and with it the indifference of foreign nations. From wheresoever they come and whithersoever they afterward go, all ships that use the canal will pass through the Caribbean. Whatever the effect produced upon the prosperity of the adjacent continent and islands by the thousand wants attendant upon maritime activity, around such a focus of trade will centre large commercial and political interests. To protect and develop its own, each nation will seek points of support and means of influence in a quarter where the United States always has been jealously sensitive to the intrusion of European powers. The precise value of the Monroe Doctrine is understood very loosely by most Americans, but the effect of the familiar phrase has been to develop a national sensitiveness, which is a more frequent cause of war than material interests; and over disputes caused by such feelings there will preside none of the calming influence due to the moral authority of international law, with its recognized principles, for the points in dispute will be of policy, of interest, not of conceded right. Already France and Great Britain are giving to ports held by them a degree of artificial strength uncalled for by their present importance. They look to the near future. Among the islands and on the mainland there are many positions of great importance, held now by weak or unstable states. Is the United States willing to see them sold to a powerful rival? But what right will she invoke against the transfer? She can allege but one, that of her reasonable policy supported by her might.

Whether they will or no, Americans must now begin to look outward. . . .

Chapter 20

THE PROGRESSIVE FERMENT

Seldom in the nation's history has the impulse for reform been more pervasive or more intense than in the Progressive Era at the turn of the twentieth century. For this was truly the Golden Age of Reform, when the fears and anxieties of middle-class Americans hard pressed between corporate power from above and the laboring masses from below had been channeled not only into an aggressive, boastful expansionism, but into a humanitarian, collectivist Progressivism as well. The task of the Progressives lay clear before them. With speed and consummate skill America's mighty Captains of Industry had created a magnificent productive plant and had presided over the rapid proliferation of national wealth. But with boundless riches came incredible poverty of purpose and spirit. If unfettered industrial capitalism had achieved for the nation vast material strength that placed her among the great powers of the world, it had also at least momentarily overridden Americans' sense of justice and fair play. Personal acquisitiveness had been substituted for social conscience, the Gospel of Wealth for the Social

Gospel. Now the Progressives had to recapture the rich human values of an earlier age, adapt them to the realities of collective economic power, and lead the nation in its quest for social justice.

From 1900 to the beginning of the First World War much of the energy of Progressivism was devoted to the formulation of new social philosophies and ideologies for a nation whose physical power had grown more rapidly than its understanding. And the seminal works of John Dewey, Thorstein Veblen, Charles A. Beard, Herbert Croly, and Walter Lippmann were powerful instruments in the ultimate reorientation of American thought. But the Progressive challenge was as pressing as it was formidable, and the overwhelming economic, social, and political problems that beset the nation demanded immediate attention and action. On every hand huge combinations of capital had emerged in the form of trusts and monopolies that dwarfed the small independent businessman and threatened the economic basis of individualistic, middle-class democracy in America. For example, in 1901 the gigantic United States Steel Corporation was organized by J. P. Morgan & Company with a capitalization that reached the staggering sum of almost one and a half billion dollars. Such industrial empires produced tremendous wealth, but while the privileged few were enriched, impoverishment was the lot of the many. Thus great fortunes and unspeakable poverty grew side by side in a nation fascinated by the spectacle of material production though little concerned with the problems of distribution. And by 1896 it was estimated that one eighth of the population owned 90% of the nation's property, while increasingly large numbers of Americans were propertyless altogether.

At the same time that unequal distribution of wealth created widely separated and deeply antagonistic economic classes, the rise of the city similarly brought social problems of unparalleled proportions. Some Americans chose to attribute the evils of urban life to the great numbers of "new" immigrants from Eastern and Southern Europe who settled in the cities. Actually, in intelligence, character, and ambition there was little to distinguish the "new" immigrant from the "old" immigrant who had come from the British Isles or Western and Northern Europe. It was America that was "new," not the immigrant. An earlier, agrarian America had offered its immigrants ample free land for settlement, but by the 1890's industrial capitalism had subdued the continent, conquered its free lands and last frontiers, and firmly established a business civilization that seemed to provide room for urban factory workers only. The newcomer from foreign shores had little choice; he must settle in the cities to earn a living. For this reason alone the "new" immigrant was identified with the poverty, slums, disease, crime, and vice peculiar to the entire movement from rural to urban areas that marked America's industrial revolution.

The systematic extension of governmental power to eliminate these evils was a major theme of the Progressive movement. In the late-nineteenth century the disciples of Henry George and Edward Bellamy, two of the most thoroughgoing philosophers of social control, had consistently been more vocal than numerous, while angry agrarians who precipitated the Populist Revolt of the 1890's had found their enthusiasm for collective social action waning with the rise of farm prices and the return of farm prosperity. Nevertheless, these early demands for State action to provide for the general welfare had made considerable inroads upon Americans' traditional adherence to laissez-faire. In the 1900's large numbers of middle-class Americans were wary of the predatory power of concentrated wealth, fearful of impending conflict between big business and the under-privileged classes generally, and profoundly disturbed by the social dislocations that accompanied urbanization. They rallied to the support of Progressive measures that called for considerable State interference in the social and economic life of the nation. And within a comparatively few years Federal and state governments alike had begun a widespread campaign to regulate those industries which vitally affected the public interest, to curb somewhat the extensive power of the trusts, to encourage fairer labor practices, and to help preserve and protect the nation's human resources through widely expanded social services.

While these first efforts at social and economic legislation laid the groundwork for the Welfare State of a later generation, Progressive leaders were equally concerned with the details of political reform. With a vast increase in its powers and responsibilities, it was imperative that government be made more responsive to the popular will and that new standards of honesty and administrative efficiency be widely adopted. Progressivism therefore stimulated an intense public interest in reform measures that promised to insure the direct and competent administration of the processes of democracy. Within the states the initiative and referendum permitted a small percentage of the electorate to petition the submission of laws directly to the general public for acceptance or rejection. The recall provided a means by which dishonest or unpopular public officials might be removed from office by majority vote before the expiration of their regular terms. And the direct primary somewhat reduced the power of political machines by giving the voters an opportunity to name party nominees as well as to choose between the final candidates for office. In the field of local government experiments were made to supplant the frequently corrupt mayoralty system with a "commission" form of government in which all municipal functions were entrusted to a small group of commissioners responsible for their respective departments. And the "city manager" plan attempted to emulate business techniques, granting all non-political functions to a managerial expert who conducted municipal affairs as he would a giant business establishment. Besides these accomplishments on the state and local levels, two reforms within the national government were of exceptional importance. Throughout the period of industrial supremacy that followed the Civil War, the Constitutional provision for the election of United States Senators by the various state legislatures had permitted a corrupt alliance between corporate wealth and purchasable state politicians to make of the national upper house a "millionaires' club" dominated by the representatives of "vested interests." But in 1913 the Seventeenth Amendment to the Constitution was ratified, providing for the direct election of Senators, and the heavy hand of privilege was somewhat lifted. Then in 1920, long after various Western states had granted the ballot to women, another Progressive demand finally met with national success when the Nineteenth Amendment was ratified and woman suffrage became a reality in every state of the Union.

Principle and plan, however, seldom contributed as importantly to the achievement of these liberal measures as did the aggressive apostles of reform who dominated the Progressive Era. Such indefatigable crusaders as "Fighting Bob" LaFollette, Governor of Wisconsin and later United States Senator, and "Golden Rule" Jones, the Mayor of Toledo, Ohio, continuously dramatized the effectiveness of honesty, intelligence, and training in the administration of public affairs. In the widely read public journals Lincoln Steffens, Ida Tarbell, Ray Stannard Baker, Upton Sinclair, David Graham Phillips, and numerous other "Muckrakers" excitingly exposed the evils of business and politics. But by far the most influential of the many stimulating personalities who lent color and character to Progressivism were the incomparably dynamic and dramatic Theodore Roosevelt and the highly intellectual, highly idealistic Woodrow Wilson. Both men were determined and inspiring leaders who considerably enhanced the power and prestige of the Presidency; both were broadly liberal in their political orientation; both advocated far-reaching changes in the national structure that later contributed importantly to the New Deal and the Fair Deal. And in 1912, when they faced each other in a bitter three-cornered race for the Presidency (with Roosevelt the third-party Bull Moose or Progressive candidate, Wilson the Democratic candidate, and William Howard Taft the standard-bearer of the Old Guard in the Republican party), their respective cries for a "New Nationalism" and a "New Freedom" seemed very much alike. Actually, however, on the issue of the trusts there existed a fundamental conflict between the two men and their respective philosophies of government that symbolized a deep confusion in Progressive thinking.

Roosevelt's sure sense of the popular—a contemporary attributed to "Teddy" the "psychology of the mutt"—made him truly the era's prophet. Nevertheless impatient critics charged that as President his bold verbal attacks upon the "malefactors of great wealth," his fiery threats to "bust the trusts," and his exhilarating promises of a Square Deal for all Americans were thoroughly out of keeping with his actual achievements. The "aggressive" Roosevelt, LaFollette insisted, had meekly and unnecessarily knuckled under to unfriendly Congressional demands that Progressive legislation be shorn of much of its potential strength. And others later pointed out that even the cautious and avowedly conservative Taft prosecuted twice as many trusts in his four years as President (1909-1913) as had the much vaunted "trust-buster" Roosevelt during nearly eight years in office (1901-1909). Yet Roosevelt had not enjoyed a free hand as President and the frequent disparity between his word and his deed was largely due to the fact that throughout his administration the Republican Square Dealer was continuously forced to seek concessions from an unsympathetic Congress dominated by ultra-conservative members of his own party. And Roosevelt *did* make numerous substantial contributions to the Progressive cause. He confounded the previously untouchable business community by invoking the long dormant Sherman Anti-Trust Act against the Northern Securities Company, an enormous consolidation of railroad interests that involved such masters of capital as E. H. Harriman and J. P. Morgan; he pushed and cajoled through Congress the Pure Food and Drug Act and various laws designed to conserve the nation's depleted natural resources; through compromise and concession he secured essential, if not thoroughly adequate, regulatory railroad legislation; and, most significantly, he led the American people in the all-important *first* steps towards meaningful national reform.

Fate, not popular choice, had taken Roosevelt from the Vice-Presidency to the highest office in the land in 1901 when an assassin's bullets ended President McKinley's life. In 1904, therefore, Roosevelt was particularly delighted to be decisively elected in his own right, and in the enthusiasm of the moment pledged himself not to seek re-election four years hence. He did choose his successor, however, and for a while there was hope that the genial and devoted Taft might competently carry on a Progressive administration. But this hope proved illusory, for Taft, conservative at heart and singularly lacking in Roosevelt's penchant for compromise, was incapable of reconciling the interests of Progressives within the Republican Party with those of the conservative standpatters who dominated party councils. This fundamental schism quickly widened and in 1910, aided by the Democratic minority, insurgent Republicans in the House of Representatives struck a vital blow at the party's conservative hierarchy by stripping "Uncle Joe" Cannon, the autocratic Speaker of the House, of much of the power he had wielded to block Progressive legislation. Yet the revolt against "Cannonism" was only a first step, and the insurgents were determined either to capture control of the Republican Party or to create an independent party that would nominate a Progressive in 1912.

Meanwhile Roosevelt returned from big-game hunting in the wilds of Africa equally convinced that a genuine Progressive, preferably himself, must be nominated. The former President had already abandoned the older formulas of economic reform he so loudly advocated a decade earlier, since "trust-busting" had proved singularly ineffective. Prosecution under the anti-trust laws dissolved monopolistic interests in a technical sense only, and effective reintegration of legally separated units (through an informal "community of interests") was not uncommon. Combination seemed truly basic to the nature of modern American business, and the "New Nationalism" that Roosevelt now espoused not only embraced most of the political and social reforms of the moment, but also accepted as both "inevitable and necessary" the concentration of extensive economic power in large corporations. Were these mammoth economic units to prove abusive, Roosevelt would regulate rather than dissolve them, maintaining instead of destroying their effective contributions to America's material wealth. In this way "big business" would be matched by "big government." This was in essence the program that Roosevelt presented to the nation in his famous speech at Osawatomie, Kansas, in August, 1910. With this program he captured the presidential nomination of an independent Progressive Party in 1912, and with it he suffered defeat at the hands of Woodrow Wilson's "New Freedom."

Trained as an historian and political scientist, Woodrow Wilson had early distinguished himself academically, rising to the presidency of Princeton University in 1902, a year after Theodore Roosevelt entered the White House. Then in 1910 Wilson abandoned academic life to become Governor of New Jersey, and two years later, on the basis of a brilliant reform record, he captured the Democratic nomination for President of the United States. Thus Wilson entered the political arena at the very height of the movement towards monopolization and the concentration of economic power. Like Roosevelt, he saw very clearly the tremendous transformation this new power had wrought in American life generally. The "Old Order Changeth," wrote the scholar in politics. "We have changed our economic conditions, absolutely, from top to bottom; and, with our economic society, the organization of our life." Both Progressive leaders, then, were aware of the collective nature of twentieth-century industrial development and of its impact upon the nation's traditionally individualistic social structure. But where Roosevelt thoroughly accepted the "new order of society," Wilson firmly rejected it, dedicating himself to restoring the economic realities of an earlier century. Indeed, the keynote of Wilson's first Inaugural Address was his assertion that "our work is a work of restoration."

Like Hamilton a century before, Theodore Roosevelt was vitally impressed by vast aggregates of power, and his "New Nationalism" sought social justice by extending the powers of the central government, particularly those of the Chief Executive, whom he regarded as peculiarly the "steward of the public welfare." "Big business" must be good or suffer regulation by "big government." Wilson, on the other hand, was essentially Jeffersonian in his orientation, and his "New Freedom" feared all bigness, whether economic or political, as potentially destructive of democracy. When he announced that the "old political formulas do not fit the present problems; they read now like documents taken out of a forgotten age," Wilson was referring primarily to the boldest type of nineteenth-century laissez-faire. An absolute "hands-off" attitude on the part of the national government would permit big business to strangle altogether the middle-class small businessman whose strength and survival Wilson regarded as vital to the nation's well-being. Therefore, government must abandon its "old formulas"; it must interfere in the economic life of the nation not only to destroy privilege but also to preserve economic competition and prevent the "men on the make" from being squeezed out of existence by the giant corporation, the trust, and the monopoly. Yet government must not expand its own power until it, too, became a threat to the individual.

In the 1912 campaign Wilson persistently attacked the plan of the "New Nationalism" merely to regulate the monopolies. If permitted to grow, Wilson insisted, big business would soon control the government itself, and governmental regulation of business would be truly a farce. Roosevelt in turn thought the advocates of the "New Freedom" were agrarian reactionaries, because they were basically out of sympathy with the growth of those giant economic units whose untrammeled productivity he considered the promise of American democracy. In theory, of course, the "New Freedom" *did* stand for the simple anti-trust policies of discontented nineteenth-century agrarians. Ironically, however, Woodrow Wilson won the election of 1912 only to preside over the extraordinary growth of business and government alike. The Underwood-Simmons Tariff Act of 1913 did revise the tariff downward to deprive monopolistic business of the usual protection of Republican trade laws; the Federal Reserve Act of 1913, by decentralizing the nation's credit resources, did attack the "money trust" that the Pujo Committee of the House of Representatives claimed was controlled by a few New York banking houses; and the Clayton Act of 1914 did give added strength to the government's anti-trust activities. Yet all of these measures, together with many other efforts towards social justice, meant the broad extension of government authority over the nation and its citizens. Thus Wilson ultimately created the "big government" Roosevelt had urged, and in 1917-1918 a wartime demand for unlimited production gave a tremendous impetus to "big business" as well. Wilson had to a large degree met the Progressive challenge, but in doing so he had sacrificed much of his basic antipathy to the subordination of the individual to power of any kind, whether in business or in government.

The New Nationalism, *Theodore Roosevelt, 1910*

We come here today to commemorate one of the epoch-making events of the long struggle for the rights of man, the long struggle for the uplift of humanity. Our country—this great republic—means nothing unless it means the triumph of a real democracy, the triumph of popular government, and, in the long run, of an economic system under which each man shall be guaranteed the opportunity to show the best that there is in him. That is why the history of America is now the central feature of the history of the world; for the world has set its face hopefully toward our democracy; and, O my fellow citizens, each one of you carries on your shoulders not only the burden of doing well for the sake of your own country, but the burden of doing well and seeing that this nation does well for the sake of mankind. . . .

At many stages in the advance of humanity, conflict between the men who possess more than they have earned and the men who have earned more than they possess is the central condition of progress. In our day it appears as the struggle of free men to gain and hold the right of self-government as against the special interests, who twist the methods of free government into machinery for defeating the popular will. At every stage, and under all circumstances, the essence of the struggle is to equalize opportunity, destroy privilege, and give to the life and citizenship of every individual the highest possible value both to himself and to the commonwealth. . . .

Practical equality of opportunity for all citizens, when we achieve it, will have two great results. First, every man will have a fair chance to make of himself all that in him lies; to reach the highest point to which his capacities, unassisted by special privilege of his own and unhampered by the special privilege of others, can carry him, and to get for himself and his family substantially what he has earned. Second, equality of opportunity means that the commonwealth will get from every citizen the highest service of which he is capable. No man who carries the burden of the special privileges of another can give to the commonwealth that service to which it is fairly entitled.

I stand for the square deal. But when I say that I am for the square deal, I mean not merely that I stand for fair play under the present rules of the game, but that I stand for having those rules changed so as to work for a more substantial equality of opportunity and of reward for equally good service. . . .

When I say I want a square deal for the poor man, I do not mean that I want a square deal for the man who remains poor because he has not got the energy to work for himself. If a man who has had a chance will not make good, then he has got to quit. . . .

Now, this means that our government, national and State, must be freed from the sinister influence or control of special interests. Exactly as the special interests of cotton and slavery threatened our political integrity before the Civil War, so now the great special business interests too often control and corrupt the men and methods of government for their own profit. We must drive the special interests out of politics. . . .

The true friend of property, the true conservative, is he who insists that property shall be the servant and not the master of the commonwealth; who insists that the creature of man's making shall be the servant and not the master of the man who made it. The citizens of the United States must effectively control the mighty commercial forces which they have themselves called into being.

There can be no effective control of corporations while their political activity remains. To put an end to it will be neither a short nor an easy task, but it can be done.

We must have complete and effective publicity of corporate affairs, so that the people may know beyond peradventure whether the corporations obey the law and whether their management entitles them to the confidence of the public. It is necessary that laws should be passed to prohibit the use of corporate funds directly or indirectly for political purposes; it is still more necessary that such laws should be thoroughly enforced. Corporate expenditures for political purposes, and especially such expenditures by public service corporations, have supplied one of the principal sources of corruption in our political affairs.

It has become entirely clear that we must have government supervision of the capitalization, not only of public service corporations, including, particularly, railways, but of all corporations doing an interstate business. I do not wish to see the nation forced into the ownership of the railways if it can possibly be avoided, and the only alternative is thoroughgoing and effective regulation, which shall be based on a full knowledge of all the facts, including a physical valuation of property. This physical valuation is not needed, or, at least, is very rarely needed, for fixing rates; but it is needed as the basis of honest capitalization.

We have come to recognize that franchises should never be granted except for a limited time, and never without proper provision for compensation to the public. It is my personal belief that the same kind and degree of control and supervision which should be exercised over public service corporations should be extended also to combinations which control necessaries of life, such as meat, oil, and coal, or which deal in them on an important scale. I have no doubt that the ordinary man who has control of them is much like ourselves. I have no doubt he would like to do well, but I want to have enough supervision to help him realize that desire to do well.

I believe that the officers, and, especially, the directors, of corporations should be held personally responsible when any corporation breaks the law.

Combinations in industry are the result of an imperative economic law which cannot be repealed by political legislation. The effort at prohibiting all combination has substantially failed. The way out lies, not in attempting to prevent such combinations, but in completely controlling them in the interest of the public welfare. . . .

No man should receive a dollar unless that dollar has been fairly earned. Every dollar received should represent a dollar's worth of service rendered—not gambling in stocks, but service rendered. The really big fortune, the swollen fortune, by the mere fact of its size acquires qualities which differentiate it in kind as well as in degree from what is possessed by men of relatively small means. Therefore, I believe in a graduated income tax on big fortunes, and in another tax which is far more easily collected and far more effective—a graduated inheritance tax on big fortunes, properly safeguarded against evasion and increasing rapidly in amount with the size of the estate.

The people of the United States suffer from periodical financial panics to a degree substantially unknown among the other nations which approach us in financial strength. There is no reason why we should suffer what they escape. It is of profound importance that our financial system should be promptly investigated, and so thoroughly and effectively revised as to make it certain that hereafter our currency will no longer fail at critical times to meet our needs. . . .

Of conservation I shall speak more at length elsewhere. Conservation means development as much as it does protection. I recognize the right and duty of this generation to develop and use the natural resources of our land; but I do not recognize the right to waste them, or to rob, by wasteful use, the generations that come after us. I ask nothing of the nation except that it so behave as each farmer here behaves with reference to his own children. That farmer is a poor creature who skins the land and leaves it worthless to his children. The farmer is a good farmer who, having enabled the land to support himself and to provide for the education of his children, leaves it to them a little better than he found it himself. I believe the same thing of a nation. . . .

Nothing is more true than that excess of every kind is followed by reaction; a fact which should be pondered by reformer and reactionary alike. We are face to face with new conceptions of the relations of property to human welfare, chiefly because certain advocates of the rights of property as against the rights of men have been pushing their claims too far. The man who wrongly holds that every human right is secondary to his profit must now give way to the advocate of human welfare, who rightly maintains that every man holds his property subject to the general right of the community to regulate its use to whatever degree the public welfare may require it. . . .

National efficiency has many factors. It is a necessary result of the principle of conservation widely applied. In the end it will determine our failure or success as a Nation. National efficiency has to do, not only with natural resources and with men, but it is equally concerned with institutions. The State must be made efficient for the work which concerns only the people of the State; and the Nation for that which concerns all the people. There must remain no neutral ground to serve as a refuge for lawbreakers, and especially for lawbreakers of great wealth, who can hire the vulpine legal cunning which will teach them how to avoid both jurisdictions. It is a misfortune when the national legislature fails to do its duty in providing a national remedy, so that the only national activity is the purely negative activity of the judiciary in forbidding the state to exercise power in the premises.

I do not ask for overcentralization; but I do ask that we work in a spirit of broad and far-reaching nationalism when we work for what concerns our people as a whole. We are all Americans. Our common interests are as broad as the continent. . . . The national Government belongs to the whole American people, and where the whole American people are interested, that interest can be guarded effectively only by the national Government. The betterment which we seek must be accomplished, I believe, mainly through the national Government.

The American people are right in demanding that New Nationalism, without which we cannot hope to deal with new problems. The New Nationalism puts the national need before sectional or personal advantage. It is impatient of the utter confusion that results from local legislatures attempting to treat national issues as local issues. It is still more impatient of the impotence which springs from overdivision of governmental powers, the impotence which makes it possible for local selfishness or for legal cunning, hired by wealthy special interests, to bring national activities to a deadlock. This New Nationalism regards the executive power as the steward of the public welfare. It demands of the judiciary that it shall be interested primarily in human welfare rather than in property, just as it demands that the representative body shall represent all the people rather than any one class or section of the people.

I believe in shaping the ends of government to protect property as well as human welfare. Normally, and in the long run, the ends are the same; but whenever the alternative must be faced, I am for men and not for property. . . .

I am far from underestimating the importance of dividends; but I rank dividends below human character. Again, I do not have any sympathy with the reformer who says he does not care for dividends. Of course, economic welfare is necessary, for a man must pull his own weight and be able to support his family. I know well that the reformers must not bring upon the people economic ruin, or the reforms themselves will go down in the ruin. But we must be ready to face temporary disaster, whether or not brought on by those who will war against us to the knife. Those who oppose all reform will do well to remember that ruin in its worst form is inevitable if our national life brings us nothing better than swollen fortunes for the few and the triumph in both politics and business of a sordid and selfish materialism.

If our political institutions were perfect, they would absolutely prevent the political domination of money in any part of our affairs. We need to make our political representatives more quickly and sensitively responsive to the people whose servants they are. More direct action by the people in their own affairs under proper safeguards is vitally necessary. The direct primary is a step in this direction, if it is associated with a corrupt practices act effective to prevent the advantage of the man willing recklessly and unscrupulously to spend money over his more honest competitor. It is particularly important that all money received or expended for campaign purposes should be publicly accounted for, not only after election, but before election as well. Political action must be made simpler, easier, and freer from confusion for every citizen. I believe that the prompt removal of unfaithful or incompetent public servants should be made easy and sure in whatever way experience shall show to be most expedient in any given class of cases.

One of the fundamental necessities in a representative government such as ours is to make certain that the men to whom the people delegate their power shall serve the people by whom they are elected, and not the special interests. I believe that every national officer, elected or appointed, should be forbidden to perform any service or receive any compensation, directly or indirectly, from interstate corporations; and a similar provision could not fail to be useful within the states.

The object of government is the welfare of the people. The material progress and prosperity of a nation are desirable chiefly so far as they lead to the moral and material welfare of all citizens. Just in proportion as the average man and woman are honest, capable of sound judgment and high ideals, active in public affairs—but, first of all, sound in their home life, and the father and mother of healthy children whom they bring up well—just so far, and no further, we may count our civilization a success. We must have—I believe we have already—a genuine and permanent moral awakening, without which no wisdom of legislation or administration really means anything; and, on the other hand, we must try to secure the social and economic legislation without which any improvement due to purely moral agitation is necessarily evanescent. . . . No matter how honest and decent we are in our private lives, if we do not have the right kind of law and the right kind of administration of the law, we cannot go forward as a nation. That is imperative; but it must be an addition to, and not a substitution for, the qualities that make up good citizens. In the last analysis, the most important elements in any man's career must be the sum of those qualities which, in the aggregate, we speak of as character. If he has not go it, then no law that the wit of man can devise, no administration of the law by the boldest and strongest executive, will avail to help him. We must have the right kind of character—character that makes a man, first of all, a good man in the home, a good father, a good husband—that makes a man a good neighbor. You must have that, and, then, in addition, you must have the kind of law and the kind of administration of the law which will give to those qualities in the private citizen the best possible chance for development. The prime problem of our nation is to get the right type of good citizenship, and, to get it, we must have progress, and our public men must be genuinely progressive.

The Old Order Changeth,* *Woodrow Wilson*, 1912

There is one great basic fact which underlies all the questions that are discussed on the political platform at the present moment. That singular fact is that nothing is done in this country as it was done twenty years ago.

We are in the presence of a new organization of society. Our life has broken away from the past. The life of America is not the life that it was twenty years ago; it is not the life that it was ten years ago. We have changed our economic conditions, absolutely, from top to bottom; and, with our economic society, the organization of our life. The old political formulas do not fit the present problems; they read now like

* From *The New Freedom* by Woodrow Wilson. Copyright 1913 by Doubleday & Company, Inc.

documents taken out of a forgotten age. The older cries sound as if they belonged to a past age which men have almost forgotten.

Things which used to be put into the party platforms of ten years ago would sound antiquated if put into a platform now. We are facing the necessity of fitting a new social organization, as we did once fit the old organization, to the happiness and prosperity of the great body of citizens; for we are conscious that the new order of society has not been made to fit and provide the convenience or prosperity of the average man. The life of the nation has grown infinitely varied. It does not center now upon questions of governmental structure or of the distribution of governmental powers. It centers upon questions of the very structure and operation of society itself, of which government is only the instrument. Our development has run so fast and so far along the lines sketched in the earlier day of constitutional definition, has so crossed and interlaced those lines, has piled upon them such novel structures of trust and combination, has elaborated within them a life so manifold, so full of forces which transcend the boundaries of the country itself and fill the eyes of the world, that a new nation seems to have been created which the old formulas do not fit or afford a vital interpretation of.

We have come upon a very different age from any that preceded us. We have come upon an age when we do not do business in the way in which we used to do business—when we do not carry on any of the operations of manufacture, sale, transportation, or communication as men used to carry them on. There is a sense in which in our day the individual has been submerged. In most parts of our country men work, not for themselves, not as partners in the old way in which they used to work, but generally as employees—in a higher or lower grade—of great corporations. There was a time when corporations played a very minor part in our business affairs, but now they play the chief part, and most men are the servants of corporations.

You know what happens when you are the servant of a corporation. You have in no instance access to the men who are really determining the policy of the corporation. If the corporation is doing the things that it ought not to do, you really have no voice in the matter and must obey the orders, and you have oftentimes with deep mortification to co-operate in the doing of things which you know are against the public interest. Your individuality is swallowed up in the individuality and purpose of a great organization.

It is true that, while most men are thus submerged in the corporation, a few, a very few, are exalted to a power which as individuals they could never have wielded. Through the great organizations of which they are the heads, a few are enabled to play a part unprecedented by anything in history in the control of the business operations of the country and in the determination of the happiness of great numbers of people.

Yesterday, and ever since history began, men were related to one another as individuals. To be sure there were the family, the Church, and the State, institutions which associated men in certain wide circles of relationship. But in the ordinary concerns of life, in the ordinary work, in the daily round, men dealt freely and directly with one another. Today, the everyday relationships of men are largely with great impersonal concerns, with organizations, not with other individual men.

Now this is nothing short of a new social age, a new era of human relationship, a new stage-setting for the drama of life.

In this new age we find, for instance, that our laws with regard to the relations of employer and employee are in many respects wholly antiquated and impossible. They were framed for another age, which nobody now living remembers, which is, indeed, so remote from our life that it would be difficult for many of us to understand it if it were described to us. The employer is now generally a corporation or a huge company of some kind; the employee is one of hundreds or of thousands brought together, not by individual masters whom they know and with whom they have personal relations, but by agents of one sort or another. Workingmen are marshaled in great numbers for the performance of a multitude of particular tasks under a common discipline. They generally use dangerous and powerful machinery, over whose repair and renewal they have no control. New rules must be devised with regard to their obligations and their rights, their obligations to their employers and their responsibilities to one another. Rules must be devised for their protection, for their compensation when injured, for their support when disabled.

There is something very new and very big and very complex about these new relations of capital and labor. A new economic society has sprung up, and we must effect a new set of adjustments. We must not pit power against weakness. The employer is generally, in our day, as I have said, not an individual, but a powerful group; and yet the workingman when dealing with his employer is still, under our existing law, an individual. . . .

What we have to discuss is, not wrongs which individuals intentionally do—I do not believe there are a great many of those—but the wrongs of a system. I want to record my protest against any discussion of this matter which would seem to indicate that there are bodies of our fellow-citizens who are trying to grind us down and do us injustice. There are some men of that sort. I don't know how they sleep o'nights, but there are men of that kind. Thank God, they are not numerous. The truth is, we are all caught in a great economic system which is heartless. The modern corporation is not engaged in business as an individual. When we deal with it, we deal with an impersonal element, an immaterial piece of society. . . .

And do our laws take note of this curious state of things? Do they even attempt to distinguish between a man's act as a corporation director and as an individual? They do not. Our laws still deal with us on the basis of the old system. The law is still living in the dead past which we have left behind. . . .

Since I entered politics, I have chiefly had men's views confided to me privately. Some of the biggest men in the United States, in the field of commerce and manufacture, are afraid of somebody, are afraid of something. They know that there is a power somewhere so organized, so subtle, so watchful, so interlocked, so complete, so pervasive, that they had better not speak above their breath when they speak in condemnation of it.

They know that America is not a place of which it can be said, as it used to be, that a man may choose his own calling and pursue it just as far as his abilities enable him to pursue it; because today, if he enters certain fields, there are organizations which will use means against him that will prevent his building up a business which they do not want to have built up; organizations that will see to it that the ground is cut from under him and the markets shut against him. For if he begins to sell to certain retail dealers, to any retail dealers, the monopoly will refuse to sell to those dealers, and those dealers, afraid, will not buy the new man's wares.

And this is the country which has lifted to the admiration of the world its ideals of absolutely free opportunity, where no man is supposed to be under any limitation except the limitations of his character and of his mind; where there is supposed to be no distinction of class, no distinction of blood, no distinction of social status, but where men win or lose on their merits.

American industry is not free, as once it was free; American enterprise is not free; the man with only a little capital is finding it harder to get into the field, more and more impossible to compete with the big fellow. Why? Because the laws of this country do not prevent the strong from crushing the weak. That is the reason, and because the strong have crushed the weak the strong dominate the industry and the economic life of this country. No man can deny that the lines of endeavor have more and more narrowed and stiffened; no man who knows anything about the development of industry in this country can have failed to observe that the larger kinds of credit are more and more difficult to obtain, unless you obtain them upon the terms of uniting your efforts with those who already control the industries of the country; and nobody can fail to observe that any man who tries to set himself up in competition with any process of manufacture which has been taken under the control of large combinations of capital will presently find himself either squeezed out or obliged to sell and allow himself to be absorbed.

There is a great deal that needs reconstruction in the United States. . . .

The present organization of business was meant for the big fellows and was not meant for the little fellows; it was meant for those who are at the top and was meant to exclude those who are at the bottom; it was meant to shut out beginners, to prevent new entries in the race, to prevent the building up of competitive enterprises that would interfere with the monopolies which the great trusts have built up.

What this country needs above everything else is a body of laws which will look after the men who are on the make rather than the men who are already made. Because the men who are already made are not going to live indefinitely, and they are not always kind enough to leave sons as able and as honest as they are.

The originative part of America, the part of America that makes new enterprises, the part into which the ambitious and gifted workingman makes his way up, the class that saves, that plans, that organizes, that presently spreads its enterprises until they have a national scope and character—that middle class is being more and more squeezed out by the processes which we have been taught to call processes of prosperity. Its members are sharing prosperity, no doubt; but what alarms me is that they are not *originating* prosperity. No country can afford to have its prosperity originated by a small controlling class. The treasury of America does not lie in the brains of the small body of men now in control of the great enterprises that have been concentrated under the direction of a very small number of persons. The treasury of America lies in those ambitions, those energies, that cannot be restricted to a special favored class. It depends upon the inventions of unknown men, upon the originations of unknown men, upon the ambitions of unknown men. Every country is renewed out of the ranks of the unknown, not out of the ranks of those already famous and powerful and in control.

There has come over the land that un-American set of

conditions which enables a small number of men who control the Government to get favors from the Government; by those favors to exclude their fellows from equal business opportunity; by those favors to extend a network of control that will presently dominate every industry in the country, and so make men forget the ancient time when America lay in every hamlet, when America was to be seen in every fair valley, when America displayed her great forces on the broad prairies, ran her fine fires of enterprise up over the mountain sides and down into the bowels of the earth, and eager men were everywhere captains of industry, not employees; not looking to a distant city to find out what they might do, but looking about among their neighbors, finding credit according to their character, not according to their connections, finding credit in proportion to what was known to be in them and behind them, not in proportion to the securities they held that were approved where they were not known. In order to start an enterprise now, you have to be authenticated, in a perfectly impersonal way, not according to yourself, but according to what you own that somebody else approves of your owning. You cannot begin such an enterprise as those that have made America until you are so authenticated, until you have succeeded in obtaining the goodwill of large allied capitalists. Is that freedom? That is dependence, not freedom.

We used to think in the old-fashioned days when life was very simple that all that government had to do was to put on a policeman's uniform, and say, "Now don't anybody hurt anybody else." We used to say that the ideal of government was for every man to be left alone and not interfered with, except when he interfered with somebody else; and that the best government was the government that did as little governing as possible. That was the idea that obtained in Jefferson's time. But we are coming now to realize that life is so complicated that we are not dealing with the old conditions, and that the law has to step in and create new conditions under which we may live, the conditions which will make it tolerable for us to live. . . .

Why are we in the presence, why are we at the threshold, of a revolution? Because we are profoundly disturbed by the influences which we see reigning in the determination of our public life and our public policy. There was a time when America was blithe with self-confidence. She boasted that she, and she alone, knew the processes of popular government; but now she sees her sky overcast; she sees that there are at work forces which she did not dream of in her hopeful youth.

Don't you know that some man with eloquent tongue, without conscience, who did not care for the nation, could put this whole country into a flame? Don't you know that this country from one end to the other believes that something is wrong? What an opportunity it would be for some man without conscience to spring up and say: "This is the way. Follow me!"—and lead in paths of destruction!

The old order changeth—changeth under our very eyes, not quietly and equably, but swiftly and with the noise and heat and tumult of reconstruction.

I suppose that all struggle for law has been conscious, that very little of it has been blind or merely instinctive. It is the fashion to say, as if with superior knowledge of affairs and of human weakness that every age has been an age of transition, and that no age is more full of change than another; yet in very few ages of the world can the struggle for change have been so widespread, so deliberate, or upon so great a scale as in this in which we are taking part.

The transition we are witnessing is no equable transition of growth and normal alteration; no silent, unconscious unfolding of one age into another, its natural heir and successor. Society is looking itself over, in our day, from top to bottom; is making fresh and critical analysis of its very elements; is questioning its oldest practices as freely as its newest, scrutinizing every arrangement and motive of its life; and it stands ready to attempt nothing less than a radical reconstruction, which only frank and honest counsels and the forces of generous co-operation can hold back from becoming a revolution. We are in a temper to reconstruct economic society, as we were once in a temper to reconstruct political society, and political society may itself undergo a radical modification in the process. I doubt if any age was ever more conscious of its task or more unanimously desirous of radical and extended changes in its economic and political practice.

We stand in the presence of a revolution—not a bloody revolution; America is not given to the spilling of blood—but a silent revolution, whereby America will insist upon recovering in practice those ideals which she has always professed, upon securing a government devoted to the general interest and not to special interests.

We are upon the eve of a great reconstruction. It calls for creative statesmanship as no age has done since that great age in which we set up the government under which we live, that government which was the admiration of the world until it suffered wrongs to grow up under it which have made many of our own compatriots question the freedom of our institutions and preach revolution against them. I do not fear revolution. I have unshaken faith in the power of America to keep its self-possession. Revolution will come in peaceful guise, as it came when we put aside the crude government of the Confederation and created the great Federal Union which governs individuals, not States, and which has been these hundred and thirty years our vehicle of progress. Some radical changes we must make in our law and practice. Some reconstructions we must push forward, which a new age and new circumstances impose upon us. But we can do it all in calm and sober fashion, like statesmen and patriots.

I do not speak of these things in apprehension, because all is open and above-board. This is not a day in which great forces rally in secret. The whole stupendous program must be publicly planned and canvassed. Good temper, the wisdom that comes of sober counsel, the energy of thoughtful and unselfish men, the habit of co-operation and compromise which has been bred in us by long years of free government, in which reason rather than passion has been made to prevail by the sheer virtue of candid and universal debate, will enable us to win through to still another great age without violence.

Chapter 21

THE GREAT CRUSADE AND AFTER

When on March 4, 1913, Woodrow Wilson became President of the United States, the American mind was far from thoughts of war and peace. Though for two decades Americans had enjoyed both the material and the emotional satisfactions of imperialist expansion, they had not yet fully accepted the limitations and responsibilities that accompany predominance in world affairs. The acquisition of a colonial empire had marked the formal abandonment of isolationism, but few were aware that now the nation's destiny might be determined in the chancelleries of the world. Most Americans were still provincial enough to believe that they could assume and divest themselves of the burden of world leadership at will, and in the heat of the 1912 Presidential campaign national energies were once again directed toward domestic issues to the exclusion of any real concern for international interests and commitments. Indeed, while Wilson's Inaugural Address solemnly pointed the way to national reconstruction, it contained not a single reference to America's relations with foreign nations or to the seething troubles of the world at large.

Nevertheless, foreign affairs became a major concern of Wilson's administration. From his first days in office there raged a bitter quarrel with Mexico's revolutionary leaders which frequently threatened to erupt into war. And the vulnerability of America's new position of power was strikingly demonstrated by her inability to remain aloof from the world conflict precipitated in the summer of 1914 by the assassination of Archduke Ferdinand, heir-apparent to the Austro-Hungarian throne. Wilson immediately issued a Proclamation of Neutrality, and at first the European conflagration seemed of small concern to a distant people intent upon domestic reform. Eventually, however, America's involvement in the stakes of world diplomacy proved stronger than the illusion of isolation, and in April, 1917, after several years of vacillation and confusion, she entered the war on the side of the Allies.

No single factor of itself "caused" America to fight, though British propaganda, American economic ties to the Allies, and unrestricted German submarine warfare all played significant roles in leading the nation on the road to war. And in molding American opinion even the outstanding success of British propaganda depended largely upon Americans' latent sympathy with the Allied cause. Numbers of German-Americans supported the Fatherland, and many citizens of Irish extraction bitterly and continuously denounced the British, but from the very beginning of the war public opinion was for the most part decidedly pro-Ally. The subtle bonds of language, custom, and a common literary and political heritage tied America more closely to England in war than ever before in peace; while traditional attachment to the French was fostered by recollections of France's gallant contributions to the American Revolution. The stage was set, then, for a widespread propaganda campaign designed to maneuver a cautious but sympathetic public into war. Throughout the nation British-inspired articles, speeches, lectures, debates and films argued the case against Germany. From college presidents to practicing journalists influential persons in every profession were enlisted to add an aura of validity to even the most outrageously false atrocity stories of German brutality. And Americans were assured on every hand that Germany alone was responsible for a war which ostensibly was a struggle between democracy and civilization on the one side and autocracy and barbarism on the other. Besides, Germany's feeble propaganda effort proved highly ineffective. It was handicapped both by an inability to grasp American modes of thought and by the bald facts that the Kaiser's troops *did* openly violate Belgian neutrality, that a German U-boat *did* torpedo the *Lusitania* with the loss of hundreds of lives, and that German espionage agents *did* attempt sabotage in American munitions plants. Thus the efficient British propaganda machine impressed upon the American mind stereotypes of German motives and ambitions that went far to prepare the nation psychologically for war against the aggressive "Hun."

Extensive business and financial ties to the Allies further jeopardized American neutrality, for they made the prospect of a German victory materially as well as ideologically unpalatable. When the war began, it had been clear to Wilson and to William Jennings Bryan, his Secretary of State, that economic involvement with either of the belligerents might compromise the nation's neutral status and lead to war. At first, therefore, the government refused to sanction loans by American bankers to the warring powers. But the President vigorously opposed an embargo that would have cut off altogether shipments abroad, and cash or credit purchases, whether of contraband or non-contraband, could still be made. Though forced to liquidate a large part of their assets in the United States to pay for these goods, the Allies alone benefited from Wilson's open policy, for control of the seas enabled them to transport foodstuffs and munitions to their own forces and to prevent neutral and enemy vessels alike from reaching Germany with American cargoes. Soon, however, Allied assets and credits in the United States were exhausted by tremendous expenditures, and Wilson was faced with an unhappy choice. If he reversed his earlier position and now approved of large scale private loans to the Allies to finance continued purchases of American goods, he would skirt the edge of belligerency and endanger American neutrality. Yet if he refused to permit these loans, not only would the Allied cause be seriously endangered, but the national economy, largely geared to war demands, would suffer serious dislocation and depression. Under intense pressure from a frightened business community and from Allied sympathizers among his advisers (the pacific and impartial Bryan had already resigned from the Cabinet), Wilson finally made his fateful choice to withdraw the government's opposition to private loans for the belligerents. And by the spring of 1917, when the United States formally entered the World War, Americans had already loaned approximately two billion dollars to the Allies (though only 27 millions to Germany) and had made their economy even more dependent upon Allied purchases of war material. The nation's economic stake in an Allied victory had grown enormously; with this huge investment, though not necessarily because of it, had come war.

Still, whatever the underlying causes of America's ultimate readiness to join forces with the Allies, it was the German U-boat that immediately plunged the nation into war. Mistress of the seas, England had again and again taken liberties with American neutral rights in her efforts to blockade the Central Powers; she had arbitrarily declared the North Sea a military zone, making that vital trade area largely inaccessible to neutral shipping; she had forced countless American ships to distant ports for visit and search; and under a vastly extended contraband list she had seized American cargoes bound directly or indirectly (through other neutral countries) for Germany. Yet British depredations had not taken American lives; American shippers had been generously compensated for their property losses; and though the State Department went through the formality of protesting these high-handed practices, the emotional and economic ties between the two countries were far too close to permit even the threat of retaliation.

On the other hand, German violations of American rights were received very differently, for here there was no reservoir of friendship and interest to temper national indignation. Early in 1915 Germany proclaimed a submarine war zone around the British Isles in order to counter the Allied blockade, warning that enemy ships would be torpedoed on sight. But now the American government refused to acquiesce as timidly as it had with the British earlier. Instead it continued to permit its citizens unlimited travel aboard Allied ships in the restricted zone, ominously declaring that Germany alone would be held to "strict accountability" if American lives or property were lost.

Submarine warfare very quickly took its toll. On May 7, 1915, a British liner, the *Lusitania*, was torpedoed and sunk without warning, with the loss of nearly 1200 persons, over 100 of whom were Americans. Other American lives and ships were lost during the year that followed, and though Wilson himself insisted that "There is such a thing as a man being too proud to fight," the bitterness and seeming finality of American protests led the Germans, on May 4, 1916, to pledge that unresisting merchantmen would not be sunk without warning and adequate provision for passengers and crew. But eight months later, in January, 1917, Germany announced that unrestricted submarine warfare would resume immediately and that U-boats would torpedo all ships, whether neutral or belligerent, found in the war zone. The logic behind this new position was clear, though mistaken. The German High Command had recognized that such a policy would be followed by war with the great Western power, but it was equally convinced that in the near future America could not aid the Allies any more as an active belligerent than she had as a "benevolent" neutral, for now German U-boats would be totally unrestricted in their efforts to send American cargoes to the bottom of the sea. Then on April 2, 1917, after several more American ships had been torpedoed, Woodrow Wilson appeared before the Congress to take up the German challenge. "Property can be paid for," said the President in his memorable war message, but "the lives of peaceful and innocent people cannot be. The present German submarine warfare against commerce is a warfare against mankind." Four days later the Congress acceded to the President's request, and war was declared against Germany.

Wilson's own role in molding America's final decision to enter the war is difficult to evaluate, for at no time was the austere reformer free from tormenting conflict on the grave issue before him. As an historian, Wilson was familiar enough with the ways of international power politics to see through many of the Allied propaganda claims, and when the war began in Europe he had called upon the American people to be "impartial in thought as well as in action" so that the nation might maintain absolute neutrality between the belligerents. Even as late as the presidential election of 1916, when the Republican Charles Evans Hughes opposed Wilson, the Democrats were able to make effective use of the slogan "He kept us out of war." But official proclamations could not change, nor even disguise, Wilson's own deep involvement with the Allied cause. His broad sympathy for the English and his intense feeling that the Allies were fighting "our fight" far outweighed his dim and merely intellectual awareness of the war's imperialist origins. Yet even these fervid sympathies did not permit him fully and satisfactorily to resolve his personal inner conflict between the choices of war and peace, for the controlled and puritanical President was not capable of lightly brushing aside his understanding and totally succumbing to his feelings. At length, of course, he chose war, but not without the gravest of misgivings engendered both by his somewhat reluctant recognition of the essentially nonideological nature of the world struggle and by his basic antipathy to war itself. To a less scrupulous, less self-demanding statesman such misgivings would have brought balance and humility; but to the perfectionist Wilson they brought only confusion and a tortured sense of guilt which convinced him that the war must be a holy crusade to "make the world safe for democracy."

Earlier Wilson had called for a "peace without victory"; now he placed America's physical and moral might behind his famous Fourteen Points for a just and lasting peace. Wilson's Fourteenth Point, providing for a "general association of nations . . . for the purpose of affording mutual guarantees of political independence and territorial integrity to great and small states alike," was the cornerstone of his plans for international order. And when the Treaty of Versailles was drawn up at the end of the war Wilson made several concessions in his other idealistic demands in order to assure the creation of a meaningful League of Nations. These concessions to Clemenceau of France, Lloyd George of England and Orlando of Italy were to no avail, however, for it was the Republican leaders of the United States Senate, not the nationalist statesmen of Europe, who fought most bitterly against Wilson's League and who contributed to its ultimate defeat by refusing American participation.

Doubtlessly partisanship played a decisive role in formulating Congressional opposition to the League. Those "irreconcilable" isolationists who bitterly opposed American participation in *any* formal international organization were alone too few to prevent the two-thirds Senate vote necessary for ratification of the Treaty of Versailles, into which was written the Covenant of the League of Nations. Indeed, Wilson's leading Republican opponent, Senator Henry Cabot Lodge, Chairman of the powerful Committee on Foreign Relations, had only a few years earlier heartily endorsed a league to enforce peace. But the Treaty before the Senate was exclusively Wilsonian and Democratic, and the Massachusetts Republican was determined either to defeat Wilson's creation or, preferably, to make it over into a Republican document through extensive reservations and amendments. Wilson was equally determined to have the treaty as it stood or not at all. Neither man was willing to give way to the other. In November, 1919, and again in March, 1920, moderate Republicans joined with the hard core of Senate isolationists to defeat the Treaty *without* the Lodge reservations. And Wilson Democrats, obeying their intransigent chief's wishes, joined with these same isolationists to defeat the Treaty *with* the Lodge reservations.

Thus Wilson must share with Lodge and his followers much of the responsibility for the defeat of the Treaty and the League in the Senate. Sincerely convinced that only a totally unqualified League could justify and atone for the death and destruction brought by the holocaust to which he had himself committed the nation, Wilson had lost all sense of political necessity. Late in 1918, on the very eve of victory, he had made a foolishly partisan appeal to the country to elect a Democratic Congress, implying that only the party in power might successfully end the war and make peace secure; and the nation had replied by electing a Republican House and a Republican Senate. When he went to Europe later that year Wilson took only one Republican adviser, and not a single Senator, to the Versailles Peace Conference, thereby antagonizing not only an already highly aroused opposition party, but also the legislative body that must ultimately accept or reject whatever treaty he might bring home. Finally in the summer of 1919 Wilson took his case to the country in an exhausting round of speeches, of which the most moving was his address at Pueblo, Colorado, where he finally succumbed to physical exhaustion and suffered a near-fatal stroke. But the President had unfortunately forgotten the role of compromise in the democratic process, and his efforts were in vain. The irony of Wilson's Presidency was that the domestic reformer should have been so completely caught up in the embroilments of world affairs. Its supreme tragedy was that his own single-minded devotion to the establishment of the machinery of international cooperation—exactly as he had conceived it, without reservation or amendment—should have helped destroy the lasting peace for which he had fought so valiantly and which he considered a personal as much as a national imperative.

War Message to Congress, *Woodrow Wilson*, 1917

Gentlemen of the Congress: I have called the Congress into extraordinary session because there are serious, very serious, choices of policy to be made, and made immediately, which it was neither right nor constitutionally permissible that I should assume the responsibility of making.

On the third of February last I officially laid before you the extraordinary announcement of the Imperial German Government that on and after the first day of February it was its purpose to put aside all restraints of law or of humanity and use its submarines to sink every vessel that sought to approach either the ports of Great Britain and Ireland or the western coasts of Europe or any of the ports controlled by the enemies of Germany within the Mediterranean. That had seemed to be the object of the German submarine warfare earlier in the war, but since April of last year the Imperialist Government had somewhat restrained the commanders of its undersea craft in conformity with its promise then given to us that passenger boats should not be sunk and that due warning would be given to all other vessels which its submarines might seek to destroy, when no resistance was offered or escape attempted, and care taken that their crews were given at least a fair chance to save their lives in their open boats. The precautions taken were meagre and haphazard enough, as was proved in distressing instance after instance in the progress of the cruel and unmanly business, but a certain degree of restraint was observed. The new policy has swept every restriction aside. Vessels of every kind, whatever their flag, their character, their cargo, their destination, their errand, have been ruthlessly sent to the bottom without warning and without thought of help or mercy for those on board, the vessels of friendly neutrals along with those of belligerents. Even hospital ships and ships carrying relief to the sorely bereaved and stricken people of Belgium, though the latter were provided with safe conduct through the proscribed areas by the German Government itself and were distinguished by unmistakable marks of identity, have been sunk with the same reckless lack of compassion or of principle.

I was for a little while unable to believe that such things would in fact be done by any government that had hitherto subscribed to the humane practices of civilized nations. International law had its origin in the attempt to set up some law which would be respected and observed upon the seas, where no nation had right of dominion and where lay the free highways of the world. By painful stage after stage has that law been built up, with meagre enough results, indeed, after all was accomplished that could be accomplished, but always with a clear view, at least, of what the heart and conscience of mankind demanded. This minimum of right the German Government has swept aside under the plea of retaliation and necessity and because it had no weapons which it could use at sea except these which it is impossible to employ as it is employing them without throwing to the winds all scruples of humanity or of respect for the understandings that were supposed to underlie the intercourse of the world. I am not now thinking of the loss of property involved, immense and serious as that is, but only of the wanton and wholesale destruction of the lives of non-combatants, men, women, and children, engaged in pursuits which have always, even in the darkest periods of modern history, been deemed innocent and legitimate. Property can be paid for; the lives of peaceful and innocent people cannot be. The present German submarine warfare against commerce is a warfare against mankind. . . .

When I addressed the Congress on the twenty-sixth of February last I thought that it would suffice to assert our neutral rights with arms, our right to use the seas against unlawful interference, our right to keep our people safe against unlawful violence. But armed neutrality, it now appears, is impracticable. Because submarines are in effect outlaws when used as the German submarines have been used against merchant shipping, it is impossible to defend ships against their attacks as the law of nations has assumed that merchantmen would defend themselves against privateers or cruisers, visible craft giving chase upon the open sea. It is common prudence in such circumstances, grim necessity indeed, to endeavour to destroy them before they have shown their own intention. They must be dealt with upon sight, if dealt with at all. The German Government denies the right of neutrals to use arms at all within the areas of the sea which it has proscribed, even in the defense of rights which no modern publicist has ever before questioned their right to defend. The intimation is conveyed that the armed guards which we have placed on our merchant ships will be treated as beyond the pale of law and subject to be dealt with as pirates would be. Armed neutrality is ineffectual enough at best; in such circumstances and in the face of such pretensions it is worse than ineffectual: it is likely only to produce what it was meant to prevent; it is practically certain to draw us into the war without either the rights or the effectiveness of belligerents. There is one choice we cannot make, we are incapable of making: we will not choose the path of submission and suffer the most sacred rights of our nation and our people to be ignored or violated. The wrongs against which we now array ourselves are no common wrongs; they cut to the very roots of human life.

With a profound sense of the solemn and even tragical character of the step I am taking and of the grave responsibilities which it involves, but in unhesitating obedience to what I deem my constitutional duty, I advise that the Congress declare the recent course of the Imperial German Government to be in fact nothing less than war against the Government and people of the United States; that it formally accept the status of belligerent which has thus been thrust upon it; and that it take immediate steps not only to put the country in a more thorough state of defense but also to exert all its power and employ all its resources to bring the Government of the German Empire to terms and end the war. . . .

While we do these things, these deeply momentous things, let us be very clear, and make very clear to all the world what our motives and our objects are. My own thought has not been driven from its habitual and normal course by the unhappy events of the last two months, and I do not believe that the thought of the nation has been altered or clouded by them. I have exactly the same things in mind now that I had in mind when I addressed the Senate on the twenty-second of January last; the same that I had in mind when I addressed the Congress on the third of February and on the twenty-sixth of February. Our object now, as then, is to vindicate the principles of peace and justice in the life of the world as against selfish and autocratic power and to set up amongst the really free and self-governed peoples of the world such a concert of purpose and of action as will henceforth ensure the observance of those principles. Neutrality is no longer feasible or desirable where the peace of the world is involved and the freedom of its peoples, and the menace to that peace and freedom lies in the existence of autocratic governments backed by organized force which is controlled wholly by their will, not by the will of their people. We have seen the last of neutrality in such circumstances. We are at the beginning of an age in which it will be insisted that the same standards of conduct and of responsibility for wrong done shall be observed among nations and their governments that are observed among the individual citizens of civilized states.

We have no quarrel with the German people. We have no feeling towards them but one of sympathy and friendship. It was not upon their impulse that their government acted in entering the war. It was not with their previous knowledge or approval. It was a war determined upon as wars used to be determined upon in the old, unhappy days when peoples were nowhere consulted by their rulers and wars were provoked and waged in the interest of dynasties or of little groups of ambitious men who were accustomed to use their fellow men as pawns and tools. Self-governed nations do not fill their neighbour states with spies or set the course of intrigue to bring about some critical posture of affairs which will give them an opportunity to strike and make conquest. Such designs can be successfully worked out only under cover and where no one has the right to ask questions. Cunningly contrived plans of deception or aggression, carried, it may be, from generation to generation, can be worked out and kept from the light only within the privacy of courts or behind the carefully guarded confidences of a narrow and privileged class. They are happily impossible where public opinion commands and insists upon full information concerning all the nation's affairs.

A steadfast concert for peace can never be maintained except by a partnership of democratic nations. No autocratic government could be trusted to keep faith within it or observe its covenants. It must be a league of honour, a partnership of opinion. Intrigue would eat its vitals away; the plottings of inner circles who could plan what they would and render account to no one would be a corruption seated at its very heart. Only free peoples can hold their purpose and their honour steady to a common end and prefer the interests of mankind to any narrow interest of their own. . . .

We are accepting this challenge of hostile purpose because we know that in such a government, following such methods, we can never have a friend; and that in the presence of its organized power, always lying in wait to accomplish we know not what purpose, there can be no assured security for the democratic governments of the world. We are now about to accept gauge of battle with this natural foe to liberty and shall, if necessary, spend the whole force of the nation to check and nullify its pretensions and its power. We are glad, now that we see the facts with no veil of false pretence about them, to fight thus for the ultimate peace of the world and for the liberation of its peoples, the German peoples included: for the rights of nations great and small and the privilege of men everywhere to choose their way of life and of obedience. The world must be made safe for democracy. Its peace must be planted upon the tested foundations of political liberty. We have no selfish ends to serve. We desire no conquest, no dominion. We seek no indemnities for ourselves, no material compensation for the sacrifices we shall freely make. We are but one of the champions of the rights of mankind. We shall be satisfied when those rights have been made as secure as the faith and the freedom of nations can make them.

Just because we fight without rancour and without selfish object, seeking nothing for ourselves but what we shall wish to share with all free peoples, we shall, I feel confident, conduct our operations as belligerents without passion and ourselves observe with proud punctilio the principles of right and of fair play we profess to be fighting for. . . .

It will be all the easier for us to conduct ourselves as belligerents in a high spirit of right and fairness because we act without animus, not in enmity towards a people or with the desire to bring any injury or disadvantage upon them, but only in armed opposition to an irresponsible government which has thrown aside all considerations of humanity and of right and is running amuck. We are, let me say again, the sincere friends of the German people, and shall desire nothing so much as the early re-establishment of intimate relations of mutual advantage between us—however hard it may be for them, for the time being, to believe that this is spoken from our hearts. We have borne with their present government through all these bitter months because of that friendship— exercising a patience and forbearance which would otherwise have been impossible. We shall, happily, still have an opportunity to prove that friendship in our daily attitude and actions towards the millions of men and women of German birth and native sympathy who live amongst us and share our life, and we shall be proud to prove it towards all who are in fact loyal to their neighbours and to the Government in the hour of test. They are, most of them, as true and loyal Americans as if they had never known any other fealty or allegiance. They will be prompt to stand with us in rebuking and restraining the few who may be of a different mind and purpose. If there should be disloyalty, it will be dealt with with a firm hand of stern repression; but, if it lifts its head at all, it will lift it only here and there and without countenance except from a lawless and malignant few.

It is a distressing and oppressive duty, Gentlemen of the Congress, which I have performed in thus addressing you. There are, it may be, many months of fiery trial and sacrifice ahead of us. It is a fearful thing to lead this great peaceful people into war, into the most terrible and disastrous of all wars, civilization itself seeming to be in the balance. But the right is more precious than peace, and we shall fight for the things which we have always carried nearest our hearts—for democracy, for the right of those who submit to authority to have a voice in their own governments, for the rights and liberties of small nations, for a universal dominion of right by such a concert of free people as shall bring peace and safety to all nations and make the world itself at last free. To such a task we can dedicate our lives and our fortunes, everything that we are and everything that we have, with the pride of those who know that the day has come when America is privileged to spend her blood and her might for the principles that gave her birth and happiness and the peace which she has treasured. God helping her, she can do no other.

The Pueblo Speech on the League of Nations,
Woodrow Wilson, 1919

. . . There have been unpleasant impressions as well as pleasant impressions, my fellow citizens, as I have crossed the continent. I have perceived more and more that men have been busy creating an absolutely false impression of what the treaty of peace and the covenant of the League of Nations contain and mean. . . . Therefore, in order to clear away the mists, in order to remove the impressions, in order to check the falsehoods that have clustered around this great subject, I want to tell you a few very simple things about the treaty and the covenant.

. . . It is a people's treaty, that accomplishes by a great sweep of practical justice the liberation of men who never could have liberated themselves, and the power of the most powerful nations has been devoted not to their aggrandizement but to the liberation of people whom they could have put under their control if they had chosen to do so. Not one foot of territory is demanded by the conquerors, not one single item of submission to their authority is demanded by them. The men who sat around that table in Paris knew that the time had come when the people were no longer going to consent to live under masters, but were going to live the lives that they chose themselves, to live under such governments as they chose themselves to erect. That is the fundamental principle of this great settlement. . . .

At the front of this great treaty is put the covenant of the League of Nations. . . . Unless you get the united, concerted purpose and power of the great Governments of the world behind this settlement, it will fall down like a house of cards. There is only one power to put behind the liberation of mankind, and that is the power of mankind. It is the power of the united moral forces of the world, and in the covenant of the League of Nations the moral forces of the world are mobilized. . . . They enter into a solemn promise to one another that they will never use their power against one another for aggression; that they never will impair the territorial integrity of a neighbor; that they never will interfere with the political independence of a neighbor; that they will abide by the principle that great populations are entitled to determine their own destiny and that they will not interfere with that destiny; and that no matter what differences arise amongst them they will never resort to war without first having . . . either submitted the matter of controversy to arbitration, in which case they agree to abide by the result without question, or submitted it to the consideration of the Council of the League of Nations . . . agreeing that there shall be six months allowed for the mature consideration of . . . the Council, and agreeing that at the expiration of the six months, even if they are not then ready to accept the advice of the Council with regard to the settlement of the dispute, they will still not go to war for another three months. In other words, they consent, no matter what happens, to submit every matter of difference between them to the judgment of mankind, and just so certainly as they do that, . . . war will be pushed out of the foreground of terror in which it has kept the world for generation after generation, and men will know that there will be a calm time of deliberate counsel. The most dangerous thing for a bad cause is to expose it to the opinion of the world. The most certain way that you can prove that a man is mistaken is by letting all his neighbors know what he thinks, by letting all his neighbors discuss what he thinks, and if he is in the wrong you will notice that he will stay at home, he will not walk on the street. He will be afraid of the eyes of his neighbors. He will be afraid of their judgment of his character. He will know that his cause is lost unless he can sustain it by the arguments of right and of justice. The same law that applies to individuals applies to nations. . . .

When you come to the heart of the covenant, my fellow citizens, you will find . . . there is something in article 10 that you ought to realize and ought to accept or reject. Article 10 is the heart of the whole matter. . . . Article 10 provides that every member of the League convenants to respect and preserve the territorial integrity and existing political independence of every other member of the League as against external aggression. Not against internal disturbance. There was not a man at that table who did not admit the sacredness of the right of self-determination, the sacredness of the right of any body of people to say that they would not continue to live under the Government they were then living under, and under article 11 of the covenant they are given a place to say whether they will live under it or not. For following article 10 is article 11, which makes it the right of any member of the League at any time to call attention to anything, anywhere, that is likely to disturb the peace of the world or the good understanding between nations upon which the peace of the world depends. . . . Now, read articles 10 and 11. You will see that international law is revolutionized by putting morals into it. Article 10 says that no member of the League, and that includes all these nations that have demanded these things unjustly of China, shall impair the territorial integrity or the political independence of any other member of the League. China is going to be a member of the League. Article 11 says that any member of the League can call attention to anything that is likely to disturb the peace of the world or the good understanding between nations, and China is for the first time in the history of mankind afforded a standing before the jury of the world. I, for my part, have a profound sympathy for China, and I am proud to have taken part in an arrangement which promises the protection of the world to the rights of China. The whole atmosphere of the world is changed by a thing like that, my fellow citizens. The whole international practice of the world is revolutionized.

But you will say, "what is the second sentence of article 10? That is what gives very disturbing thoughts." The second sentence is that the Council of the League shall advise what steps, if any, are necessary to carry out the guaranty of the first sentence, namely, that the members will respect and preserve the territorial integrity and political independence of the other members. I do not know any other meaning for the word "advise" except "advise." The Council advises, and it can not advise without the vote of the United States. Why gentlemen should fear that the Congress of the United States would be advised to do something that it did not want to do I frankly can not imagine, because they can not even be advised to do anything unless their own representative has participated in the advice. It may be that that will impair somewhat the vigor of the League, but, nevertheless, the fact is so, that we are not obliged to take any advice except our own, which to any man who wants to go his own course is a very satisfactory state of affairs. Every man regards his own advice as best, and I dare say every man mixes his own advice with some thought of his own interest. Whether we use it wisely or unwisely, we can use the vote of the United States to make impossible drawing the United States into any enterprise that she does not care to be drawn into.

Yet article 10 strikes at the taproot of war. Article 10 is a statement that the very things that have always been sought in imperialistic wars are henceforth forgone by every ambitious nation in the world. I would have felt very lonely, my fellow countrymen, and I would have felt very much disturbed if, sitting at the peace table in Paris, I had supposed that I was expounding my own ideas. Whether you believe it or not, I know the relative size of my own ideas; I know how they stand related in bulk and proportion to the moral judgments of my fellow countrymen, and I proposed nothing whatever at the peace table at Paris that I had not sufficiently certain knowledge embodied the moral judgment of the citizens of the United States. I had gone over there with, so to say, explicit instructions. Don't you remember that we laid down fourteen points which should contain the principles of the settlement? They were not my points. In every one of them I was conscientiously trying to read the thought of the people of the United States, and after I uttered those points I had every assurance given me that could be given me that they did speak the moral judgment of the United States and not my single judgment. . . .

I am dwelling upon these points, my fellow citizens, in spite of the fact that I dare say to most of you they are perfectly well known, because in order to meet the present situation we have got to know what we are dealing with. We are not dealing with the kind of document which this is represented by some gentlemen to be; and inasmuch as we are dealing with a document simon-pure in respect of the very principles we have professed and lived up to, we have got to do one or other of two things—we have got to adopt it or reject it. There is no middle course. You can not go in on a special-privilege basis of your own. I take it that you are too proud to ask to be exempted from responsibilities which the other members of the League will carry. We go in upon equal terms or we do not go in at all; and if we do not go in, my fellow citizens, think of the tragedy of that result—the only sufficient guaranty to the peace of the world withheld! Ourselves drawn apart with that dangerous pride which means that we shall be ready to take care of ourselves, and that means that we shall maintain great standing armies and an irresistible navy; that means we shall have the organization of a military nation; that means we shall have a general staff, with the kind of power that the general staff of Germany had, to mobilize this great manhood of the Nation when it pleases, all the energy of our young men drawn into the thought and preparation for war. What of our pledges to the men that lie dead in France? We said that they went over there, not to prove the prowess of America or her readiness for another war but to see to it that there never was such a war again. It always seems to make it difficult for me to say anything, my fellow citizens, when I think of my clients in this case. My clients are the children; my clients are the next generation. They do not know what promises and bonds I undertook when I ordered the armies of the United States to the soil of France, but I know, and I intend to redeem my pledges to the children; they shall not be sent upon a similar errand.

Again and again, my fellow citizens, mothers who lost their sons in France have come to me and, taking my hand, have shed tears upon it not only, but they had added, "God bless you, Mr. President!" Why, my fellow citizens, should they pray God to bless me? I advised the Congress of the United States to create the situation that led to the death of their sons. I ordered their sons overseas. I consented to their sons being put in the most difficult parts of the battle line, where death was certain, as in the impenetrable difficulties of the forest of Argonne. Why should they weep upon my hand and call down the blessings of God upon me? Because they believe that their boys died for something that vastly transcends any of the immediate and palpable objects of the war. They believe, and they rightly believe, that their sons saved the liberty of the world. They believe that wrapped up with the liberty of the world is the continuous protection of that liberty by the concerted powers of all civilized people. They believe that this sacrifice was made in order that other sons should not be called upon for a similar gift—the gift of life, the gift of all that died—and if we did not see this thing through, if we fulfilled the dearest present wish of Germany and now dissociated ourselves from those alongside whom we fought in the war, would not something of the halo go away from the gun over the mantelpiece, or the sword? Would not the old uniform lose something of its significance? These men were crusaders. They were not going forth to prove the might of the United States. They were going forth to prove the might of justice and right, and all the world accepted them as crusaders, and their transcendent achievement has made all the world believe in America as it believes in no other nation organized in the modern world. There seems to me to stand between us and the rejection or qualification of this treaty the serried ranks of those boys in khaki, not only these boys who came home, but those dear ghosts that still deploy upon the fields of France.

My friends, on last Decoration Day I went to a beautiful hillside near Paris, where was located the cemetery of Suresnes, a cemetery given over to the burial of the American dead. Behind me on the slopes was rank upon rank of living American soldiers, and lying before me upon the levels of the plain was rank upon rank of departed American soldiers. Right by the side of the stand where I spoke there was a little group of French women who had adopted those graves, had made themselves mothers of those dear ghosts by putting flowers every day upon those graves, taking them as their own sons, their own beloved, because they had died in the same cause—France was free and the world was free because America had come! I wish some men in public life who are now opposing the settlement for which these men died could visit such a spot as that. I wish that the thought that comes out of those graves could penetrate their consciousness. I wish that they could feel the moral obligation that rests upon us not to go back on those boys, but to see the thing through, to see it through to the end and make good their redemption of the world. For nothing less depends upon this decision, nothing less than the liberation and salvation of the world. . . .

Chapter 22

BOOM AND BUST

In the Presidential election of 1920 a war-weary and disillusioned America formally abandoned the enlightened Progressivism it had embraced in the early years of the century and embarked upon a decade-long quest for "normalcy." Though plans for domestic reform had been set aside and liberalism generally had been subordinated to oppressive demands for war-time conformity, the energies of

Progressivism had not been entirely dissipated during the World War, for Woodrow Wilson had successfully channeled them into commanding aspirations for international understanding and world peace. But when the war to "make the world safe for democracy" was over, when the peace had been won—and then lost—and the lofty visions of Wilsonian idealism had been largely dispelled, then Americans shed the burdens both of internationalism and of social experimentation. Despairing of crusades and crusaders, they sent to the White House a handsome, genial mediocrity who promised "not heroics, but healing; not nostrums, but normalcy; not revolution, but restoration; not experimentation, but equipoise." Warren Gamaliel Harding was surely not a great leader, but his "folksiness," his small town ways, his easy identification with the average citizen, and particularly his conviction that America's salvation lay in a return to the simple formulas of McKinley Republicanism thoroughly endeared the Ohio politician to a tired and rather indifferent nation that eschewed reform and longed for nothing more strenuous than "equipoise" and "normalcy."

"Normalcy" itself was a complex phenomenon that defied analysis if not description, and two of its major themes, license and intolerance, were patently self-contradictory. War had wrought absolute havoc with the Victorian moral code that long dominated American life, and the boisterous, roaring twenties were marked with a widespread moral laxity undreamed of only a few years before. Now movies, magazines and books designed for mass consumption dealt frankly and rather heatedly with sex; taboos against vulgarity were flagrantly disregarded, even in public; brazen flappers cut and bobbed their hair, rouged and lipsticked their faces, and immodestly wore their skirts higher and higher above the ankle; and a defiant younger generation loudly proclaimed that its new-found freedom was the only thing it would take at all seriously. Meanwhile the Eighteenth Amendment to the Constitution had brought Prohibition with the speakeasy, the hip-flask, the rum-runner and the beginnings of organized crime. And on a political level a series of outrageous scandals high up in the Harding administration reflected an unmistakable break-down in public as well as private morals.

But if lawlessness and a profound revolt in manners and morals characterized the post-war era, Americans more than compensated for this liberal self-indulgence with a political conservatism that bred fear and intolerance. For most middle-class Americans these were golden years of plenty and they thoroughly despised the unorthodox few whose attacks upon the established order threatened to undermine the nation's prosperity and material well-being. In an atmosphere charged with suspicion and bigotry, criticism was soon equated with disloyalty; vigilante groups sprang up all over the country to brand as "un-American" those who dared question the political and economic status quo; and the imposition of loyalty oaths, the arrest and deportation of alien agitators, and the purging of radicals from their seats in various state legislatures heralded an official crusade against the bogeys of "Bolshevism" and the "Red Menace." Besides, in a nation where mass production and mass communication had standardized nearly every aspect of daily living (Americans everywhere wore the same factory-made clothes, saw the same movies, listened to the same radio programs, drove the same cars and read the same advertisements and canned editorials in chain newspapers) an enormous premium was placed upon conformity, while unorthodoxy and innovation were regarded with distrust. And though the revival of the Ku Klux Klan was a particularly extreme example of the national temper, it was undeniably true that Negroes, Jews, Catholics and members of other minorities that stood outside the carefully molded and guarded pattern of 100% White Protestant Americanism suffered frequent discrimination or attack.

Still, not even the hysterical intolerance of the twenties could destroy entirely the American tradition of liberal protest, and though far less successful than H. L. Mencken, Ernest Hemingway, John Dos Passos and other writers who attacked traditionalism in literature, there were many who dared challenge traditionalism in politics. Laborers and farmers who failed to enjoy a much vaunted Republican prosperity were particularly aware of the necessity for political action to stem the tide of conservatism, and in 1924 various farm and labor groups banded together to form an independent Progressive Party with Senator Robert M. La-Follette of Wisconsin as its candidate for President. For the first time in its history the American Federation of Labor officially endorsed a Presidential candidate and the Progressive ticket polled an impressive 5,000,000 votes. Yet it was clear that a complacent nation had overwhelmingly heeded the Republican admonition that its choice was "Coolidge or Chaos," and the new third party was quickly abandoned when a final tabulation revealed that its candidate had run far behind the 8,000,000 votes for conservative Democrat John W. Davis and the nearly 16,000,000 votes for Calvin Coolidge, an extremely conservative Republican who had succeeded to the Presidency upon Harding's death in 1923.

Liberal agitation did not end with Coolidge's triumph, however, and a vociferous Farm Bloc in Congress continued to press for legislation to aid underprivileged and hard-pressed agrarians who were caught between soaring costs and a rapidly declining farm income. Nevertheless Coolidge was convinced that "the business of America is business," not agriculture nor even the welfare of all citizens, and the President twice vetoed the McNary-Haugen Bill that was designed, through government support, to keep an exportable agriculture surplus from depressing farm prices by glutting the domestic market. Other efforts at relief for the farmer and the worker were equally unsuccessful.

But the chief prophet and high priest of Republican prosperity and conservatism was neither Harding (who longed for a time when there would be "less government in business and more business in government") nor the dour Coolidge. Rather it was Herbert Clark Hoover, who had served under both men as Secretary of Commerce and who was himself the Republican standard-bearer in the Presidential election of 1928. In that year the liberal, urban element in the Democratic party had asserted itself once again, forcing the nomination of Alfred E. Smith. Smith's Catholicism was undoubtedly an important factor in his defeat, for even in the traditionally Solid South, Democrats passed over their party's candidate to vote for the Protestant Hoover. But Smith's record of progressive social reform as Governor of New York compelled Hoover to express the political philosophy that was to dominate Republican thinking in the harsh depression years of his own administration (1929-1933) no less than it had in the era of prosperity presided over by Harding and Coolidge. And Hoover's speech on "Rugged Individualism," delivered at the very end of the 1928 campaign, ranks with Carnegie's defense of the Gospel of Wealth as a classic statement of American conservatism.

Answering those who called upon government to assume a greater and more positive responsibility for the general welfare, Hoover argued that the "American system of rugged individualism" had brought untold prosperity and strength to the nation. On the other hand, the "doctrines of paternalism and state socialism" would mean "the destruction of self-government through centralization of government" and "the undermining of the individual initiative and enterprise through which our people have grown to unparalleled greatness." Implying that government interference in economic activities must necessarily lead to socialism, Hoover insisted that its ultimate effect would be to "impair the very basis of liberty and freedom," for "You cannot extend the mastery of the Government over the daily working life of a people without at the same time making it the master of the people's souls and thoughts."

To his critics it seemed ironic that Hoover should argue so vehemently against government intervention in the economic life of the nation. For as chief architect of the Republican business program of the twenties Hoover had approved government aid to *business* that took not only the negative forms of stringent economies (usually in social services), huge tax reductions, the elimination of government competition with private industry, and the practical suspension of the anti-trust laws, but also the very positive form of subsidies and incredibly high tariffs. Besides, as Secretary of Commerce, Hoover had enthusiastically given official sanction and encouragement to large-scale private investment abroad and to the creation of vast domestic business and trade associations designed primarily to increase industrial efficiency and profit. Possibly these blatant examples of government assistance to the business community were uppermost in Hoover's mind when he spoke of "ordered liberty" and denied that his was a "system of laissez-faire" or that the "United States is free-for-all and devil-take-the-hindmost." For surely there was little else in Hoover's philosophy of "Rugged Individualism" to distinguish it, in theory or in practice, from the rampant Social Darwinism of the late-nineteenth century.

Though "Rugged Individualism" was doubtlessly in the mainstream of an American ideology which had at least temporarily rejected Progressive notions of reform and social control, Hoover was in office less than a year before his philosophy of government was tested and found tragically inadequate. In October, 1929, the bottom literally dropped out of a bullish, speculative stock market and a decade of unparalleled prosperity came abruptly to an end. A nation which only a few months before had complacently assumed that it had reached the high "permanent plateau of prosperity," found itself in the doldrums of depression, and desperate years of unemployment, poverty and insecurity soon provided a grim contrast to the feverish, booming twenties. Yet Hoover's conception of the role of the State remained fundamentally unchanged; just as earlier the administration had denied any responsibility to temper the fantastic orgy of speculation which finally precipitated the 1929 Crash, so now Hoover and his followers steadfastly refused to summon the full resources of government to succor the needy and provide relief for the homeless and jobless. Eventually, of course, an aroused public opinion forced Hoover to combat the Great Depression with more than the futile assurances of the day that "Prosperity is just around the corner," and the Republican statesman actually departed considerably from the traditional practice of permitting panic and depression simply to run their course. But even his rather grudging efforts at government intervention were consistent with an immovably conservative orientation, for though the President favored a Reconstruction Finance Corporation to bolster failing *industries* with Federal funds, he firmly opposed government assistance to *individuals*. Some had assumed that the exigencies of depression would necessarily make important inroads upon Hoover's devotion to "Rugged Individualism." Actually, however, neither this nineteenth-century ideal nor its practitioners were flexible enough to adapt to the shock of depression or to meet the pressing need for an appropriate new understanding of the relationship between the State and the individual in twentieth-century industrial America. And early in the thirties the American people rejected those whom they regarded as the false prophets of conservatism and turned with renewed faith and hope to the Progressivism of Theodore Roosevelt, Robert M. LaFollette, Woodrow Wilson, and now Franklin D. Roosevelt.

Rugged Individualism,* *Herbert C. Hoover, 1928*

This campaign now draws to a close. The platforms of the two parties defining principles and offering solutions of various national problems have been presented and are being earnestly considered by our people. . . .

In my acceptance speech I endeavored to outline the spirit and ideals by which I would be guided in carrying that platform into administration. Tonight, I will not deal with the multitude of issues which have been already well canvassed. I intend rather to discuss some of those more fundamental principles and ideals upon which I believe the Government of the United States should be conducted. . . .

But in addition to this great record of contributions of the Republican Party to progress, there has been a further fundamental contribution—a contribution underlying and sustaining all the others—and that is the resistance of the

* Reprinted from *The New Day* by Herbert Hoover by permission of the author and of the publishers, Stanford University Press.

Republican Party to every attempt to inject the Government into business in competition with its citizens.

After the war, when the Republican Party assumed administration of the country, we were faced with the problem of determination of the very nature of our national life. During 150 years we have builded up a form of self-government and a social system which is peculiarly our own. It differs essentially from all others in the world. It is the American system. It is just as definite and positive a political and social system as has ever been developed on earth. It is founded upon a particular conception of self-government in which decentralized local responsibility is the very base. Further than this, it is founded upon the conception that only through ordered liberty, freedom, and equal opportunity to the individual will his initiative and enterprise spur on the march of progress. And in our insistence upon equality of opportunity has our system advanced beyond all the world.

During the war we necessarily turned to the Government to solve every difficult economic problem. The Government having absorbed every energy of our people for war, there was no other solution. For the preservation of the State the Federal Government became a centralized despotism which undertook unprecedented responsibilities, assumed autocratic powers, and took over the business of citizens. To a large degree we regimented our whole people temporarily into a socialistic state. However justified in time of war, if continued in peace time it would destroy not only our American system but with it our progress and freedom as well.

When the war closed, the most vital of all issues both in our own country and throughout the world was whether Governments should continue their wartime ownership and operation of many instrumentalities of production and distribution. We were challenged with a peace-time choice between the American system of rugged individualism and a European philosophy of diametrically opposed doctrines—doctrines of paternalism and state socialism. The acceptance of these ideas would have meant the destruction of self-government through centralization of government. It would have meant the undermining of the individual initiative and enterprise through which our people have grown to unparalleled greatness.

The Republican Party from the beginning resolutely turned its face away from these ideas and these war practices. A Republican Congress cooperated with the Democratic Administration to demobilize many of our war activities. At that time the two parties were in accord upon that point. When the Republican Party came into full power it went at once resolutely back to our fundamental conception of the State and the rights and responsibilities of the individual. Thereby it restored confidence and hope in the American people, it freed and stimulated enterprise, it restored the Government to its position as an umpire instead of a player in the economic game. For these reasons the American people have gone forward in progress while the rest of the world has halted, and some countries have even gone backward. If any one will study the causes of retarded recuperation in Europe, he will find much of it due to the stifling of private initiative on one hand, and overloading of the Government with business on the other.

There has been revived in this campaign, however, a series of proposals which, if adopted, would be a long step toward the abandonment of our American system and a surrender to the destructive operation of governmental conduct of commercial business. Because the country is faced with difficulty and doubt over certain national problems—that is, prohibition, farm relief and electrical power—our opponents propose that we must thrust government a long way into the businesses which give rise to these problems. In effect, they abandon the tenets of their own party and turn to State socialism as a solution for the difficulties presented by all three. It is proposed that we shall change from prohibition to the State purchase and sale of liquor. If their agricultural relief program means anything, it means that the Government shall directly or indirectly buy and sell and fix prices of agricultural products. And we are to go into the hydro-electric power business. In other words, we are confronted with a huge program of government in business.

There is, therefore, submitted to the American people a question of fundamental principle. That is, shall we depart from the principles of our American political and economic system, upon which we have advanced beyond all the rest of the world, in order to adopt methods based on principles destructive of its very foundations? And I wish to emphasize the seriousness of these proposals. I wish to make my position clear; for this goes to the very roots of American life and progress.

I should like to state to you the effect that this projection of government in business would have upon our system of self-government and our economic system. That effect would reach to the daily life of every man and woman. It would impair the very basis of liberty and freedom not only for those left outside the fold of expanded bureaucracy but for those embraced within it.

Let us first see the effect upon self-government. When the Federal Government undertakes to go into commercial business it must at once set up the organization and administration of that business, and it immediately finds itself in a labyrinth, every alley of which leads to the destruction of self-government.

Commercial business requires a concentration of responsibility. Self-government requires decentralization and many checks and balances to safeguard liberty. Our Government to succeed in business would need become in effect a despotism. There at once begins the destruction of self-government.

The first problem of the Government about to adventure in commercial business is to determine a method of administration. It must secure leadership and direction. Shall this leadership be chosen by political agencies or shall we make it elective? The hard practical fact is that leadership in business must come through the sheer rise in ability and character. That rise can only take place in the free atmosphere of competition. Competition is closed by bureaucracy. Political agencies are feeble channels through which to select able leaders to conduct commercial business.

Government, in order to avoid the possible incompetence, corruption, and tyranny of too great authority in individuals entrusted with commercial business, inevitably turns to boards and commissions. To make sure that there are checks and balances, each member of such boards and commissions must have equal authority. Each has his separate responsibility to the public, and at once we have the conflict of ideas and the lack of decision which would ruin any commercial business. It has contributed greatly to the demoralization of our shipping business. Moreover, these commissions must be representative of different sections and different political parties, so that at once we have an entire blight upon coordinated action within their ranks which destroys any possibility of effective administration.

Moreover, our legislative bodies cannot in fact delegate their full authority to commissions or to individuals for the conduct of matters vital to the American people; for if we would preserve government by the people we must preserve the authority of our legislators in the activities of our Government.

Thus every time the Federal Government goes into a commercial business, five hundred and thirty-one Senators and Congressmen become the actual board of directors of that business. Every time a State government goes into business one or two hundred state Senators and Legislators become the actual directors of that business. Even if they were supermen and if there were no politics in the United States, no body of such numbers could competently direct commercial activities; for that requires initiative, instant decision, and action. It took Congress six years of constant discussion to even decide what the method of administration of Muscle Shoals should be.

When the Federal Government undertakes to go into business, the State governments are at once deprived of control and taxation of that business; when a State government undertakes to go into business, it at once deprives the municipalities of taxation and control of that business. Municipalities, being local and close to the people, can, at times, succeed in business where Federal and State Governments must fail. We have trouble enough with log-rolling in legislative bodies today. It originates naturally from desires of citizens to advance their particular section or to secure some necessary service. It would be multiplied a thousandfold were the Federal and State Governments in these businesses.

The effect upon our economic progress would be even worse. Business progressiveness is dependent on competition. New methods and new ideas are the outgrowth of the spirit of adventure, of individual initiative, and of individual enterprise. Without adventure there is no progress. No Government administration can rightly take chances with taxpayers' money. . . .

The Government in commercial business does not tolerate amongst its customers the freedom of competitive reprisals to which private business is subject. Bureaucracy does not tolerate the spirit of independence; it spreads the spirit of submission into our daily life and penetrates the temper of our people not with the habit of powerful resistance to wrong but with the habit of timid acceptance of irresistible might.

Bureaucracy is ever desirous of spreading its influence and its power. You cannot extend the mastery of the Government over the daily working life of a people without at the same time making it the master of the people's souls and thoughts. Every expansion of Government in business means that Government in order to protect itself from the political consequences of its errors and wrongs is driven irresistibly without peace to greater and greater control of the nation's press and platform. Free speech does not live many hours after free industry and free commerce die.

It is a false liberalism that interprets itself into the Government operation of commercial business. Every step of bureaucratizing of the business of our country poisons the very roots of liberalism—that is, political equality, free speech, free assembly, free press, and equality of opportunity. It is the road not to more liberty but to less liberty. Liberalism should be found not striving to spread bureaucracy but striving to set bounds to it. True liberalism seeks all legitimate freedom, first in the confident belief that without such freedom the pursuit of all other blessings and benefits is vain. That belief is the foundation of all American progress, political as well as economic.

Liberalism is a force truly of the spirit, a force proceeding from the deep realization that economic freedom cannot be sacrificed if political freedom is to be preserved. Even if governmental conduct of business could give us more efficiency instead of less efficiency, the fundamental objection to it would remain unaltered and unabated. It would destroy political equality. It would increase rather than decrease abuse and corruption. It would stifle initiative and invention. It would undermine the development of leadership. It would cramp and cripple the mental and spiritual energies of our people. It would extinguish equality and opportunity. It would dry up the spirit of liberty and progress. For these reasons primarily it must be resisted. For a hundred and fifty years liberalism has found its true spirit in the American system, not in the European systems.

I do not wish to be misunderstood in this statement. I am defining a general policy. It does not mean that our Government is to part with one iota of its national resources without complete protection to the public interest. I have already stated that where the Government is engaged in public works for purposes of flood control, of navigation, of irrigation, of scientific research or national defense, or in pioneering a new art, it will at times necessarily produce power or commodities as a by-product. But they must be a by-product of the major purpose, not the major purpose itself.

Nor do I wish to be misinterpreted as believing that the United States is free-for-all and devil-take-the-hindmost. The very essence of equality of opportunity and of American individualism is that there shall be no domination by any group or combination in this Republic, whether it be business or political. On the contrary, it demands economic justice as well as political and social justice. It is no system of laissez-faire.

I feel deeply on this subject because during the war I had some practical experience with governmental operation and control. I have witnessed not only at home but abroad the many failures of Government in business. I have seen its tyrannies, its injustices, its destructions of self-government, its undermining of the very instincts which carry our people forward to progress. I have witnessed the lack of advance, the lowered standards of living, the depressed spirits of people working under such a system. My objection is based not upon theory or upon a failure to recognize wrong or abuse, but I know the adoption of such methods would strike at the very roots of American life and would destroy the very basis of American progress.

Our people have the right to know whether we can continue to solve our great problems without abandonment of our American system. I know we can. We have demonstrated that our system is responsive enough to meet any new and intricate development in our economic and business life. We have demonstrated that we can meet any economic problem and still maintain our democracy as master in its own house and that we can at the same time preserve equality of opportunity and individual freedom. . . .

And what have been the results of our American system? Our country has become the land of opportunity to those born without inheritance, not merely because of the wealth of its resources and industry, but because of this freedom of initiative and enterprise. Russia has natural resources equal to ours. Her people are equally industrious, but she has not had the blessings of one hundred and fifty years of our form of government and of our social system.

By adherence to the principles of decentralized self-government, ordered liberty, equal opportunity, and freedom to the individual our American experiment in human welfare has yielded a degree of well-being unparalleled in all the world. It has come nearer to the abolition of poverty, to the abolition of fear of want, than humanity has ever reached before. Progress of the past seven years is the proof of it. This alone furnishes the answer to our opponents who ask us to introduce destructive elements into the system by which this has been accomplished.

Let us see what this system has done for us in our recent years of difficult and trying reconstruction and let us then solemnly ask ourselves if we now wish to abandon it.

As a nation we came out of the war with great losses. We made no profits from it. The apparent increases in wages were at that time fictitious. We were poorer as a nation when we emerged from the war. Yet during these last eight years we have recovered from these losses and increased our national income by over one-third, even if we discount the inflation of the dollar. That there has been a wide diffusion of our gain in wealth and income is marked by a hundred proofs. I know of no better test of the improved conditions of the average family than the combined increase in assets of life and industrial insurance, building and loan associations, and savings deposits. These are the savings banks of the average man. These agencies alone have in seven years increased by nearly 100 per cent to the gigantic sum of over fifty billions of dollars, or nearly one-sixth of our whole national wealth. We have increased in home ownership, we have expanded the investments of the average man.

. . . We have in this short period decreased the fear of poverty, the fear of unemployment, the fear of old age; and these are fears that are the greatest calamities of human kind. . . .

In bringing this address to a conclusion I should like to restate to you some of the fundamental things I have endeavored to bring out.

The foundations of progress and prosperity are dependent as never before upon the wise policies of government, for government now touches at a thousand points the intricate web of economic and social life.

Under administration by the Republican Party in the last seven and one-half years our country as a whole has made unparalleled progress and this has been in generous part reflected to this great city. Prosperity is no idle expression. It is a job for every worker; it is the safety and the safeguard of every business and every home. A continuation of the policies of the Republican Party is fundamentally necessary to the further building up of this prosperity.

I have dwelt at some length on the principles of relationship between the Government and business. I make no apologies for dealing with this subject. The first necessity of any nation is the smooth functioning of the vast business machinery for employment, feeding, clothing, housing, and providing luxuries and comforts to a people. Unless these basic elements are properly organized and function, there can be no progress in business, in education, literature, music, or art. There can be no advance in the fundamental ideas of a people. A people cannot make progress in poverty.

I have endeavored to present to you that the greatness of America has grown out of a political and social system and a method of control of economic forces distinctly its own— our American system—which has carried this great experiment in human welfare further than ever before in all history. We are nearer today to the ideal of the abolition of poverty and fear from the lives of men and women than ever before in any land. And I again repeat that the departure from our American system by injecting principles destructive to it which our opponents propose will jeopardize the very liberty and freedom of our people, will destroy equality of opportunity, not alone to ourselves but to our children. . . .

Chapter 23

THE ROOSEVELT REVOLUTION

The triumphant election in 1932 of Franklin D. Roosevelt, the liberal Democratic Governor of New York, was in the largest sense a profound reaffirmation of America's continuing faith in the essential capacity of democracy to survive the crises of depression and economic instability. A generation devoted to the quest for security had witnessed the rise of Communist, Fascist, and Nazi dictatorships in other nations. And in the United States the Great Depression, with its long years of poverty and acute distress, its breadlines, its soup kitchens, and its ever-mounting unemployment rolls, led many Americans to question seriously the efficacy of the democratic process. Indeed, had the depression grown worse, and had the national government continued to deny its responsibility to provide for those of its citizens who had been overcome by disaster, then the counsel of extremists might have been heeded and democracy abandoned in despair. But Americans turned instead to a liberal statesman whose purpose was to strengthen rather than to destroy traditional American values and institutions, and who pledged himself to devote unstintingly the full resources of democratic government to the rehabilitation of the depression-worn nation.

Ultimately it was the reforms of the New Deal that preserved American democracy from immediate collapse and protected it against the threatened inroads of totalitarianism of both the Left and Right. Not only did the New Deal seek to maintain the essential fabric of America's free economy, but its widely debated techniques of government regulation were entirely within the framework of a long-established American tradition of social control. Over a half century earlier state Granger laws had attempted rigorous control of railroad abuses; and the Interstate Commerce Act of 1887 and the Sherman Anti-Trust Act of 1890 had committed the national government as well to a real, if rather limited, role in the regulation of industry. The Populists of the 1890's had demanded specific reforms which pre-dated much of the Roosevelt farm program. And the extensive governmental activities of Theodore Roosevelt's Square Deal, his proposed New Nationalism, and Woodrow Wilson's New Freedom provided ample precedent for many of the New Deal's experiments in liberal reform. Even Herbert Hoover's minimal efforts at government intervention anticipated somewhat the substance, if not the spirit, of his successor's bold acts.

Nevertheless the New Deal did reflect a significant change in the nation's concept of the proper relationship between the State and the individual, and to many Americans it seemed that the election of 1932, as Jefferson had written of his own election in 1800, was "as real a revolution in the principles of our government as that of 1776 was in its form." Government participation in the economic life of the country could no longer be considered an entirely novel response to national crisis, but in the Roosevelt administration such activity became the *dominant* pattern and government assumed a broad and continuous new responsibility for the social and economic well-being of all the people. In a 1932 campaign address to the Commonwealth Club of San Francisco, Roosevelt had stated very clearly his belief that the economic basis of the nineteenth century's expansive, laissez-faire individualism had disappeared with the end of the last frontier and the completion of "our industrial plant," and that "our task now is not discovery or exploitation of natural resources, or necessarily producing more goods." The times called for a "reappraisal of values." Now government must play a major role in "the soberer, less dramatic business of administering resources and plants already in hand, of seeking to re-establish foreign markets for our surplus production, of meeting the problem of underconsumption, of adjusting production to consumption, of distributing wealth and products more equitably, of adapting existing economic organizations to the service of the people." Leftist critics scored the New Deal as disorganized and haphazard, totally without plan or philosophy, but this new orientation towards the State as the active, permanent guardian of the general welfare actually formed the persistent central theme of the "Roosevelt Revolution."

Yet the essence of the New Deal was as much in its spirit as in its ideology, for Roosevelt shrewdly sensed that a distressed and disheartened people needed most of all the strong moral conviction of his famous First Inaugural Address: "This great Nation will endure as it has endured, will revive and will prosper. . . . The only thing we have to fear is fear itself—nameless, unreasoning, unjustified terror which paralyzes needed efforts to convert retreat into advance." Graced with a warm and winning personality, Roosevelt again and again employed the masterful device of radio "fireside chats" to report directly to an anxious national audience, and his calm assurance did much to restore Americans' confidence in themselves and in their government. But brave words were not enough, and the exciting first hundred days of the Roosevelt Era saw an effective leadership translate the President's Inaugural assertion that "we must act, and act quickly" into a rapid succession of dramatic measures. To avert the total collapse of an already badly shaken banking system, the President proclaimed a national "bank holiday," closing the banks until steps might be taken to protect the savings of vast numbers of small depositors. A Federal Emergency Relief Administration (FERA) was created to make direct and immediate contributions to the states for relief purposes. A Civilian Conservation Corps (CCC) quickly put over a quarter of a million idle young men to the constructive task of preserving the nation's natural resources. A Works Progress Administration (WPA) restored the self-respect of millions of older unemployed by taking them from the relief rolls and employing their talents on public projects of permanent value—whether they were unskilled laborers or writers, artists, historians or musicians. Like many of the alphabetical agencies created during the depression emergency, these work-relief projects were temporary and frankly experimental, but they thoroughly vindicated the New Deal's assumption that needy Americans wanted work, not the dole, and they amply demonstrated the government's new and continuing determination to provide for the underprivileged "forgotten man."

Relief measures of necessity received highest priority in the grim early years of the Roosevelt administration, but recovery and reform ranked importantly too. The long-range objective of the New Deal was to place the American economy back on its feet, in good working order and with adequate safeguards against the inequities and maladjustments responsible for the tragic boom and bust of the twenties. Here again the Congress followed strong Executive leadership, adopting almost in its entirety each of the legislative proposals made by the President and his remarkable group of advisers known collectively—and sometimes derisively—as the "Brain Trust." An expanded and "democratized" Reconstruction Finance Corporation (RFC) was authorized to lend enormous sums of Federal monies not only to the largest financial institutions—as it had under Hoover—but to smaller faltering industries as well. And a Public Works Administration (PWA) was created to "prime" the "pump" of national economic activity through an extensive program of government spending. The New Dealers were convinced that Hoover's technique (as Roosevelt described it) of helping "only those at the top, in the pious hope that the few at the top would in their benevolence or generosity pass that help on" was inadequate to the times and that the key to recovery lay instead in increased consumer purchasing power. To this end an Agricultural Adjustment Administration (AAA) brought about an enormously expanded national farm income through a program of crop curtailment and government-supported price levels, and a National Recovery Administration (NRA) attempted the same for the urban industrial worker.

It was, of course, in the realm of labor relations that the New Deal accomplished its most sweeping economic reforms. Formal guarantees of labor's right to organize and to bargain collectively were written into Section 7(a) of the act which created the NRA and later into the National Labor Relations Act. And in 1938 the Fair Labor Standards Act established a legal floor under wages and a ceiling over working hours for employees engaged in interstate commerce. These measures and the administration's obvious eagerness to deal with labor as industry's equal gave a tremendous impetus to the growth of organized labor. But labor's gains were quickly challenged by management, and the mid-thirties were marred by a long series of sit-down strikes, boycotts, and lockouts that frequently were accompanied by violence and bloodshed. Besides, all was not well within labor's own house. A long-standing conflict between the respective advocates of trade and industrial unionism had resulted in a schism within the venerable and rather conservative American Federation of Labor and in the creation of a rival Congress of Industrial Organizations. Inter-union struggles were particularly bitter and continuous jurisdictional disputes seriously threatened labor's recent strides forward. But under the dynamic leadership of John L. Lewis the CIO proved remarkably successful in recruiting large armies of unorganized industrial workers, and by the end of the decade each of the giant labor organizations could claim a membership of 4,000,000.

Important reforms were enacted in other areas as well. The nation's anti-trust laws were enforced with renewed vigor in a concerted effort to control the trend towards monopoly and the concentration of wealth that was so clearly revealed in the reports of the Temporary National Economic Committee (TNEC). A Securities and Exchange Commission (SEC) was created to guard against a recurrence of the fraudulent and speculative stock market practices that had contributed so much to the 1929 Crash. A generously conceived Social Security Act inaugurated a program of old-age insurance, unemployment insurance, and financial assistance for dependent children, the crippled, and the blind. And a Tennessee Valley Authority (TVA) that was empowered not only to generate and to sell cheap electricity, but also to conduct flood-control, reforestation, community organization and educational programs for the impoverished people of the Valley, provided a daring experiment in social planning.

All of these measures for relief, recovery and reform were designed to insure a free, democratic society against the ravages of poverty and insecurity, for Roosevelt was firmly convinced that the "liberty of a democracy is not safe if its business system does not provide employment and produce and distribute goods in such a way as to sustain an acceptable standard of living." To critics who vigorously opposed the New Deal in the name of a Jeffersonian tradition of limited government, the President cogently replied that in twentieth-century industrial America the real threat to individual freedom lay not in the expanding services of democratic government, but rather in the irresponsible power of concentrated wealth. Now Americans' liberties were seriously endangered by privileged, monopolistic economic power, and a limited Welfare State must supplant the Laissez-Faire State of the nineteenth century, not to hamper individualism, but to protect it.

Though there were some who accused the President of creating a vast Federal bureaucracy merely to foster his own political ambitions, and though the cry of "dictator" was heard over and over again, most Americans heartily approved of the New Deal. In the Congressional elections of 1934 an already sizable Democratic legislative majority was substantially increased; and in the Presidential election of 1936 Roosevelt soundly defeated Alfred M. Landon, the "Kansas Coolidge," who carried only Maine and Vermont for the Republican Party. But these handsome victories at the polls made no impression at all upon the judicial branch of the national Government, and it was in the rarefied, though hardly unprejudicial atmosphere of a conservative and largely hostile Supreme Court that Roosevelt, as Jefferson before him, encountered his most formidable opposition. Here a majority of the "nine old men"—whose tenure had begun long before the "Roosevelt Revolution"—interpreted the Constitution in such a manner as to invalidate vital portions of the New Deal's liberal legislative program. The Court had long been a bulwark of conservatism, but seldom before had the Justices so flagrantly flouted the will of the popularly chosen Congress and Chief Executive or so consistently read into the Constitution what Justice (later Chief Justice) Harlan F. Stone described as their own "personal economic predilections." And when the NRA, the AAA, the Municipal Bankruptcy Act, the Farm Mortgage Act, and the Guffey Coal Act were all declared unconstitutional, then the President realized that the entire New Deal would suffer judicial emasculation if drastic action were not quickly taken. Thus, early in 1937 the administration proposed legislation which permitted Justices of the high court to retire on full pay at the age of 70 and which empowered the President to appoint an additional Justice—until the Supreme Court numbered 15 —for each of the judges who remained on the bench after the retirement age. Roosevelt argued that his plan would "save our National Constitution from hardening of the judicial arteries," but his opponents joined in attacking it as a "court-packing" measure, and when the Congress defeated the court reform bill the administration suffered a major political setback.

The Court was not unimpressed by this attack upon its prerogatives, however, and even as the controversial bill was being debated and defeated in Congress the Justices conceded that an aroused public might someday impose even more stringent limitations upon judicial review were the popular will further denied. Bowing to expediency, the Court very quickly became more receptive to social legislation, and in 1937 the New Deal was upheld in several particularly important decisions. In N.L.R.B. v. Jones & Laughlin Steel Corporation the Court sustained the National Labor Relations Act, despite the fact that distinguished lawyers who had studied the Court's earlier decisions on related matters had strongly advised their clients that the law was unconstitutional. In Helvering v. Davis the Court sustained the Social Security Act in a decision which liberally construed Congressional power to tax for the general welfare. In West Coast Hotel Co. v. Parrish the Court upheld the right of the State of Washington to pass minimum wage legislation, though less than a year before a similar law in New York had been invalidated, and though in 1923 a Federal minimum wage act for the District of Columbia had been set aside in Adkins v. Children's Hospital.

The Supreme Court's voluntary about-face was historic— some called it "the switch in time that saved nine." But within a few years death and resignation permitted Roosevelt to remake the membership himself. Soon conservatives such as McReynolds, Sutherland and Van Devanter were replaced by the liberals Hugo Black, Felix Frankfurter, William O. Douglas, Frank Murphy and Robert Jackson, and the Court withdrew farther and farther from the realm of law-making. Besides, by the end of the decade comparatively few Americans entirely rejected the New Deal philosophy of social control. There were many who continued bitterly to criticize the President as incompetent or dictatorial, and even less partisan observers seriously questioned both the desirability of extreme centralization of power in the Federal government at Washington and the essential wisdom of continuously strengthening the power of the Chief Executive at the expense of the power and prestige of the Congress and the Supreme Court. But for the most part the "Roosevelt Revolution" had made its permanent impression upon national life and it was doubtful if Americans would ever again enjoy —or regret—an era of laissez-faire.

Franklin D. Roosevelt's First Inaugural Address, *1933*

President Hoover, Mr. Chief Justice, my friends:

This is a day of national consecration, and I am certain that my fellow-Americans expect that on my induction into the Presidency I will address them with a candor and a decision which the present situation of our nation impels.

This is pre-eminently the time to speak the truth, the whole truth, frankly and boldly. Nor need we shrink from honestly facing conditions in our country today. This great nation will endure as it has endured, will revive and will prosper.

So first of all let me assert my firm belief that the only thing we have to fear is fear itself—nameless, unreasoning, unjustified terror which paralyzes needed efforts to convert retreat into advance.

In every dark hour of our national life a leadership of frankness and vigor has met with that understanding and support of the people themselves which is essential to victory. I am convinced that you will again give that support to leadership in these critical days.

In such a spirit on my part and on yours we face our common difficulties. They concern, thank God, only material things. Values have shrunken to fantastic levels; taxes have risen; our ability to pay has fallen, government of all kinds is faced by serious curtailment of income; the means of exchange are frozen in the currents of trade; the withered leaves of industrial enterprise lie on every side; farmers find no markets for their produce; the savings of many years in thousands of families are gone.

More important, a host of unemployed citizens face the grim problem of existence, and an equally great number toil with little return. Only a foolish optimist can deny the dark realities of the moment.

Yet our distress comes from no failure of substance. We are stricken by no plague of locusts. Compared with the perils which our forefathers conquered because they believed and were not afraid, we have still much to be thankful for. Nature still offers her bounty and human efforts have multiplied it. Plenty is at our doorstep, but a generous use of it languishes in the very sight of the supply.

Primarily, this is because the rulers of the exchange of mankind's goods have failed through their own stubbornness and their own incompetence, have admitted that failure and abdicated. Practices of the unscrupulous money changers stand indicted in the court of public opinion, rejected by the hearts and minds of men.

True, they have tried, but their efforts have been cast in the pattern of an outworn tradition. Faced by failure of credit, they have proposed only the lending of more money.

Stripped of the lure of profit by which to induce our people to follow their false leadership, they have resorted to exhortations, pleading tearfully for restored confidence. They know only the rules of a generation of self-seekers.

They have no vision, and when there is no vision the people perish.

The money changers have fled from their high seats in the temple of our civilization. We may now restore that temple to the ancient truths.

The measure of the restoration lies in the extent to which we apply social values more noble than mere monetary profit.

Happiness lies not in the mere possession of money; it lies in the joy of achievement, in the thrill of creative effort.

The joy and moral stimulation of work no longer must be forgotten in the mad chase of evanescent profits. These dark days will be worth all they cost us if they teach us that our true destiny is not to be ministered unto but to minister to ourselves and to our fellow-men.

Recognition of the falsity of material wealth as the standard of success goes hand in hand with the abandonment of the false belief that public office and high political position are to be valued only by the standards of pride of place and personal profit; and there must be an end to a conduct in banking and in business which too often has given to a a sacred trust the likeness of callous and selfish wrongdoing.

Small wonder that confidence languishes, for it thrives

only on honesty, on honor, on the sacredness of obligations, on faithful protection, on unselfish performance. Without them it cannot live.

Restoration calls, however, not for changes in ethics alone. This nation asks for action, and action now.

Our greatest primary task is to put people to work. This is no unsolvable problem if we face it wisely and courageously.

It can be accomplished in part by direct recruiting by the government itself, treating the task as we would treat the emergency of a war, but at the same time, through this employment, accomplishing greatly needed projects to stimulate the use of our natural resources.

Hand in hand with this, we must frankly recognize the overbalance of population in our industrial centers and, by engaging on a national scale in the redistribution, endeavor to provide a better use of the land for those best fitted for the land.

The task can be helped by definite efforts to raise the values of agricultural products and with this the power to purchase the output of our cities.

It can be helped by preventing realistically the tragedy of the growing loss, through foreclosure, of our small homes and our farms.

It can be helped by insistence that the Federal, State and local governments act forthwith on the demand that their cost be drastically reduced.

It can be helped by the unifying of relief activities which today are often scattered, uneconomical and unequal. It can be helped by national planning for and supervision of all forms of transportation and of communications and other utilities which have a definitely public character.

There are many ways in which it can be helped, but it can never be helped merely by talking about it. We must act, and act quickly.

Finally, in our progress toward a resumption of work we require two safeguards against a return to the evils of the old order; there must be a strict supervision of all banking and credits and investments; there must be an end to speculation with other people's money, and there must be provision for an adequate but sound currency.

These are the lines of attack. I shall presently urge upon a new Congress in special session detailed measures for their fulfillment, and I shall seek the immediate assistance of the several States.

Through this program of action we address ourselves to putting our own national house in order and making income balance outgo.

Our international trade relations, though vastly important,

are, in point of time and necessity, secondary to the establishment of a sound national economy.

I favor as a practical policy the putting of first things first. I shall spare no effort to restore world trade by international economic readjustment, but the emergency at home cannot wait on that accomplishment.

The basic thought that guides these specific means of national recovery is not narrowly nationalistic.

It is the insistence, as a first consideration, upon the interdependence of the various elements in, and parts of, the United States—a recognition of the old and permanently important manifestation of the American spirit of the pioneer.

It is the way to recovery. It is the immediate way. It is the strongest assurance that the recovery will endure.

In the field of world policy I would dedicate this nation to the policy of the good neighbor—the neighbor who resolutely respects himself and, because he does so, respects the rights of others—the neighbor who respects his obligations and respects the sanctity of his agreements in and with a world of neighbors.

If I read the temper of our people correctly, we now realize as we have never before, our interdependence on each other; that we cannot merely take, but we must give as well; that if we are to go forward we must move as a trained and loyal army willing to sacrifice for the good of a common discipline, because, without such discipline, no progress is made, no leadership becomes effective.

We are, I know, ready and willing to submit our lives and property to such discipline because it makes possible a leadership which aims at a larger good.

This I propose to offer, pledging that the larger purposes will bind upon us all as a sacred obligation with a unity of duty hitherto evoked only in time of armed strife.

With this pledge taken, I assume unhesitatingly the leadership of this great army of our people, dedicated to a disciplined attack upon our common problems.

Action in this image and to this end is feasible under the form of government which we have inherited from our ancestors.

Our Constitution is so simple and practical that it is possible always to meet extraordinary needs by changes in emphasis and arrangement without loss of essential form.

That is why our constitutional system has proved itself the most superbly enduring political mechanism the modern world has produced. It has met every stress of vast expansion of territory, of foreign wars, of bitter internal strife, of world relations.

It is to be hoped that the normal balance of executive and legislative authority may be wholly adequate to meet the unprecedented task before us. But it may be that an unprecedented demand and need for undelayed action may call for temporary departure from that normal balance of public procedure.

I am prepared under my constitutional duty to recommend the measures that a stricken nation in the midst of a stricken world may require.

These measures, or such other measures as the Congress may build out of its experience and wisdom, I shall seek, within my constitutional authority, to bring to speedy adoption.

But in the event that the Congress shall fail to take one of these two courses, and in the event that the national emergency is still critical, I shall not evade the clear course of duty that will then confront me.

I shall ask the Congress for the one remaining instrument to meet the crisis—broad executive power to wage a war against the emergency as great as the power that would be given me if we were in fact invaded by a foreign foe.

For the trust resposed in me I will return the courage and the devotion that befit the time. I can do no less.

We face the arduous days that lie before us in the warm courage of national unity; with the clear consciousness of seeking old and precious moral values; with the clean satisfaction that comes from the stern performance of duty by old and young alike.

We aim at the assurance of a rounded and permanent national life.

We do not distrust the future of essential democracy. The people of the United States have not failed. In their need they have registered a mandate that they want direct, vigorous action.

They have asked for discipline and direction under leadership. They have made me the present instrument of their wishes. In the spirit of the gift I take it.

In this dedication of a nation we humbly ask the blessing of God. May He protect each and every one of us! May He guide me in the days to come!

N.L.R.B. v. Jones & Laughlin
Steel Corporation, *1937*

In a proceeding under the National Labor Relations Act of 1935, the National Labor Relations Board found that the petitioner, Jones & Laughlin Steel Corporation, had violated the Act by engaging in unfair labor practices affecting commerce. . . . The unfair labor practices charged were that the corporation was discriminating against members of the union with regard to hire and tenure of employment, and was coercing and intimidating its employees in order to interfere with their self-organization. The discriminatory and coercive action alleged was the discharge of certain employees. . . .

Contesting the ruling of the Board, the respondent argues (1) that the Act is in reality a regulation of labor relations and not of interstate commerce; (2) that the Act can have no application to the respondent's relations with its production employees because they are not subject to regulation by the Federal Government; and (3) that the provisions of the Act violate Section 2 of Article III and the Fifth and Seventh Amendments of the Constitution of the United States. . . .

Respondent says that whatever may be said of employees engaged in interstate commerce, the industrial relations and activities in the manufacturing department of respondent's enterprise are not subject to federal regulations. The argument rests upon the proposition that manufacturing in itself is not commerce. . . .

The Government distinguishes these cases. The various parts of respondent's enterprise are described as interdependent and as thus involving "a great movement of iron ore, coal and limestone along well-defined paths to the steel mills, thence through them, and thence in the form of steel products into the consuming centers of the country—a definite and well-understood course of business." It is urged that these activities constitute a "stream" or "flow" of commerce, of which the Aliquippa manufacturing plant is the focal point, and that industrial strife at that point would cripple the entire movement. Reference is made to our decision sustaining the Packers and Stockyards Act. The Court found that the stockyards were but a "throat" through which the current of commerce flowed and the transactions which there occurred could not be separated from that movement. . . .

We do not find it necessary to determine whether these features of defendant's business dispose of the asserted analogy to the "stream of commerce" cases. The congressional authority to protect interstate commerce from burdens and obstructions is not limited to transactions which can be deemed to be an essential part of a "flow" of interstate or foreign commerce. Burdens and obstructions may be due to injurious action springing from other sources. The fundamental principle is that the power to regulate commerce is the power to enact "all appropriate legislation" for "its protection and advancement"; to adopt measures "to promote its growth and insure its safety"; "to foster, protect, control and restrain." That power is plenary and may be exerted to protect interstate commerce "no matter what the source of the dangers which threaten it." Although activities may be intrastate in character when separately considered, if they have such a close and substantial relation to interstate commerce that their control is essential or appropriate to protect that commerce from burdens and obstructions, Congress cannot be denied the power to exercise that control. Undoubtedly the scope of this power must be considered in the light of our dual system of government and may not be extended so as to embrace effects upon interstate commerce so indirect and remote that to embrace them, in view of our complex society, would effectually obliterate the distinction between what is national and what is local and create a completely centralized government. The question is necessarily one of degree. . . .

It is thus apparent that the fact that the employees here concerned were engaged in production is not determinative. The question remains as to the effect upon interstate commerce of the labor practice involved. . . .

Giving full weight to respondent's contention with respect to a break in the complete continuity of the "stream of commerce" by reason of respondent's manufacturing operations, the fact remains that the stoppage of those operations by industrial strife would have a most serious effect upon interstate commerce. In view of respondent's far-flung activities, it is idle to say that the effect would be indirect or remote. It is obvious that it would be immediate and might be catastrophic. We are asked to shut our eyes to the plainest facts of our national life and to deal with the question of direct and indirect effects in an intellectual vacuum. Because there may be but indirect and remote effects upon interstate commerce in connection with a host of local enterprises throughout the country, it does not follow that other industrial activities do not have such a close and intimate relation to interstate commerce as to make the presence of industrial strife a matter of the most urgent national concern. When industries organize themselves on a national scale, making their relation to interstate commerce the dominant factor in their activities, how can it be maintained that their industrial labor relations constitute a forbidden field into which Congress may not enter when it is necessary to protect interstate commerce from the paralyzing consequences of industrial war? We have often said that interstate commerce itself is a practical conception. It is equally true that interferences with that commerce must be appraised by a judgment that does not ignore actual experience.

Experience has abundantly demonstrated that the recognition of the right of employees to self-organization and to have representatives of their own choosing for the purpose of collective bargaining is often an essential condition of industrial peace. Refusal to confer and negotiate has been one of the most prolific causes of strife. This is such an outstanding fact in the history of labor disturbances that it is a proper subject of judicial notice and requires no citation of instances. But with respect to the appropriateness of the recognition of self-organization and representation in the promotion of peace, the question is not essentially different in the case of employees in industries of such a character that interstate commerce is put in jeopardy from the case of employees of transportation companies. And of what avail is it to protect the facility of transportation, if interstate commerce is throttled with respect to the commodities to be transported!

These questions have frequently engaged the attention of Congress and have been the subject of many inquiries. The steel industry is one of the great basic industries of the United States, with ramifying activities affecting interstate commerce at every point. The Government aptly refers to the steel strike of 1919-1920 with its far-reaching consequences. The fact that there appears to have been no major disturbance in that industry in the more recent period did not dispose of the possibilities of future and like dangers to interstate commerce which Congress was entitled to foresee and to exercise its protective power to forestall. It is not necessary again to detail the facts as to respondent's enterprise. Instead of being beyond the pale, we think that it presents in a most striking way the close and intimate relation which a manufacturing industry may have to interstate commerce and we have no doubt that Congress had constitutional authority to safeguard the right of respondent's employees to self-organization and freedom in the choice of representatives for collective bargaining. . . .

Our conclusion is that the order of the Board was within its competency and that the Act is valid. . . .

Helvering et al. v. Davis, *1937*

The Social Security Act is challenged once again. . . .

The purge of nation-wide calamity that began in 1929 has taught us many lessons. Not the least is the solidarity of interests that may once have seemed to be divided. Unemployment spreads from state to state, the hinterland now settled that in pioneer days gave an avenue of escape. Spreading from state to state, unemployment is an ill not particular but general, which may be checked, if Congress so determines, by the resources of the Nation. . . .

But the ill is all one or at least not greatly different whether men are thrown out of work because there is no longer work to do or because the disabilities of age make them incapable of doing it. Rescue becomes necessary irrespective of the cause. The hope behind this statute is to save men and women from the rigors of the poor house as well as from the haunting fear that such a lot awaits them when journey's end is near. . . .

A recent study of the Social Security Board informs us that "one-fifth of the aged in the United States were receiving old-age assistance, emergency relief, institutional care, employment under the works program, or some other form of aid from public or private funds; two-fifths to one-half were dependent on friends and relatives; one-eighth had some income from earnings; and possibly one-sixth had some savings or property. Approximately three out of four persons 65 or over were probably dependent wholly or partially on others for support." We summarize in the margin the results of other studies by state and national commissions. They point the same way.

The problem is plainly national in area and dimensions. Moreover, laws of the separate states cannot deal with it effectively. Congress, at least, had a basis for that belief. States and local governments are often lacking in the resources that are necessary to finance an adequate program of security for the aged. This is brought out with a wealth of illustration in recent studies of the problem. Apart from the failure of resources, states and local governments are at times reluctant to increase so heavily the burden of taxation to be borne by their residents for fear of placing themselves in a position of economic disadvantage as compared with neighbors or competitors. . . .

A system of old age pensions has special dangers of its own, if put in force in one state and rejected in another. The existence of such a system is a bait to the needy and dependent elsewhere, encouraging them to migrate and seek a haven of repose. Only a power that is national can serve the interests of all.

Whether wisdom or unwisdom resides in the scheme of benefits it is not for us to say. The answer to such inquiries must come from Congress, not the courts. Our concern here as often is with power, not with wisdom. Counsel for respondent has recalled to us the virtues of self-reliance and frugality. There is a possibility, he says, that aid from a paternal government may sap those sturdy virtues and breed a race of weaklings. If Massachusetts so believes and shapes her laws in that conviction, must her breed of sons be changed, he asks, because some other philosophy of government finds favor in the halls of Congress? But the answer is not doubtful. One might ask with equal reason whether the system of protective tariffs is to be set aside at will in one state or another whenever local policy prefers the rule of *laissez faire*. The issue is a closed one. It was fought out long ago. When money is spent to promote the general welfare, the concept of welfare or the opposite is shaped by Congress, not the states. So the concept be not arbitrary, the locality must yield. Constitution, Art. VI, Par. 2.

Ordered Accordingly.

West Coast Hotel Co. v. Parrish, *1937*

This case presents the question of the constitutional validity of the minimum wage law of the State of Washington.

The Act, entitled "Minimum Wages for Women," authorizes the fixing of minimum wages for women and minors. . . .

The appellant conducts a hotel. The appellee Elsie Parrish was employed as a chambermaid and (with her husband) brought this suit to recover the difference between the wages paid her and the minimum wage fixed pursuant to the state law. The minimum wage was $14.50 per week of 48 hours. The appellant challenged the act as repugnant to the due process clause of the Fourteenth Amendment of the Constitution of the United States. The Supreme Court of the State, reversing the trial court, sustained the statute and directed judgment for the plaintiff. . . .

The case is here on appeal.

The appellant relies upon the decision of this Court in *Adkins v. Children's Hospital*, which held invalid the District of Columbia Minimum Wage Act which was attacked under the due process clause of the Fifth Amendment. . . .

The Supreme Court of Washington has upheld the minimum wage statute of this State. It has decided that the statute is a reasonable exercise of the police power of the State. In reaching that conclusion the State court has invoked principles long established by this Court in the application of the Fourteenth Amendment. The State court has refused to regard the decision in the *Adkins* case as determinative and has pointed to our decisions both before and since that case as justifying its position. We are of the opinion that this ruling of the State court demands on our part a re-examination of the *Adkins* case. The importance of the question, in which many States having similar laws are concerned, the close division by which the decision in the *Adkins* case was reached, and the economic conditions which have supervened, and in the light of which the reasonableness of the exercise of the protective power of the State must be considered, make it not only appropriate, but we think imperative, that in deciding the present case the subject should receive fresh consideration. . . .

The principle which must control our decision is not in doubt. The constitutional provision invoked is the due process clause of the Fourteenth Amendment governing the States, as the due process clause invoked in the *Adkins* case governed Congress. In each case the violation alleged by those attacking minimum wage regulation for women is deprivation of freedom of contract. What is this freedom? The Constitution does not speak of freedom of contract. It speaks of liberty and prohibits the deprivation of liberty without due process of law. In prohibiting that deprivation the Constitution does not recognize an absolute and uncontrollable liberty. Liberty in each of its phases has its history and connotation. But the liberty safeguarded is liberty in a social organization which requires the protection of law against the evils which menace the health, safety, morals and welfare of the people. Liberty under the Constitution is thus necessarily subject to the restraints of due process, and regulation which is reasonable in relation to its subject and is adopted in the interests of the community is due process. . . .

The minimum wage to be paid under the Washington statute is fixed after full consideration by representatives of employers, employees and the public. It may be assumed that the minimum wage is fixed in consideration of the services that are performed in the particular occupations under normal conditions. Provision is made for special licenses at less wages in the case of women who are incapable of full service. The statement of Mr. Justice Holmes in the *Adkins* case is pertinent:

This statute does not compel anybody to pay anything. It simply forbids employment at rates below those fixed as the minimum requirement of health and right living. It is safe to assume that women will not be employed at even the lowest wages allowed unless they earn them, or unless the employer's business can sustain the burden. In short the law in its character and operation is like hundreds of so-called police laws that have been upheld. . . .

What can be closer to the public interest than the health of women and their protection from unscrupulous and overreaching employers? And if the protection of women is a legitimate end of the exercise of state power, how can it be said that the requirement of the payment of a minimum wage fairly fixed in order to meet the very necessities of existence is not an admissible means to that end? The legislature of the State was clearly entitled to consider the situation of women in employment, the fact that they are in the class receiving the least pay, that their bargaining power is relatively weak, and that they are the ready victims of those who would take advantage of their necessitous circumstances. The legislature was entitled to adopt measures to reduce the evils of the "sweating system," the exploiting of workers at wages so low as to be insufficient to meet the bare cost of living, thus making their very helplessness the occasion of a most injurious competition. The legislature had the right to consider that its minimum wage requirements would be an important aid in carrying out its policy of protection. The adoption of similar requirements by many States evidences a deepseated conviction both as to the presence of the evil and as to the means adopted to check it. Legislative response to that conviction cannot be regarded as arbitrary or capricious and that is all we have to decide. Even if the wisdom of the policy be regarded as debatable and its effects uncertain, still the legislature is entitled to its judgment.

There is an additional and compelling consideration which recent economic experience has brought into a strong light. The exploitation of a class of workers who are in an unequal position with respect to bargaining power and are thus relatively defenceless against the denial of a living wage is not only detrimental to their health and well being but casts a direct burden for their support upon the community. What these workers lose in wages the taxpayers are called upon to pay. The bare cost of living must be met. We may take judicial notice of the unparalleled demands for relief which arose during the recent period of depression and still continue to an alarming extent despite the degree of economic recovery which has been achieved. It is unnecessary to cite official statistics to establish what is of common knowledge through the length and breadth of the land. While in the instant case no factual brief has been presented, there is no reason to doubt that the State of Washington has encountered the same social problem that is present elsewhere. The community is not bound to provide what is in effect a subsidy for unconscionable employers. The community may direct its law-making power to correct the abuse which springs from their selfish disregard of the public interest. . . .

Our conclusion is that the case of *Adkins v. Children's*

Hospital, supra, should be, and is overruled. The judgment of the Supreme Court of the State of Washington is affirmed.

Chapter 24

THE END OF ISOLATION

However far-reaching the social and economic reforms that constituted the "Roosevelt Revolution," it was as war leader rather than as domestic reformer that Franklin D. Roosevelt made his most profound impression upon the course of American life. Under his bold leadership American foreign policy ultimately underwent a transformation even more revolutionary than that in political thought, and by the time of the President's death in April, 1945, the nation seemed permanently to have abandoned isolationism and accepted its full responsibilities as a great world power. Yet like Woodrow Wilson before him, Roosevelt entered the Presidency with a minor concern for foreign affairs, and during the early thirties America's relations with the world around her were generally conducted on a rather narrow, nationalistic basis which offered little suggestion of the broadly conceived program of international co-operation of Roosevelt's second and third administrations.

In only two areas did Roosevelt immediately indicate an attitude which differed importantly from the provincial nationalism long characteristic of American foreign policy. Convinced that economic reform depended largely upon the removal of the barriers to international trade, he heartily endorsed the reciprocal trade program of Secretary of State Cordell Hull. The prohibitive Hawley-Smoot Tariff, which Hoover signed in 1930 over the strenuous objections of 1000 professional economists, had brought extensive foreign retaliation against American goods. But the Trade Agreements Act of 1934 authorized the reduction of tariff rates by as much as fifty per cent in return for similar concessions from other nations, and within a few years reciprocal agreements had brought a vastly increased foreign trade.

Meanwhile Roosevelt abandoned the threatening "Big Stick" policy in Latin-American relations and adopted instead "the policy of the good neighbor—the neighbor who resolutely respects himself and, because he does so, respects the rights of others—the neighbor who respects his obligations and respects the sanctity of his agreements in and with a world of neighbors." The United States ended its protectorate over Cuba, pledging non-intervention in the internal affairs of her sister republics to the South; the last American marines were withdrawn from Haiti; and the Monroe Doctrine was reinterpreted as an expression of multilateral Pan-American policy rather than merely the unilateral pronouncement of the United States. It would take many years before the once aggressively self-assertive "Colossus of the North" could entirely dispel the fears of her Latin-American neighbors, but the Good Neighbor Policy proved a wise and eminently successful first step in that direction.

Aside from these departures from tradition, however, in the early days of the New Deal there were few indications of the outstanding leadership Franklin D. Roosevelt was eventually to offer the democratic world in its fight for freedom. Setting the nation's own house in order demanded the President's full attention and energies and seemed to leave little time for concern with the world at large. Besides, in the thirties American public opinion was firmly set against embroilment in foreign affairs. To the general disillusionment which followed World War I had been added intense chagrin at the failure of former Allies to pay their war debts. Then when the Nye Committee of the Senate revealed that munitions makers had enjoyed huge earnings from 1914 to 1918, a great many Americans cynically concluded that the war had been fought merely for the profit of a greedy few. From 1935 to 1937 these feelings all found expression in a series of Neutrality Acts which were designed to keep America out of future wars by placing an embargo upon the export of arms to belligerent nations, by prohibiting the extension of loans and credits to belligerents, by forbidding Americans to travel on belligerent vessels, and by preventing the arming of American merchant ships.

Yet war clouds were rapidly gathering throughout the world, and neutrality was hardly possible for a democracy surrounded by totalitarian aggressors. In 1931 Imperial Japan seized Manchuria from China, and in 1937 she launched another vicious and unprovoked attack upon that near-defenseless nation in an effort to establish a Japanese dominated "New Order" in the Far East. In 1935 Benito Mussolini, the "sawdust Caesar" of Fascist Italy, began an imperialist war against Ethiopia. And in 1936, after Japanese and Italian aggressions had indicated very clearly the collapse of collective security and the ineffectiveness of the League of Nations, Nazi Germany remilitarized the Rhineland as a prelude to Adolf Hitler's mad quest for world domination.

Most Americans thoroughly deplored the rise of totalitarianism and their sympathies were sincerely extended to persecuted minorities within the dictator nations and to the hapless victims of totalitarian aggression. But the national temper was still largely isolationist, and there seemed little likelihood that popular opinion would tolerate active intervention abroad. Thus Roosevelt's course was all the more difficult. Though at first he had been somewhat indifferent to world politics, he actually had come much sooner than most of his countrymen to a real understanding of the formidable threat that aggressive dictatorship anywhere in the world posed to the United States and to democracy everywhere. It was clearly the President's task to educate the nation to the imminent danger to its security, and in his famous "Quarantine" speech of 1937 he warned that there is a "solidarity and interdependence about the modern world, both technically and morally, which makes it impossible for any nation completely to isolate itself from economic and political upheavals in the rest of the world. . . ." "The epidemic of world lawlessness is spreading . . ." he argued, and America must join the free world in quarantining aggressors as she would quarantine those who suffer from physical disease. "Let no one imagine that America will escape, that it may expect mercy, that this Western Hemisphere will not be attacked, and that it will continue tranquilly and peacefully to carry on the ethics and the arts of civilization."

Internationalists cheered the "Quarantine" speech as an unequivocal statement of America's stake in collective security, but most Americans were less far-sighted, and the President's grim lecture on the realities of international politics was greeted with widespread public apathy or hostility. Yet the dictator nations themselves soon provided the basis for Roosevelt's eloquent and increasingly frequent lessons in world diplomacy. Interventionist sentiment was immeasurably strengthened by further Japanese assaults upon China; by Hitler's demand that democratic Czechoslovakia surrender the Sudetenland to Germany or face total war; by appeasement at Munich, where England and France deserted that small republic to guarantee what British Prime Minister Neville Chamberlain naïvely called "peace in our time"; by Hitler's armed march into what remained of Czechoslovakia after the Munich betrayal; and by Mussolini's rape of Albania. Then in August, 1939, the signature of a non-aggression pact between Nazi Germany and Communist Russia further shocked Americans from their complacency. Now protected against war on two fronts, Hitler ordered his armies to march into Poland, and when England and France finally resisted the Nazi aggressor, World War II began.

Even after England and France had taken up Hitler's challenge to peace and to democracy, America was largely opposed to direct involvement in war. Though there was little pro-German sentiment within the nation, and though most Americans fervently prayed for an Allied victory over totalitarian aggression, American assistance in 1939 was limited to repealing the arms embargo of the Neutrality Acts and permitting "cash and carry" sales of war supplies to the belligerents. In the Spring of 1940, however, when Denmark, Norway, Belgium, Holland, Luxembourg, and finally France all fell in rapid order before Hitler's onrushing armies, Americans finally awoke to the menace to their own safety and freedom and embraced more enthusiastically the realistic leadership of Franklin D. Roosevelt. There remained those who damned the President as a "war-monger," and the isolationist "America First Committee" proved a powerful antidote to the interventionist "Committee to Defend America by Aiding the Allies." But there was a general approval of the government's intensive preparedness program for "total defense," and in September, 1940, Congress enacted the nation's first peace-time conscription law.

By 1940 most Americans had come to agree with the President that "we must make America the arsenal of democracy" and in September they warmly applauded the transfer —by Executive Order— of 50 over-age destroyers to the hard-pressed British. Though generally a fervent supporter of the Allied cause, Wendell Willkie, the popular Republican candidate for President in the election of 1940, roundly denounced the destroyer deal as a "dictatorial action" and rebuked the President for not seeking prior Congressional approval. But Roosevelt easily overrode these criticisms and was re-elected despite bitter partisan opposition and traditional objections to a third term for any President. His foreign aid program continued unabated. Early in 1941 he submitted to the Congress a plan which would permit the government to lend or lease or otherwise transfer military supplies to any nation whose defense was essential to American security. Then in his "Four Freedoms" speech the President summoned the full moral strength of America in support of the Lend-Lease Bill, announcing to the world—as Wilson had in his Fourteen Points—that America's goal was a post-war world which would enjoy freedom of speech, freedom of religion, freedom from want, and freedom from fear. In the Summer of 1941 Roosevelt and British Prime Minister Winston Churchill held a secret shipboard rendezvous in the Atlantic, where the senior statesmen of the free world drew up an "Atlantic Charter" to state precisely the ideological nature of the war against totalitarianism.

Even at this point Americans spoke hopefully of all-out aid to the Allies *short of war*, but the Rome-Berlin-Tokyo Axis soon determined the nation's fate otherwise. On December 7, 1941—"a day that will live in infamy"—the Japanese launched a disastrous surprise attack upon Pearl Harbor and other American outposts in the Pacific. Within a week the United States was officially at war with the Axis powers. Americans fought because they had been attacked; yet it was also true that the attack would not have come had they been willing to appease the dictators as England and France had done so futilely at Munich, had they been willing to sacrifice their ideals, to abandon their fellow democracies to total destruction, and to postpone the day when they would ultimately stand alone against a hostile, Axis-dominated world. Thus the nation was not forced or tricked into war; rather out of enlightened self-interest she had deliberately chosen what Winston Churchill so dramatically described as the path of "blood, toil, tears, and sweat."

The "Four Freedoms" Speech, *Franklin D. Roosevelt, 1941*

I address you, the Members of the Seventy-seventh Congress, at a moment unprecedented in the history of the Union. I use the word "unprecedented," because at no previous time has American security been as seriously threatened from without as it is today.

Since the permanent formation of our Government under the Constitution, in 1789, most of the periods of crisis in our history have related to our domestic affairs. Fortunately, only one of these—the four-year War between the States —ever threatened our national unity. Today, thank God, one hundred and thirty million Americans, in forty-eight States, have forgotten points of the compass in our national unity.

It is true that prior to 1914 the United States often had been disturbed by events in other Continents. We had even engaged in two wars with European nations and in a number of undeclared wars in the West Indies, in the Mediterranean and in the Pacific for the maintenance of American rights and for the principles of peaceful commerce. But in no case had a serious threat been raised against out national safety or our continued independence.

What I seek to convey is the historic truth that the United States as a nation has at all times maintained clear, definite opposition, to any attempt to lock us in behind an ancient Chinese wall while the procession of civilization went past. Today, thinking of our children and of their children, we oppose enforced isolation for ourselves or for any other part of the Americas.

That determination of ours, extending over all these years, was proved, for example, during the quarter century of wars following the French Revolution.

While the Napoleonic struggles did threaten interests of the United States because of the French foothold in the West Indies and in Louisiana, and while we engaged in the War of 1812 to vindicate our right to peaceful trade, it is nevertheless clear that neither France nor Great Britain, nor any other nation, was aiming at domination of the whole world.

In like fashion, from 1815 to 1914—ninety-nine years— no single war in Europe or in Asia constituted a real threat against our future or against the future of any other American nation.

Except in the Maximilian interlude in Mexico, no foreign power sought to establish itself in this Hemisphere; and the strength of the British fleet in the Atlantic has been a friendly strength. It is still a friendly strength.

Even when World War broke out in 1914, it seemed to contain only small threat of danger to our own American future. But, as time went on, the American people began to visualize what the downfall of democratic nations might mean to our own democracy.

We need not overemphasize imperfections in the Peace of Versailles. We need not harp on failure of the democracies to deal with problems of world reconstruction. We should remember that the Peace of 1919 was far less unjust than the kind of "pacification" which began even before Munich, and which is being carried on under the new order of tyranny that seeks to spread over every continent today. The American people have unalterably set their faces against that tyranny.

Every realist knows that the democratic way of life is at this moment being directly assailed in every part of the world—assailed either by arms, or by secret spreading of poisonous propaganda by those who seek to destroy unity and promote discord in nations that are still at peace.

During sixteen long months this assault has blotted out the whole pattern of democratic life in an appalling number of independent nations, great and small. The assailants are still on the march, threatening other nations, great and small.

Therefore, as your President, performing my constitutional duty to "give to the Congress information of the state of the Union," I find it, unhappily, necessary to report that the future and the safety of our country and of our democracy are overwhelmingly involved in events far beyond our borders.

Armed defense of democratic existence is now being gallantly waged in four continents. If that defense fails, all the population and all the resources of Europe, Asia, Africa and Australasia will be dominated by the conquerors. Let us remember that the total of those populations and their resources in those four continents greatly exceeds the sum total of the population and the resources of the whole of the Western Hemisphere many times over.

In times like these it is immature—and incidentally, untrue—for anybody to brag that an unprepared America, single-handed, and with one hand tied behind its back, can hold off the whole world.

No realistic American can expect from a dictator's peace international generosity, or return of true independence, or world disarmament, or freedom of expression, or freedom of religion, or even good business.

Such a peace would bring no security for us or for our neighbors. "Those, who would give up essential liberty to purchase a little temporary safety, deserve neither liberty nor safety."

As a nation, we may take pride in the fact that we are soft-hearted; but we cannot afford to be soft-headed.

We must always be wary of those who with sounding brass and a tinkling cymbal preach the "ism" of appeasement.

We must especially beware of that small group of selfish men who would clip the wings of the American eagle in order to feather their own nests.

I have recently pointed out how quickly the tempo of modern warfare could bring into our very midst the physical attack which we must eventually expect if the dictator nations win this war.

There is much loose talk of our immunity from immediate and direct invasion from across the seas. Obviously, as long as the British Navy retains its power, no such danger exists. Even if there were no British Navy, it is not probable that any enemy would be stupid enough to attack us by landing troops in the United States from across thousands of miles of ocean, until it had acquired strategic bases from which to operate.

But we learn much from the lessons of the past years in Europe—particularly the lesson of Norway, whose essential seaports were captured by treachery and surprise built up over a series of years.

The first phase of the invasion of this Hemisphere would not be the landing of regular troops. The necessary strategic points would be occupied by secret agents and their dupes, and great numbers of them are already here, and in Latin America.

As long as the aggressor nations maintain the offensive, they—not we—will choose the time and the place and the method of their attack.

That is why the future of all the American Republics is today in serious danger.

That is why this Annual Message to the Congress is unique in our history.

That is why every member of the Executive Branch of the Government and every member of the Congress faces great responsibility and great accountability.

The need of the moment is that our actions and our policy should be devoted primarily—almost exclusively—to meeting this foreign peril. For all our domestic problems are now a part of the great emergency.

Just as our national policy in internal affairs has been based upon a decent respect for the rights and the dignity of all our fellow men within our gates, so our national policy in foreign affairs has been based on a decent respect for the rights and dignity of all nations, large and small. And the justice of morality must and will win in the end.

Our national policy is this:

First, by an impressive expression of the public will and without regard to partisanship, we are committed to all-inclusive national defense.

Second, by an impressive expression of the public will and without regard to partisanship, we are committed to full support of all those resolute peoples, everywhere, who are resisting aggression and are thereby keeping war away from our Hemisphere. By this support, we express our determination that the democratic cause shall prevail; and we strengthen the defense and the security of our own nation.

Third, by an impressive expression of the public will and without regard to partisanship, we are committed to the proposition that principles of morality and considerations for our own security will never permit us to acquiesce in a peace dictated by aggressors and sponsored by appeasers. We know that enduring peace cannot be bought at the cost of other people's freedom.

In the recent national election there was no substantial difference between the two great parties in respect to that national policy. No issue was fought out on this line before the American electorate. Today it is abundantly evident that

American citizens everywhere are demanding and supporting speedy and complete action in recognition of obvious danger.

Therefore, the immediate need is a swift and driving increase in our armament production. . . .

New circumstances are constantly begetting new needs for our safety. I shall ask this Congress for greatly increased new appropriations and authorizations to carry on what we have begun.

I also ask this Congress for authority and for funds sufficient to manufacture additional munitions and war supplies of many kinds, to be turned over to those nations which are now in actual war with aggressor nations.

Our most useful and immediate role is to act as an arsenal for them as well as for ourselves. They do not need man power, but they do need billions of dollars worth of the weapons of defense.

The time is near when they will not be able to pay for them all in ready cash. We cannot, and we will not, tell them that they must surrender, merely because of inability to pay for the weapons which we know they must have.

I do not recommend that we make them a loan of dollars with which to pay for these weapons—a loan to be repaid in dollars.

I recommend that we make it possible for those nations to continue to obtain war materials in the United States, fitting their orders into our own program. Nearly all their matériel would, if the time ever came, be useful for our own defense.

Taking counsel of expert military and naval authorities, considering what is best for our own security, we are free to decide how much should be kept here and how much should be sent abroad to our friends who by their determined and heroic resistance are giving us time in which to make ready our own defense.

For what we send abroad, we shall be repaid within a reasonable time following the close of hostilities, in similar materials, or, at our option, in other goods of many kinds, which they can produce and which we need.

Let us say to the democracies: "We Americans are vitally concerned in your defense of freedom. We are putting forth our energies, our resources and our organizing powers to give you the strength to regain and maintain a free world. We shall send you, in ever-increasing numbers, ships, planes, tanks, guns. This is our purpose and our pledge."

In fulfillment of this purpose we will not be intimidated by the threats of dictators that they will regard as a breach of international law or as an act of war our aid to the democracies which dare to resist their aggression. Such aid is not an act of war, even if a dictator should unilaterally proclaim it so to be.

When the dictators, if the dictators, are ready to make war upon us, they will not wait for an act of war on our part. They did not wait for Norway or Belgium or the Netherlands to commit an act of war.

Their only interest is in a new one-way international law, which lacks mutuality in its observance, and, therefore, becomes an instrument of oppression.

The happiness of future generations of Americans may well depend upon how effective and how immediate we can make our aid felt. No one can tell the exact character of the emergency situations that we may be called upon to meet. The Nation's hands must not be tied when the Nation's life is in danger.

We must all prepare to make the sacrifices that the emergency—almost as serious as war itself—demands. Whatever stands in the way of speed and efficiency in defense preparations must give way to the national need.

A free nation has the right to expect full cooperation from all groups. A free nation has the right to look to the leaders of business, of labor, and of agriculture to take the lead in stimulating effort, not among other groups but within their own groups.

The best way of dealing with the few slackers or trouble makers in our midst is, first, to shame them by patriotic example, and, if that fails, to use the sovereignty of Government to save Government.

As men do not live by bread alone, they do not fight by armaments alone. Those who man our defenses, and those behind them who build our defenses, must have the stamina and the courage which come from unshakeable belief in the manner of life which they are defending. The mighty action that we are calling for cannot be based on a disregard of all things worth fighting for.

The Nation takes great satisfaction and much strength from the things which have been done to make its people conscious of their individual stake in the preservation of democratic life in America. Those things have toughened the fibre of our people, have renewed their faith and strengthened their devotion to the institutions we make ready to protect.

Certainly this is no time for any of us to stop thinking about the social and economic problems which are the root cause of the social revolution which is today a supreme factor in the world.

For there is nothing mysterious about the foundations of a healthy and strong democracy. The basic things expected by our people of their political and economic systems are simple. They are:

Equality of opportunity for youth and for others.

Jobs for those who can work.

Security for those who need it.

The ending of special privilege for the few.

The preservation of civil liberties for all.

The enjoyment of the fruits of scientific progress in a wider and constantly rising standard of living.

These are the simple, basic things that must never be lost sight of in the turmoil and unbelievable complexity of our modern world. The inner and abiding strength of our economic and political systems is dependent upon the degree to which they fulfill these expectations.

Many subjects connected with our social economy call for immediate improvement.

As examples:

We should bring more citizens under the coverage of old-age pensions and unemployment insurance.

We should widen the opportunities for adequate medical care.

We should plan a better system by which persons deserving or needing gainful employment may obtain it.

I have called for personal sacrifice. I am assured of the willingness of almost all Americans to respond to that call.

A part of the sacrifice means the payment of more money in taxes. In my Budget Message I shall recommend that a greater portion of this great defense program be paid for from taxation than we are paying today. No person should try, or be allowed, to get rich out of this program; and the principle of tax payments in accordance with ability to pay should be constantly before our eyes to guide our legislation.

If the Congress maintains these principles, the voters, putting patriotism ahead of pocketbooks, will give you their applause.

In the future days, which we seek to make secure, we look forward to a world founded upon four essential human freedoms.

The first is freedom of speech and expression—everywhere in the world.

The second is freedom of every person to worship God in his own way—everywhere in the world.

The third is freedom from want—which, translated into world terms, means economic understandings which will secure to every nation a healthy peacetime life for its inhabitants—everywhere in the world.

The fourth is freedom from fear—which, translated into world terms, means a world-wide reduction of armaments to such a point and in such a thorough fashion that no nation will be in a position to commit an act of physical aggression against any neighbor—anywhere in the world.

That is no vision of a distant millennium. It is a definite basis for a kind of world attainable in our own time and generation. That kind of world is the very antithesis of the so-called new order of tyranny which the dictators seek to create with the crash of a bomb.

To that new order we oppose the greater conception—the moral order. A good society is able to face schemes of world domination and foreign revolutions alike without fear.

Since the beginning of our American history, we have been engaged in change—in a perpetual peaceful revolution—a revolution which goes on steadily, quietly adjusting itself to changing conditions—without the concentration camp or the quick-lime in the ditch. The world order which we seek is the cooperation of free countries, working together in a friendly, civilized society.

This nation has placed its destiny in the hands and heads and hearts of its millions of free men and women; and its faith in freedom under the guidance of God. Freedom means the supremacy of human rights everywhere. Our support goes to those who struggle to gain those rights or keep them. Our strength is our unity of purpose.

To that high concept there can be no end save victory.

The Atlantic Charter, *1941*

Joint declaration of the President of the United States of America and the Prime Minister, Mr. Churchill, representing His Majesty's Government in the United Kingdom, being met together, deem it right to make known certain common principles in the national policies of their respective countries on which they base their hopes for a better future for the world.

First, their countries seek no aggrandizement, territorial or other;

Second, they desire to see no territorial changes that do not accord with the freely expressed wishes of the peoples concerned;

Third, they respect the right of all peoples to choose the form of government under which they will live; and they wish to see sovereign rights and self-government restored to those who have been forcibly deprived of them;

Fourth, they will endeavor, with due respect for their existing obligations, to further the enjoyment by all states, great or small, victor or vanquished, of access, on equal terms, to the trade and to the raw materials of the world which are needed for their economic prosperity;

Fifth, they desire to bring about the fullest collaboration between all nations in the economic field with the object of securing, for all, improved labor standards, economic advancement, and social security;

Sixth, after the final destruction of the Nazi tyranny, they hope to see established a peace which will afford to all nations the means of dwelling in safety within their own boundaries, and which will afford assurance that all the men in all the lands may live out their lives in freedom from fear and want;

Seventh, such a peace should enable all men to traverse the high seas and oceans without hindrance;

Eighth, they believe that all of the nations of the world, for realistic as well as spiritual reasons, must come to the abandonment of the use of force. Since no future peace can be maintained if land, sea, or air armaments continue to be employed by nations which threaten, or may threaten, aggression outside of their frontiers, they believe, pending the establishment of a wider and permanent system of general security, that the disarmament of such nations is essential. They will likewise aid and encourage all other practicable measures which will lighten for peace-loving peoples the crushing burden of armaments.

Chapter 25

THE COLD WAR

On January 1, 1942, less than a month after Pearl Harbor, 26 nations at war with the Axis powers signed the historic Declaration of the United Nations, thus binding themselves to full and unstinting efforts against the common enemy and unifying themselves in the struggle against totalitarian aggression. Equally significant in the development of collective security were the frequent international conferences at Quebec, Casablanca, Cairo, Teheran, and Yalta which marked continuous, close cooperation on military and diplomatic matters among the major Allied powers, particularly England, Russia, and the United States. When this war-time harmony and singleness of purpose culminated in the defeat of the Axis powers and in creation of the United Nations world organization at the San Francisco Conference in April, 1945, it seemed to hopeful men everywhere that global war must soon give way to a new world founded upon the principles of law and order.

The United States was now fully prepared to abandon the disastrous isolationism of the post-Versailles generation. Diehards remained who opposed American involvement in any scheme for international cooperation, but war had taught the overwhelming majority of Americans that world interdependence was an inescapable reality, and the United Nations was enthusiastically cheered throughout the country. Besides, Franklin D. Roosevelt had proved too skillful a politician to repeat Wilson's tragic blunder of making world organization both a party and a personal issue. Instead the President had shrewdly identified the administration's war and peace policies with such outstanding Republican statesmen as Wendell L. Willkie, Henry L. Stimson, Frank Knox, and Senator Arthur H. Vandenburg (a former isolationist and ranking minority member of the important Senate Foreign Relations Committee). Bipartisanship worked well, for even in the election of 1944, when Roosevelt defeated Thomas E. Dewey to win a precedent-shattering fourth term, conflict over foreign policy was at a minimum. At the San Francisco Conference and for some time thereafter the leaders of both major parties assumed the responsibility of assuring official American support for the United Nations.

Nazi Germany collapsed in May, 1945, under the combined pressures of Western forces led by General Dwight D. Eisenhower and of Russian forces from the East. Four months later, after the cities of Hiroshima and Nagasaki had been almost totally destroyed by America's newly developed, incredibly powerful atom bomb, the Japanese surrendered, and the war was over. But peace and security were not to be long enjoyed by a war-weary world, for disunity among the former allies was apparent almost as soon as the war ended. A bitter "cold war" broke out between the East and the West, and the United Nations very quickly became the scene of continuous disagreements between the Soviet Union and the United States.

Then in March, 1947, when the American government believed that the independence of Greece and Turkey was being seriously threatened by Soviet imperial ambitions, President Harry S Truman (who had succeeded to the Presidency after Roosevelt's untimely death in April, 1945) appeared before Congress to announce a revolutionary change in American foreign policy:

At the present moment in world history nearly every nation must choose between alternative ways of life. The

choice is too often not a free one. One way of life is
based upon the will of the majority. . . . The second way
of life is based upon the will of the minority forcibly
imposed upon the majority. It relies upon terror and oppression, a controlled press and radio, fixed elections,
and the suppression of personal freedoms. I believe that
it must be the policy of the United States to support
free peoples who are resisting attempted subjugation by
armed minorities or by outside pressures. . . .

Then the President further urged financial support for the administration's new plan to "contain" Communist power
through economic and military assistance abroad.

Congress quickly approved the Truman Doctrine and
granted the President's initial request for $400,000,000. Yet it
was clear that the war-devastated nations of Western Europe
could not long survive an extensive cold war with the East
unless their economies were reconstructed and strengthened,
for Communism fed upon poverty and chaos. Thus in a
speech at Harvard University in June, 1947, Secretary of
State George C. Marshall announced that if Europe were to
indicate a willingness to work hard at its own recovery, then
the United States would make large sums of money available
for economic reconstruction. The Russians bitterly denounced
the Marshall Plan, and within the United States itself the administration encountered considerable resistance from former
isolationists who once again argued for American withdrawal
from foreign commitments. Nevertheless the European
Recovery Program was enacted in April, 1948, and an
Economic Cooperation Administration was established under
the direction of Paul G. Hoffman, a Republican industrialist,
to administer the multi-billion-dollar American grants.

The Marshall Plan proved immediately effective in Western
Europe, and Americans hoped that economic rehabilitation
would prove an insurmountable barrier to further Communist
penetration. That this faith in mutual aid and cooperation was
justified was indicated in 1948-1949 when the strengthened
free nations of Europe supported America's successful efforts
to break a Russian blockade of Berlin, and again in the spring
of 1949 when they joined with the United States and Canada
to form the North Atlantic Alliance. But continuing tension
and conflict, following so soon worldwide holocaust and the
unleashing of what seemed ultimate atomic weaponry, terri-
fied thoughtful persons everywhere with the further specter of
mutual annihilation. And it remained for American novelist
William Faulkner, as he received the 1949 Nobel Prize for
Literature, most sensitively to sum up mankind's best hope for
survival: the triumph of the human spirit, even as nations
locked in cold war appeared unceasingly to denigrate it.

The Marshall Plan, *George C. Marshall, 1947*

I need not tell you, gentlemen, that the world situation is very serious. That must be apparent to all intelligent people. I think one difficulty is that the problem is one of such enormous complexity that the very mass of facts presented to the public by press and radio make it exceedingly difficult for the man in the street to reach a clear appraisement of the situation. Furthermore, the people of this country are distant from the troubled areas of the earth and it is hard for them to comprehend the plight and consequent reactions of the long-suffering peoples, and the effect of those reactions on their governments in connection with our efforts to promote peace in the world.

In considering the requirements for the rehabilitation of Europe, the physical loss of life, the visible destruction of cities, factories, mines and railroads was correctly estimated, but it has become obvious during recent months that this visible destruction was probably less serious than the dislocation of the entire fabric of European economy. For the past ten years conditions have been highly abnormal.

The feverish preparation for war and the more feverish maintenance of the war effort engulfed all aspects of national economies. Machinery has fallen into disrepair or is entirely obsolete. Under the arbitrary and destructive Nazi rule, virtually every possible enterprise was geared into the German war machine. Long-standing commercial ties, private institutions, banks, insurance companies and shipping companies disappeared, through loss of capital, absorption through nationalization or by simple destruction.

In many countries, confidence in the local currency has been severely shaken. The breakdown of the business structure of Europe during the war was complete. Recovery has been seriously retarded by the fact that two years after the close of hostilities a peace settlement with Germany and Austria has not been agreed upon. But even given a more prompt solution of these difficult problems, the rehabilitation of the economic structure of Europe quite evidently will require a much longer time and greater effort than had been foreseen.

There is a phase of this matter which is both interesting and serious. The farmer has always produced the foodstuffs to exchange with the city dweller for the other necessities of life. This division of labor is the basis of modern civilization. At the present time it is threatened with breakdown. The town and city industries are not producing adequate goods to exchange with the food-producing farmer. Raw materials and fuel are in short supply. Machinery is lacking or worn out.

The farmer or the peasant cannot find the goods for sale

which he desires to purchase. So the sale of his farm produce for money which he cannot use, seems to him an unprofitable transaction. He, therefore, has withdrawn many fields from crop cultivation and is using them for grazing. He feeds more grain to stock and finds for himself and his family an ample supply of food, however, short he may be on clothing and the other ordinary gadgets of civilization. Meanwhile, people in the cities are short of food and fuel. So the governments are forced to use their foreign money and credits to procure these necessities abroad. This process exhausts funds which are urgently needed for reconstruction. Thus a very serious situation is rapidly developing which bodes no good for the world. The modern system of the division of labor upon which the exchange of products is based is in danger of breaking down.

The truth of the matter is that Europe's requirements for the next three or four years of foreign food and other essential products—principally from America—are so much greater than her present ability to pay that she must have substantial additional help, or face economic, social and political deterioration of a very grave character.

The remedy lies in breaking the vicious circle and restoring the confidence of the European people in the economic future of their own countries and of Europe as a whole. The manufacturer and the farmer throughout wide areas must be able and willing to exchange their products for currencies, the continuing value of which is not open to question.

Aside from the demoralizing effect on the world at large and the possibilities of disturbances arising as a result of the desperation of the people concerned, the consequences to the economy of the United States should be apparent to all. It is logical that the United States should do whatever it is able to do to assist in the return of normal economic health in the world, without which there can be no political stability and no assured peace.

Our policy is directed not against any country or doctrine but against hunger, poverty, desperation and chaos. Its purpose should be the revival of a working economy in the world so as to permit the emergence of political and social conditions in which free institutions can exist. Such assistance, I am convinced, must not be on a piecemeal basis as various crises develop. Any assistance that this Government may render in the future should provide a cure rather than a mere palliative.

Any government that is willing to assist in the task of recovery will find full cooperation, I am sure, on the part of the United States Government. Any government which maneuvers to block the recovery of other countries cannot expect help from us. Furthermore, governments, political parties or groups which seek to perpetuate human misery in order to profit therefrom politically or otherwise will encounter the opposition of the United States.

It is already evident that, before the United States Government can proceed much further in its efforts to alleviate the situation and help start the European world on its way to recovery, there must be some agreement among the countries of Europe as to the requirements of the situation and the part those countries themselves will take in order to give proper effect to whatever action might be undertaken by this Government. It would be neither fitting nor efficacious for this Government to undertake to draw up unilaterally a program designed to place Europe on its feet economically. This is the business of the Europeans. The initiative, I think, must come from Europe. The role of this country should consist of friendly aid in the drafting of a European program and of later support of such a program so far as it may be practical for us to do so. The program should be a joint one, agreed to by a number, if not all European nations.

An essential part of any successful action on the part of the United States is an understanding on the part of the people of America of the character of the problem and the remedies to be applied. Political passion and prejudice should have no part. With foresight, and a willingness on the part of our people to face up to the vast responsibility which history has clearly placed upon our country, the difficulties I have outlined can and will be overcome.

William Faulkner's Acceptance Speech for the 1949 Nobel Prize for Literature

I feel that this award was not made to me as a man, but to my work—a life's work in the agony and sweat of the human spirit, not for glory and least of all for profit, but to create out of the materials of the human spirit something which did not exist before. So this award is only mine in trust. It will not be difficult to find a dedication for the money part of it commensurate with the purpose and significance of its origin. But I would like to do the same with the acclaim too, by using this moment as a pinnacle from which I might be listened to by the young men and women already dedicated to the same anguish and travail, among whom is already that one who will some day stand here where I am standing.

Our tragedy today is a general and universal physical fear so long sustained by now that we can even bear it. There are no longer problems of the spirit. There is only the question: When will I be blown up? Because of this, the young man or woman writing today has forgotten the problem of the human heart in conflict with itself which alone can make good writing because only that is worth writing about, worth the agony and the sweat.

He must learn them again. He must teach himself that the

basest of all things is to be afraid; and, teaching himself that, forget it forever, leaving no room in his workshop for anything but the old verities and truths of the heart, the old universal truths lacking which any story is ephemeral and doomed—love and honor and pity and pride and compassion and sacrifice. Until he does so, he labors under a curse. He writes not of love but of lust, of defeats in which nobody loses anything of value, of victories without hope and, worst of all, without pity or compassion. His griefs grieve on no universal bones, leaving no scars. He writes not of the heart but of the glands.

Until he relearns these things, he will write as though he stood among and watched the end of man. I decline to accept the end of man. It is easy enough to say that man is immortal simply because he will endure: that when the last dingdong of doom has clanged and faded from the last worthless rock hanging tideless in the last red and dying evening, that even then there will still be one more sound: that of his puny inexhaustible voice, still talking. I refuse to accept this. I believe that man will not merely endure: he will prevail. He is immortal, not because he alone among creatures has an inexhaustible voice, but because he has a soul, a spirit capable of compassion and sacrifice and endurance. The poet's, the writer's, duty is to write about these things. It is his privilege to help man endure by lifting his heart, by reminding him of the courage and honor and hope and pride and compassion and pity and sacrifice which have been the glory of his past. The poet's voice need not merely be the record of man, it can be one of the props, the pillars to help him endure and prevail.

Chapter 26

AMERICA AT MID-CENTURY

Just as in the field of foreign affairs post-World War II America had no real intention of giving up its new sense of international responsibility and returning to pre-war isolationism, so in domestic affairs it showed no overwhelming desire to return to "normalcy," to forsake outright the liberalism and social progress of the 1930's for the more conservative political formulas of the distant past. To be sure, there no longer seemed to be any great sense of urgency about domestic reform, and possibly the extension and liberalization of Social Security benefits marked the only major step toward such reform, while housing, health, and education proposals languished. Yet essentially this was a period when the social experiments, and to a considerable extent even the very ideology of the New Deal, were being ever more thoroughly institutionalized and consolidated within the fabric of American life.

Despite President Harry S Truman's warnings, conservative elements in Congress forced the end of price controls soon after the war, much to the acute dismay of the "little man" (no longer Franklin D. Roosevelt's "forgotten man"), for inflation took over and the cost of living soared to distressing heights. Also, the Taft-Hartley Act of 1947, passed over President Truman's vigorous veto, threatened to curb unions somewhat. But ever-rising incomes within the booming American economy offset high living costs; and the Taft-Hartley "slave labor law," as it was labeled, surely failed to cripple the labor movement, as both the A.F. of L. and the C.I.O. grew and flourished until their merger into one giant labor organization in 1955.

Besides, the Presidential election of 1948 also indicated few particularly conservative tendencies in the United States. On the much-favored Republican ticket, both Presidential nominee Thomas E. Dewey and Vice-Presidential nominee Earl Warren represented the liberal wing of their party and promised a continuation of basic New Deal measures. Ex-Vice-President Henry A. Wallace ran on a left-wing Progressive Party ticket. And underdog Harry S Truman, who conducted the most dynamic campaign Americans had seen in a good many years, barnstormed on an unabashedly liberal platform to win the Presidency in an astonishing upset victory. Pollsters, prophets, and politicians had all picked Republican Dewey as the sure winner. But aside from a widespread admiration for Democrat Truman's "guts" in running against overwhelming odds, one deciding factor in the electoral upset probably was the President's promise of continued high price supports for the farmer. Rising costs and the end of a wartime agricultural boom had left the American farmer in desperate straits, ever more dependent upon government subsidies, and thus upon political promises. Nor was this situation remedied—or even importantly relieved—in the following decades.

But still another factor in the 1948 Democratic victory, and a domestic theme that more than any other dominated post-war America, was the civil rights issue. President Truman had taken a firm stand against the concept of second class citizenship, and he had urged strong national legislation to guarantee full civil rights for America's Negro population. This had caused Southern "Dixiecrats" to bolt the 1948 Democratic Convention and to nominate for President South Carolina's Governor J. Strom Thurmond on a States' Rights Party ticket. Thus, in the face of this Democratic split, Truman's ultimate victory was all the more miraculous, and it served all the more dramatically to point up America's new willingness to go farther and farther towards guaranteeing equal rights to all, towards justifying in practice the nation's older heritage of Jeffersonian democratic beliefs.

In 1952, of course, the United States finally experienced a change in national political power, when in the Presidential election of that year Republican Dwight D. Eisenhower defeated Democrat Adlai E. Stevenson, to end twenty years of Democratic rule. There continued to be partisan differences of opinion over such issues as high prices, unemployment, taxes, farm subsidies, public power, reductions in our armed forces and the proper techniques of insuring both internal security and individual liberties. And, until he was finally censured by his colleagues in the Senate, Republican Senator Joseph R. McCarthy of Wisconsin dominated the nation's headlines with violent attacks on what he called Democratic "softness" towards Communism. (Ultimately in his much publicized hunt for Communists in government McCarthy would attack the Republican Eisenhower Administration, which had not rejected him, but with which he disagreed on many issues almost as fiercely as the Democratic Truman Administration before it.)

Generally, however, the new Republican "team" made few fundamental changes in the domestic policies set down by Democratic Presidents Roosevelt and Truman. And on one point at least—with the singular exception of the South— there seemed to be widespread national and partisan agreement: that on May 17, 1954, Chief Justice Earl Warren, recently appointed by President Eisenhower, had struck a most dramatic blow for America's historic principles of democracy and equality. On that date, speaking for a unanimous Supreme Court, the Chief Justice of the United States declared that segregation of Negro and white children in our public schools is unconstitutional (Brown v. Board of Education). This was a radical reversal of the Court's earlier finding (in Plessy v. Ferguson, 1896) in favor of the "separate but equal" doctrine that segregation generally is permissible when equal facilities are provided for Negro and white. In 1896 Justice John Marshall Harlan had dissented vigorously from the majority decision, arguing that "our Constitution is color-blind, and neither knows nor tolerates classes among citizens." And this was the position the Court unanimously came to in 1954, speaking through Chief Justice Warren. There were some who felt that the Warren opinion was based more on ethics and sociology than on history and law, but one thing was certain: it was thoroughly and vigorously consistent with the spirit of the American heritage.

Recognizing the pressures of custom and precedent within the South itself, and sympathizing with that region's enormous task in revamping its entire educational structure, the Court permitted desegregation to progress at a moderate tempo, "with all deliberate speed." But moderation was not to be a substitute for action, and the Court continued to strike down the barriers to equality for all Americans raised by those who would not accept the inevitable triumph of democracy.

The Warren decision was a significant milestone in America's domestic development; even more than that, however, it was also a profound contribution to our foreign policy. It added true moral substance to what President Eisenhower had said in his Inaugural Address of January 20, 1953: ". . . destiny has laid upon our country the responsibility of the free world's leadership." And, indeed, President Eisenhower's efforts during his years in office were to be mainly concerned with America's posture in relation to foreign affairs. Even as the United States grew to fifty states with the admission in 1959 first of Alaska and then of Hawaii, the world itself appeared to shrink, and its many danger points seemed ever closer to home. The technological advances that took place with incredible rapidity in the 1950's and 1960's increased speeds, shortened distances, and made it ever more necessary that men learn to live together in peace.

The Space Age officially began in October, 1957, when Russia announced the successful launching of Sputnik I, the first man-made satellite. The Russian achievement drastically spurred American space-science efforts, and within a few years both nations had orbited astronaut-manned vehicles many times around the earth, were vying to see which would first land a man on the moon, and were otherwise venturing more and more boldly into outer space.

Meanwhile, on earth, conflict between East and West still preoccupied men concerned with human survival. Behind an impenetrable "Iron Curtain," Russian-inspired puppet governments continued to dominate European "satellite" states, while Soviet propaganda and Soviet pressures in other parts of the world promised no easy resolution of the Cold War. In response, determined to build up its military power, the West had created the North Atlantic Treaty Organization (NATO) to take major steps toward unity and collective strength in the face of aggression.

Actually, it was in the Far East that collective security was put to its most severe test. For in June, 1950, Soviet-trained and -equipped North Korean troops had launched a large-scale invasion of South Korea. The United Nations Security Council immediately called upon member nations to help repel the invaders, and President Harry S Truman boldly dispatched American armed forces to support the UN "police action." The Communist invaders were finally halted, and this new determination to stand firm against aggression anywhere seemed to be a decisive move in the struggle between two worlds. But the fighting in Korea was long and bitter; it stirred up unrest at home that was partially responsible for the Democratic defeat in 1952, and it wasn't until July, 1953, that the new Eisenhower Administration arranged an armistice that in truth was no more a total victory than it was a total defeat. Besides Communist-led forces intensified their drive to control Southeast Asia, and it seemed clear that the Far East would long remain a source of international conflict.

Conflict had begun to assume somewhat different dimensions, however, when in March, 1953, the Kremlin announced that Joseph Stalin was dead. The Soviet Union gradually adopted a so-called new look and began a "peace offensive," which some people thought resulted only from the Communists' realization that ultimate possession by both Russia and the United States of all-destructive thermonuclear weapons had made war intolerable. Under Nikita Khrushchev the Iron Curtain was raised somewhat; there were more and more frequent exchanges of visits between East and West, and Russia's top leaders made good-will trips far beyond their country's borders.

But in the Western world cautious and experienced observers remained thoroughly skeptical of the Soviet Union's real intentions. In the midst of continued thermonuclear weapon-testing and Russian rejection of meaningful disarmament proposals, they argued convincingly that the West must remain strong in military, industrial, and scientific areas. And yet others argued as cogently that to a democracy nurtured in peace there may also be danger inherent in the continuing buildup of such strengths. After eight years as President of mid-twentieth-century America, Dwight D. Eisenhower in his extraordinary Farewell Address of January 17, 1961, warned his fellow countrymen to be ever strong, but also to guard against both "the acquisition of unwarranted influence" over American life by "the military-industrial complex," and the Cold War danger that "public policy could itself become the captive of a scientific-technological elite." These words Americans carried with them as they looked to the long future.

Segregation Decision,
Chief Justice Earl Warren
for the Supreme Court, 1954

These cases come to us from the States of Kansas, South Carolina, Virginia, and Delaware. They are premised on different facts and different local conditions, but a common legal question justifies their consideration together in this consolidated opinion.

In each of the cases, minors of the Negro race, through their legal representatives, seek the aid of the courts in obtaining admission to the public schools of their community on a nonsegregated basis. In each instance, they had been denied admission to schools attended by white children under laws requiring or permitting segregation according to race.

This segregation was alleged to deprive the plaintiffs of the equal protection of the laws under the Fourteenth Amendment. In each of the cases other than the Delaware case, a three-judge Federal District Court denied relief to the plaintiffs on the so-called "separate but equal" doctrine announced by this court in Plessy v. Ferguson.

Under that doctrine, equality of treatment is accorded when the races are provided substantially equal facilities, even though these facilities be separate. In the Delaware case, the Supreme Court of Delaware adhered to that doctrine, but ordered that the plaintiffs be admitted to the white schools because of their superiority to the Negro schools.

The plaintiffs contend that segregated public schools are not "equal" and cannot be made "equal" and that, hence, they are deprived of the equal protection of the laws. Because of the obvious importance of the question presented, the Court took jurisdiction. Argument was heard in the 1952 term, and reargument was heard this term on certain questions propounded by the Court.

Reargument was largely devoted to the circumstances surrounding the adoption of the Fourteenth Amendment in 1868. It covered, exhaustively, consideration of the Amendment in Congress, ratification by the states, then existing practices in racial segregation. and the views of proponents and opponents of the Amendment.

This discussion and our own investigation convince us that although these sources cast some light, it is not enough to resolve the problem with which we are faced.

At best, they are inconclusive. The most avid proponents of the postwar Amendments undoubtedly intended them to remove all legal distinctions among "all persons born or naturalized in the United States."

Their opponents, just as certainly, were antagonistic to both the letter and the spirit of the Amendments and wished them to have the most limited effect. What others in Congress and the State Legislature had in mind cannot be determined with any degree of certainty.

An additional reason for the inclusive nature of the Amendment's history, with respect to segregated schools, is the status of public education at that time. In the South, the movement toward free common schools, supported by general taxation, had not yet taken hold. Education of white children was largely in the hands of private groups. Education of Negroes was almost nonexistent, and practically all of the race was illiterate. In fact, any education of Negroes was forbidden by law in some states.

Today, in contrast, many Negroes have achieved outstanding success in the arts and sciences as well as in the business and professional world. It is true that public education has already advanced further in the North, but the effect of the Amendment on Northern States was generally ignored in the Congressional debates.

Even in the North, the conditions of public education did not approximate those existing today. The curriculum was usually rudimentary; ungraded schools were common in rural areas; the school term was but three months a year in many states; and compulsory school attendance was virtually unknown.

As a consequence, it is not surprising that there should be so little in the history of the Fourteenth Amendment relating to its intended effect on public education.

In the first cases in this court construing the Fourteenth Amendment, decided shortly after its adoption, the court interpreted it as proscribing all state-imposed discriminations against the Negro race.

The doctrine of "Separate but Equal" did not make its appearance in this court until 1896 in the case of Plessy v. Ferguson, supra, involving not education but transportation.

American courts have since labored with the doctrine for over half a century. In this court, there have been six cases involving the "separate but equal" doctrine in the field of public education.

In Cumming v. County Board of Education, and Gong Lum v. Rice, the validity of the doctrine itself was not challenged. In most recent cases, all on the graduate school level, inequality was found in that specific benefits enjoyed by white students were denied to Negro students of the same educational qualifications. Missouri ex rel. Gaines v. Canada, 305 U.S. 337; Sipuel v. Oklahoma, 332 U.S. 331; Sweatt v. Painter, 339 U.S. 629; McLaurin v. Oklahoma State Regents, 339 U.S. 637.

In nine of these cases it was necessary to re-examine the doctrine to grant relief to the Negro plaintiff. And in Sweatt v. Painter, supra, the court expressly reserved decision on the question whether Plessy v. Ferguson should be held inapplicable to public education.

In the instant cases, that question is directly presented. Here, unlike Sweatt v. Painter, there are findings below that the Negro and white schools involved have been equalized or are being equalized, with respect to buildings, curricula, qualifications and salaries of teachers, and other "tangible" factors.

Our decision, therefore, cannot turn on merely a comparison of these tangible factors in the Negro and white schools involved in each of the cases. We must look instead to the effect of segregation itself on public education.

In approaching this problem, we cannot turn the clock back to 1868, when the Amendment was adopted, or even to 1896, when Plessy v. Ferguson was written. We must consider public education in the light of its full development and its present place in American life throughout the nation. Only in this way can it be determined if segregation in public schools deprives these plaintiffs of the equal protection of the laws.

Today, education is perhaps the most important function of state and local governments. Compulsory school attendance laws and the great expenditures for education both demonstrate our recognition of the importance of education to our democratic society. It is required in the performance of our most basic public responsibilities, even service in the armed forces. It is the very foundation of good citizenship. Today, it is a principal instrument in awakening the child to cultural values, in preparing him for later professional training, and in helping him to adjust normally to his environment.

In these days, it is doubtful that any child may reasonably be expected to succeed in life if he is denied the opportunity of an education. Such an opportunity, where the state has undertaken to provide it, is a right which must be made available to all on equal terms.

We come then to the question presented: Does segregation of children in public schools solely on the basis of race, even though the physical facilities and other "tangible" factors may be equal, deprive the children of the minority group of equal educational opportunities? We believe that it does.

In Sweatt v. Painter, supra, in finding that a segregated law school for Negroes could not provide them equal educational opportunities, this court relied in large part on "those qualities which are incapable of objective measurement but which make for greatness in a law school."

In McLaurin v. Oklahoma State Regents, supra, the court, in requiring that a Negro admitted to a white graduate school be treated like all other students, again resorted to intangible considerations: "* * * his ability to study, engage in discussions and exchange views with other students, and, in general, to learn his profession."

Such considerations apply with added force to children in grade and high schools. To separate them from others of similar age and qualifications solely because of their race generates a feeling of inferiority as to their status in the community that may affect their hearts and minds in a way unlikely ever to be undone.

The effect of this separation on their education opportunities was well stated by a finding in the Kansas case by a court which nevertheless felt compelled to rule against the Negro plaintiffs:

> Segregation of white and colored children in public schools has a detrimental effect upon the colored children. The impact is greater when it has the sanction of the law; for the policy of separating the races is usually interpreted as denoting the inferiority of the Negro group. . . .
> A sense of inferiority affects the motivation of a child to learn. Segregation with the sanction of law, therefore, has a tendency to retard the educational and mental development of Negro children and to deprive them of some of the benefits they would receive in a racially integrated school system.

Whatever may have been the extent of psychological knowledge at the time of Plessy v. Ferguson, this finding is amply supported by modern authority. Any language in Plessy v. Ferguson contrary to this finding is rejected.

We conclude that in the field of public education the doctrine of "separate but equal" has no place. Separate educational facilities are inherently unequal. Therefore, we hold that the plaintiffs and others similarly situated for whom the actions have been brought are, by reason of the segregation complained of, deprived of the equal protection of the laws guaranteed by the Fourteenth Amendment. This disposition makes unnecessary any discussion whether such segregation also violates the Due Process Clause of the fourteenth Amendment.

Because these are class actions, because of the wide applicability of this decison, and because of the great variety of local conditions, the formulation of decrees in these cases presents problems of considerable complexity. On reargument, the consideration of appropriate relief was necessarily subordinated to the primary question—the constitutionality of segregation in public education.

We have now announced that such segregation is a denial of the equal protection of the laws. In order that we may have the full assistance of the parties in formulating decrees, the cases will be restored to the docket, and the parties are requested to present further argument. . . .

The Attorney General of the United States is again invited to participate. The Attorneys General of the states requiring or permitting segregation in public education will also be permitted to appear as amici curiae upon request to do so. . . .

IT IS SO ORDERED.

Dwight D. Eisenhower's Farewell Address, *1961*

Good evening, my fellow Americans. . . .

Three days from now, after half a century in the service of our country, I shall lay down the responsibilities of office as, in traditional and solemn ceremony, the authority of the Presidency is vested in my successor.

This evening I come to you with a message of leavetaking and farewell, and to share a few final thoughts with you, my countrymen. . . .

I wish the new President, and all who will labor with him, Godspeed. I pray that the coming years will be blessed with peace and prosperity for all. . . .

We now stand ten years past the midpoint of a century that has witnessed four major wars among great nations—three of these involved our own country.

Despite these holocausts America is today the strongest, the most influential and most productive nation in the world. Understandably proud of this pre-eminence, we yet realize that America's leadership and prestige depend, not merely upon our unmatched material progress, riches and military strength, but on how we use our power in the interests of world peace and human betterment.

Throughout America's adventure in free government, our basic purposes have been to keep the peace; to foster progress in human achievement, and to enhance liberty, dignity and integrity among peoples and among nations.

To strive for less would be unworthy of a free and religious people.

Any failure traceable to arrogance or our lack of comprehension or readiness to sacrifice would inflict upon us grievous hurt, both at home and abroad.

Progress toward these noble goals is persistently threatened by the conflict now engulfing the world. It commands our whole attention, absorbs our very beings. . . .

Threats, new in kind or degree, constantly arise. Of these, I mention two only.

A vital element in keeping the peace is our military establishment. Our arms must be mighty, ready for instant action, so that no potential aggressor may be tempted to risk his own destruction.

Our military organization today bears little relation to that known of any of my predecessors in peacetime—or, indeed, by the fighting men of World War II or Korea.

Until the latest of our world conflicts, the United States had no armaments industry. American makers of plowshares could, with time and as required, make swords as well.

But we can no longer risk emergency improvisation of national defense. We have been compelled to create a permanent armaments industry of vast proportions. Added to this, three and a half million men and women are directly engaged in the defense establishment. We annually spend on military security alone more than the net income of all United States corporations.

Now this conjunction of an immense military establishment and a large arms industry is new in the American experience. The total influence—economic, political, even spiritual—is felt in every city, every state house, every office of the Federal Government. We recognize the imperative need for this development. Yet we must not fail to comprehend its grave implications. Our toil, resources and livelihood are all involved; so is the very structure of our society.

In the councils of Government, we must guard against the acquisition of unwarranted influence, whether sought or unsought, by the military-industrial complex. The potential for the disastrous rise of misplaced power exists and will persist.

We must never let the weight of this combination endanger our liberties or democratic processes. We should take nothing for granted. Only an alert and knowledgeable citizenry can compel the proper meshing of the huge industrial and military machinery of defense with our peaceful methods and goals, so that security and liberty may prosper together.

Akin to, and largely responsible for the sweeping changes in our industrial-military posture has been the technological revolution during recent decades.

In this revolution research has become central. It also becomes more formalized, complex and costly. A steadily increasing share is conducted for, by, or at the direction of the Federal Government.

Today the solitary inventor, tinkering in his shop, has been overshadowed by task forces of scientists, in laboratories and testing fields. In the same fashion, the free university, historically the fountainhead of free ideas and scientific discovery, has experienced a revolution in the conduct of research. Partly because of the huge costs involved, a Government contract becomes virtually a substitute for intellectual curiosity.

For every old blackboard there are now hundreds of new electronic computers.

The prospect of domination of the nation's scholars by Federal employment, project allocations and the power of money is ever present, and is gravely to be regarded.

Yet, in holding scientific research and discovery in respect, as we should, we must also be alert to the equal and opposite danger that public policy could itself become the captive of a scientific-technological elite.

It is the task of statesmanship to mold, to balance, and to integrate these and other forces, new and old, within the principles of our democratic system ever aiming toward the supreme goals of our free society. . . .

Disarmament, with mutual honor and confidence, is a continuing imperative. Together we must learn how to compose differences—not with arms, but with intellect and decent purpose. Because this need is so sharp and apparent, I confess that I lay down my official responsibilities in this field with a definite sense of disappointment. As one who has witnessed the horror and the lingering sadness of war, as one who knows that another war could utterly destroy this civilization which has been so slowly and painfully built over thousands of years, I wish I could say tonight that a lasting peace is in sight.

Happily, I can say that war has been avoided. Steady progress toward our ultimate goal has been made. But so much remains to be done. . . .

To all the peoples of the world, I once more give expression to America's prayerful and continuing aspiration:

We pray that peoples of all faiths, all races, all nations, may have their great human needs satisfied; that those now denied opportunity shall come to enjoy it to the full; that all who yearn for freedom may experience its spiritual blessings, those who have freedom will understand, also, its heavy responsibility; that all who are insensitive to the needs of others, will learn charity, and that the sources—scourges of poverty, disease and ignorance will be made to disappear from the earth; and that in the goodness of time, all peoples will come to live together in a peace guaranteed by the binding force of mutual respect and love. . . .

Thank you, and, good night.

Chapter 27

FROM THE NEW FRONTIER TO THE GREAT SOCIETY

"So let us begin anew." With these Inaugural words, on January 20, 1961, John Fitzgerald Kennedy set his country upon the thousand extraordinary days of national self-renewal that were given to his Presidency. And ultimately those words—and his deeds—would be judged less by the traditional criterion of legislative enactment than within the larger, more meaningful context of national enrichment: of America's rededication to justice and to the life of reason, to a renewed movement forward, to the dynamic, underlying principles of the American heritage that the vigorous and courageous leader seemed somehow to sum up in his very person.

The youngest man ever to be elected President, Democrat Kennedy at 43 succeeded Republican Eisenhower—at 70 the oldest man to preside over this nation's destiny. And to many the change was both profound and symbolic; the bold, articulate New Englander—intellectual, politician, historian, war hero, with a style and grace and vigor that inspired to self-sacrifice so many young Americans—proclaimed in his Inaugural Address "to friend and foe alike, that the torch has been passed to a new generation of Americans—born in this century, tempered by war, disciplined by a hard and bitter peace, proud of our ancient heritage."

John F. Kennedy had by no means been thrust into the Presidency by an overwhelming national consensus. Indeed, in November, 1960, out of a total vote of almost 69,000,000, his popular lead over Republican Vice-President Richard M. Nixon was only slightly more than 100,000 votes. Presumably even that bare margin of victory had been attained only because the unprecedented nationwide series of Nixon-Kennedy face-to-face television and radio debates had brought both candidates into the homes of some 70,000,000 Americans, showing the handsome, less-well-known junior Senator from Massachusetts to be knowledgeable, cool, serious, and purposeful beyond his years and reputation, and perhaps modifying the political liability that if elected he would be the first Roman Catholic in the White House.

Thus, as he assumed the Presidency, John F. Kennedy was acutely aware of being handicapped by having far less than a popular mandate. From the White House he eschewed undue executive pressure upon House and Senate when legislative independence ran high and when wisdom and reason commanded otherwise—much to the undisguised despair of those liberals whose concept of Presidential leadership was limited by their passion for counting Administration bills passed by the Congress. But even while the more astute President bided his legislative time, the New Frontier for which he had campaigned so strenuously was made real by the tone his Administration set, by the healthy, hopeful readiness with which he actively sought out new approaches to the monumental domestic and international problems before the country, and by the infectious enthusiasm and penchant for excellence that enabled him to attract to the nation's service dedicated men and women of high standards and intellect whose absence and aloofness from the world of public affairs had too long been noted.

To many the Peace Corps seemed best and most dramatically to symbolize President Kennedy's capacity to help America—particularly her younger citizens—to recognize and then to realize the nation's highest and most honorable instincts. Mobilizing skilled manpower in teaching, child care, agriculture, public health, and many other fields of service as it trained young Americans to assist less fortunate peoples around the world, the Peace Corps also mobilized the nation's deep idealism, providing a bright cornerstone to the Administration's efforts to utilize America's potential for achievement and leadership both at home and abroad.

Indeed, in an age of science, when America's astronauts were performing incredible feats of courage and daring, constantly pushing back even the newest frontiers of man's knowledge of the physical world, such leadership was most appropriate. Nor was it less so when attention was turned to the myriad social and economic problems that still plagued the nation. Inroads were made upon the ever-destructive scourge of unemployment; efforts were made to encourage business and general economic activity, to increase the nation's productivity, and to extend the material benefits of a more and more affluent society to those who shared in it to only the smallest degree. These actions necessarily took place on a national level, but the states could not avoid their responsibilities either. And as it became abundantly clear that the complexities of industrialized urban and suburban American life called for drastically modernized state governments, the Supreme Court handed down major decisions requiring the reappointment of state legislatures that were historically but undemocratically weighted in favor of rural areas, on the more equitable basis of one man, one vote, in order to make them more representative and presumably better equipped to deal with contemporary challenges.

Even more important in this period of domestic upheaval, however, was a basic decision made in June, 1963, in the White House itself: that in the strife-torn area of civil rights the appropriate and politically feasible time had finally come for the President of the United States to exercise the decisive leadership that alone could set America's moral house in order. Before, the time had not been right; now it was. Before, the national climate of opinion would not have tolerated, would not in its response have made effective and meaningful, the full exercise of Presidential leadership in civil rights. But now public opinion was receptive. The nation had finally been roused by continued violence against the American Negro as well as by the Negroes' own newly militant and forthright demands for a final realization of the concern for human rights that is so deeply rooted in the American heritage. And as no President before him had done, John F. Kennedy, on June 11, 1963, in a dramatic and emotion-laden television address appealed to what Lincoln had once called "the better angels of our nature" to help set right the relationship of American to American, asking the Congress to quicken the long process of providing adequate national legislative guarantees of the rights of all men. That year, too, having written from a Birmingham jail his extraordinary "unwise and untimely" response to criticism of civil disobedience, Dr. Martin Luther King would lead a massive civil rights March on Kennedy's Washington, and "have a dream" of

> that day when all of God's children, black men and white men, Jews and Gentiles, Protestants and Catholics, will be able to join hands and sing in the words of the old Negro spiritual, "Free at last, Free at last, Great God a-mighty, We are free at last."

It was, of course, in the realm of world affairs that the short-lived Kennedy Administration made its most obvious contributions—despite the early Bay of Pigs fiasco, which the new President blundered into by halfheartedly endorsing a plan, launched during the previous Administration, to support an abortive attempt by Cuban refugees to "invade" Cuba and to overthrow Communist dictator Fidel Castro.

No such mistake was made again. When Russia's Khrushchev threatened the President at a 1961 summit meeting and later built the infamous Berlin Wall, the United States stood firm, held its temper and its ground. And in the fall of 1962, when threatening Russian missile bases in Cuba brought civilization to the very brink of nuclear holocaust, John F. Kennedy's cool firmness and decisiveness forced the Soviet Union to back down before what clearly would be American retaliation, and, more important, forced the entire world, particularly the prime antagonists, to realize how vital it was to accommodate national differences before another such confrontation might—even accidentally—take us all over the brink.

For as important as President Kennedy's posture of strength and firmness, so was his famous Inaugural plea: "Let us never negotiate out of fear. But let us never fear to negotiate." Nor was this an idle thought, for the President—knowing as no man else could the enormous danger in continuing and escalating the nuclear arms race—was determined to take important and realistic first steps toward a ban on the nuclear testing that for generations to come could poison our atmosphere and then toward bilateral disarmament itself. To Kennedy, man's fate depended wholly upon a lessening of tensions, upon accommodation rather than war between East and West. Thus, in the summer of 1963 the Soviet Union and the United States agreed upon a "hot line" to facilitate instant communications and to minimize the danger of critical, fatal misunderstanding between Moscow and Washington. And in June, 1963, President Kennedy delivered his historic "Strategy of Peace" address at American University, urging the two great powers, under the assumption that peace is possible and war not inevitable, to reexamine areas of conflict between themselves and their basic attitudes toward each other. Asserting that the United States would refrain from nuclear testing in the atmosphere so long as others did so too, President Kennedy proposed a "strategy of peace" to lead the United States and the Soviet Union out of the "vicious and dangerous cycle" of cold war. Less than two months later men of goodwill everywhere applauded as the United States, Great Britain, and the Soviet Union signed a formal test ban treaty that would considerably diminish the further contamination of the atmosphere shared by East and West and would at least to some degree begin to thaw relations between them. With this stunning diplomatic achievement, John F. Kennedy's major place in man's history was assured.

And not too soon. For on November 22, 1963, the youthful President was dead, murdered by an assassin's bullets. America's splendid rendezvous with uncommon greatness was over.

"Let us continue" was Lyndon B. Johnson's singular plea to his countrymen as he succeeded to the Presidency. Long experienced as a Congressman, then a Senator from Texas, and under Kennedy a most active and responsible Vice-President, Johnson took up the reins of government with a calmness and command that gave the shaken nation both renewed confidence in its future and, once again, deep appreciation for its cherished principle of continuity in high office. Picking up precisely where the fallen leader had been stopped, the skilled new Chief Executive brought all of his legislative experience to bear upon making a reality of Kennedy's promised program. Seemingly with a national consensus—built perhaps upon sadness and grief—that Kennedy had not achieved in 1960, President Johnson broke through the long-standing Congressional logjam that had so plagued his predecessor, even achieving the strong Civil Rights bill for which John F. Kennedy had pleaded. In a May, 1964, landmark speech at the University of Michigan, the President gave stirring expression to his vision of a Great Society not only resting on "abundance and liberty for all" but challenged also to use its great wealth and resources "to enrich and elevate our national life, and to advance the quality of our American civilization." Translating his aspirations into action at almost every level of government, he initiated a wide range of innovative social and economic programs that appeared vastly to enhance his popularity. And in November, 1964, Lyndon Johnson was elected President in his own right, defeating Arizona's Republican Senator Barry M. Goldwater in an unprecedented landslide victory that gave him over 61 percent of the total popular vote.

Nor did the world outside stand still. By this time Khrushchev had been removed from office in Russia without this signaling an end to a seemingly decisive ideological split between Communist leaders in China and the Soviet Union; the Chinese had exploded their first nuclear bomb; conflict in Vietnam worsened; and the many international problems that beset the new President grew ever more horrendous. But there were now new opportunities, too, largely because on the world stage a great man had come and played his brief role; in the long future John Fitzgerald Kennedy would not be forgotten.

John F. Kennedy's Inaugural Address, *1961*

We observe today not a victory of party but a celebration of freedom—symbolizing an end as well as a beginning—signifying renewal as well as change. For I have sworn before you and Almighty God the same solemn oath our forebears prescribed nearly a century and three-quarters ago.

The world is very different now. For man holds in his mortal hands the power to abolish all forms of human poverty and all forms of human life. And yet the same revolutionary beliefs for which our forebears fought are still at issue around the globe—the belief that the rights of man come not from the generosity of the state but from the hand of God.

We dare not forget today that we are the heirs of that first revolution. Let the word go forth from this time and place, to friend and foe alike, that the torch has been passed to a new generation of Americans—born in this century, tempered by war, disciplined by a hard and bitter peace, proud of our ancient heritage—and unwilling to witness to or permit the slow undoing of those human rights to which this nation has always been committed, and to which we are committed today at home and around the world.

Let every nation know, whether it wishes us well or ill, that we shall pay any price, bear any burden, meet any hardship, support any friend. oppose any foe to assure the survival and the success of liberty.

This much we pledge—and more.

To those old allies whose cultural and spiritual origins we share, we pledge the loyalty of faithful friends. United, there is little we cannot do in a host of new cooperative ventures. Divided, there is little we can do—for we dare not meet a powerful challenge at odds and split asunder.

To those new states whom we welcome to the ranks of the free, we pledge our word that one form of colonial control shall not have passed away merely to be replaced by a far more iron tyranny. We shall not always expect to find them supporting our view. But we shall always hope to find them strongly supporting their own freedom—and to remember that. in the past. those who foolishly sought power by riding the back of the tiger ended up inside.

To those people in the huts and villages of half the globe struggling to break the bonds of mass misery, we pledge our best efforts to help them help themselves, for whatever period is required—not because the Communists may be doing it, not because we seek their votes, but because it is right. If a free society cannot help the many who are poor, it cannot save the few who are rich.

To our sister republics south of our border, we offer a special pledge—to convert our good words into good deeds—in a new alliance for progress—to assist free men and free governments in casting off the chains of poverty. But this peaceful revolution of hope cannot become the prey of hostile powers. Let all our neighbors know that we shall join with them to oppose aggression or subversion anywhere in the Americas. And let every other power know that this hemisphere intends to remain the master of its own house.

To that world assembly of sovereign states, the United Nations, our last best hope in an age where the instruments of war have far outpaced the instruments of peace, we renew our pledge of support—to prevent it from becoming merely a forum for invective—to strengthen its shield of the new and the weak—and to enlarge the area in which its writ may run.

Finally, to those nations who would make themselves our adversary, we offer not a pledge but a request: that both sides begin anew the quest for peace, before the dark powers of destruction unleashed by science engulf all humanity in planned or accidental self-destruction.

We dare not tempt them with weakness. For only when our arms are sufficient beyond doubt can we be certain beyond doubt that they will never be employed.

But neither can two great and powerful groups of nations take comfort from our present course—both sides overburdened by the cost of modern weapons, both rightly alarmed by the steady spread of the deadly atom, yet both racing to alter that uncertain balance of terror that stays the hand of mankind's final war.

So let us begin anew—remembering on both sides that civility is not a sign of weakness, and sincerity is always subject to proof. Let us never negotiate out of fear. But let us never fear to negotiate.

Let both sides explore what problems unit us instead of belaboring those problems which divide us.

Let both sides, for the first time, formulate serious and precise proposals for the inspection and control of arms—and bring the absolute power to destroy other nations under the absolute control of all nations.

Let both sides seek to invoke the wonders of science instead of its terrors. Together let us explore the stars, conquer the deserts, eradicate disease, tap the ocean depths and encourage the arts and commerce.

Let both sides unite to heed in all corners of the earth the command of Isaiah—to "undo the heavy burdens ... [and] let the oppressed go free."

And if a beachhead of cooperation may push back the jungles of suspicion, let both sides join in creating a new endeavor—not a new balance of power, but a new world of law, where the strong are just and the weak secure and the peace preserved.

All this will not be finished in the first 100 days. Nor will it be finished in the first 1,000 days, nor in the life of this Administration, nor even perhaps in our lifetime on this planet. But let us begin.

In your hands, my fellow citizens, more than mine, will rest the final success or failure of our course. Since this country was founded, each generation of Americans has been summoned to give testimony to its national loyalty. The graves of young Americans who answered the call to service surround the globe.

Now the trumpet summons us again—not as a call to bear arms, though arms we need—not as a call to battle, though embattled we are—but a call to bear the burden of a long twilight struggle year in and year out, "rejoicing in hope, patient in tribulation"—a struggle against the common enemies of man: tyranny, poverty, disease and war itself.

Can we forge against these enemies a grand and global alliance, north and south, east and west, that can assure a more fruitful life for all mankind? Will you join in that historic effort?

In the long history of the world, only a few generations have been granted the role of defending freedom in its hour of maximum danger. I do not shrink from this responsibility—I welcome it. I do not believe that any of us would exchange places with any other people or any other generation. The energy, the faith, the devotion which we bring to this endeavor will light our country and all who serve it—and the glow from that fire can truly light the world.

And so, my fellow Americans: ask not what your country can do for you—ask what you can do for your country.

My fellow citizens of the world: ask not what America will do for you, but what together we can do for the freedom of man.

Finally, whether you are citizens of America or citizens of the world, ask of us here the same high standards of strength and sacrifice which we ask of you. With a good conscience our only sure reward, with history the final judge of our deeds, let us go forth to lead the land we love, asking His blessing and His help, but knowing that here on earth God's work must truly be our own.

The American University "Strategy of Peace" Speech, *John F. Kennedy, 1963*

... I have, therefore, chosen this time and place to discuss a topic on which ignorance too often abounds and the truth is too rarely perceived—and that is the most important topic on earth: peace.

What kind of peace do I mean and what kind of peace do we seek? Not a Pax Americana enforced on the world by American weapons of war. Not the peace of the grave or the security of the slave. I am talking about genuine peace—the kind of peace that makes life on earth worth living—and the kind that enables men and nations to grow and to hope and build a better life for their children—not merely peace for Americans but peace for all men and women—not merely peace in our time but peace in all time.

I speak of peace because of the new face of war. Total war makes no sense in an age where great powers can maintain large and relatively invulnerable nuclear forces and refuse to surrender without resort to those forces. It makes no sense in an age when a single nuclear weapon contains almost ten times the explosive force delivered by all the Allied air forces in the second world war. It makes no sense in an age when the deadly poisons produced by a nuclear exchange would be carried by wind and water and soil and seed to the far corners of the globe and to generations yet unborn.

Today the expenditure of billions of dollars every year on weapons acquired for the purpose of making sure we never need them is essential to the keeping of peace. But surely the acquisition of such idle stockpiles—which can only destroy and can never create—is not the only, much less the most efficient, means of assuring peace.

I speak of peace, therefore, as the necessary rational end of rational men. I realize the pursuit of peace is not as dramatic as the pursuit of war—and frequently the words of the pursuer fall on deaf ears. But we have no more urgent task.

Some say that it is useless to speak of peace or world law or world disarmament—and that it will be useless until the leaders of the Soviet Union adopt a more enlightened attitude. I hope they do. I believe we can help them do it.

But I also believe that we must re-examine our own attitudes—as individuals and as a nation—for our attitude is as essential as theirs. And every graduate of this school, every thoughtful citizen who despairs of war and wishes to bring peace, should begin by looking inward—by examining his own attitude toward the course of the cold war and toward freedom and peace here at home.

First: Examine our attitude toward peace itself. Too many

of us think it is impossible. Too many think it is unreal. But that is a dangerous, defeatist belief. It leads to the conclusion that war is inevitable—that mankind is doomed—that we are gripped by forces we cannot control.

We need not accept that view. Our problems are man-made. Therefore, they can be solved by man. And man can be as big as he wants. No problem of human destiny is beyond human beings. Man's reason and spirit have often solved the seemingly unsolvable—and we believe they can do it again.

I am not referring to the absolute, infinite concepts of universal peace and goodwill of which some fantasies and fanatics dream. I do not deny the value of hopes and dreams but we merely invite discouragement and incredulity by making that our only and immediate goal.

Let us focus instead on a more practical, more attainable peace—based not on a sudden revolution in human nature but on a gradual evolution in human institutions—on a series of concrete actions and effective agreement which are in the interests of all concerned.

There is no single, simple key to this peace—no grand or magic formula to be adopted by one or two powers. Genuine peace must be the product of many nations, the sum of many acts. It must be dynamic, not static, changing to meet the challenge of each new generation. For peace is a process—a way of solving problems.

With such a peace, there will still be quarrels and conflicting interests, as there are within families and nations. World peace, like community peace, does not require that each man love his neighbor—it requires only that they live together with mutual tolerance, submitting their disputes to a just and peaceful settlement. And history teaches us that enmities between nations, as between individuals, do not last forever. However fixed our likes and dislikes may seem, the tide of time and events will often bring surprising changes in the relations between nations and neighbors.

So let us persevere. Peace need not be impracticable—and war need not be inevitable. By defining our goal more clearly—by making it seem more manageable and less remote—we can help all people to see it, to draw hope from it, and to move irresistibly towards it.

And second: Let us re-examine our attitude towards the Soviet Union. It is discouraging to think that their leaders may actually believe what their propagandists write.

It is discouraging to read a recent authoritative Soviet text on military strategy and find, on page after page, wholly baseless and incredible claims—such as the allegation that "American imperialist circles are preparing to unleash different types of war . . . that there is a very real threat of a preventative war being unleashed by American imperialists against the Soviet Union . . . (and that) the political aims," and I quote, "of the American imperialists are to enslave economically and politically the European and other capitalist countries . . . (and) to achieve world domination . . . by means of aggressive war."

Truly, as it was written long ago: "The wicked flee when no man pursueth." Yet it is sad to read these Soviet statements—to realize the extent of the gulf between us. But it is also a warning—a warning to the American people not to fall into the same trap as the Soviets, not to see only a distorted and desperate view of the other side, not to see conflict as inevitable, accommodation as impossible and communication as nothing more than an exchange of threats.

No government or social system is so evil that its people must be considered as lacking in virtue. As Americans, we find Communism profoundly repugnant as a negation of personal freedom and dignity. But we can still hail the Russian people for their many achievements—in science and space, in economic and industrial growth, in culture, in acts of courage.

Among the many traits the peoples of our two countries have in common, none is stronger than our mutual abhorrence of war. Almost unique among the major world powers, we have never been at war with each other. And no nation in the history of battle ever suffered more than the Soviet Union in the second world war. At least 20,000,000 lost their lives. Countless millions of homes and families were burned or sacked. A third of the nation's territory, including two-thirds of its industrial base, was turned into a wasteland—a loss equivalent to the destruction of this country east of Chicago.

Today, should total war ever break out again—no matter how—our two countries will be the primary targets. It is an ironic but accurate fact that the two strongest powers are the two in the most danger of devastation. All we have built, all we have worked for, would be destroyed in the first 24 hours. And even in the cold war—which brings burdens and dangers to so many countries, including this nation's closest allies—our two countries bear the heaviest burdens. For we are both devoting massive sums of money to weapons that could be better devoted to combat ignorance, poverty and disease.

We are both caught up in a vicious and dangerous cycle with suspicion on one side breeding suspicion on the other, and new weapons begetting counter-weapons.

In short, both the United States and its allies, and the Soviet Union and its allies, have a mutually deep interest in a just and genuine peace and in halting the arms race. Agreements to this end are in the interests of the Soviet Union as well as ours—and even the most hostile nations can be relied upon to accept and keep those treaty obligations and only those treaty obligations, which are in their own interest.

So, let us not be blind in our differences—but let us also direct attention to our common interests and the means by which those differences can be resolved. And if we cannot end now our differences, at least we can help make the world safe for diversity. For, in the final analysis, our most basic common link is that we all inhabit this small planet. We all breathe the same air. We all cherish our children's future. And we are all mortal.

Third: Let us re-examine our attitude towards the cold war, remembering we are not engaged in a debate, seeking to pile up debating points. We are not here distributing blame or pointing the finger of judgment. We must deal with the world as it is, and not as it might have been had the history of the last eighteen years been different.

We must, therefore, persevere in the search for peace in the hope that constructive changes within the Communist bloc might bring within reach solutions which now seem beyond us. We must conduct our affairs in such a way that it becomes in the Communists' interest to agree on a genuine peace. And above all, while defending our own vital interests, nuclear powers must avert those confrontations which bring an adversary to a choice of either a humiliating retreat or a nuclear war. To adopt that kind of course in the unclear age would be evidence only of the bankruptcy of our policy—or of a collective death-wish for the world.

To secure these ends, America's weapons are non-provocative, carefully controlled, designed to deter and capable of selective use. Our military forces are committed to peace and disciplined in self-restraint. Our diplomats are instructed to avoid unnecessary irritants and purely rhetorical hostility.

For we can seek a relaxation of tensions without relaxing our guard. And, for our part, we do not need to use threats to prove that we are resolute. We do not need to jam foreign broadcasts out of fear our faith will be eroded. We are unwilling to impose our system on any unwilling people—but we are willing and able to engage in peaceful competition with any people on earth.

Meanwhile, we seek to strengthen the United Nations, to help solve its financial problems, to make it a more effective instrument for peace, to develop it into a genuine world security system—a system capable of resolving disputes on the basis of law, of insuring the security of the large and the small, and of creating conditions under which arms can finally be abolished.

At the same time we seek to keep peace inside the non-Communist world, where many nations, all of them our friends, are divided over issues which weaken Western unity, which invite Communist intervention, or which threaten to erupt into war.

Our efforts in West New Guinea, in the Congo, in the Middle East and the Indian subcontinent have been persistent and patient despite criticism from both sides. We have also tried to set an example for others—by seeking to adjust small out significant differences with our own closest neighbors in Mexico and Canada.

Speaking of other nations, I wish to make one point clear. We are bound to many nations by alliances. These alliances exist because our concern and theirs substantially overlap. Our commitment to defend Western Europe and West Berlin, for example, stands undiminished because of the identity of our vital interests. The United States will make no deal with the Soviet Union at the expense of other nations and other peoples, not merely because they are our partners, but also because their interests and ours converge.

Our interests converge, however, not only in defending the frontiers of freedom, but in pursuing the paths of peace.

It is our hope—and the purpose of allied policies—to convince the Soviet Union that she, too, should let each nation choose its own future, so long as that choice does not interfere with the choices of others. The communist drive to impose their political and economic system on others is the primary cause of world tension today. For there can be no doubt that, if all nations could refrain from interfering in the self-determination of others, the peace would be much more assured.

This will require a new effort to achieve world law—a new context for world discussions. It will require increased understanding between the Soviets and ourselves. And increased understanding will require increased contact and communication.

One step in this direction is the proposed arrangement for a direct line between Moscow and Washington, to avoid on each side the dangerous delays, misunderstanding, and misreadings of the other's actions which might occur in a time of crisis.

We have also been talking in Geneva about other first-step measures of arms control, designed to limit the intensity of the arms race and reduce the risks of accidental war.

Our primary long-range interest in Geneva, however, is general and complete disarmament—designed to take place by stages, permitting parallel political developments to build the new institutions of peace which would take the place of arms. The pursuit of disarmament has been an effort of this Government since the 1920's. It has been urgently sought by the past three Administrations. And however dim the prospects are today, we intend to continue this effort—to continue it in order that all countries, including our own, can better grasp what the problems and the possibilities of disarmament are.

The only major area of these negotiations where the end is in sight—yet where a fresh start is badly needed—is in a treaty to outlaw nuclear tests. The conclusion of such a treaty—so near and yet so far—would check the spiraling arms race in one of the most dangerous areas. It would place the nuclear powers in a position to deal more effectively with one of the greatest hazards which man faces in 1963—the further spread of nuclear weapons. It would increase our security—it would decrease the prospects of war.

Surely this goal is sufficiently important to require our steady pursuit, yielding neither to the temptation to give up the whole effort nor the temptation to give up our insistence on vital and responsible safeguards.

I am taking this opportunity, therefore, to announce two important decision in this regard:

First: Chairman Khrushchev, Prime Minister Macmillan and I have agreed that high-level discussions will shortly begin in Moscow towards early agreement on a comprehensive test ban treaty. Our hopes must be tempered with the caution of history—but with our hopes go the hopes of all mankind.

Second: To make clear our good faith and solemn convictions on the matter, I now declare that the United States does not propose to conduct nuclear tests in the atmosphere so long as other states do not do so. We will not be the first to resume. Such a declaration is no substitute for a formal binding treaty—but I hope it will help us achieve one. Nor would such a treaty be a substitute for disarmament—but I hope it will help us achieve it.

Finally, my fellow Americans, let us examine our attitude towards peace and freedom here at home. The quality and spirit of our own society must justify and support our efforts abroad. We must show it in the dedication of our own lives—as many of you who are graduating today will have an opportunity to do, by serving without pay in the Peace Corps abroad or in the proposed National Service Corps here at home.

But wherever we are, we must all, in our daily lives, live up to the age-old faith that peace and freedom walk together. In too many of our cities today, the peace is not secure because freedom is incomplete.

It is the responsibility of the executive branch at all levels of government—local, state and national—to provide and protect that freedom for all of our citizens by all means within our authority. It is the responsibility of the legislative branch at all levels, wherever the authority is not now adequate, to make it adequate. And it is the responsibility of all citizens in all sections of this country to respect the rights of others and respect the law of the land.

All this is not unrelated to world peace. "When a man's ways please the Lord," the scriptures tell us, "he maketh even his enemies to be at peace with him." And is not peace, in the last analysis, basically a matter of human rights—the right to live out our lives without fear of devastation—the right to

reathe air as nature provided it—the right of future generations to a healthy existence?

While we proceed to safeguard our national interests, let us
also safeguard human interests. And the elimination of war
and arms is clearly in the interest of both.

No treaty, however much it may be to the advantage of all,
however tightly it may be worded, can provide absolute security against the risks of deception and evasion. But it
can—if it is sufficiently effective in its enforcement and it is
sufficiently in the interests of its signers—offer far more security and far fewer risks than an unabated, uncontrolled, un-
predictable arms race.

The United States, as the world knows, will never start a
war. We do not want a war. We do not now expect a war.
This generation of Americans has already had enough—more
than enough—of war and hate and oppression. We shall be
prepared if others wish it. We shall be alert to try to stop it.
But we shall also do our part to build a world of peace where
the weak are safe and the strong are just.

We are not helpless before that task or hopeless of its
success. Confident and unafraid, we labor on—not toward a
strategy of annihilation but toward a strategy of peace. Thank
you.

Civil Rights Speech, *John F. Kennedy, 1963*

Good evening, my fellow citizens.

This afternoon, following a series of threats and defiant
statements, the presence of Alabama National Guardsmen
was required on the University of Alabama to carry out the
final and unequivocal order of the United States District
Court of the Northern District of Alabama.

That order called for the admission of two clearly qualified
young Alabama residents who happened to have been born
Negro.

That they were admitted peacefully on the campus is due in
good measure to the conduct of the students of the University
of Alabama who met their responsibilities in a constructive
way.

I hope that every American, regardless of where he lives,
will stop and examine his conscience about this and other
related incidents.

This nation was founded by men of many nations and
backgrounds. It was founded on the principle that all men are
created equal, and that the rights of every man are diminished
when the rights of one man are threatened.

Today we are committed to a worldwide struggle to promote and protect the rights of all who wish to be free. And
when Americans are sent to Vietnam or West Berlin we do
not ask for whites only.

It ought to be possible, therefore, for American students of any color to attend any public institution they select without having to be backed up by troops. It ought to be possible for American consumers of any color to receive equal service in places of public accommodation, such as hotels and restaurants, and theaters and retail stores without being forced to resort to demonstrations in the street.

And it ought to be possible for American citizens of any color to register and to vote in a free election without interference or fear of reprisal.

It ought to be possible, in short, for every American to enjoy the privileges of being American without regard to his race or his color.

In short, every American ought to have the right to be treated as he would wish to be treated, as one would wish his children to be treated. But this is not the case.

The Negro baby born in America today, regardless of the section or the state in which he is born, has about one-half as much chance of completing a high school as a white baby born in the same place, on the same day; one-third as much chance of becoming a professional man; twice as much chance of becoming unemployed; about one-seventh as much chance of earning $10,000 a year; a life expectancy which is seven years shorter and the prospects of earning only half as much.

This is not a sectional issue. Difficulties over segregation and discrimination exist in every city, in every state of the Union, producing in many cities a rising tide of discontent that threatens the public safety.

Nor is this a partisan issue. In a time of domestic crisis men of goodwill and generosity should be able to unite regardless of party or politics.

This is not even a legal or legislative issue alone. It is better to settle these matters in the courts than on the streets, and new laws are needed at every level. But law alone cannot make men see right.

We are confronted primarily with a moral issue. It is as old as the Scriptures and is as clear as the American Constitution. The heart of the question is whether all Americans are to be afforded equal rights and equal opportunities; whether we are going to treat our fellow Americans as we want to be treated.

If an American, because his skin is dark, cannot eat lunch in a restaurant open to the public; if he cannot send his children to the best public school available; if he cannot vote for the public officials who represent him; if, in short, he cannot enjoy the full and free life which all of us want, then who among us would be content to have the color of his skin changed and stand in his place?

Who among us would then be content with the counsels of patience and delay? One hundred years of delay have passed nce President Lincoln freed the slaves, yet their heirs, their grandsons, are not fully free. They are not yet freed from the bonds of injustice; they are not yet freed from social and economic oppression.

And this nation, for all its hopes and all its boasts, will not be fully free until all its citizens are free.

We preach freedom around the world, and we mean it. And we cherish our freedom here at home. But are we to say to the world—and much more importantly to each other—that this is the land of the free, except for the Negroes; that we have no second-class citizens, except Negroes; that we have no class or caste system, no ghettos, no master race, except with respect to Negroes?

Now the time has come for this nation to fulfill its promise. The events in Birmingham and elsewhere have so increased the cries for equality that no city or state or legislative body can prudently choose to ignore them.

The fires of frustration and discord are burning in every city, North and South. Where legal remedies are not at hand, redress is sought in the streets in demonstrations, parades and protests, which create tensions and threaten violence—and threaten lives.

We face, therefore, a moral crisis as a country and a people. It cannot be met by repressive police action. It cannot be left to increased demonstrations in the streets. It cannot be quieted by token moves or talk. It is a time to act in the Congress, in your state and local legislative body, and, above all, in all of our daily lives.

It is not enough to pin the blame on others, to say this is a problem of one section of the country or another, or deplore the facts that we face. A great change is at hand, and our task, our obligation is to make that revolution, that change peaceful and constructive for all.

Those who do nothing are inviting shame as well as violence. Those who act boldly are recognizing right as well as reality.

Next week I shall ask the Congress of the United States to act, to make a commitment it has not fully made in this century to the proposition that race has no place in American life or law.

The Federal judiciary has upheld that proposition in a series of forthright cases. The Executive Branch has adopted that proposition in the conduct of its affairs, including the employment of Federal personnel, and the use of Federal facilities, and the sale of Federally financed housing.

But there are other necessary measures which only the Congress can provide, and they must be provided at this session.

The old code of equity law under which we live commands for every wrong a remedy. But in too many communities, in too many parts of the country wrongs are inflicted on Negro citizens and there are no remedies in law.

Unless the Congress acts their only remedy is the street.

I am, therefore, asking the Congress to enact legislation giving all Americans the right to be served in facilities which are open to the public—hotels, restaurants and theaters, retail stores and similar establishments. This seems to me to be an elementary right.

Its denial is an arbitrary indignity that no American in 1963 should have to endure, but many do.

I have recently met with scores of business leaders, urging them to take voluntary action to end this discrimination. And I've been encouraged by their response. And in the last two weeks over 75 cities have seen progress made in desegregating these kinds of facilities.

But many are unwilling to act alone. And for this reason nationwide legislation is needed, if we are to move this problem from the streets to the courts.

I'm also asking Congress to authorize the Federal Government to participate more fully in lawsuits designed to end segregation in public education. We have succeeded in persuading many districts to desegregate voluntarily. Dozens have admitted Negroes without violence.

Today a Negro is attending a state-supported institution in every one of our 50 states. But the pace is very slow.

Too many Negro children entering segregated grade schools at the time of the Supreme Court's decision nine years ago will enter segregated high schools this fall, having suffered a loss which can never be restored.

The lack of an adequate education denies the Negro a chance to get a decent job. The orderly implementation of the Supreme Court decision therefore, cannot be left solely to those who may not have the economic resources to carry their legal action or who may be subject to harrassment.

Other features will be also requested, including greater protection for the right to vote.

But legislation, I repeat, cannot solve this problem alone. It must be solved in the homes of every American in every community across our country.

In this respect, I want to pay tribute to those citizens North and South, who've been working in their communities to make life better for all.

They are acting not out of a sense of legal duty but out of a sense of human decency. Like our soldiers and sailors in all parts of the world, they are meeting freedom's challenge on the firing line and I salute them for their honor—their courage.

My fellow Americans, this is a problem which faces us all in every city of the North as well as the South.

Today there are Negroes unemployed—two or three times

is many compared to whites—inadequate education; moving into the large cities, unable to find work; young people particularly out of work, without hope, denied equal rights, denied the opportunity to eat at a restaurant or a lunch counter, or go to a movie theater; denied the right to a decent education; denied, almost today, the right to attend a state university even though qualified.

It seems to me that these are matters which concern us all—not merely Presidents, or Congressmen, or Governors, but every citizen of the United States.

This is one country. It has become one country because all of us and all the people who came here had an equal chance to develop their talents.

We cannot say to 10 per cent of the population that "you can't have that right. Your children can't have the chance to develop whatever talents they have, that the only way that they're going to get their rights is to go in the street and demonstrate."

I think we owe them and we owe ourselves a better country than that.

Therefore, I'm asking for your help in making it easier for us to move ahead and provide the kind of equality of treatment which we would want ourselves—to give a chance for every child to be educated to the limit of his talent.

As I've said before, not every child has an equal talent or an equal ability or equal motivation. But they should have the equal right to develop their talent and their ability and their motivation to make something of themselves.

We have a right to expect that the Negro community will be responsible, will uphold the law. But they have a right to expect the law will be fair, that the Constitution will be color blind, as Justice Harlan said at the turn of the century.

This is what we're talking about. This is a matter which concerns this country and what it stands for, and in meeting it I ask the support of all of our citizens.

Thank you very much.

The Birmingham City Jail
"Unwise and Untimely" Letter,
Martin Luther King, Jr., 1963

My dear Fellow Clergymen,

While confined here in the Birmingham City Jail, I came across your recent statement calling our present activities "unwise and untimely" . . . since I feel that you are men of genuine goodwill and your criticisms are sincerely set forth, I would like to answer your statement in what I hope will be patient and reasonable terms.

I think I should give the reason for my being in Bi mingham, since you have been influenced by the argument ("outsiders coming in" . . . Several months ago our local affi ate here in Birmingham invited us to be on call to engage in nonviolent direct action program if such were deemed nece sary. . . . So I am here, along with several members of m staff, because we were invited here. I am here because I hav basic organizational ties here.

Beyond this, I am in Birmingham because injustice is here Just as the eighth-century prophets left their little villages an carried their "thus saith the Lord" far beyond the boundarie of their home towns; and just as the Apostle Paul left his littl village of Tarsus and carried the gospel of Jesus Christ t practically every hamlet and city of the Graeco-Roma world, I too am compelled to carry the gospel of freedom be yond my particular home town. Like Paul, I must constantl respond to the Macedonian call for aid.

Moreover, I am cognizant of the interrelatedness of al communities and states. I cannot sit idly by in Atlanta and no be concerned about what happens in Birmingham. Injustic anywhere is a threat to justice everywhere. We are caught i an inescapable network of mutuality, tied in a single garmen of destiny. Whatever affects one directly affects all indirectly Never again can we afford to live with the narrow, provincia "outside agitator" idea. Anyone who lives inside the Unitec States can never be considered an outsider anywhere in thi country.

You deplore the demonstrations that are presently taking place in Birmingham. But I am sorry that your statement dic not express a similar concern for the conditions that brough the demonstrations into being. I am sure that each of you would want to go beyond the superficial social analyst who looks merely at effects, and does not grapple with underlying causes. I would not hesitate to say that it is unfortunate that so-called demonstrations are taking place in Birmingham at this time, but I would say in more emphatic terms that it is even more unfortunate that the white power-structure of this city left the Negro community with no other alternative . . .

Birmingham is probably the most thoroughly segregated city in the United States. Its ugly record of police brutality is known in every section of this country. Its unjust treatment of Negroes in the courts is a notorious reality. There have been more unsolved bombings of Negro homes and churches in Birmingham than any city in this nation. These are the hard, brutal, and unbelievable facts. On the basis of these conditions Negro leaders sought to negotiate with the city fathers. But the political leaders consistently refused to engage in good-faith negotiation. . . .

You may well ask, "Why direct action? Why sit-ins, marches, etc.? Isn't negotiation a better path?" You are ex-

ctly right in your call for negotiation. Indeed, this is the pur-
ose of direct action. Nonviolent direct action seeks to create
uch a crisis and establish such creative tension that a commu-
ity that has constantly refused to negotiate is forced to con-
ront the issue. It seeks so to dramatize the issue that it can
o longer be ignored. I just referred to the creation of tension
s a part of the work of the nonviolent resister. This may
ound rather shocking. But I must confess that I am not
fraid of the word tension. I have earnestly worked and
reached against violent tension, but there is a type of con-
tructive nonviolent tension that is necessary for growth. Just
s Socrates felt that it was necessary to create a tension in the
nind so that individuals could rise from the bondage of myths
nd half-truths to the unfettered realm of creative analysis
nd objective appraisal, we must see the need of having nonviolent gadflies to create the kind of tension in society that
vill help men to rise from the dark depths of prejudice and
acism to the majestic heights of understanding and brother-
ood. So the purpose of the direct action is to create a situa-
ion so crisis-packed that it will inevitably open the door to
negotiation. We, therefore, concur with you in your call for
negotiation. Too long has our beloved Southland been bogged
down in the tragic attempt to live in monologue rather than
dialogue. . . .

My friends, I must say to you that we have not made a
single gain in civil rights without determined legal and nonvio-
ent pressure. History is the long and tragic story of the fact
hat privileged groups seldom give up their privileges volun-
arily. Individuals may see the moral light and voluntarily give
up their unjust posture; but as Reinhold Neibuhr has reminded us, groups are more immoral than individuals.

We know through painful experience that freedom is
never voluntarily given by the oppressor; it must be demanded
by the oppressed. Frankly, I have never yet engaged in a
direct-action movement that was "well timed," according to
he timetable of those who have not suffered unduly from the
disease of segregation. For years now I have heard the word
"Wait!" It rings in the ear of every Negro with a piercing
amiliarity. This "wait" has almost always meant "never." It
has been a tranquilizing thalidomide, relieving the emotional
tress for a moment, only to give birth to an ill-formed infant
of frustration. We must come to see with the distinguished ju-
ist of yesterday that "justice too long delayed is justice denied." We have waited for more than three hundred and forty
years for our constitutional and God-given rights. The nations
of Asia and Africa are moving with jetlike speed toward the
goal of political independence, and we still creep at horse and
buggy pace toward the gaining of a cup of coffee at a lunch
ounter. I guess it is easy for those who have never felt the
stinging darts of segregation to say, "Wait." But when you

have seen vicious mobs lynch your mothers and fathers at will and drown your sisters and brothers at whim; when you have seen hate-filled policemen curse, kick, brutalize, and even kill your black brothers and sisters with impunity; when you see the vast majority of your twenty million Negro brothers smothering in an airtight cage of poverty in the midst of an affluent society; when you suddenly find your tongue twisted and your speech stammering as you seek to explain to your six-year-old daughter why she can't go to the public amusement park that has just been advertised on television, and see tears welling up in her little eyes when she is told that Funtown is closed to colored children, and see the depressing clouds of inferiority begin to form in her little mental sky, and see her begin to distort her little personality by unconsciously developing a bitterness toward white people; when you have to concoct an answer for a five-year-old son asking in agonizing pathos: "Daddy, who do white people treat colored people so mean?"; when you take a cross-country drive and find it necessary to sleep night after night in the uncomfortable corners of your automobile because no motel will accept you; when you are humiliated day in and day out by nagging signs reading "white" and "colored"; when your first name becomes "nigger" and your middle name becomes "boy" (however old you are) and your last name becomes "John," and when your wife and mother are never given the respected title "Mrs."; when you are harried by day and haunted at night by the fact that you are a Negro, living constantly at tip-toe stance never quite knowing what to expect next, and plagued with inner fears and outer resentments; when you are forever fighting a degenerating sense of "nobodiness"; then you will understand why we find it difficult to wait. There comes a time when the cup of endurance runs over, and men are no longer willing to be plunged into an abyss of injustice where they experience the blackness of corroding despair. I hope, sirs, you can understand our legitimate and unavoidable impatience.

You express a great deal of anxiety over our willingness to break laws. This is certainly a legitimate concern. Since we so diligently urge people to obey the Supreme Court's decision of 1954 outlawing segregation in the public schools, it is rather strange and paradoxical to find us consciously breaking laws. One may well ask, "How can you advocate breaking some laws and obeying others?" The answer is found in the fact that there are two types of laws: There are *just* and there are *unjust* laws. I would agree with Saint Augustine that "an unjust law is no law at all."

Now what is the difference between the two? How does one determine when a law is just or unjust? A just law is a man-made code that squares with the moral law or the law of God. An unjust law is a code that is out of harmony with the moral law. To put it in the terms of Saint Thomas Aquinas, an unjust law is a human law that is not rooted in eternal and natural law. Any law that uplifts human personality is just. Any law that degrades human personality is unjust. All segregation statutes are unjust because segregation distorts the soul and damages the personality. It gives the segregator a false sense of superiority, and the segregated a false sense of inferiority. To use the words of Martin Buber, the great Jewish philosopher, segregation substitutes an "I-it" relationship for the "I-thou" relationship, and ends up relegating persons to the status of things. So segregation is not only politically, economically, and sociologically unsound, but it is morally wrong and sinful. Paul Tillich has said that sin is separation. Isn't segregation an existential expression of man's tragic separation, an expression of his awful estrangement, his terrible sinfulness? So I can urge men to disobey segregation ordinances because they are morally wrong. . . .

There are some instances when a law is just on its face and unjust in its application. For instance, I was arrested Friday on a charge of parading without a permit. Now there is nothing wrong with an ordinance which requires a permit for a parade, but when the ordinance is used to preserve segregation and to deny citizens the First Amendment privilege of peaceful assembly and peaceful protest, then it becomes unjust.

I hope you can see the distinction I am trying to point out. In no sense do I advocate evading or defying the law as the rabid segregationist would do. This would lead to anarchy. One who breaks an unjust law must do it *openly, lovingly* (not hatefully as the white mothers did in New Orleans when they were seen on television screaming "nigger, nigger, nigger"), and with a willingness to accept the penalty. I submit that an individual who breaks a law that conscience tells him is unjust, and willingly accepts the penalty by staying in jail to arouse the conscience of the community over its injustice, is in reality expressing the very highest respect for law.

Of course, there is nothing new about this kind of civil disobedience. It was seen sublimely in the refusal of Shadrach, Meshach, and Abednego to obey the laws of Nebuchadnezzar because a higher moral law was involved. It was practiced superbly by the early Christians who were willing to face hungry lions and the excruciating pain of chopping blocks, before submitting to certain unjust laws of the Roman empire. To a degree academic freedom is a reality today because Socrates practiced civil disobedience.

We can never forget that everything Hitler did in German was "legal" and everything the Hungarian freedom fighters did in Hungary was "illegal." It was "illegal" to aid and comfort a Jew in Hitler's Germany. But I am sure that if I had lived in Germany during that time, I would have aided and comforted my Jewish brothers even though it was illegal. If I lived in a Communist country today, where certain principles dear to the Christian faith are suppressed, I believe I would openly advocate disobeying these anti-religious laws. I must make two honest confessions to you, my Christian and Jewish brothers. First I must confess that over the last few years I have been gravely disappointed with the white moderate. I have almost reached the regrettable conclusion that the Negro's great stumbling block in the stride toward freedom is not the White Citizen's Council-er or the Ku Klux Klanner, but the white moderate who is more devoted to "order" than to justice; who prefers a negative peace which is the absence of tension to a positive peace which is the presence of justice; who constantly says "I agree with you in the goal you seek, but I can't agree with your methods of direct action"; who paternalistically feels that he can set the timetable for another man's freedom; who lives by the myth of time and who constantly advises the Negro to wait until a "more convenient season." Shallow understanding from people of goodwill is more frustrating than absolute misunderstanding from people of ill will. Lukewarm acceptance is much more bewildering than outright rejection.

I had hoped that the white moderate would understand that law and order exist for the purpose of establishing justice, and that when they fail to do this they become dangerously structured dams that block the flow of social progress. I had hoped that the white moderate would understand that the present tension in the South is merely a necessary phase of the transition from an obnoxious negative peace, where the Negro passively accepted his unjust plight, to a substance-filled positive peace, where all men will respect the dignity and worth of human personality. Actually, we who engage in nonviolent direct action are not the creators of tension. We merely bring to the surface the hidden tension that is already alive. We bring it out in the open where it can be seen and dealt with. Like a boil that can never be cured as long as it is covered up but must be opened with all its pus-flowing ugliness to the natural medicines of air and light, injustice must likewise be exposed, with all of the tension its exposing creates, to the light of human conscience and the air of national opinion before it can be cured.

In your statement you asserted that our actions, even though peaceful, must be condemned because they precipitate violence. But can this assertion be logically made? Isn't this like condemning the robbed man because his possession of money precipitated the evil act of robbery? Isn't this like condemning Socrates because his unswerving commitment to truth and his philosophical delvings precipitated the misguided popular mind to make him drink the hemlock? Isn't this like condemning Jesus because His unique God-Consciousness and never-ceasing devotion to His will precipitated the evil act of crucifixion? We must come to see, as federal courts have consistently affirmed, that it is immoral to urge an individual to withdraw his efforts to gain his basic constitutional rights because the quest precipitates violence. Society must protect the robbed and punish the robber.

I had also hoped that the white moderate would reject the myth of time. I received a letter this morning from a white brother in Texas which said: "All Christians know that the colored people will receive equal rights eventually, but it is possible that you are in too great of a religious hurry. It has taken Christianity almost two thousand years to accomplish what it has. The teachings of Christ take time to come to earth." All that is said here grows out of a tragic misconception of time. It is the strangely irrational notion that there is something in the very flow of time that will inevitably cure all ills. Actually time is neutral. It can be used either destructively or constructively. I am coming to feel that the people of ill-will have used time much more effectively than the people of good will. We will have to repent in this generation not merely for the vitriolic words and actions of the bad people, but for the appalling silence of good people. We must come to see that human progress never rolls in on wheels of inevitability. It comes through the tireless efforts and persistent work of men willing to be coworkers with God, and without this hard work time itself becomes an ally of the forces of social stagnation. We must use time creatively, and forever realize that the time is always ripe to do right. Now is the time to make real the promise of democracy, and transform our pending national elegy into a creative psalm of brotherhood. Now is the time to lift our national policy from the quicksand of racial injustice to the solid rock of human dignity. . . .

. . . I stand in the middle of two opposing forces in the Negro community. One is a force of complacency made up of Negroes who, as a result of long years of oppression, have been so completely drained of self-respect and a sense of "somebodiness" that they have adjusted to segregation, and of a few Negroes in the middle class who, because of a degree of academic and economic security, and because at points they profit by segregation, have unconsciously become insensitive to the problems of the masses. The other force is one of bitterness and hatred, and comes perilously close to advocating violence. It is expressed in the various black-nationalist groups that are springing up over the nation, the largest and best known being Elijah Muhammad's Muslim movement. This movement is nourished by the contemporary frustration over the continued existence of racial discrimination. It is made up of people who have lost faith in America, who have absolutely repudiated Christianity, and who have concluded that the white man is an incurable "devil." I have tried to stand between these two forces, saying that we need not follow the "do-nothingism" of the complacent or the hatred and despair of the black nationalist. There is the more excellent way of love and nonviolent protest. I'm grateful to God that, through the Negro church, the dimension of nonviolence entered our struggle. If this philosophy had not emerged, I am convinced that by now many streets of the South would be flowing with floods of blood. And I am further convinced that if our white brothers dismiss as "rabble-rousers" and "outside agitators" those of us who are working through the channels of nonviolent direct action and refuse to support our nonviolent efforts, millions of Negroes, out of frustration and despair, will seek solace and security in black-nationalist ideologies, a development that will lead inevitably to a frightening racial nightmare.

Oppressed people cannot remain oppressed forever. The urge for freedom will eventually come. This is what happened to the American Negro. Something within has reminded him of his birthright of freedom; something without has reminded him that he can gain it. Consciously and unconsciously, he has been swept in by what the Germans call the *Zeitgeist*, and with his black brothers of Africa, and his brown and yellow brothers of Asia, South America, and the Caribbean, he is moving with a sense of cosmic urgency toward the promised land of racial justice. Recognizing this vital urge that has engulfed the Negro community, one should readily understand public demonstrations. The Negro has many pent-up resentments and latent frustrations. He has to get them out. So let him march sometime; let him have his prayer pilgrimages to the city hall; understand why he must have sit-ins and freedom rides. If his repressed emotions do not come out in these nonviolent ways, they will come out in ominous expressions of violence. This is not a threat; it is a fact of history. So I have not said to my people "get rid of your discontent." But I have tried to say that this normal and healthy discontent can be channelized through the creative outlet of nonviolent direct action. Now this approach is being dismissed as extremist. I must admit that I was initially disappointed in being so categorized.

But as I continued to think about the mater I gradually gained a bit of satisfaction from being considered an extremist. Was not Jesus an extremist in love—"Love your enemies, bless them that curse you, pray for them that despitefully use you." Was not Amos an extremist for justice—"Let justice roll down like waters and righteousness like a mighty stream." Was not Paul an extremist for the gospel of Jesus Christ—"I bear in my body the marks of the Lord Jesus." Was not Martin Luther an extremist—"Here I stand; I can do none other so help me God." Was not John Bunyan an extremist—"I will tay in jail to the end of my days before I make a butchery of ny conscience." Was not Abraham Lincoln an extremist— "This nation cannot survive half slave and half free." Was not Thomas Jefferson an extremist—"We hold these truths to be elf-evident, that all men are created equal." So the question s not whether we will be extremist but what kind of extremist vill we be. Will we be extremists for hate or will be be extremists for love? Will we be extremists for the preservation of injustice—or will we be extremists for the cause of justice? n that dramatic scene on Calvary's hill, three men were crucified. We must not forget that all three were crucified for the ame crime—the crime of extremism. Two were extremists or immorality, and thusly fell below their environment. The other, Jesus Christ, was an extremist for love, truth, and goodness, and thereby rose above his environment. So, after all, maybe the South, the nation, and the world are in dire need of creative extremists. . . .

I hope the church as a whole will meet the challenge of this decisive hour. But even if the church does not come to the aid of justice, I have no despair about the future. I have no fear about the outcome of our struggle in Birmingham, even if our motives are presently misunderstood. We will reach the goal of freedom in Birmingham and all over the nation, because the goal of America is freedom. Abused and scorned though we may be, our destiny is tied up with the destiny of America. Before the pilgrims landed at Plymouth we were here. Before the pen of Jefferson etched across the pages of history the majestic words of the Declaration of Independence, we were here. For more than two centuries our fore-parents labored in his country without wages; they made cotton king, and they built the homes of their masters in the midst of brutal injustice and shameful humiliation—and yet out of a bottomless vitality they continued to thrive and develop. If the inexpressible cruelties of slavery could not stop us, the opposition we now face will surely fail. We will win our freedom because the sacred heritage of our nation and the eternal will of God are embodied in our echoing demands.

> Yours for the cause of Peace and Brotherhood,
> Martin Luther King, Jr.

The "Great Society" Speech,
Lyndon B. Johnson, 1964

. . . The purpose of protecting the life of our Nation and preserving the liberty of our citizens is to pursue the happiness of our people. Our success in that pursuit is the test of our success as a Nation.

For a century we labored to settle and to subdue a continent. For half a century we called upon unbounded invention and untiring industry to create an order of plenty for all of our people.

The challenge of the next half century is whether we have the wisdom to use that wealth to enrich and elevate our national life, and to advance the quality of our American civilization.

Your imagination, your initiative, and your indignation will determine whether we build a society where progress is the servant of our needs, or a society where old values and new visions are buried under unbridled growth. For in your time we have the opportunity to move not only toward the rich society and the powerful society, but upward to the Great Society.

The Great Society rests on abundance and liberty for all. It demands an end to poverty and racial injustice, to which we are totally committed in our time. But that is just the beginning.

The Great Society is a place where every child can find knowledge to enrich his mind and to enlarge his talents. It is a place where leisure is a welcome chance to build and reflect, not a feared cause of boredom and restlessness. It is a place where the city of man serves not only the needs of the body and the demands of commerce but the desire for beauty and the hunger for community.

It is a place where man can renew contact with nature. It is a place which honors creation for its own sake and for what it adds to the understanding of the race. It is a place where men are more concerned with the quality of their goals than the quantity of their goods.

But most of all, the Great Society is not a safe harbor, a resting place, a final objective, a finished work. It is a challenge constantly renewed, beckoning us toward a destiny where the meaning of our lives matches the marvelous products of our labor.

So I want to talk to you today about three places where we begin to build the Great Society—in our cities, in our countryside, and in our classrooms.

Many of you will live to see the day, perhaps fifty years from now, when there will be 400 million Americans—four-fifths of them in urban areas. In the remainder of this century urban population will double, city land will double, and we will have to build homes, highways, and facilities equal to all those built since this country was first settled. So in the next forty years we must rebuild the entire urban United States.

Aristotle said: "Men come together in cities in order to live; but they remain together in order to live the good life." It is harder and harder to live the good life in American cities today.

The catalog of ills is long: There is the decay of the centers and the despoiling of the suburbs. There is not enough housing for our people or transportation for our traffic. Open land is vanishing and old landmarks are violated.

Worst of all, expansion is eroding the precious and time-honored values of community with neighbors and communion with nature. The loss of these values breeds loneliness and boredom and indifference.

Our society will never be great until our cities are great. Today the frontier of imagination and innovation is inside those cities and not beyond their borders.

New experiments are already going on. It will be the task of your generation to make the American city a place where future generations will come, not only to live but to live the good life. . . .

A second place where we begin to build the Great Society is in our countryside. We have always prided ourselves on being not only America the strong and America the free, but America the beautiful. Today that beauty is in danger. The water we drink, the food we eat, the very air that we breathe, are threatened with pollution. Our parks are overcrowded, our seashores overburdened. Green fields and dense forests are disappearing.

A few years ago we were greatly concerned about the "Ugly American." Today we must act to prevent an ugly America.

For once the battle is lost, once our natural splendor is destroyed, it can never be recaptured. And once man can no longer walk with beauty or wonder at nature his spirit will wither and his sustenance be wasted.

A third place to build the Great Society is in the classrooms of America. There your children's lives will be shaped. Our society will not be great until every young mind is set free to scan the farthest reaches of thought and imagination. We are still far from that goal. . . .

In many places, classrooms are overcrowded and curricula are outdated. Most of our qualified teachers are underpaid, and many of our paid teachers are unqualified. So we must give every child a place to sit and a teacher to learn from. Poverty must not be a bar to learning, and learning must offer an escape from poverty.

But more classrooms and more teachers are not enough. We must seek an educational system which grows in excellence as it grows in size. This means better training for our teachers. It means preparing youth to enjoy their hours of leisure as well as their hours of labor. It means exploring new techniques of teaching, to find new ways to stimulate the love of learning and the capacity for creation.

These are three of the central issues of the Great Society. While our government has many programs directed at those issues, I do not pretend that we have the full answer to those problems.

But I do promise this: We are going to assemble the best thought and the broadest knowledge from all over the world to find those answers for America. . . .

The solution to these problems does not rest on a massive program in Washington, nor can it rely solely on the strained resources of local authority. They require us to create new concepts of cooperation, a creative federalism, between the national capital and the leaders of local communities.

Woodrow Wilson once wrote: "Every man sent out from his university should be a man of his nation as well as a man of his time."

Within your lifetime powerful forces, already loosed, will take us toward a way of life beyond the realm of our experience, almost beyond the bounds of our imagination.

For better or for worse, your generation has been appointed by history to deal with those problems and to lead America toward a new age. You have the chance never before afforded to any people in any age. You can help build a society where the demands of morality, and the needs of the spirit, can be realized in the life of the nation.

So, will you join in the battle to give every citizen the full equality which God enjoins and the law requires, whatever his belief, or race, or the color of his skin?

Will you join in the battle to give every citizen an escape from the crushing weight of poverty?

Will you join in the battle to make it possible for all nations to live in enduring peace—as neighbors and not as mortal enemies?

Will you join in the battle to build the Great Society, to prove that our material progress is only the foundation on which we will build a richer life of mind and spirit?

There are those timid souls who say this battle cannot be won; that we are condemned to a soulless wealth. I do not agree. We have the power to shape the civilization that we want. But we need your will, your labor, your hearts, if we are to build that kind of society.

Those who came to this land sought to build more than just a new country. They sought a new world. So I have come here today to your campus to say that you can make their vision our reality. So let us from this moment begin our work so that in the future men will look back and say: It was then, after a long and weary way, that man turned the exploits of his genius to the full enrichment of his life.

Chapter 28

DECADE OF TURMOIL

Most of the decade before America's 1976 Bicentennial was marred by the politics not only of upheaval, but of deep division and internal conflict as well. Black militant demands for economic and social equality and for meaningful civil rights programs ultimately came to be pursued vigorously by national leadership, but not in time to avoid the most polarizing racial conflicts since the Civil War. Besides, violence seemed to confront Americans everywhere. Martin Luther King was assassinated in April, 1968; Senator Robert F. Kennedy was murdered two months later; and in the 1972 Presidential campaign, Alabama Governor George C. Wallace was paralyzed by an assassin's bullets.

Violence on a larger scale threatened the fabric of American life, too. Mired in an undeclared yet bitterly controversial war in Vietnam that had begun with American involvement in Southeast Asia literally as far back as Dwight Eisenhower's Presidency, the nation's sense of well-being was shaken more severely perhaps than at any time in its two-hundred-year history. Eventually America would withdraw from Vietnam in what most would consider defeat, but not before angry debates over her reasons for the war as well as her conduct of the war would lead many Americans—particularly the young—cynically to question their nation's very purposes and integrity. Not before campus discontent with the war had flared into pitched battles and had found its parallel in large-scale draft dodging and desertion that further demonstrated the destructive ugliness of the Vietnamese encounter. Not before the revelations of American atrocities at My Lai were followed by tragedy at Ohio's Kent State University, where National Guardsmen fired into a group of antiwar demonstrators, killing four students, wounding more, and alarming all Americans with concern for what they were doing to themselves. Not before the pilfered Pentagon Papers had further undermined the confidence of many Americans in "the best and the brightest" of both national parties who had taken and kept us in what became America's most unwanted war, her symbol to many both of diminished world power and of moral irresponsibility.

Perhaps what astounded Americans most as they prepared for their Bicentennial was the seeming new vulnerability to

345

public criticism and disparagement of their most highly placed leaders even as ever-expanding Executive decision-making led to fears of an emerging "Imperial Presidency." Despite his huge majorities in 1964, Lyndon B. Johnson chose not to run for reelection as President in 1968 because of widely demonstrated opposition to his war policies. And his speech on the role of the new electronic media in American life and politics, delivered immediately after he withdrew from the Presidential race, significantly pointed to broadcasting as an instrument of political activism, an interpretation not previously shared by most Americans who consider the medium essentially as an entertainment. That year Republican Richard M. Nixon defeated Democratic Vice President Hubert H. Humphrey for the Presidency; and in 1972 he literally overwhelmed Democratic Senator George S. McGovern in what was to become his virulently controversial campaign for reelection. But Nixon, who had purposely used Vice President Spiro T. Agnew to attack American television for supposedly pressing upon the nation political views contrary to the Administration's, would also soon come to feel the power of the media. Instantaneous and widespread electronic and print coverage of scandals touching on his Vice President quickly forced Agnew to resign from office, to be replaced under provisions of the never-before-used 25th Amendment to the Constitution by the appointment of Michigan Congressman Gerald R. Ford, Republican leader in the House of Representatives. And soon after that, when this nation had literally been deluged with the mass media's boldly revealing and incessant reporting of Watergate and the other scandals that suddenly disgraced his Presidency, Nixon himself was forced to resign under threat of impeachment. Appointed, not elected, to the second highest office of the land just months before, Gerald Ford now succeeded to the Presidency of the United States and in a brief, humble but thoroughly welcomed Inaugural Address made the first of his touching efforts to lead a nation deeply shaken by tragedy and scandal from suspicion to faith, from despair to hope.

The "Power of the Media" Speech,

Lyndon B. Johnson, 1968

Once again we are entering the period of national festivity which Henry Adams called the dance of democracy. At its best, that can be a time of debate and enlightenment. At its worst, it can be a period of frenzy. But always it is a time when emotion threatens to substitute for reason. Yet the basic hope of a democracy is that somehow amid all the frenzy and all the emotion that in the end reason will prevail.

Reason just must prevail if democracy itself is to survive. . . .

But the real problem of informing the people is still with us, and I think I can speak with some authority about the problem of communication. I understand far better than some of my severe and perhaps intolerant critics would admit my own shortcomings as a communicator.

How does a public leader find just the right word or the right way to say no more or no less than he means to say, bearing in mind that anything he says may topple governments and may involve the lives of innocent men?

How does that leader speak the right phrase in the right way under the right conditions to suit the accuracies and contingencies of the moment when he's discussing questions of policy so that he does not stir a thousand misinterpretations and leave the wrong connotation or impression?

How does he reach the immediate audience and how does he communicate with the millions of others who are out there listening from afar? . . .

You men and women who are masters of the broadcast media I think surely must know what I am talking about. It was a long time ago a President once said, "The printing press is the most powerful weapon with which man has ever armed himself." And in our age the electronic media have added immeasurably to man's power.

You have within your hands the means to make our nation as intimate and as informed as a New England town meeting. Yet the use of broadcasting has not cleared away all the problems that we still have of communication.

In some ways, I think, sometimes it has complicated them. Because it tends to put the leader in a time capsule. It requires him often to abbreviate what he has to say. Too often it may catch a random phrase from his rather lengthy discourse and project it as the whole story.

How many men . . . in public life have watched themselves on a TV newscast and then been tempted to exclaim: "Can that really be me?"

Well, there is no denying it. You, the broadcast industry, have enormous power in your hands. You have the power to clarify. And you have the power to confuse.

Men in public life cannot remotely rival your opportunities, because day after day, night after night, hour after hour, on the hour, you shape—and the half-hour sometimes—you shape the nation's dialogue. The words that you choose, hopefully always accurate, hopefully always just, are the words that are carried out for all the people to hear.

The commentary that you provide can give the real meaning to the issues of the day or it can distort them beyond all meaning.

By your standards of what is news you can cultivate with

them or you could nurture misguided passions. Your commentary carries an element of uncertainty.

Unlike the print media, television writes on the wind. There is no accumulated record which the historian can examine later with the 20-20 vision of hindsight, asking this question: How fair was he tonight? How impartial was he today? How honest was he all along?

Well, I hope the National Association of Broadcasters, with whom I have had a pleasant association for many years, will point the way to all of us in developing this kind of a record because history is going to be asking very hard questions about our times and the period through which we are passing. And I think that we all owe it to history to complete the record.

But I did not come here this morning to sermonize in matters of fairness and judgment. No law and no set of regulations and no words of mine can improve you or dictate your daily responsibility. All I mean to do—what I'm trying to do—is to remind you where there's great power there must also be great responsibility.

This is true for broadcasters just as it's true for Presidents and seekers for the Presidency.

What we say and what we do now will shape the kind of a world that we pass along to our children and our grandchildren. And I keep this thought constantly in my mind during the long days and the somewhat longer nights when crisis comes at home and abroad.

I took a little of your prime time last night. I wouldn't have done that except for a very prime purpose. I reported on the prospects for peace in Vietnam. I announced that the United States is taking a very important unilateral act of de-escalation which could—and I fervently pray, will—lead to mutual moves to reduce the level of violence and to de-escalate the war.

As I sat in my office last evening waiting to speak, thought of the many times each week when television brings the war into the American home. No one can say exactly what effect those vivid scenes have on American opinion.

Historians must only guess at the effect that television would have had during earlier conflicts on the future of this nation. During the Korean War, for example, at that time when our forces were pushed back there to Pusan. Or World War II, the Battle of the Bulge, or when our men were slugging it out in Europe, or when most of our Air Force was shot down that day in June, 1942, off Australia.

But last night television was being used to carry a different message. It was a message of peace and it occurred to me that the medium may be somewhat better suited to conveying the actions of conflict than to dramatizing the words that the leaders use in trying and hoping to end the conflict.

Certainly it is more dramatic to show policemen and rioters locked in combat than to show men trying to cooperate with one another.

The face of hatred and of bigotry comes through much more clearly, no matter what its color, and the face of tolerance I seem to find is rarely newsworthy.

Progress, whether it's a man being trained for a job or millions being trained, or whether it's a child in Head Start learning to read or an older person, seventy-two, in adult education, or being cared for in Medicare, rarely makes the news, although more than twenty-million of them are affected by it.

Perhaps this is because tolerance and progress are not dynamic events such as riots and conflict are events.

So peace in the new sense is a condition. War is an end. Part of your responsibility is simply to understand the consequences of that fact, the consequences of your own acts. And part of that responsibility, I think, is to try as very best we all can to draw the attention of our people to the real business of society in our system, finding and securing peace in the world, at home and abroad and for all that you have done. And that you are doing and that you will do to the end, I thank you and I commend you. . . .

Speaking as I did to the nation last night, I was moved by the very deep convictions that I entertain about the nature of the office that it's my present privilege to hold.

The office of the Presidency is the only office in this land of all the people.

Whatever may be the personal wishes or the preferences of any man who holds it, a President of all the people can afford no thought of self. At no time and in no way and for no reason can a President allow the integrity or the responsibility or the freedom of the office ever to be compromised or diluted or destroyed because when you destroy it, you destroy yourselves. And I hope and I pray by not allowing the Presidency to be involved in division and deep partisanship I shall be able to pass on to my successor a stronger office, strong enough to guard and defend all the people against all the storms that the future may bring us. . . .

You are yourselves the trustees—legally accepted trustees, legally selected trustees—of a great institution on which the freedom of our land utterly depends.

The security, the success of our country, what happens to us tomorrow rests squarely upon the media which disseminates the truth on which the decisions of democracy are made. We get a great deal of our information from you, and an informed mind is the guardian genius of democracy.

So you are the keepers of a trust and you must be just. You must guard and you must defend your media against a spirit of action, against the works of divisiveness, against bigotry, against the corrupting evils of partisanship in any guise.

For America's press as for the American Presidency, the integrity and the responsibility and the freedom—the freedom to know the truth and let the truth make us free—must never be compromised or diluted or destroyed.

The defense of our media is your responsibility. Government cannot and must not and never will, as long as I have anything to do about it, intervene in that role.

But I do want to leave this thought with you as I leave you this morning. I hope that you will give this trust your closest care. Acting as I know you can to guard not only against the obvious but to watch for the hidden, the sometimes unintentional, the often petty intrusion upon the integrity of the information by which Americans decide.

Men and women of the airways fully as much as men and women of public service have a public trust, and if liberty is to survive and to succeed that solemn trust must be faithfully kept.

I do not want and I don't think you want to wake up some morning and find America changed because we slept when we should have been awake, because we remained silent when we should have spoken up, because we went along with what was popular and fashionable and "in," rather than what was necessary and what was right.

Being faithful to our trust ought to be the prime test of any public trustee in office or on the airways and in any society all you students of history know that a time of division is a time of danger, and in these times now we must never forget that eternal vigilance is the price of liberty.

Thank you for wanting me to come. I've enjoyed it.

Gerald R. Ford's Inaugural Address, 1974

Mr. Chief Justice, my dear friends, my fellow Americans: The oath that I have taken is the same oath that was taken by George Washington and by every Persident under the Constitution.

But I assume the Presidency under extraordinary circumstances never before experienced by Americans. This is an hour of history that troubles our minds and hurts our hearts.

Therefore, I feel it is my first duty to make an unprecedented compact with my countrymen. Not an inaugural address, not a fireside chat, not a campaign speech, just a little straight talk among friends. And I intend it to be the first of many.

I am acutely aware that you have not elected me as your President by your ballots. So I ask you to confirm me as your President with your prayers. And I hope that such prayers will also be the first of many.

If you have not chosen me by secret ballot, neither have I gained office by any secret promises. I have not campaigned ither for the Presidency or the Vice Presidency. I have not subscribed to any partisan platform. I am indebted to no man and only to one woman, my dear wife.

As I begin this very difficult job, I have not sought this enormous responsibility, but I will not shirk it. Those who nominated and confirmed me as Vice President were my friends and are my friends. They were of both parties, elected by all the people and acting under the Constitution in their name.

It is only fitting then that I should pledge to them and to you that I will be the President of all the people.

Thomas Jefferson said the people are the only sure reliance for the preservation of our liberty. And down the years, Abraham Lincoln renewed this American article of faith asking is there any better way for equal hopes in the world.

I intend on next Monday to request of the Speaker of the House of Representatives and the President pro tempore of the Senate the privilege of appearing before the Congress to share with my former colleagues and with you, the American people, my views on the priority business of the nation and to solicit your views and their views.

And may I say to the Speaker and the others, if I could meet with you right after this—these remarks—I would appreciate it.

Even though this is late in an election year there is no way we can go forward except together and no way anybody can win except by serving the people's urgent needs.

We cannot stand still or slip backward. We must go forward now together.

To the peoples and the governments of all friendly nations, and I hope that could encompass the whole world, I pledge an uninterrupted and sincere search for peace. America will remain strong and united.

But its strength will remain dedicated to the safety and sanity of the entire family of man as well as to our own precious freedom.

I believe that truth is the glue that holds governments together, not only our government but civilization itself. That bond, though stained, is unbroken at home and abroad.

In all my public and private acts as your President, I expect to follow my instincts of openness and candor with full confidence that honesty is always the best policy in the end.

My fellow Americans, our long national nightmare is over. Our Constitution works. Our great republic is a government of laws and not of men. Here, the people rule.

But there is a higher power, by whatever name we honor Him, who ordains not only righteousness but love, not only justice but mercy.

As we bind up the internal wounds of Watergate, more painful and more poisonous than those of foreign wars, let us restore the golden rule to our political process. And let brotherly love purge our hearts of suspicion and of hate.

In the beginning, I asked you to pray for me. Before closing, I ask again your prayers for Richard Nixon and for his family. May our former President who brought peace to millions find it for himself.

May God bless and comfort his wonderful wife and daughters whose love and loyalty will forever be a shining legacy to all who bear the lonely burden of the White House.

I can only guess at those burdens although I witnessed at close hand the tragedies that befell three Presidents and the lesser trials of others.

With all the strength and all the good sense I have gained from life, with all the confidence my family, my friends, and dedicated staff impart to me, and with the goodwill of countless Americans I have encountered in recent visits to forty states, I now solemnly reaffirm my promise I made to you last December 6 to uphold the Constitution, to do what is right as God gives me to see the right, and to do the very best I can for America.

God helping me, I will not let you down.

Thank you.